PRAISE FOR
Destined to Witness

"An incredible tale. . . . Exceptional. . . . It is reviving and heartening to learn of this intrepid black child and young man who through a combination of guts, smarts, and a really good mother, manages to waltz through the darkest abyss of the twentieth century and come out whistling."

   —*Chicago Sun-Times*

"His story is truly a fascinating one, and in this absorbing memoir, he tells it with vividness and considerable verve. Written with clarity, directiveness, and sharply evocative detail, Mr. Massaquoi's book offers a unique perspective on a period of organized madness, destruction, and turmoil that continues to demand our attention and evade our comprehension."

   —*Washington Times*

"A revelation . . . a modest account of a remarkable life . . . filled with emotional intensity, humor and frankness. . . . *Destined to Witness* [is] a cry against racism, a survivor's tale, a wartime adventure, a coming-of-age story, and a powerful tribute to a mother's love, and her son's willingness to make something of his life."

   —*New Orleans Times-Picayune*

"*Destined to Witness* examines a roller coaster of racism from different cultures and continents. Massaquoi concludes that 'true human decency is . . . simply a matter of the human heart.' "

   —*New York Times Book Review*

"Filled with courage, feeling, and intelligence. . . . Intriguing."

   —*Jet*

"To say that Hans Massaquoi had it all, is not to say only that he had black skin, in Germany, where and when white skin and Aryan blood were revered, nor to suggest that he lived without money when only money could have saved him and his mother from the degradation of racial hate and deprivation. Massaquoi, indeed, did have it all: keen observation, an important intelligence, and a remarkable memory. Here is a story rarely lived and even more rarely told. We need this book for a balanced picture of the Holocaust, which was not only a 'Jewish thing.' Hate is hate, it knows no color, and knows all colors all too well."

—Maya Angelou

"A unique addition to life under the Third Reich . . . thoughtful and well-written."

—*Publishers Weekly*

"Massaquoi's background and experiences provide incredible context to this personal story of overcoming racism."

—*Booklist*

"A nuanced, startling memoir . . . Massaquoi's unique, pathos-filled childhood in extremis is rendered superlatively, as is his portrait of a prewar Germany giddily embarked on its own destruction."

—*Kirkus Reviews*

DESTINED TO WITNESS

GROWING UP BLACK IN NAZI GERMANY

HANS J. MASSAQUOI

Perennial

An Imprint of HarperCollins*Publishers*

A hardcover edition of this book was published in 1999 by William Morrow and Company, Inc.

DESTINED TO WITNESS. Copyright © 1999 by Hans J. Massaquoi. All rights reserved. Printed in the United States of America. No part of this book may be used or reproduced in any manner whatsoever without written permission except in the case of brief quotations embodied in critical articles and reviews. For information address HarperCollins Publishers Inc., 10 East 53rd Street, New York, NY 10022.

HarperCollins books may be purchased for educational, business, or sales promotional use. For information please write: Special Markets Department, HarperCollins Publishers Inc., 10 East 53rd Street, New York, NY 10022.

First Perennial edition published 2001.

Designed by Nicola Ferguson

The Library of Congress has catalogued the hardcover edition as follows:

Massaquoi, Hans J.
Destined to witness: growing up black in Nazi Germany / Hans J. Massaquoi
p.   cm.
ISBN 0-688-17155-9
1. Massaquoi, Hans J.   2. Blacks—Germany Biography.
3. Racism—Germany.   4. Germany—Social conditions—
1933–1945.   5. National socialism.   I. Title.
DD78.B55M38   1999
943'.00496'0092—dc21
[B]   99-34221
CIP

ISBN 0-06-095961-4 (pbk.)

09 WB/RRD 20 19 18 17 16 15 14

To my mother,
Bertha Nikodijevic (1903–1986)
with deep gratitude

ACKNOWLEDGMENTS

Not unlike raising a child, it usually takes a "village" of loyal relatives, friends, and professionals to "raise" a book. *Destined to Witness* is no exception. Without the help of a small but dedicated cadre of supporters, it would still be a pipe dream in the remote recesses of my mind.

Much of the credit for helping me turn an idea into a book goes to my wife and best friend, Katharine, who throughout the various stages of the manuscript put up with the erratic behavior of a genius at work while assuming the multiple duties of inspiring muse, sounding board, gourmet cook, chauffeur, critic, et cetera, et cetera, et cetera. On numerous occasions, she literally saved the day by matching wits with my Power PC, bending the disgustingly obstinate gadget to her will whenever it went on strike or otherwise refused to cooperate with me.

Similar praise goes to my two sons, Steve G. Massaquoi, M.D., Ph. D., assistant professor at the Massachusetts Institute of Technology (MIT), and Atty. Hans J. Massaquoi Jr., partner at the law firm Lewis and Munday in Detroit. In spite of their taxing professional careers, they took the time to become deeply involved with the project, from reading and critiquing the text to (in the case of Atty. Hans Jr.) helping me with free (I think) legal advice in the preparation of contracts with publishers and agents and the obtaining of copyrights.

Equally deserving of my gratitude are my wife's brother and sister, Numa Rousseve of White Plains, New York, and Elaine Thompson of San Jose, California, and my friend Ed Morris, professor of television at Columbia College in Chicago. The three separately took on the reading and editing of the manuscript as a labor of love and offered many constructive comments.

Even if belatedly, I must give major praise to my late friend Alex Haley. Just a few months before his untimely death on February 10, 1992, he returned my unfinished manuscript, which he had kindly agreed to critique, with many invaluable suggestions.

I could not write this page of acknowledgments without mentioning my lifetime friend and established author of bestselling books, Ralph Giordano of Cologne, Germany, who started the ball rolling, so to speak. After years of encouraging me to write my memoir, he called me one day to tell me that he had meetings scheduled with important German editors and that if I would rush him a copy of my in-progress manuscript, he would see to it that the right people would see it. Shortly after I mailed my manuscript to Ralph, German publishers' interest in my book was kindled and *Destined to Witness* was on its way.

I also would like to take this opportunity to thank Prof. Raymond J. Smyke of Morges, Switzerland, who is preparing a biography of my grandfather, the Hon. Momolu Massaquoi (1870–1938), for providing me with some valuable information about him.

The person who deserves credit for introducing me to the arcane and bewildering world of book-publishing and who, in the process, convinced me that the writing of a book is the easy part is my literary agent Sarah Lazin of Sarah Lazin Books in New York City. Sarah has been tireless in representing my interest in Europe as well as the United States. I am deeply grateful to Claire Wachtel, executive editor at William Morrow, for having the faith in my work to publish it. I am also indebted to Greg Villepique, copy editor, who, with a keen eye and deft touch, put the finishing touches on my manuscript.

Last but not least, I must mention here my two faithful companions, (Don) Quixote and Sancho (Panza), our two Welsh terriers, who patiently kept me company during the many lonesome vigils that are the lot of anyone who embarks on the adventure of writing a book.

To write of one's self, in such a manner as not to incur
the imputation of weakness, vanity, and egotism, is a
work within the ability of but few; and I have little
reason to believe that I belong to that fortunate few.

—FREDERICK DOUGLASS

I could not agree more with the above sentiments, expressed so eloquently over a century ago by the great abolitionist in the preface to his autobiography, *My Bondage, My Freedom*. If, like Mr. Douglass, I nonetheless decided to risk being thought of as weak, vain, and egocentric by making public the story of my life, it was mainly because of the persistent urging of persons whose literary judgment I felt was above reproach, such as my longtime friends Alex Haley, the author of *Roots;* Ralph Giordano, of Cologne, Germany, author of *Die Bertinis;* and my former employer and mentor, *Ebony* publisher John H. Johnson. Each convinced me that my experiences as a black youngster growing into manhood and surviving in Nazi Germany—an eyewitness to, and frequent victim of, both Nazi racial madness and Allied bombings—followed by my years in Africa were so unique that it was my duty as a journalist to share this rather different perspective on the Holocaust. Alex felt that because I was both an insider in Nazi Germany and, paradoxically, an endangered outsider, I had a rare perspective on some of the Third Reich's major catastrophic events. He also urged me to record my equally unique experience of finding my own African roots.

Four fundamental aspects set the private hell I endured under the Nazis apart from both the pogroms suffered by my Jewish compatriots in Germany and from the racial persecution inflicted on my African-American brothers and sisters in the United States.

As a black person in white Nazi Germany, I was highly visible and thus could neither run nor hide, to paraphrase my childhood idol Joe Louis.

Unlike African-Americans, I did not have the benefit of inherited survival techniques created and perfected by countless ancestors and passed down from generation to generation of oppressed people. Instead, I was forced to traverse a minefield of potential disasters and to develop my own instincts to tell me how best to survive physically and psychologically in a country consumed by racial arrogance and racial hatred and openly committed to the destruction of all "non-Aryans."

Nazi racists, unlike their white American counterparts, did not commit their atrocities anonymously, disguised in white sheets and under the protection of night. Nor did they operate like some contemporary American politicians who advance their racist agendas by dividing black and white Americans with cleverly disguised code words about "unfair quotas," "reverse discrimination," and "states' rights." Racists in Nazi Germany did their dirty work openly and brazenly with the full protection, cooperation, and encouragement of the government, which had declared the pollution of Aryan blood with "inferior" non-Aryan blood the nation's cardinal sin.

For all practical purposes—except for the courageous and unflagging support I received from my German mother, who taught me to believe in myself by believing in me and my potential—I faced the constant threat that Nazi ethnic-cleansing policies posed to my safety alone. I faced this threat without the sense of security and feeling of belonging that humans derive from being members of a group, even an embattled one. Because of the absence of black females and the government-imposed taboo of race mixing, I had no legal social outlet when I reached puberty. Unlike the thousands of Africans and so-called "brown babies"—children of black GI fathers and German mothers—who reside in the Federal Republic of Germany today, there simply was no black population to speak of in Germany during the Hitler years, certainly none that I encountered. Not until long after the war did I learn that a small number of black Germans—the tragic so-called "Rhineland bastards" fathered by World War I French and Belgian colonial occupation troops—were exterminated in Hitler's death camps.

Because Germans of my generation were expected to be fair skinned and of Aryan stock, it became my lot in life to explain ad nauseam why someone who had a brown complexion and black, kinky hair spoke accent-free German and claimed Germany as his place of birth. So let me state here once again, for the record, that I was born in 1926 in Hamburg, Germany's second-largest city, because my grandfather, then consul general of Liberia to Hamburg, had brought with him his sizable family. His oldest son became my father after an intense courtship with my mother, a German nurse. Shortly before Hitler's rise to power, my grandfather and father returned to Liberia, leaving my mother and me to fend for ourselves in an increasingly hostile racist environment.

Our ordeal of living in constant fear of both Gestapo executioners and Allied bombs ended in the spring of 1945, when Karl Kaufmann, Hamburg's Nazi governor, surrendered the nearly destroyed city to the advancing British troops in defiance of Hitler's order to defend Hamburg "to the last man." That which Studs Terkel in his oral history of World War II calls *The Good War* was everything but. It certainly was not for my mother and me, who narrowly escaped death in Hamburg's inferno after surviving some two hundred British and American air attacks, the killing of more than forty-one thousand civilians, and the destruction of more than half of the city's homes, including our own.

Three years after the war, in 1948, I joined my father in Liberia. While in Africa, I not only developed an appreciation for African culture, but also got my first taste of colonial racism, both French and British style. In 1950 I was admitted to the United States on a one-year student visa. Not quite nine months after my arrival, about a third of the way into the Korean "conflict," I, a noncitizen, was ordered to report for military service due to an apparent clerical error, and served two years as a paratrooper in the 82nd Airborne Division.

There were numerous occasions, inside and outside the military, when I had the opportunity to see the ugly side of America, to sample U.S.–style racism and compare it with its Nazi counterpart. In one incident that clearly demonstrated that racism was not confined to the Jim Crow South, as is often alleged, I joined a "march for open housing" led by Dr. Martin Luther King Jr., in 1966 in Chicago's all-white Gage Park neighborhood. As Dr. King led our peaceful group in prayer, we were pelted with rocks and assaulted with profanities by an enraged white community barely held at bay by the thin ranks of police assigned to protect us.

In another incident, dressed in my army uniform, I was riding a train from Chicago to Fayetteville, North Carolina, on my way back to my post at Fort Bragg, when I was assaulted by a white train conductor after I had fallen asleep and missed moving to a segregated "colored car" when the Southbound train reached the Mason-Dixon Line. "Get your black ass out of here and go where you niggers belong!" the conductor, a shriveled white man, had screamed at me after kicking me from behind. Rather than risk being lynched for beating an old white man, as was my deep-felt inclination, I controlled my anger, picked up my duffel bag, and did as I had been told.

Such indignities were almost too much to bear, but I learned early in life that survival is the name of the game. My reward for having endured was the GI Bill, which enabled me to obtain the college education denied to me in Nazi Germany. Between studies, I managed to woo, win, and marry a young social worker from St. Louis. Although the marriage ended in divorce after fourteen years, it blessed us with two fine sons who provided much of the impetus for the modest success I have enjoyed.

Armed with a degree in journalism and communication from the University of Illinois, I held minor editorial jobs until I joined Johnson Publishing Company as an associate editor of the weekly black newsmagazine *Jet*. Within a year I was transferred to a similar position on *Ebony*, the company's flagship monthly photo-feature magazine.

Overnight, I became an active participant, observer, and reporter of the greatest social and political movement of the century—the black struggle for racial equality waged during the fifties, sixties, and seventies in the United States, in colonial Africa, and in the West Indies. Throughout my nearly forty-year career with *Ebony*, during which I rose to the rank of managing editor and became a member of the publication's editorial board, I had a ringside seat to some of the most important historic events of our times and came face-to-face with some of the best-known personalities of our age, including three U.S. presidents (Carter, Reagan, and Bush) while covering a wide range of assignments in the United States, Africa, Europe, Asia, and the Caribbean. My diverse assignments ran the gamut from exclusive interviews with statesmen, including Presidents Nnamdi Azikiwe of Nigeria, Tseretse Kama of Botswana, William Tolbert of Liberia, and Sam Njomo of Namibia; Jamaican Prime Ministers Michael Manley and Edward Seaga; civil-rights activists, such as Dr. Martin Luther King Jr., the Reverend Jesse Jackson, and Malcolm X, to a fair number of "living legends," such as Lena Horne, Diana Ross, Shirley Temple Black, Joe Louis, Max Schmeling, and Muhammad Ali.

Researching and reporting the achievements of black people for so long had many rewards. The most important one for me was that it allowed me to find my own psychological moorings after twelve years of dehumanizing and degrading mistreatment under the Nazis. It was the solution to the conflict which so many biracial people experience regarding their racial identity. I could not be a living witness to the ongoing heroic struggle for black survival and equality in racist America, document in article after article the countless achievements of blacks in the face of staggering odds, and not feel black and proud myself. The finest hour of the civil-rights struggle, the 1963 March on Washington, during which I stood at the Lincoln Memorial and heard Dr. King give his unforgettable "I Have a Dream" speech, is still one of my proudest and most cherished memories.

As a youngster growing up among ordinary German working people, I witnessed the rise of one of the most oppressive governments ever devised by man and—twelve agonizingly slow years later—its well-earned, cataclysmic demise. From my vantage point I observed firsthand how the Nazi poison—concocted by Hitler and served by a clever manipulator named Joseph Goebbels, the Third Reich's Minister of Public Enlightenment and Propaganda—slowly but surely did its contaminating work until it had transformed decent, caring, reasonable men and women into fanatical racists who approved the destruction of anyone and anything that did not conform to their vision of a new world order that took their national anthem, *"Deutschland Über Alles,"* literally. That Germans as a people were more than willing to take their racist marching orders from a bunch of unscrupulous political opportunists headed by a bloodthirsty madman is often cited as proof that all Germans were tainted and thus culpable. I disagree. I know that a large number—unfortunately not enough to have made a crucial difference—remained decent human beings despite pressures exerted by the Nazi leadership and the fact that decency had gone totally out of style. It is owing to some of these individuals who resisted the temptation to go with the prevailing flow of racial madness and who never regarded me as anything less than a worthwhile fellow human being that I survived largely unscathed. That I, a certified non-Aryan, was spared extermination, sterilization, or medical experimentation in one of Hitler's death camps I attribute largely to two fortunate coincidences. Unlike Jews, blacks were so few in numbers that they were relegated to low-priority status in the Nazis' lineup for extermination. Also, the unexpectedly rapid advance of the Allied military juggernaut kept the Nazis preoccupied with their own survival and in many cases crushed the Gestapo executioners before they could put the finishing touches on their racial cleansing. Thus, I fell through the cracks of modern history's most extensive, most systematic mass-murder scheme, with the fortunate result that I am still around and able to write this account of my life.

In retracing the events of more than seven decades, I relied heavily on my own memory and personal records and—in the case of events that preceded my birth or ability to remember—on the memories of my mother and other family members in Germany, the United States, and Liberia. Since not all of the incidents described are flattering, I have changed some of the names in order to spare the people involved undue embarrassment.

DESTINED
TO
WITNESS

BRIEF ENCOUNTER

One beautiful summer morning in 1934, I arrived at school to hear our third-grade teacher, Herr Grimmelshäuser, inform the class that Herr Wriede, our *Schulleiter* (principal), had ordered the entire student body and faculty to assemble in the schoolyard. There, dressed as he often was on special occasions in his brown Nazi uniform, Herr Wriede announced that "the biggest moment of [our] young lives" was imminent, that fate had chosen us to be among the lucky ones privileged to behold "our beloved Führer Adolf Hitler" with our own eyes. It was a privilege for which, he assured us, our yet-to-be-born children and children's children would one day envy us. At the time I was eight years old and it had not yet dawned on me that of the nearly six hundred boys assembled in the schoolyard, the only pupil Herr Wriede was not addressing was me.

Taking Wriede at his word, the entire school soon buzzed with anticipation of this rare, totally unexpected treat of a virtually school-free day. We had all been thoroughly indoctrinated in the Führer's heroic rise to power and his superhuman efforts to free Germany from the enslavement endured since its defeat in World War I and to restore its old glory and preeminence. Already we had come to feel the Führer's omnipresence. His likenesses appeared everywhere—throughout the school, in public buildings of the city, on posters and postage stamps, in newspapers and magazines. Even more vivid were his by now familiar voice on radio and his compelling appearances in the weekly newsreels at the neighborhood cinema. Now we would get a chance to see with our own eyes this legendary savior and benefactor of the *Vaterland*. To most of the students, myself included, the thrills in store for us seemed beyond our ability to comprehend.

Buoyed by our enthusiasm and flanked by our teachers, we marched for nearly an hour to a point along Alsterkrugchaussee, a major thoroughfare leading to Hamburg's airport in suburban Fuhlsbüttel. The entire route from the airport to Hamburg's venerable *Rathaus* downtown, which the Führer's fleet of cars was scheduled to travel, was lined with thousands of nearly hysterical people. They were kept from spilling into the street by stern brownshirts who, with clasped hands, formed an endless human chain. Seated along the curb behind the SS and SA troopers, we children endured an agonizing wait that dragged on for several hours. But just as our strained patience was reaching the breaking point, the roar of the crowds began to swell to a deafening crescendo. A nearby SS marching band intoned the opening fanfares of the *"Badenweiler Marsch,"* a Hitler favorite designated as the official signal of the Führer's arrival. The moment everyone had been waiting for was here. Standing erect beside the driver of his black Mercedes convertible, his right arm outstretched in the familiar Nazi salute, the Führer rolled past at a brisk walking pace, his eyes staring expressionlessly ahead.

The "biggest moment in our lives" for which Principal Wriede had prepared us had lasted only a few seconds, but to me they seemed like an eternity. There I was, a kinky-haired, brown-skinned eight-year-old boy amid a sea of blond and blue-eyed kids, filled with childlike patriotism, still shielded by blissful ignorance. Like everyone around me, I cheered the man whose every waking hour was dedicated to the destruction of "inferior non-Aryan people" like myself, the same man who only a few years later would lead his own nation to the greatest catastrophe in its long history and bring the world to the brink of destruction.

MOMOLU MASSAQUOI

The story of how I became part of that fanatically cheering crowd did not begin on January 19, 1926, the day of my birth. Neither did it begin, as one might suspect, in Hamburg, the city of my birth. Instead, it began five years earlier, more than three thousand miles away in the West African capital city of Monrovia, Liberia, with the shrewd decision of a president to rid himself of a potential political rival, Momolu Massaquoi, my paternal grandfather-to-be.

Charles Dunbar King, the fourteenth president of Liberia, had for some time considered the rising popularity of the ambitious Massaquoi as potentially dangerous. The American-educated Massaquoi had been the hereditary ruler of the indigenous Vai nation, which straddled Liberia and the adjacent British colony of Sierra Leone. At age thirty, after having been forced in a tribal dispute to abdicate the crown he had inherited upon the death of his parents, King Lahai and Queen Sandimannie, and that he had worn for ten years as Momolu IV, he had sought his fortune in Monrovian politics. He helped his cause immensely by divesting himself of five tribal wives and marrying a young beauty, Rachel Johnson, who—by a fortuitous coincidence—happened to be the politically and financially well-connected granddaughter of Hilary W. R. Johnson, the country's first Liberian-born president. The marriage proved gratifying not only to Massaquoi's boundless appreciation for feminine beauty, but to his ambitions, for it gave him something without which no one in Liberia could hope to succeed in politics—social acceptance by the country's "Americo-Liberian" ruling class. ("Americo-Liberian" was the name favored by the descendants of American slaves who had founded the republic in 1847 before setting up a rigid caste system designed to keep the indigenous population in a perpetual state of political and economic impotence.)

Aided by his political savvy, charm, and rugged good looks, Massaquoi quickly advanced with a number of appointments to important government posts, including Secretary of the Interior, charged with the responsibilities of bringing tribal chiefs and the Liberian government closer together, investigating tribal grievances, and settling intertribal disputes. With broad popular support from his adopted Americo-Liberian class as well as his tribal people in the hinterland, the aristocratic Massaquoi became a political power to be reckoned with. He also became the subject of whispers in high political circles that touted him as the next occupant of the Executive Mansion. Some of these whispers reached President King, who decided that it was high time to put an end to them. The question was how? Before long, he would have his answer.

It came in the form of a visit from a representative of Germany's first postwar government, which was headed by President Friedrich Ebert. The German envoy, a Dr. Busing, met with President King in the Executive Mansion to discuss closer cooperation between Liberia and Germany. Also present at the meeting was Secretary of the Interior Momolu Massaquoi.

The president and Massaquoi rose as the short, slightly obese envoy entered King's office in the Executive Mansion. The German was dressed in a rumpled white linen suit and held a white sun helmet with which he fanned himself perpetually in a futile attempt to obtain a measure of relief from the stifling tropical heat.

Unlike the visitor, the two Liberians seemed comfortably cool. King, a tall and elegant man with a heavy mustache, and Massaquoi, a stocky, clean-shaven man with bold features, were both impeccably attired in dark gray, London-tailored suits and fashionable high stiff collars whose pristine white contrasted sharply with their dark faces.

After the three had lighted their cigars and sat down, the German came to the point of his visit. Speaking in precise and fluent, heavily German-accented English, he explained that both President Ebert and Foreign Minister Walther Rathenau had asked him to convey their gratitude to President King for his willingness to listen to their proposal.

His government, he continued, felt that the time had come for Germany and Liberia to establish diplomatic relations through an exchange of consul generals. Such an exchange, Dr. Busing explained, would be mutually beneficial in that it could facilitate the opening of a much-needed market for Liberian raw materials and products such as rubber, cocoa, and palm oil, while giving Germany unencumbered access to these vital commodities, access it had forfeited when it lost the war and was stripped by the Allies of its African colonies.

President King not only expressed interest in the proposal but urged that the plan be put into action as soon as possible. Much of the success of such a plan, the envoy cautioned, would depend on choosing the right man for the job. What the president needed, he pointed out, was a man of extraordinary qualities. He must be highly intelligent, articulate, and have a well-rounded education. He must also have a thorough knowledge of Africa in general and Liberia and its culture in particular, and finally, to succeed in class-conscious Germany, he should have excellent social skills.

"I think I have precisely who you are looking for," the president responded, with an unmistakable look at his Secretary of the Interior. "In fact, I know I have."

Six months after the visit of the German emissary, on June 12, 1922, Momolu Massaquoi, newly appointed Liberian consul general to Germany, arrived in Hamburg with his wife, Rachel, sons Nathaniel, seventeen, and Arthur, one, and daughter Fatima, ten, on the German Woermann Line's S.S. *Wigbert* to assume his new post. Five of his six adult sons from his previous marriages, Jaiah, Manna, Jawa, Bei James, and Abraham, stayed behind in Africa. His oldest son, Al-Haj, had already preceded him to Europe as a student in Dublin, Ireland.

HERMANN BAETZ

It was a Sunday morning in February and bitterly cold. The year was 1905. As many times before, quarry master Hermann Baetz made his way through the wintry forest landscape of central Germany's scenic Harz Mountains near the small town of Uftrungen. He was headed for the powder hut, the depository of large quantities of dynamite, to fetch a few sticks for a blasting job scheduled for the next morning. Normally, it was only a brief walk from the stone quarry to the powder hut, but now, with the snow almost a foot high, Meister Baetz made only slow progress. He was of sturdy build and medium height and, like most self-respecting German men of his era, wore the symbol of manhood, a heavy handlebar mustache.

This particular morning, he was apprehensive, and for good reason. Twice during the last month he had survived narrow brushes with death. The first time he had been climbing a rope ladder in the quarry to mark drilling holes in a steep wall in preparation for blasting when one of the ladder's two main ropes broke. Fortunately, he was able to hold on to a rung long enough for several of his men to pull him to safety. A few days later, when he was almost crushed to death by a falling boulder that missed him by only a few centimeters, he realized that these weren't accidents. A careful inspection of the broken ladder and the dislodged boulder confirmed his suspicion. Both had been tampered with; somebody wanted him dead.

Even before the "accidents" he had been warned by his wife, Martha, to be extra careful. Ever since he told her that he had fired six Italian workers in order to replace them with unemployed Germans, she had been fearing for his safety. While he felt no animosity toward the foreigners, he was a patriotic German of simple principles, which included the firm conviction that charity begins at home. For years, several Italians had worked at the quarry when jobs were plentiful. But the unwritten rule had always been that they were the last to be hired and, if there was a shortage of jobs, the first to be fired. Feeling unwanted or, at best, tolerated as necessary evils, the Italians were mostly resentful of the Germans, but wisely kept their resentment to themselves. They all lived in the worst houses on the outskirts of town and kept their contact with the native townfolk to a bare minimum, which suited the natives just fine.

Mindful of his wife's warning, Meister Baetz approached the hut with caution. When he entered it, an ear-shattering explosion ripped through the silent forest, causing the ground to tremble and setting off a chain of echoes that were heard by everyone within a radius of many kilometers—by everyone, that is, except Meister Baetz.

When Martha heard the explosion, she immediately knew that something dreadful had happened to her husband. Although nearly eight months pregnant, she hurriedly gathered the three youngest of her eight children, Bertha, two, Frieda, five, and Karl, seven, and they ran as fast as their legs would carry them to summon help in town. But several quarry workers, alerted by the unusual blast on a Sunday, had already formed a small expedition and were on their way to the quarry. Martha prepared to follow them, but was held back by sympathetic quarry wives. When the men returned late that night, their faces were grim. The news they brought was even worse than Martha had feared. All they had found on the powder-hut site was a gigantic crater, some fragments from the hut's logs, and a piece of heavy chain that had been cut with a saw. There was not a trace of Meister Baetz, except a mother-of-pearl button from his vest and the grisly remnants of his severed right big toe.

At an inquest held the day after the disaster, it was concluded that Hermann Baetz had been the victim of an assassin or assassins, who by some undetermined means had set off the explosion the moment the quarry master entered the hut. There were strong suspicions that it had been an act of vengeance by some of the fired Italian workers, but no conclusive evidence turned up to link any person to the crime. Within a few weeks, after the shock over the disaster had subsided, life in Uftrungen returned pretty much to where it had been before the disaster. For Martha and her children, however, the explosion on that Sunday morning in February 1905 had shattered their entire world. A day after her husband's funeral and the burial of his meager remains, Martha was obliged to vacate the little company-owned cottage to make room for the new quarry master and his family. Adding to her woes was the fact that her already sizable brood increased even further with the untimely arrival of another baby girl, Clara, bringing the total to nine. Despite seemingly insurmountable handicaps, Martha, barely forty, dug in and raised her children the best she could. Moving from town to town wherever she could find work and lodgings she could afford, she cleaned homes, took in laundry, and helped out at baptisms, weddings, and funerals. Eventually, she and her children settled in Nordhausen, a picturesque medieval town. There, falling back on her early training as a midwife, she was able to make a comfortable living by helping little Nordhausers into the world.

By the time World War I broke out in July 1914, Martha, now nearing fifty, had almost achieved the goal she had set for herself, which was to raise her children as decent human beings until they could fend for themselves. Anna, thirty-one, her oldest, was happily married to a well-to-do butcher and had children of her own. Hermann, twenty-eight, was a foreman on a large farm. Her daughter Martha, twenty-five, was employed as a skilled seamstress. Hedwig, twenty-four, was earning a living as a cook in the household of a wealthy family. Paul, eighteen, had just completed his apprenticeship as a pastry baker, and Karl, sixteen, was winding up his tailoring apprenticeship. The only ones still living with Martha at home were her three youngest daughters, Frieda, fourteen, Bertha, eleven (who, in due time, would become my mother), and Clara, nine. While each of Martha's children differed widely in disposition, temperament, and outlook on life, they all shared their mother's irreconcilable distrust of Italians, a prejudice that over the years she had broadened to include all Catholics.

As the war dragged on, one Baetz boy after another joined the Imperial

Army of His Majesty Kaiser Wilhelm II—Hermann joining the artillery, Paul the infantry, and Karl the cavalry. All three served with valor and distinction on the battlefields of France, the way they knew their father would have wanted them to. Hermann, in the process, earned the Iron Cross First Class but lost his right eye. When the brothers returned to civilian life in 1918, after the German army surrendered and the Kaiser took up exile in Holland, unemployment in Germany was widespread, and the future looked dim. This gave Hermann, the most adventurous of the brothers, the idea to try his luck in the United States, the land of unlimited opportunities where, he had heard, jobs were said "to go begging." The plan was that as soon as he had gotten a toehold in the New World, he would send for the rest of the family. During the early 1920s, Hermann sailed for New York, then proceeded to Chicago, where he had been promised a job as a handyman in a German restaurant. Within three years of putting away every dime he could spare, he had saved up enough money to make good on his promise to send for Paul, Martha, Hedwig, and Clara. Karl and Frieda were to be next, but they had gotten married and decided to remain in Nordhausen with their mother, whose diabetic condition had worsened to a point where emigrating to the United States was out of the question. Bertha, who had just finished her training as a nurse's aide at a local hospital and who also had been preparing to join her siblings in America, suddenly changed her mind. Hearing of an opening at a small private hospital in Hamburg, the seaport city that had always fascinated her, she packed her suitcase, kissed her mother and small-town life goodbye, and jumped on the next Hamburg-bound train. In due time she would find out that it had been a much bigger jump than she could have imagined in her wildest dreams.

GERMANY'S FIRST AFRICAN "AMBASSADOR"

The post–World War I Weimar Republic, where newly appointed Consul General Massaquoi made his diplomatic debut in the spring of 1922, was a volatile volcano ready to erupt. Street riots brought on by dissatisfaction with high unemployment and runaway inflation were the order of the day. There were repeated violent clashes between opposing political parties that ran the gamut from the extreme left to the extreme right. Nationalists, enraged by the punitive terms of the Treaty of Versailles that had been dictated to Germany by the victors of World War I, vented their anger by lashing out at Jews, whom they branded as traitors and conspirators. Within two weeks of Massaquoi's taking office in Hamburg, Germany's Jewish Foreign Minister Walther Rathenau, who was instrumental in beginning the reparations payments required under the Treaty of Versailles, was gunned down by anti-Semitic right-wing fanatics as he was riding in an open car to his office in Berlin. The abortive Beer-Hall Putsch in Munich the following November, in which an unknown Austrian by the name of Adolf Hitler tried to topple the Bavarian state government and the central government in Berlin, was only one of many attempts to destabilize the already shaky Weimar Republic.

Such inauspicious conditions notwithstanding, the Liberian envoy took to his new diplomatic post and life in the thriving Hanseatic metropolis like the proverbial duck to water. As the first official representative of Africa since Germany's loss of more than one million square miles of African colonial territory with more than fourteen million inhabitants, Momolu Massaquoi became the most visible African personality on the European continent. Within a few years, he had firmly established himself as one of the best known and most popular members of the seaport city's consular corps and as a much sought-after host to some of the most prominent and distinguished residents of and visitors to Hamburg. African nationalists who, like Jomo Kenyatta of Kenya, were fighting colonialism from exile in Europe found the congenial atmosphere at Massaquoi's villa near the Alster on Johnsallee 22, in the upscale Rotherbaum district, an ideal setting for their secret strategy meetings. Other personalities who at one time or another enjoyed the Liberian envoy's hospitality included civil-rights activists, entertainers, intellectuals, and athletes from the United States. The most notable among these were singer-actor-activist Paul Robeson, NAACP cofounder W. E. B. Du Bois, poet Langston Hughes, jazz star Louis Armstrong, ex–heavyweight champion Jack Johnson, concert singer Roland Hayes, and scholar Alain Locke. Some of them Momolu had known since his student days in the United States.

In addition to tending to his many consular responsibilities, Momolu still found time to write, teach, and lecture on African languages, especially Vai, at various institutions, including the prestigious University of Hamburg, and translating the Bible into Vai. Proving himself years ahead of his time as a communicator, he authored and published a handsome illustrated booklet entitled *The Republic of Liberia,* which, as far as Germany was concerned, literally put Liberia on the map. Written in English with German translations on facing pages, the booklet clearly stated the author's aim "to make clear what Liberia is, what the ideal is for which she stands, and what she offers to the world's market to perpetuate the progress of civilization and the advancement of the human race." In addition to winning friends for Liberia and influencing people, the booklet also revealed his sure touch as a politician and diplomat. On its opening page it featured a full-page photo of President King, resplendently attired in order-bedecked tails, while a much smaller photo of himself in a regular business suit was buried on page 25.

By this time, the major elements for my pending arrival on this earth were gradually falling into place. But destiny still required a few little nudges here and there to bring about the "oddity" of my German birth. One such nudge came in the form of tonsillitis suffered by my grandfather-to-be. During his brief hospital stay to have his tonsils removed, the chivalrous VIP charmed the doctors and nurses and quickly became the most popular, and hence the most pampered, patient on the ward. Upon discharge from the hospital, the ex-king was moved to reciprocate the befittingly royal treatment he had received by throwing a lavish bash at his villa for the doctors and nurses who had cared for him.

Present at the party—and here's another little nudge from destiny—was Momolu's oldest son, twenty-six-year-old Al-Haj, who happened to be on holiday from his studies at Trinity College in Dublin. Overindulged ever since he was a baby by his father and mother, a London-educated "Americo-Liberian" beauty from Cape Palmas, Al-Haj had duly turned into a spoiled, self-centered young man who was used to having his way. In addition to these rather negative, learned attributes, he had the good fortune to have inherited a fair amount of his father's intellectual powers and his ability to charm, especially members of the opposite sex. On the evening of the party, while circulating among his father's guests, he spotted a pretty, brown-haired young woman, barely out of her teens, who was standing alone in a corner of the crowded reception room. "I'm Al-Haj Massaquoi," he introduced himself, amused at the young woman's obvious discomfort at being spoken to by a stranger. "Do you speak English?"

The young woman shook her head. "*Es tut mir leid. Ich verstehe nicht* (I'm sorry. I don't understand)."

"In that case, we'll have to make do with what little German I know," he responded in fluent yet heavily accented German. "What's your name?"

"Bertha," she replied while shyly studying the elegant young African, his impeccably tailored Savile Row suit, his handsome, velvety dark face, his close-cropped black hair, and his meticulously clipped mustache. She especially noticed his well-shaped yet strong-looking hands and his flawless, incredibly white teeth. Bertha thought how very different he was from the awkward, rough-talking and crude-acting young men in her hometown of Nordhausen. Most of the fellows she had gone to dances with were farmworkers or tradesmen.

"You don't have to be afraid of me," Al-Haj told her. "I don't bite. I don't know what they have told you about us Africans, but I can assure you that I'm not a cannibal."

Embarrassed that he had mistaken her reticence for fear, she hastened to tell him that no such thoughts had crossed her mind. That's why she didn't hesitate to say yes when he asked her whether she would join him the next day for a ride in his new automobile, a gift from his indulgent father. That automobile ride, which was followed by many more, was the beginning of a whirlwind courtship during which Al-Haj swept the unsophisticated Bertha off her feet. Commuting between Dublin and Hamburg as often as his studies permitted, Al-Haj took Bertha to all the popular nightspots on St. Pauli's Reeperbahn, to the horse races, the theater, the opera, and even boxing matches. Occasionally, they would take trips to other cities, such as Berlin. In the rush of activities, Al-Haj kept postponing the long-promised trip to the altar, explaining, whenever Bertha raised the subject, that his exams didn't leave him enough time to plan and execute a wedding grand enough for the son of the Liberian Consul General. But destiny had already given its final nudge. I made my unheralded debut at Eppendorfer *Krankenhaus* two months prematurely on Tuesday, January 19, 1926. My mother named me Hans-Jürgen, in keeping with the prevailing popularity of hyphenated names, and in due time, like most German children, I started calling her Mutti. By an unusual coincidence, only six months later, on July 31, Momolu's wife, Rachel, presented him with another son—and me with a baby uncle—whom they named Fritz.

Meanwhile, my maternal grandmother, Martha Baetz, who was gravely ill with diabetes, had traveled to the United States for "one last visit" with her children who had settled in and around Chicago. Before Mutti's letter announcing my arrival could reach my grandmother, Mutti received a black-rimmed letter from one of her sisters informing her that their mother had died and had been buried in Chicago.

THE GOOD LIFE AT THE ALSTER

Eventually, Momolu, who had become quite fond of my mother, insisted that she and I join the rest of the Massaquois in their villa on Johnsallee while my father spent most of his time pursuing his law studies—and whatever else—in Ireland. Immediately, the mansion became a house linguistically divided, with everyone speaking German to my mother and me while conversing in English among themselves. Soon the stately mansion in one of Hamburg's most exclusive neighborhoods was filled with the screams of two willful toddlers, while my mother, who had quit her hospital job in order to take care of me, tried to arbitrate the never-ending disputes between "Uncle" Fritz and me to keep us from disturbing Momolu. Since Fatima had been farmed out to some fancy boarding school in the suburbs, and Nat and Arthur attended high school and kindergarten, respectively, Fritz and I had the run of the house. That went on until, at age two, we were joined by Fritz's baby sister, my "Auntie" Fasia, who became the new apple of Momolu's eye.

If, during my toddler days following my first contact with the outside world, I believed that the universe revolved around me and that I was something quite rare and extraordinarily precious, I came by my belief honestly enough. Not a day went by without people craning their necks at me and rapturously exclaiming "*Ist der nicht süss* (Isn't he sweet)?" or *"Wie niedlich* (How cute)!" At times, during strolls with Mutti, this adulation was tangible as passersby offered me candy, fruit, or even money, all of which, to my chagrin, my mother made me refuse. I soon became aware that other children my age didn't receive as much attention as I did, and when I asked Mutti why, she explained that it was because everybody admired my "beautiful brown skin and black curly hair." It had never occurred to me that there were physical differences that set me apart from other people, including my own mother. Suddenly, I became keenly aware of the differences between European and African racial traits. Since my grandfather—a very dark man—was the dominant figure of my universe, with most whites playing deferential if not subordinate roles, I came to regard a dark complexion and kinky hair as superior attributes and accepted the celebrity treatment accorded me by the public as my well-deserved due.

Grandpa Momolu was an unabashed lover of children who spent as much time as his many consular duties permitted with us kids. In fact, I saw much more of him than I did of my father, who was winding up his studies in Dublin while working in various Hamburg businesses, including the Woermann Line, in order to gain practical experience in the import-export trade. Since Momolu, Fritz, and I were early risers, we three started each day having our breakfast—cantaloupes and a bowl of porridge—on the glass-enclosed terrace overlooking a tree-shaded backyard. While we ate, I would regale the old gentleman with German children's rhymes, including scary *Struwwelpeter* (Sloppy Peter) rhymes that my mother had often read to me from an illustrated book, and that I could recite by heart. The rhyme that got the greatest reaction from my grandfather was that of *"Die Drei Tintenjungen* (The Three Ink Boys),"* who started out as white boys but ended up black. After making fun of a loinclothed young "blackamoor" who happened by, they were punished by Santa who, by dunking them into a giant ink bottle, made them even blacker than the blackamoor. Each time I recited this condescendingly racist German children's classic, my grandfather would roar with laughter that could be heard throughout the house. In return for my efforts, he would tell me stories of great ancient African kingdoms. He even told me that once he had been a king himself, something I found extremely hard to believe until he showed me a photograph of himself as a young man wearing a robe and a crown. He explained that he left the crown in Liberia and promised that one day he would take me there and show it to me. No matter how often he explained to me that he had passed on the crown and title to a younger cousin of his because he had gotten tired of being king, I could never understand why anyone in his right mind would not want to be a king.

Every Sunday afternoon, Momolu would take Arthur, Fritz, and me for a stroll through a park along the Alster. We were an imposing group, my grandfather in his homburg hat, fur-collared ulster, and fashionable spats, and we boys in matching blue sailor suits and hats, which were the fashion rage of the day. These outings always climaxed in a much-anticipated stop at a small, exclusive café, or *Konditorei,* where the air was filled with the irresistible aroma of hot chocolate, fresh-brewed coffee, and fresh-baked pastries, and where the inevitable violin and piano background of schmaltzy Viennese waltzes provided that uniquely cozy atmosphere that Germans call *Gemütlichkeit.* As soon as we arrived, an obsequious, tail-coated maître d', amid much bowing from the waist, would seat our small yet ever-so-distinguished party at one of the establishment's better tables, which had been especially reserved for *Seine Excellenz.* Invariably, the patrons at neighboring tables would stare at us, however discreetly, and invariably, to my great delight, my grandfather would ask me to order the various treats to show off my authentic German. Nothing seemed to please him more than to watch the surprised expressions on the faces of the other patrons as I, fully aware of my importance, rose to the occasion with enthusiastic narcissism.

There were even times when Momolu had my mother wake me up after I had already gone to bed because he wanted me to demonstrate my linguistic prowess to some African and German dinner guests. On such occasions, the old man would ask me to sing a German nursery song, such as *"Hänschen Klein Ging Allein* (Little Hans Walked Alone),'' and I would be only too happy to oblige. For my trouble, I could bask in the adulation of the guests, who never failed to be impressed by the fact that not only did I speak accent-free German, but that I did so with an unmistakably Hamburgian brogue.

To me, Momolu was simply *Opa* (Granddad), an infinitely kind and indulgent man whose main purpose in life, it seemed to me, was to see that my every wish and desire was fulfilled. Only much later did I learn and appreciate what an important and distinguished statesman he was and what a vital, pioneering role he played as a spokesman for Africa in general and Liberia in particular.

Meanwhile, allegations of an international scandal involving Liberia produced a fallout that had far-reaching consequences for my grandfather, and ultimately for all of the Massaquois, including me. Ever since the latter part of the twenties, reports had been surfacing that sent shock waves of indignation around the world, and that threatened the very existence of modern history's first black-ruled republic on the African continent. It was alleged that the Liberian government under President King was not only condoning but actively participating in the extremely lucrative export of Liberian tribal people to the Spanish island colony of Fernando Po (now Bioko) off the coast of Nigeria as forced labor. Liberia, the nation founded by freed slaves for the express purpose of providing a haven from oppression, and whose motto was "The love of liberty brought us here," stood accused of practicing slavery.

Stung by the accusation, President King demanded a full investigation by an impartial League of Nations commission of inquiry to clear his and his country's honor. The League obliged and, following an exhaustive investigation, concluded that charges of slavery, as defined by the League's Anti-Slavery Convention, were unfounded. The commission did, however, censure Liberia for the practice of "pawning" whereby persons, especially children of tribal background, were literally given away by their families to work in households of well-to-do Americo-Liberians, usually without any remuneration other than the most primitive room and board, ostensibly as part of their "education." Despite the fact that pawning was widely practiced and condoned throughout West Africa, including the vast British, French, Belgian, and Portuguese colonies, it was Liberia, the tiny black-ruled republic, that was singled out for international condemnation. As a result, pressure mounted, especially in the United States and Britain, for the resignation of President King and Vice President Allen Yancy.

At this point, a wild scramble to fill the political vacuum that could result from a King resignation erupted in Monrovia. Much of the behind-the-scenes maneuvering took place thirty-five hundred miles away from Monrovia at the Liberian Consulate General in Hamburg, right under my toddler nose. There, a steady stream of Liberian visitors—all leading members of the opposition People's Party—tried to convince my grandfather that he was the logical person to lead Liberia out of its darkest hour. It took some doing to convince him to consider a bid for the presidency, especially since that meant changing his political allegiance from the ruling True Whig Party and being pitted against his longtime friend and political ally, Secretary of State Edwin Barclay. But when President King asked Momolu to return to Liberia in order to take over the post of Postmaster General, he regarded the offer as a fortunate omen and accepted. On December 8, 1929, his mind made up to face whatever political challenges lay ahead, Momolu Massaquoi sailed aboard the S.S. *Livadia* of the Hamburg-Afrika Linie toward Monrovia and an uncertain political future.

As my grandfather's oldest son, my father was expected to play an active role in his father's still clandestine quest for the presidency. This meant that my father had to end his law studies in Dublin and return to Liberia as well, a disruption that he used as further excuse that the time wasn't right for a wedding. When my grandfather invited us to leave for Liberia with the rest of the family, my mother refused. Although she had been looking forward to our living in Africa one day, she quickly changed her mind when our family physician sternly warned her against such a drastic change of climate for me because of my generally frail health. In quick succession, I had been stricken with diphtheria, whooping cough, scarlet fever, and a touch of pneumonia, and had barely survived. The doctor convinced my mother that taking me to one of Africa's most inhospitable climates, a country plagued by malaria and a host of other tropical diseases, and that at the time had only the most rudimentary medical facilities, was tantamount to sending me to certain death. That's all my mother needed to hear. Not bothering to get a second opinion, she told my grandfather that, at least for the time being, she and I would remain in Germany. Her decision was nonnegotiable. Determined not to put my life in jeopardy regardless of the consequences to our financial security or her marital status, she gave up her long-harbored dream of a future in Liberia without blinking an eye.

THE NEW KID ON THE BLOCK

With the departure of my grandfather, my father, and the other Massaquois, our comfortable lifestyle in one of Hamburg's most exclusive residential areas came to an abrupt halt. The only Massaquoi who remained behind in Europe was my aunt Fatima, who at the time was attending a boarding school in Bern, Switzerland.

Left virtually to her own devices, Mutti was forced to make it on her own. This meant finding a job and an apartment she could afford. Luckily, there was an opening for a nurse's aide in the ear, nose, and throat clinic of St. Georg Hospital, a huge government facility, near the center of Hamburg. Acting on a tip from a fellow hospital worker, she found a tiny, one-room, cold-water, attic flat on the third floor of a tenement building that could be reached from a rear entrance by negotiating two of the steepest and creakiest flights of stairs I had ever seen. Our new address was No. 3 Stückenstrasse in Barmbek, a sprawling, predominantly working-class section on the city's northeast side. In addition to the affordable rent, what persuaded my mother to take this particular flat was the fact that on the floor directly below ours there lived an elderly widow, Frau Elisabeth Möller, who, for a modest weekly fee and the stipulation that I call her Tante (Aunt) Möller, agreed to look after me and feed me during the day while my mother was at work.

Being the new kid on the block is never easy, but as far as my new neighborhood was concerned, I was not only a new kid, but a most unusual new kid. Consequently, it took a while before my new neighbors became used to me and—equally important—I became used to them. In the upscale, cosmopolitan environment I had left behind, an environment in which black people of my grandfather's stature were treated with the utmost respect, I had learned to look upon my racial traits as enviable assets. All at once I was forced to regard them as liabilities, as I noticed a drastic change in the way people related to me. Instead of the friendly glances and flattering comments I had been used to, I suddenly drew curious, at times even hostile stares and insulting remarks. Most offensive to me were two words that I had never heard before and that I soon discovered were used by people for the sole purpose of describing the way I looked. One word was *Mischling,* which, after pressing Mutti for an explanation, she defined as someone who, like me, was of racially mixed parentage. The other word was *Neger*—according to Mutti, a misnomer as far as I was concerned, since she insisted that I was definitely not a *Neger,* a term that she said applied only to black people in America. But street urchins, who were my worst tormentors, apparently did not know, or care, about such fine distinctions. As soon as they spotted me, they would start to chant, *"Neger, Neger, Schornsteinfeger* (Negro, Negro, chimney sweep)!" and they would keep it up with sadistic insistence until I was out of their sight. Luckily, after a short time, the stares and taunts became fewer as the novelty of my exotic appearance began to wear off. Soon, some of the kids who had shouted the loudest became my closest pals. To my great relief, it seemed as if all of a sudden they had become oblivious to the visual differences that set us apart.

Occasionally, I still missed my former, sheltered life in Rotherbaum— my daily breakfast ritual with my grandfather, our walks at the edge of the Alster, and the feeling of being the center of the universe. But whatever feelings of nostalgia remained, they had nothing to do with our drastically lowered standard of living, of which I was hardly aware. From my perspective, our new environment entailed a different lifestyle, not a lower one. Today I realize that my mother saw it differently.

Instead of hot and cold running water, we now had only cold. This meant that instead of taking daily showers or baths, I now had to wait until Saturday evenings for my mother to heat a huge pot of water on a coal-burning hearth in the kitchen and empty it into a zinc washtub that doubled as my bathtub. After soaking me for a while, my mother would give me a thorough workover with a soapy sponge. The best part was always the rinsing, when my mother, improvising a shower, would dump several pitchers full of warm water on me. During the week, I had to make do with a cold-water "birdie bath" at the kitchen sink.

Other amenities that were conspicuous by their absence in our apartment were a telephone and a refrigerator. The absence of the latter was typical for the majority of pre–World War II German households, and made daily shopping trips for food an absolute necessity. Private telephones were found only in the homes of the affluent. The one thing, however, that set our apartment apart from every other apartment in the neighborhood, including those in our building, was that it was not wired for electricity and instead was lighted by gas. I had no problem with that. On the contrary, I enjoyed watching my mother each evening hold a lighted match to the ceiling fixture and turn on the gas, then wait for the bright light to come on with a muffled mini-explosion.

I found my new world far more exciting than the staid, quiet villa and the serene, parklike atmosphere I used to call home. Our new neighborhood consisted mainly of old, dingy-looking three- and four-story tenements, some with balconies and tiny backyards, and terraces of two-story row houses. This was long before it became customary to keep the facades of houses freshly painted in a variety of bright colors, which gave post–World War II West German cities that characteristic "economic miracle" look of prosperity. In the working-class sections of prewar Hamburg, buildings were covered with a rich patina of grime that rendered all an undistinguishable shade of gray. But despite their grimy exteriors, homes in Barmbek were immaculate inside, since housewives spent practically the entire day scrubbing, brushing, sweeping, dusting, polishing, beating rugs, and doing the laundry. Unlike the quiet boulevards of Rotherbaum, the streets of Barmbek were alive with people who were doing exciting things that were enormously appealing to a five-year-old boy's curiosity. I did most of my explorations of my new surroundings while tagging along with my babysitter, Tante Möller, as she made her daily rounds to an assortment of shops—the milkman's, the grocer's, the butcher's, the greengrocer's and, once a week, the fishmonger's. In each of these mostly mom-and-pop shops, she would hold lengthy discussions with the proprietors about virtually everything, from the weather to her rheumatism, and from the high cost of living to "the good old days" before World War I. Each shop held its own special attraction for me, not the least of which were the small samples of cheese, candy, sausage, or fruit that the kindly shopkeepers would invariably hand me. These "donations" became even more bountiful after the shopkeepers learned from Tante Möller that, appearances notwithstanding, I was a genuine, born-and-bred Hamburger and not, as everybody assumed, a *Quiddje,* which was a contemptuous slang term Hamburgers reserved for people who had the monumental misfortune not to have been born within Hamburg's city limits.

On a typical morning of shopping with Tante Möller, I would watch with fascination as a tailor sat cross-legged on a table near the window of his shop while sewing a suit, a blacksmith inside a smoke-filled smithy nailed new horseshoes onto the hoofs of a giant brewery horse, an iceman unloaded huge slabs of ice from a truck in front of a tavern, and a soot-covered, top-hatted chimney sweep balanced precariously on top of a roof while lowering a weighted brush at the end of a cable down a chimney. Occasionally, the alternating sounds of horns and bells would signal the approach of a fleet of fire engines manned by helmeted firemen. Bordering Stückenstrasse, our street, was the main thoroughfare, Am Markt, which bustled with squealing streetcars while clanking elevated trains, called *Hochbahn,* passed overhead. Unaccustomed to noise at all hours of night, my mother and I would awaken every time an el train thundered by, but within a few weeks we had become so accustomed to the sound that we became totally oblivious to it.

Among the more intriguing neighborhood events was the occasional sighting of a siren-blaring police paddy wagon, nicknamed *Grüner August* because of its dark green color. Tante Möller, with her penchant to exaggerate, had explained that its purpose was to haul criminals to jail. In reality, the "criminals" delivered at the nearby precinct were, for the most part, hard-working and law-abiding men from the neighborhood who, after a few beers too many at their pub, had become a bit boisterous.

Directly across from our home was the rear exit of the Europa Palast, the neighborhood movie theater, which was soon to become my favorite week-end hangout, thanks to its Sunday matinees. Half a block up the street stood the *Waffelfabrik,* an old, ugly-looking, four-storied red-brick building that, despite its unprepossessing appearance, was held in high esteem by the children of the neighborhood. I soon learned that after I ascended a flight of stairs and rang a bell, a little window would open through which, in exchange for five pfennig, an old lady would hand me an enormous paper bag filled with delicious waffle scraps. Within a few years, the old waffle factory would assume an entirely different, largely sinister importance for the neighborhood and me. But like so many other things I encountered during those wonder years, it had an innocence and charm that I would later see with different eyes.

Since daily shopping for food was a necessity, I not only learned to put up with Hamburg's notoriously cold, drizzly, and foggy weather, but actually learned to like it, which is a trait that sets Hamburgers apart from the vast majority of people and animals on the globe. Via Tante Möller's kitchen, I also became hooked on such Hamburg delicacies as smoked eel; boiled rice topped with a mixture of sugar and cinnamon; pear soup; pig snouts and feet; flounder fried in bacon; fried, raw, and smoked herring; and *Rote Grütze,* a red fruit puddinglike dish. Because of Tante Möller, I learned to think and feel like a Hamburger, and if she taught me anything, it was that people born and living in Hamburg were blessed with the most beautiful, the most exciting, and the most desirable hometown on the face of the earth.

About once a month, Tante Möller would take me shopping downtown via streetcar *Linie* 6 where we would visit big department stores like Karstadt, Toedt, Epa, and Woolworth, the recent import from the United States, and look at the colorful window and indoor displays. Invariably, we would conclude our excursion with a visit to the elegant Alster Pavilion on Jungfernstieg (Hamburg's answer to New York's Fifth Avenue) or the roof garden of Karstadt to sample a variety of confectionery delights. Occasionally, we would take the Alster ferry instead of the streetcar home, where I would give a detailed report to my mother about all the things I had seen and heard. Unfortunately, these downtown excursions came to a sudden halt after Tante Möller, who was getting up in years and a bit feeble, lost her grip while stepping off a streetcar and fell. The incident caused a big commotion, with people standing around us and staring while a policeman helped her back on her feet. Although she was not seriously hurt, she lost her nerve for venturing and never rode the streetcar again.

One day, not far from our home, Tante Möller and I encountered three dark-skinned, keen-featured women approaching. Their black hair was flowing in the wind while their long, colorful dresses were sweeping the ground. The three were followed by several kids who were taunting them the way I often had been taunted. But instead of the black chimney-sweeper chant that I had to endure, they were chanting something about a "Gypsy boy who shit in his pants." When I asked Tante Möller who those strange ladies were, she whispered to me that they were Gypsies. She explained that while she didn't approve of what the kids where doing, Gypsies really had it coming. "Gypsies," she told me, "are very dangerous people. They never stay put or work and they steal anything that isn't nailed down—especially little children." I looked with terror at the three approaching women, and when they returned my stares with their dark, penetrating eyes, I nearly died of fear. I, too, became a staunch believer in the popular German myth that

Gypsies steal children—especially blond children—and raise them as their own in order to bring "fresh blood" into their "tribes" and thereby avoid problems from repeated inbreeding. Although I realized that my black hair made me a less desired target of Gypsy kidnappers, I wasn't about to take chances. I always made sure to keep as much distance between them and me as possible.

Eventually, Tante Möller let me venture into the street by myself and play with the kids, but with the stern admonition to stay within the audible range of her voice, which was roughly a two-block area bordered by Stückenstrasse, Am Markt, Haferkamp, and Langenrehm. This meant that as long as I returned home within a few minutes of being summoned by her from a window of her apartment, I was considered within bounds. The moment I strayed beyond hearing range or was too engrossed in playing to respond to her clarion call, "Haaaans-Jüüüürgen!," I was considered at large and subject to being retrieved by the old lady herself. In that case, the inevitable punishment was not being allowed to go outside the next day, a sentence for which there was no appeal.

Tante Möller also instructed me to always keep on the lookout for *Mitschnacker,* a special Hamburg variety of male kidnappers who derived their name from their modus operandi of talking children into following them. Remembering the three sinister Gypsy women with spine-chilling vividness, I promised not to accept invitations to go along with strangers in general and *Mitschnacker* in particular.

If there was one thing I had learned in a hurry, it was to respect Tante Möller's no-nonsense approach to discipline. Having reared three sons and a daughter to respectable adulthood by herself following her husband's death in the famed World War I battle of Verdun in France, she had emerged as an expert at making kids mind. For my own benefit, she quickly disabused me of my long-held notion that I was the center of the universe. Nevertheless, she was a kind and soft-hearted woman who, although somewhat gruff in demeanor, never spanked me or in any way became physical when I stepped over the line. She didn't have to. For those not altogether rare occasions, she had a handy deterrent that never failed to do the trick. Intoning the old German proverb "He who doesn't listen must feel," she'd reach into her broom closet and fetch her notorious *Rute,* consisting of a bundle of thin twigs tied together at one end, which, she claimed, Santa

Claus had left behind for precisely such occurrences. Just waving this vaunted instrument of mayhem in my face was all she needed to do to make me return in a hurry to the straight and narrow path of righteousness.

QUALITY TIME

Although I really liked Tante Möller a lot and didn't mind staying with her during the week, I always looked forward to evenings, when Mutti came home from work, and especially Sundays, when she didn't have to go to the hospital and could spend the entire day with me. (Prior to World War II, Germans still worked a six-day week.) Following an old German custom, my mother would invariably dress me up in my *Sonntagsanzug* (Sunday suit) and we would head outdoors. Often we would walk to City Park at the edge of town, which on summer weekends buzzed with the activities of thousands of pent-up Hamburgers yearning to breathe free. People were rowing boats or paddling canoes, while others played soccer or tennis, flew kites, had a picnic, rode horses or bicycles, or swam in the huge outdoor pool. But most people were doing exactly what my mother and I were doing, simply walking and enjoying watching others at play.

When we got hungry and tired from walking, we would stop at one of the many wooden benches and tables and feast on the delicious sandwiches my mother had brought. For dessert, she let me buy a giant, double-scoop vanilla and strawberry ice cream cone for a *Groschen* (about a dime) from one of the ubiquitous tricycle vendors.

Another popular destination for our summertime Sunday excursions was Blankenese, with its many miles of sandy beaches and packed beach cafés along the Elbe, which was less than an hour-long train ride away. In Blankenese we would join the thousands of sun worshippers on the beach, change into our swimsuits, build sand castles, watch the majestic ocean liners appear and disappear over the Elbe's horizon, or simply lie on our backs, stare into the sky, and watch the clouds go by. Before starting our journey home, we would walk up the hundreds of zigzagging steps leading to the upper level of Blankenese and marvel at the quaint hillside homes.

Occasionally, we would attend special events, like the popular air shows near Hamburg's airport. There we would join thousands of spectators to watch the legendary World War I flying ace Ernst Udet risk his life in breathtaking aerial stunts and parachute jumps. When, only a few years later, Udet emerged as one of the major architects of the vaunted *Luftwaffe,* the weapon that emboldened Hitler to embark on his conquest of the world, I often thought back to the carefree time I spent in Fuhlsbüttel under a cloudless sky, thrilled to the core by one of the first heroes of my early years.

The constant stares of people that followed us wherever my mother and I went didn't bother me in the least. Since I was convinced that my mother was about the prettiest woman around and that I, too, looked absolutely spiffy in my neatly pressed suit and shined shoes, I wouldn't have had it any other way. Only when I sensed that the gawkers' curiosity was uncomplimentary, mean-spirited, or intrusive, as when someone pointed at me and laughed or used the hated word *Neger,* did I feel offended and angry. When that happened, I'd usually retaliate by sticking out my tongue at the person or tapping my forehead with my index finger, which is German sign language for *Du bist verrückt* (You're crazy). Sensing my frustration, my mother never chided me for giving vent to my anger in this way, although she frequently told me that the best way to deal with ignoramuses was to simply ignore them, something I found exceedingly difficult to do.

"CULTURE SHOW" AT HAGENBECKS ZOO

One of the most popular attractions for Hamburgers, both young and old, was Hagenbecks *Tierpark* (animal park), the internationally famous zoo in suburban Stellingen. Named for its innovative founder, Carl Hagenbeck, it reputedly was the world's first zoo where wild animals could be viewed in spacious outdoor runs patterned after their natural habitats instead of in cramped cages and behind bars. A confirmed Hagenbeck fan, I was in full agreement when Mutti suggested one day that it was time for another visit to the zoo. This time, she had arranged for a fellow nurse's daughter, Ingeborg, a somewhat brattish but otherwise cute girl my age, to come along.

As soon as we arrived at the zoo after a lengthy streetcar ride, Ingeborg demanded to see the *Indianer* (Native Americans). My mother and I had never heard of people being exhibited at an animal park, but Ingeborg insisted that on her last visit she had seen real live "Indians." When my mother asked a zoo guide whether there were any Indians to be seen, he told her they were fresh out of Indians but that there was an equally interesting African exhibit, just a few minutes' walk away. The guide explained that the "primitive peoples" exhibits were part of Hagenbeck's famous "Culture Shows."

Ingeborg and I were disappointed, as we had looked forward to seeing Indians attired in resplendent feather headgear, but we agreed to settle for the African exhibit although none of us had the slightest idea of what to expect. I was totally unprepared for what we found. After walking past spectacular exhibits of monkeys, giraffes, lions, elephants, and other African wildlife, we arrived at the "African Village," replete with half a dozen or so thatch-roofed clay huts and peopled, we were told, by "authentic Africans." Like the animal exhibits, the "village" was bordered by a chest-high wooden fence to keep the viewers out and the viewees in. The only thing that distinguished the human exhibit from the animal exhibits was the absence of the deep, water-filled moat that separated men from beasts.

Except for their skin color and hair, the Africans on display looked nothing like my relatives or any of the Africans I had met at my grandfather's house. All of the villagers were barefoot and dressed in tattered rags. Two women, draped in dingy-looking cloths, were rhythmically pounding a heavy wooden stick into a mortar. A guide explained that they were making corn flour in preparation for their dinner. The men were sitting around in small groups, intently watching the spectators while chatting away in an unintelligible language between puffs from short, primitive-looking pipes. It was difficult to say who was more interested in whom, the Africans in the Europeans or the Europeans in the Africans. Each group studied the other across the wooden fence with the same undisguised curiosity.

Suddenly, something happened that I had feared from the moment I caught sight of the exhibit. Despite the fact that I had carefully tried to stay in the background in order to see without being seen, one of the Africans spotted me in the crowd. All at once the entire village took notice of me. The two women stopped pounding and the men stopped puffing. As if they had seen a long-lost relative, they were all pointing and grinning at me.

Desperately, I tried to hide behind one of the spectators, but to no avail. Tipped off by the Africans' finger-pointing, one of the zoo visitors spun around and, after realizing what the Africans' excitement was all about, pointed his own stubby index finger at me. "Look!" he alerted his female companion. "Here's one of their kids." This set off a chain reaction among the rest of the spectators until everyone, both African and German, was looking at me.

Just when I felt that I would die from embarrassment for having been mistaken for one of "them," Mutti grabbed me and Ingeborg by the hand and, over Ingeborg's protest, quietly led us away.

Later that evening, after we were home alone, my mother told me that I had no reason to feel embarrassed at the zoo. The Africans we saw, she explained, were simple but good people from the hinterland who deserved to be pitied rather than ridiculed. She suspected that they had been tricked by somebody into leaving their homeland and appearing in the exhibit. Mutti made me understand that even if the Africans had not been taken by force to Germany, it was still terribly wrong to display human beings in a zoo behind fences and side by side with animals. "I can't understand the mentality of people who let something like that happen and who see nothing wrong with it," she said over and over.

As much as we both liked zoos, my mother and I vowed that evening never to set foot on Hagenbecks Tierpark again. I kept that vow for about fifteen years until after the war, when, as a young man, I obliged a young lady when she asked me to take her to Hagenbeck. The zoo was still largely the way I remembered it from my childhood, but, not to my surprise, the "African Village" had disappeared.

A COMEDOWN FOR A KING

To my frequent question, "When will Daddy be back?" Mutti always responded with a helpless shrug and the standard reply, "I really don't know." She was telling the truth. What she didn't tell me was that she had received bad news from Liberia via Tante Fatima. It wasn't until several years later that she let me read the letter. The gist of the letter, sent from Bern, was that my grandfather had failed in his quest for the presidency, that he was held on a trumped-up charge of embezzling postal funds, that my father and several of his brothers were in hiding among fellow Vai tribesmen in the Liberian hinterland and that my Uncle Nat was in jail on charges of having plotted to kill the newly appointed President Barclay and overthrow the government. During his trial on sedition charges, Nat denied the assassination plot but admitted that a youth group he had helped organize was aimed at destroying the America-Liberian political monopoly and replacing it with a government by the aborigines.

Tante Fatima's letter contained a lengthy explanation of the circumstances that caused the Massaquois' fortunes to take a turn for the worse. It seems that President King and Vice President Yancy, faced with the prospect of Liberia being stripped of its independence and placed under League of Nations trusteeship because of the Fernando Po slavery charges, resigned on December 3, 1930. On that same day, Secretary of State Edwin Barclay was sworn in as president to serve out President King's unexpired term. In an apparent attempt to destroy his strongest political rival and former close friend, Barclay immediately launched his anti-Massaquoi vendetta, which culminated in the jailing of both my grandfather and my Uncle Nat.

Fatima's letter concluded that this was by no means all the bad news she had. The loss of his postmaster general's post and the fact that he had mortgaged all of his properties in order to raise funds to mount a political campaign also meant that Momolu was financially ruined. Out of a job and out of political favor, he had no way of paying when the payments fell due.

For Fatima, it meant that she was suddenly financially dependent on the generosity of Momolu's many European friends. For my mother, it meant the end of all hope that one day my father and grandfather would contribute at least in a small measure to my financial support.

HEAD START

The fact that Tante Möller lived comfortably on her widow's pension enabled her to devote a good portion of her time to her one remaining passion—the gathering and disseminating of gossip. Toward that end, she had founded, and was now the most respected member of, the Thursday Knitting Club, made up of a dozen or so pensioned old ladies like herself. Each Thursday, on a rotating basis, members would entertain each other with coffee, cake, knitting, crocheting, and—most important—the latest "news."

For me, the weekly meetings of the old ladies were a welcome interruption of my daily routine. There were two reasons in particular why I looked forward to them. One was that I could always count on getting my fill of delicious cake; the other, equally important, was that it gave me a chance to play with Erika. Erika was a frisky redhead a year younger than I, whose maternal grandmother, Frau Häselich, was her baby-sitter and a charter member of the club. By coincidence, Erika's father, Walter Schmedemann, was a *Stationsarbeiter* (station worker) at my mother's hospital. Station workers did menial tasks such as delivering food from the kitchen to the various hospital wards by way of a two-wheeled pushcart. I learned later that Onkel Walter was also a prominent functionary in anti-Hitler Social Democratic politics.

This particular Thursday it was Tante Möller's turn to entertain. As always, after Erika and I had finished our plates of pastry, we were banished from the *Gute Stube* (good room) where the old ladies had gathered and told to play and not to make any noise. Thus instructed, we repaired to an adjacent bedroom where we kept busy for a while with various children's games. Eventually, we ran out of things to do and boredom set in. All of a sudden, Erika—ever ready for mischief—signaled that she had an idea. Before I could fully comprehend what was taking place, she had stepped out of her panties, lifted her little skirt, turned around, and bent over to give me an unobstructed close-up of the lower part of the female anatomy. Since I had never seen anything as funny as that in all of my four years, I broke out in uproarious laughter. Soon my voice was joined by the high squeals of Erika, who relished my enthusiastic response to her impromptu striptease. At precisely that moment—at the height of our mirth over a successful performance—the door to the *Gute Stube* opened and Frau Häselich stepped into the room. Apparently made curious by our boisterous laughter, she had come to investigate.

"What in heavens is going on here?" the old lady demanded to know after recovering from her initial shock. Literally caught with her panties down by her nonplussed grandmother, Erika shifted into reverse and started to cry. With instant tears streaming down her cheeks, she pointed an accusing finger at me.

"He told me to do it! Hans-Jürgen told me to take off my panties!" she screamed at the top of her lungs.

Taken totally by surprise by the sudden turn of events and the accusation of my playmate, I was too dumbfounded to speak up in defense of my good name.

"Well, what do you have to say for yourself, you rascal?" Frau Häselich, blue in the face with anger, wanted to know.

Gradually, I recovered my composure. In a halting, barely audible voice I presented my version of the unspeakable act to a summary court-martial that had been hastily convened by—and consisted of—the Thursday Knitting Club. Immediately, the court split into two factions. One, headed by Frau Häselich, held that I was guilty as charged. The other, headed by Tante Möller, believed that Erika was a shrewd and conniving femme fatale who had led poor Hans-Jürgen astray. For a moment it looked as though the anti-Hans-Jürgen faction would win out as Erika backed her testimony with a new deluge of crocodile tears, but eventually Tante Möller prevailed. Convincing everyone, except Frau Häselich, that Erika's testimony was highly suspect because she had been caught telling fibs before, Tante Möller persuaded her peers to dismiss the case. Not long thereafter, the club adjourned until the following Thursday, leaving behind a bewildered four-year-old boy whose view of women—for more than one reason—would never be quite the same.

The lessons I gleaned from this traumatic interlude were (1) that there

was a distinct anatomical difference between boys and girls, (2) that there
was something about that difference that for some unfathomable reason
made grown-ups uptight, and (3) that a girl could get a fellow into a whole
lot of trouble. Having had my share, I decided to leave well enough alone
and in the future to avoid girls like the plague. But as the best-laid plans of
men and mice sometimes go awry, so eventually did mine.

GOING TO TANTE TILLI

The only person who shared the attic floor of our apartment building with
us was a gaunt, gray-haired spinster of indeterminable age whom everybody
called Tante Tilli, and who was the great-aunt of my little friend Erika. Tilli
was a fountain-pen polisher in the local Mont Blanc factory whose once
well-to-do family used to own the building in which we were living. When
hard times forced her family to sell the building, they made an agreement
with the buyer to have her live in the small apartment rent-free in perpetuity.

Since our one-room apartment lacked, among numerous other conve-
niences, a toilet, an arrangement had been worked out with Tante Tilli
whereby we had a key to her apartment and unrestricted access to her toilet.
While my mother had cautioned me repeatedly that whenever I had to "go
to Tante Tilli" to do so as quickly and unobtrusively as possible so as not
to disturb our neighbor, I usually managed to make my presence known to
the old lady before leaving by closing the bathroom door just a little louder
than necessary. I had a reason.

Unfailingly, as I was leaving she would offer me a treat from a big brown
paper bag that she kept filled with an assortment of candy and cookies.
While waiting for her, I would sneak glances around the dim, kerosene-
lamp-lit room. Lined along the walls and piled on every piece of furniture,
including her bed, were stacks and stacks of folded brown paper bags, all
neatly arranged according to size, and stacks and stacks of newspapers, some
reaching almost to the ceiling. When I asked her once what she intended to
do with her voluminous paper collection, she told me she hadn't decided
yet, then left me with a piece of advice.

"Never throw anything away that is not *kaput*. You never know when it will come in handy."

Little did I realize at the time that this reasoning, which seemed like an obsessive quirk of an eccentric old lady, would half a century later become the basis of the well-respected and ecologically correct recycling movement.

As time went by, having to "go to Tante Tilli" became a code my mother and I used whenever we had to go to the toilet, no matter whose toilet and where.

The remarkable thing about Tante Tilli was that in spite of her age, which unconfirmed rumors put at about sixty-five, she was an avid hiker and swimmer who spent all of her weekends alone at her rented one-room beach cabin, on the northern bank of the Elbe River. Her ascetic, reclusive lifestyle included leaving for the factory at dawn and returning at dusk. Once she had reached her apartment, she wouldn't leave the house until it was time to go back to work. When she returned from work in the evening, her tall, angular figure draped in a heavy, dark green loden cape and hood that gave her the silhouette of a capuchin monk, she was always trailed by a flock of urchins. They had discovered the strange old lady's kind heart and were never disappointed when they asked her for candy, which she always carried in a brown paper bag beneath her cape. While she loved children, she had little use for grown people—nor they for her—and consequently kept her contact with them to a bare minimum.

All grown-ups, including my mother, thought that Tante Tilli was a bit odd, but she was all right in my book. Somehow I sensed that she was marching to the beat of a different drummer, and her aura of adventure and free-spiritedness appealed to me.

Except during the coldest days of winter, Tante Tilli would spend weekends swimming in the Elbe River and resting in her beach cabin. Eschewing any form of public transportation, she would cover the twenty-odd miles to and from the cabin on foot.

Her love for water almost became her undoing. One Saturday night, while sleeping in her cabin, she was awakened by howling winds, cascading rain, and strange gurgling noises. Instead of the usual lights of boats going up- and downstream, all she could see as she peered through the window was ink-black night. Gradually, she realized that she was in the midst of a flood. Her cabin was completely surrounded by water and the water level inside was almost up to the top bunk on which she was lying. With the water still rising, she climbed out of the window and onto the cabin's roof. Swimming ashore, she decided, was out of the question since the impenetrable darkness could easily cause her to lose her bearing and head in the wrong direction. Thus, while the water around her kept rising agonizing inch by agonizing inch, she spent the entire night clinging to the roof while shivering in her drenched clothes. It was not until dawn that she was spotted by a fishing boat and rescued and taken to shore.

I remember that Sunday morning. Two police officers in a squad car had delivered Tante Tilli, still soaking wet and shivering from her ordeal, to our door after she had refused to be taken to a hospital. After drying her off, putting her to bed, and plying her with hot tea, my mother made her promise to stay in bed for a few days—to no avail. On Monday morning, before dawn, we heard her leave her apartment as usual and go to work.

Eventually, Mont Blanc sent Tante Tilli into retirement and she moved from the neighborhood into a retirement home. Since we were in desperate need of additional living space, Mutti jumped at the opportunity of renting her vacated apartment. At the same time, we—especially I—hated to see the kind old lady go. Before she departed, she took me aside and left me with a bit of advice: "Always do what you think is right, no matter what others have to say about it." As young as I was at the time, I realized that she was speaking from experience.

I don't know what ever happened to her thousands of newspapers and brown paper bags, but after she packed them and left, her bedroom became my bedroom and—thank God—was never the same.

WYK AUF FÖHR

Seemingly out of the blue, my mother asked me one day whether I would be interested in spending a few weeks at a children's summer camp. At first the idea of being separated from her for more than a day seemed too frightening to contemplate, but when she explained that I'd be with lots of other children my age who were there for one purpose only and that was to have fun, I changed my mind.

Thus, barely five years old, I arrived via train and ferryboat with several hundred children on the tiny North Sea island of Föhr, whose small town of Wyk included a large *Kinderheim* (children's home). Following our arrival, we were grouped according to age, and a counselor, a pleasant red-haired young woman whose name has escaped me, assigned us to our dormitory. For the first time in my life I was required to follow a strict daily routine that included getting up at 7 A.M. and taking a cold shower, making up my bed, being ready for breakfast in the huge dining hall at exactly 8 A.M., and participating in organized games such as building sand castles on the beach, collecting seashells, wading in the surf, and playing soccer. At night, our counselor would read us a bedtime story, *Emil und die Detektive,* for half an hour, then turn off the lights at 9 P.M. on the dot.

The most popular person at the home was the *Heimleiter* (camp director), a tall lean *Friese* (a member of a Northern German ethnic group) whom everybody called Onkel Tamm. I adored Onkel Tamm because he singled me out with special bonbon treats whenever he ran into me. One day, after asking my counselor's permission to "borrow" me for a few hours, Onkel Tamm took me for a walk in town, which consisted largely of picturesque old straw-roof farmhouses, until we reached a house where, he told me, he was born and grew up. Inside, he introduced me to his ancient-looking parents, who looked at me in utter disbelief as if I had just descended from Mars. While at the time I felt extremely proud of having been singled out for special attention by Onkel Tamm, since I imagined that of all the children at the camp he liked me best, I now can't escape the nagging suspicion that the good uncle used me to provide his old parents with an exotic treat, their own private Hagenbeck "culture show," so to speak.

THE FIRST SCHOOL DAY

The first weekday after Easter 1932 marked an important milestone in my life. It was Germany's traditional beginning of school and my first school day. Like most of my peers, I had longed for it and dreaded it with equal intensity. The prospect of being transformed from "just a kid" into a "schoolkid" filled me with a sense of accomplishment and pride. On the other hand, I dreaded venturing beyond my familiar surroundings into a new, and—by my perception—largely hostile world.

According to the older boys on our block, school was a no-fun, no-nonsense place where if you got into trouble with the teacher, neither your parents nor God could help you. After listening to hundreds of the most detailed and vivid accounts of atrocities committed by teachers, I had become convinced that teachers were a subhuman species of sadists who derived their sole pleasure in life from beating up on kids. I recalled with terror the cluster of thick, angry-red welts on the buttocks of Eugen Braun, the neighborhood blacksmith's eight-year-old son. Eugen had invited us boys to a special viewing to prove his ability to take everything his teacher could dish out. Right then and there I disavowed any such ambition. I had no intention of ever becoming acquainted with that three-foot bamboo switch, which, Eugen told us, was as much a teacher's standard equipment as were blackboard and chalk.

But fear of teachers, which I shared with most school beginners, was only one of my problems. My biggest worry, which I carefully tried to keep to myself, was having to face hundreds of strange children and the certainty of racial taunts and ridicule. In an obvious attempt to make me less conspicuous, my mother told my barber—albeit with a heavy heart—to get rid of my generous Afro, which I wore decades before it became the rage among African-Americans in the United States and that my mother loved as much as I detested it. Sensing my growing anxiety, she tried to reassure me that I had nothing to worry about and that I would love school once I got the hang of it. But her words seemed to lack conviction, and I sensed that she, too, was becoming anxious as the day drew near.

Finally, the big day arrived. Since Mutti was unable to take time off from her job, the chore of taking me to school fell to Tante Möller. All scrubbed and dressed up in my spanking-new "school clothes," and with my new leather school satchel strapped to my back, I glumly walked beside Tante Möller the two blocks from our house to the school, across Am Markt into Hufnerstrasse, past the venerable straw-roofed farmhouse of *Bauer* (farmer) Lembcke, the only surviving reminder of Barmbek's rural past. Lest I be thought of as a mama's boy by other kids, I refused to hold the old lady's hand, except when we crossed streets as she insisted on it.

Her attempts to cheer me up with an account of her own "wonderful" first school day an eternity earlier became an exercise in futility. There was no way I could relate to the image of gray-haired and bent-by-age Tante Möller as a little schoolgirl even if I had tried. The closer we got to the school, the more miserable I became. Not even the sight of several fellow sufferers going my way comforted me. Like all German first-day pupils of the time, I was carrying a traditional *Ostertüte* (Easter bag), a brightly colored cardboard cone nearly my own size, which well-wishing neighbors and friends had filled with chocolate Easter bunnies, marzipan eggs, and other candy gifts. It was the largest *Ostertüte* Mutti could find, but even the thought of getting my hands on its delicious contents after school did little to dispel my gloom. After turning a corner, we stood in front of Kätner-kampschule, my new home away from home. Like all Hamburg public schools at the time, it was named after the street on which it was located, and consisted of two identical wings, one for boys and the other for girls. As I beheld its massive walls for the first time from close up, the old, fortresslike four-story structure assumed an especially sinister aura for me. The sudden realization that for years to come I would spend the greater part of my waking hours in this forbidding, cheerless edifice filled me with palpable terror.

It appeared that at least one of my new schoolmates harbored similar thoughts. He was screaming at the top of his lungs that he wasn't going into that school no matter what his mother or anybody had to say. While I knew exactly how he felt, I was determined not to make a scene like that and thus draw unnecessary attention to myself. Taking advantage of the diversion he created, I handed Tante Möller my *Ostertüte,* quickly climbed the school's broad steps, and, without looking back, entered the cavernous building. Once inside, I and my fellow first-day initiates were ushered along a seemingly endless corridor and into a first floor classroom. There, instead of the grim, switch-wielding male teacher I had expected to find, we were greeted by a pleasant-looking, plumpish woman with short-cropped gray hair. Like the other teachers I had seen in the hall, she was wearing a white smock.

"Good morning, boys! I am Fräulein Beyle, your teacher," she introduced herself with a friendly smile. "The first thing I want you to do is to find a seat on these benches and to sit down." After selecting a seat on the back row, I carefully sneaked a glimpse of the other boys to see if any of them displayed any undue interest in me. To my great relief, I recognized several of my pals from the Stückenstrasse. There was Karl Morell, who lived in an alley just around the corner from me, and Karl-Heinz Ratje, who lived just down the street. As far as the other boys were concerned, they all seemed too awed by their new surroundings to be inclined to make fun of me or anyone.

"Remember you are in Class 8A," Fräulein Beyle continued. "From now on, you never talk, stand up, leave your seat or the classroom without my permission. If you have a question, or you need to go to the toilet, which is down the hall to the right, you raise your hand until I call on you. Does everyone understand that?

"Now let's see if everyone who is supposed to be here is actually here," she resumed. "When you hear me call your name, you raise your right hand, stand up so I can see you, and answer, 'Here!' " With that, she started calling roll. When my turn came to say *here* and stand up, some boys looked at me and started to giggle.

"Those boys who were laughing just now are very ignorant. In fact, they are too ignorant to be in my class," Fräulein Beyle scolded. "The next time anyone laughs at Hans-Jürgen or anybody else, he will have to leave the classroom and wait outside in the hall until class is over." Then, turning to me, she said, "I hope you won't let stupid boys like that upset you. You are a fine boy. Don't let anybody make you think otherwise."

I could have hugged the teacher for putting my tormentors in their place, but of course I did no such thing and merely responded with a barely audible, "Yes."

When the bell signaled the end of class, Fräulein Beyle instructed us to leave the classroom quietly and walk in a double file along the hall and down to the schoolyard for recess. Quite pleased with the outcome of my first class in spite of that little "incident," I was beginning to feel my anxiety about school disappear. If that was all there was to it, I thought, then school and I would get along just fine. But no sooner had I reached the schoolyard than a big, sandy-haired boy with coarse, ugly features and nearly a head taller than I, took one look at me and started to holler, *"Neger, Neger, Schornsteinfeger!"*

Soon, other kids had taken up the chant, and within seconds I was the center of attention of the entire school. All of a sudden *"Neger, Neger, Schornsteinfeger!"* became the rallying cry of literally hundreds of boys, until the entire schoolyard reverberated around me in a deafening crescendo of the hated chant.

Desperate, I looked for an escape route through the dense mass of jeering boys that surrounded me, but without success. Recognizing the hopelessness of my situation, my first inclination was to simply cry. But my feelings of despair and humiliation quickly turned to blind rage when the big ugly boy who had started the commotion stepped forward, put his hand on my head and mockingly stroked my hair. "Why do Negroes grow sheep wool instead of hair on their heads?" he asked me, to the delight of the crowd. Before even I had become fully aware of my reaction, my right foot had hauled back in a wide arc and, with all the muscle power I could muster, came crashing forward against the bare shin of my tormentor. The impact of my hard leather boot on my adversary's leg was audible and, quite apparently, excruciatingly painful to him.

As if struck by lightning, he collapsed. Still shaking with rage, yet emboldened by the effect of my fancy footwork, I surveyed the crowd for other potential attackers, prepared to give anyone who dared to touch me a dose of the same medicine. But, to my surprise, if not disappointment, there were no takers. On the contrary, the same boys who seconds earlier had been taunting me now turned their ridicule and jeers on the vanquished bully who was still writhing on the ground in pain.

Abruptly, the jeers stopped as Fräulein Beyle appeared on the scene. Sizing up the situation, she turned to my attacker, who was holding his badly bruised and swollen shin. "What's the matter with you?" she demanded to know.

"He kicked me," he blurted out while pointing accusingly at me.

"Why do you think he did that?" Fräulein Beyle demanded to know.

"I don't know."

"What's your name?"

"Gerhard Rademeier."

"And who's your teacher?"

"Fräulein Rodewald."

She then turned to me. "Well, Hans-Jürgen, is it true that you kicked him?"

"Yes."

"Can you tell me why you kicked him?"

"Because he was touching my hair and making fun of me and calling me names."

"Did you touch his hair and call him names?" Fräulein Beyle continued her interrogation.

"Yes, but I didn't hit him or anything," my adversary conceded under the mounting pressure of the investigation.

"Then you deserve what you got," Fräulein Beyle ruled sternly. "You have no business calling people names or making fun of the way they look. In the future, if you ever bother Hans-Jürgen again, I will report you to Fräulein Rodewald for punishment and, in addition, have a word with your parents. Now run along and never let me catch you picking on anyone again!"

While my adversary limped away, physically and morally crushed, Fräulein Beyle admonished me never again to take the law into my own hands—or feet, for that matter—but instead to report any abuse by fellow pupils to her or the nearest teacher. It was an admonition that I was never able, nor willing, to heed. A quick, violent temper kept compelling me to retaliate instantly. And besides, I realized that my unexpected attack upon my adversary's shin had decisively leveled the playing field and snatched for me victory from almost certain defeat.

Looking around the schoolyard that had turned back to normal, Fräulein Beyle waved to a tall, handsome teenager whose height and white-blond hair made him stand out in a group of older boys. "Come here a minute, Wolfgang," Fräulein Beyle called.

When the boy stood before her, she introduced us. "This is Hans-Jürgen; he's just started school, and this is Wolfgang Neumann, who started school exactly seven years ago on this day, also in my class. The reason I called you, Wolfgang," she continued, "is that it looks as if Hans-Jürgen here could use someone to look after him. How would you like to be his bodyguard?"

Wolfgang replied that he'd like it a lot.

"Well, then, this is how it's going to work," Fräulein Beyle explained. "Each recess you keep an eye on Hans-Jürgen and make sure nobody bothers him. If there is a situation you can't handle, you report it to the teacher on duty or come to me."

"Don't you worry about a thing, Fräulein Beyle. Nobody's going to bother him. I'll make sure of that."

"I know I can depend on you, Wolfgang," Fräulein Beyle replied, "and you, Hans-Jürgen," she continued, "be sure to let Wolfgang know whenever you run into a problem during recess, like today. I'm awfully sorry about what happened to you today. There's just so much ignorance in the world— so much ignorance," she kept repeating, more to herself.

After I shook hands with Wolfgang, my new hero and bodyguard, the school bell signaled the end of recess and we returned to our respective classes. When I entered the room, all eyes of my new classmates turned to me. For a moment I feared another verbal attack. To my surprise and great relief, the entire class broke out in loud cheers mixed with praise of the way I had brought the bully to his knees. The tumult did not end until Fräulein Beyle entered the room. She didn't ask for the reason of the commotion, but I had a feeling that she knew exactly what happened.

Within a few days it seemed as if everybody had forgotten that ugly scene on my first day of school—everybody, that is, but the bully and me. Occasionally, I would spot him in the schoolyard or in the hall looking at me sheepishly or altogether averting his eyes. Having learned his lesson the hard way, he made sure to always stay out of my boots' range. Wolfgang, true to his word, kept a watchful eye on me until he graduated the following spring. After that, I was more or less on my own. But by that time, I had become a toughy of sorts in my own right and no longer needed a bodyguard.

Quite contrary to my earlier expectations, I had come to like—no, love— school, and apparently school had come to like me. I got on well with my classmates, and several had become my closest friends. I also liked my teachers, especially Fräulein Beyle, who helped me discover the immense joy of learning for learning's sake. At the same time I appreciated the respect and status that my newly acquired knowledge and skills conferred on me. I found that there was a strong correlation between doing well in school and being respected and accepted, and since learning came easy to me, I had every reason to feel that I had it made. That view seemed to be shared by Fräulein Beyle, whose brief evaluation of my first year in school contained the following observations:

"Hans-Jürgen is a remarkable pupil who has made a good adjustment to school. He is unusually talented in reading, writing, drawing, music, and athletics. In arithmetic he is average, but manages to find the correct answers with the aid of his fingers. He is a born leader who is always willing to help out slower classmates. Due to some teasing he suffered in the beginning and the need to defend himself, he has become a bit more aggressive than he ought to be. Judging by his first-year performance, I am expecting good things from him. Hans-Jürgen will be promoted to Class 7A [2nd grade] and I am looking forward with pleasure to again having him in my class."

By the time Mutti had finished reading my first school report to all of her friends and acquaintances, and anyone else who would listen, I could recite Fräulein Beyle's laudatory words by heart.

OUR NEW NEIGHBORS

On January 30, 1933, three months before I entered second grade, Adolf Hitler became *Reichskanzler* of Germany. It was an event that stirred barely a ripple in Barmbek, a former Communist stronghold, although its lethal impact would eventually be felt throughout the world.

I had heard the words *Hitler* and *Nazi* and the letters *NSDAP* (National Socialist German Labor Party) many times, but at first they were largely meaningless to me. That, however, was soon to change. While we kids hadn't a clue what political parties were all about, we nevertheless began to choose our favorite parties the way we did soccer teams based on what we heard and saw at home, in the streets, and at school. Before we realized what had happened, the unprepossessing man with the Chaplinesque mustache had ceased to be an object of ridicule to us. Barely seven, I, of all people, became an unabashed proponent of the Nazis simply because they put on the best shows with the best-looking uniforms, best-sounding marching bands, and best-drilled marching columns, all of which appealed to my budding sense of masculinity. The Communists, or Komune, as well as the Social Democrats, or Sozis, by contrast, often looked ragged and undisciplined to me during their demonstrations, having chosen to project an exaggerated proletarian image rather than one of Prussian militarism. Thus, when I had gotten my hands on an embroidered swastika emblem, I had Tante Möller—who didn't know any better—sew it on a sweater of mine, where it remained until my mother removed it over my vigorous protest.

Except for the increasing number of swastika flags flying from the tenement windows, and the abrupt disappearance of the hammer-and-sickle flags of the Komune and the "three iron arrows" banner of the Sozis after the new Nazi government outlawed all political parties, there were no visible signs in the Stückenstrasse indicating that a major change had taken place.

In school, the revered national father figure and symbol of authority had been *Reichspräsident* Paul von Hindenburg, the aged field marshal who represented Germany's old military aristocracy and who in his heyday, in World War I, had crushed the Russian army at the battle of Tannenberg. When he died in 1934, the first indications of change were the introduction of *Heil Hitler* as the official form of greeting and the replacement of Hindenburg portraits with those of Hitler throughout the school building. From the walls of every classroom, corridor, and office, Hitler's piercing blue eyes seemed to follow us kids wherever we went, as if intent on casting a hypnotic spell. Before we realized it, the face of the Führer had become as familiar to us as that of Fräulein Beyle, who was again our teacher. Yet even more intrusive on our consciousness than Hitler's portraits was his extraordinary guttural voice—a curious marvel of range, stamina, and flexibility. Whenever the Führer addressed the German people, which happened with increasing frequency, all instruction came to a mandated halt. Our entire school, like all other schools throughout Germany, would assemble in the auditorium, where we would listen to the broadcast speech in its entirety. Most of Hitler's speeches lasted over one hour. Yet in spite of the length of the speeches and the fact that much of what the Führer had to say was beyond our comprehension, we never were bored or failed to be fascinated and moved by the sound of his voice. One minute, that voice would be a low, measured, and reassuring baritone, as Hitler spoke calmly of his trials and tribulations during his rise to power. The next minute it would explode into a high-pitched, angry crescendo as he lashed out at groups and individuals whom he deemed his—and therefore Germany's—enemies. Jews, non-Aryans, Marxists, Communists, liberals, reactionaries, and democrats were the most frequent targets of his wrath. While we kids were too young to understand the meaning of these words, we nevertheless sensed the power that emanated from the speaker, and we took pride in an emerging, all-powerful father figure who was courageous and not intimidated by Germany's adversaries.

Calling Hamburg's venerable *Rathausmarkt* in front of City Hall "Adolf Hitler Square" after it had been renamed took some getting used to, but as the months went by, we managed. Before long, raising our right hand and shouting *"Heil Hitler!"* instead of simply greeting people with *Guten Tag,* as we used to do, had ceased to strike us as somewhat peculiar, as it had at first. It also didn't seem unusual to us that we had gotten into the habit of sitting and standing at attention and clicking our heels. Like soldiers, we wore nail-studded boots and tiny "horseshoes" on our heels that made our school and the streets reverberate under our feet. We also became accustomed to what at first appeared to us as a strange Monday morning school-yard ritual before the beginning of classes. While we stood at rigid attention with our right arms raised, a Hitler Youth "honor guard" would raise our two new national flags—the traditional black, white, and red banner of pre-Weimar Germany and the Nazis' *Hakenkreuz* flag. This was followed by our singing of Germany's dual national anthems, *"Deutschland Über Alles"* and *"Das Horst Wessel Lied."* The latter was named after its composer, a young SA trooper who was gunned down in 1930 by Communists during street clashes over turf in Berlin, and whom we were taught to worship as the Nazi movement's star martyr No. 1. Star martyr No. 2, we learned, was Albert Leo Schlageter, a *Freikorps* officer in the French-occupied Ruhr after World War I, who was executed by the French in 1923 for sabotage and espionage.

To help us gain an appreciation for Hamburg's naval tradition and inspire an interest in the German navy, our entire school was transported to Hamburg Harbor for a sight-seeing tour of the newly built and commissioned school ship *Gorch Fock,* a three-mast sailboat used for the training of naval cadets. The vessel was named in honor of the renowned North German folk poet and author of seamen's tales Gorch Fock (the nom de plume of Johannes Kinau), who was killed in action during the famed sea battle against the British at Skagerrak in World War I. Following the tour, one of the teachers, a navy veteran, lectured us for an hour on the bright future that awaited young German boys who early in life decided to make the navy their career. I wondered whether Gorch Fock, who was killed at age thirty-five, would have agreed with that, but knew better than to voice my thoughts.

Once Hitler was firmly in control of the nation, there literally was never a dull moment in Hamburg. Each week brought new major events and excitement. Nobody felt the excitement more than we schoolchildren, especially after our teachers had whipped our youthful enthusiasm into a wild frenzy. And there was so much for us to be enthusiastic about. There were endless processions of SS, SA, and Hitler Youth units marching through the city to the traditional martial strains of old Prussia and the new fighting marches of the Nazi movement, dramatic torchlight parades at night, and fireworks over the Alster. There were *Massenkundgebungen* (mass demonstrations) in the Stadt Park and on the Moorweide, a large parade ground in front of Dammtor railroad station, and speeches by party bigwigs, all trying to outdo each other with their flatteries of the now near-divine Führer.

None of these events, however, did I recognize as presenting any particular personal threat—not until the bizarre drama that nearly swept me away one day. It happened in the early part of 1934, when I was in the third grade. On that particular day, at age eight, I got my first inkling of the danger the Nazi regime might pose to me.

It was a bizarre twist of fate that the newly formed local Nazi chapter chose for its weekly meeting place Zanoletti's tavern and meeting hall, directly adjacent to the apartment building in which we lived. For several months, our new neighbors and I were oblivious to each other's existence, since the Nazis held their regular meetings at night after I had gone to bed. Then the inevitable occurred. It happened on a beautiful spring Sunday that had started upbeat with a giant paramilitary parade through our neighborhood. For more than two hours, column after column of brown-shirted SA and black-uniformed SS strutted through the neighborhood. The occasion, which had no meaning for me at the time, was one of Hitler's infamous sham referendums, in which the German people were ostensibly given an opportunity to accept or reject a Nazi proposal by voting *Ja* or *Nein* in polls that had been flagrantly rigged to favor the Nazis' agenda and tighten their stranglehold on Germany.

The colorful procession had attracted large crowds of spectators, who were lining the parade route along Am Markt that intersected the usually quiet Stückenstrasse. Like all the other kids, I had gone to watch the parade and, like everyone else, become caught up in the excitement. I was especially thrilled when I saw Wolfgang, my former bodyguard, marching at the head of a troop of Hitler Youth. And I nearly burst with pride when, after spotting me in the crowd, he waved and smiled at me. I watched until the last unit of storm troopers had marched by and the crowd started to disperse.

As I walked home, I heard loud singing and shouting coming from the building next to ours. My curiosity aroused, I tried to catch a glimpse through the wide open door of Zanoletti's meeting hall. It was packed to overflowing with beer-guzzling, smoking, shouting, laughing, and singing brownshirts who were celebrating their spurious election victory. None of them seemed to notice me—the living antithesis to their obsession with racial purity—as I peered into the meeting hall. Or so I thought. Suddenly, I felt myself grabbed from behind by two huge fists and lifted into the air. Instinctively, I stretched and bent in rapid succession like a fish on a hook. The next thing I knew, I had slipped from the grip of the two fists and was running as fast as I could to escape my captor. Looking over my shoulder, I caught my first glimpse of my attacker, a huge SA trooper with short-cropped white-blond hair and mean little eyes set deep in a ruddy, beer-flushed face. I might have made good my escape had it not been for two other brownshirts who, alerted by the shouts of my pursuer, blocked my path. Like a hawk descending on his prey, the SA trooper reclaimed his hapless quarry and this time, none of my kicking, wiggling, and biting could loosen his viselike grip.

Triumphantly, he dragged me through a dense throng of drunken comrades toward a speaker's platform at the end of the hall. I felt nauseated from fear, the cacophony of rough male voices, and the stench of beer and tobacco smoke. With superhuman effort I managed to suppress an instinctive urge to vent my panic by screaming, sensing somehow that I could only expect more abuse—certainly not help—from this crowd. Fortunately for me, almost no one had become aware of the drama that was unfolding in their midst, mainly because of the din and their visible drunkenness. The SA trooper was about to lift me to the speaker's platform, apparently as an exhibit of *Rassenschande* (racial defilement), when he found himself confronted by an enraged woman who was staring at him with hate-filled eyes.

Mutti had spent the Sunday morning enjoying a well-deserved respite from her hospital chores. Unlike me, she had paid little attention to the election activities in the neighborhood, except for an occasional glance out of the window in a futile effort to spot me in the crowd below. The heavy presence of brownshirts gave her a growing sense of foreboding as the hours went by. When she could no longer contain her anxiety, she started to look for me. She had barely reached the stairs when she ran into Tante Möller, who in breathless tones reported that she had just seen an SA man drag me into the beer hall next door. Mutti did not wait for the end of Tante Möller's report. With the fury of a tigress protecting her cub, she dashed downstairs, raced through the crowd in the street and into the beer hall. Then, like an unstoppable force, she plowed a path through the drunken troopers who were blocking her way until she had reached the speaker's platform and the man who had kidnapped me. Momentarily startled by this trembling, yet apparently fearless woman, the giant SA trooper loosened his grip. Before he, I, or anyone else could comprehend what was taking place, I was once again snatched and dragged through the carousing throng, but this time by my mother, who hauled me off to the relative safety of our home.

Although the experience in Zanoletti's beer hall haunted me for months, perhaps years, at the time I was still reluctant to fully connect those raucous, drunken SA troopers and the man who was increasingly presented to us children as Germany's messiah, the man who, our teachers told us, would restore Germany to its rightful place of dominance in the world. To me, as to virtually all of my peers, Hitler had taken on a near-godlike nimbus that placed him beyond blame or criticism. Thus, it never occurred to me that the brutality I—an eight-year-old boy—had experienced at the hands of a Nazi bully was merely a mild expression of the most brutal racist policies and that the mastermind of that policy was Adolf Hitler, the man I was being taught to worship.

But from that Sunday on, my unreserved admiration of Hitler and the

Nazis changed into a strange mixture of fear and fascination. I began to sense that the brownshirts, the swastika, the martial music were harbingers of danger. Even so, it would take several years and numerous humiliations at the hands of Nazi-inspired racists before I could clearly see Hitler's evil and the disastrous course he was charting.

PARADISE LOST

It took me a while to realize that the beer hall incident was not an isolated occurrence triggered by some rowdies in Nazi uniforms who had a few beers too many, but that I belonged to a group targeted by a government-directed conspiracy. I made that shattering discovery a few weeks later at a place where one would have least expected it—at a neighborhood public playground a few blocks from my home. As I had done many times before, I had gone to the playground after school for an afternoon of innocent play. My favorite attraction, like everybody else's, was the seesaw, which meant that there was always a waiting line. After patiently awaiting our turn, a boy and I were about to mount when a mother with her young son in tow blocked my way. "Where do you think you are going?" she inquired, her voice shrill with aggravation. I had no idea why she was questioning me about the obvious and helplessly pointed to the seesaw where her son had already taken my seat.

"It's my turn," I said in feeble protest.

"What do you mean 'my turn'?" she shrieked. "You people had your turn! Now it's our turn. You aren't even supposed to be in this playground. Can't you read?" With that, she pointed to a painted sign near the playground's entrance that I had never noticed before.

Several mothers had witnessed the woman's outburst, and although they seemed to sympathize with me, none spoke up in my behalf.

Thoroughly embarrassed and crushed, I walked away. Before leaving the playground, I studied the sign with eyes blurred with suppressed tears. The sign read:

NICHTARIERN

IST DAS BETRETEN DIESES

SPIELPLATZES

STRENGSTENS

VERBOTEN

(Non-Aryans are sternly prohibited
from entering this playground)

Although I had heard the term *non-Aryan* before, I never felt that it had anything to do with me. But if the woman was right, *Nichtariern* meant me. I still didn't comprehend the reason for her outburst, except that for some reason I could not yet fully fathom, I had been banished from a place where I had spent countless happy hours, a place I had always regarded as belonging to me as much as to all the other kids.

That evening after my mother had returned from work, I pointedly asked her, "Am I a non-Aryan?"

Taken totally by surprise, Mutti demanded to know what prompted my question. When I told her what had happened on the playground, she conceded that Africans were among several racial groups that had been classified non-Aryans by the Nazi government.

"Since your father is African and you are his son," she explained, "you, too, are classified non-Aryan."

"Are you a non-Aryan, too?" I kept pressing.

"No, I'm not."

"Why not?"

"Because I'm not African; I am European."

"Then why am I a non-Aryan because I'm Dad's son and not an Aryan like you when I'm your son also?" I tried to reason with her. "And why," I added, "aren't non-Aryans allowed to play in the playground?"

"I agree that it doesn't make any sense," Mutti conceded. "Tomorrow I'll speak to the park warden. I'm sure he'll make an exception and let you play in the park."

"I don't want you to talk to the warden," I told her. "I don't ever want to play in that park again."

Despite my protest, my mother did have a talk with the warden and he told her that I shouldn't pay any attention to the sign. But nothing Mutti said could make me break my vow never to set foot in that park again.

FAMILY FEUD

While I tried hard not to let my experience in the park ruin my life, I found it difficult to dismiss what had happened and its implications. One reason was that whenever Tante Möller's grown sons were visiting her, they would inevitably wind up in a heated argument about politics. Otto, who was pro-Nazi although not a member of the party, almost came to blows with his younger brother Fritz, an avowed Communist, when the latter suggested that the Nazis were nothing but a bunch of thugs who would soon get their comeuppance. "I used to look up to you because I thought you were smart," Fritz screamed, "but not anymore. How can you be so stupid and let these crooks pull the wool over your eyes?"

"I should report you and have them take you away for making such irresponsible remarks," Otto screamed back.

As on many previous occasions, Tante Möller would tell them to stop fighting, especially in front of me, or leave since she had gotten sick and tired of hearing about both the Nazis *and* the Communists. Out of respect for their mother, they would hold their tongues, only to resume the arguments the next time they came around.

To Fritz's chagrin, Willi, the oldest brother, had developed a strong anti-Communist bias while living in the United States during World War I, and since he knew very little about German party politics, he became more and more receptive to Otto's arguments. To the utter delight of Otto, Willi, the chief steward of a Hamburg-Amerika liner, announced that he had joined the *Marine* (Navy) SA, a branch of the storm troopers that was tailor-made for members of the merchant marines. I was all in favor, and he even took me along when he bought his uniform: a brown shirt, navy blue breeches and matching hat with visor, a brown belt and shoulder strap, as well as a pair of brown riding boots.

The first major event scheduled after Willi joined the *Marine* SA was a marathon *Gepäckmarsch* during which different units of the SA, SS, NSDAP, and Hitler Youth demonstrated their endurance while loaded down with heavy field packs. A strapping six-footer, Willi looked splendid in his new uniform when he stopped at his mother's in the morning before joining his comrades-in-arms. Obviously pleased with his new military appearance, the always dapper man of the world stuck out his chest and strutted about as he looked approvingly at himself in the mirror. I could have burst with pride as I walked this magnificent specimen of a storm trooper to the corner where he caught a streetcar for a ride downtown. I only hoped that some of my cronies would see us, but as it turned out, they were not around. Before Willi left, he gave me the approximate time when his unit would reach Am Markt to give me a chance to watch him and his new Nazi buddies march by.

I spent most of the afternoon watching sweat-drenched formation after formation pass in review. When the first distinctly dressed *Marine* SA unit arrived, I concentrated on spotting Onkel Willi. But as hard as I looked, no Onkel Willi came in sight. Finally, when the last marcher had straggled by, I gave up and went home to tell Tante Möller that Onkel Willi was missing. Just as I was ready to join my mother upstairs, my hero limped in. Unlike the proud warrior of the morning, he was a pitiful sight, soaking wet with perspiration and moaning in agony with every step. To add insult to injury, Fritz dropped in just in time to witness his sibling's unheroic return and to heckle him for letting Otto talk him into making a fool of himself.

According to Willi, his trouble started less than an hour after the march began. His brand-new boots, which he had never broken in, started to give him trouble. Both feet felt as if they were clamped by iron vises that tightened with every step. When he couldn't stand the pain any longer, he said, he stepped out of formation while his comrades booed and laughed. This, he said, hurt him more than his feet.

When Fritz tried to pull off his brother's boots through the time-tested method of straddling one boot while Willi gave him a kick in the rear, the boots would not budge. Willi winced in agony with every tug and pull. When Willi couldn't take the pain any longer, he told Fritz to get their mother's big scissors and cut the boots off. I couldn't understand why anyone would ruin a pair of brand-new boots until I saw Willi's feet, which were a swollen, gory mess of blood and blisters.

Within a few weeks Willi was able to wear regular footwear again and walk without pain. But the painful experience, plus being booed by his SA comrades, were enough for him to get the Nazis out of his system. Much to Otto's chagrin, and to the delight of Fritz, he never went to another SA meeting and swore off activist politics for good.

SUNDAYS AT THE MOVIES

On Sundays, rain or shine, one of my favorite pastimes was going to the 1 P.M. matinee for children at the Europa Palast, an art deco theater just around the corner. The admission price was thirty pfennig and since, according to Mutti, money didn't grow on trees, she tried to limit my attendance to one performance per month. But her plan was doomed to failure from the start, since she could rarely resist my pleading and begging, especially when I "reasoned" with her that all my friends were going, so why couldn't I?

There was one movie star even Mutti couldn't resist. Whenever a Shirley Temple movie was shown, my attendance was a foregone conclusion because Mutti not only wanted me to go, she insisted on coming along. Films featuring the curly-headed, dimple-cheeked moppet from America drew longer lines than any other stars', foreign and domestic, and invariably resulted in a sold-out house. Practically all Germans went bananas over Shirley, and I was no exception. Since all American films were dubbed with German soundtracks, I was hardly aware of the fact that Shirley wasn't German. Whether she played the intrepid little orphan in *Lachende Augen (Bright Eyes)* in which she popularized the song, "On the Good Ship Lollipop," or the tap-dance partner of Bill Robinson in the Civil War epic *Der Kleinste Rebel (The Littlest Rebel)*, when Shirley laughed, I laughed, and when Shirley cried, I cried. Had someone told me at the time that one day I would not only meet and talk with my little idol of my childhood years but even dance with her, I would have had that person declared mentally challenged. But that is exactly what happened. In 1975, I was dispatched by *Ebony* to Accra, Ghana, to interview the U.S. ambassador to Ghana, who was none other than Mrs. Shirley Temple Black (her married name), an appointee of President Gerald Ford. During the lengthy interview my childhood idol revealed to me how shocked she was as a child when she discovered that her black costar Bill Robinson, of whom she had become quite fond, couldn't stay in the same Florida hotel where she stayed because of the strictly enforced Jim Crow laws. Later that evening, at a Ghanaian function in honor of the ambassador, the former child star invited me to dance with her. How I wished that my former cronies from the Stückenstrasse, who stood in line with me at the Europa Palast to see Shirley Temple movies, could have seen me then.

Just as intriguing as the main features were the weekly newsreels that preceded them. There would always be a hush of great expectation in the audience as the announcer intoned slowly in a voice dripping with gravity Fox's signature opening of its newsreels, "We are bringing you the most interesting and most current news from all lands of the world, in picture and sound." It was through the newsreels that I received my first, albeit lopsided, impression of the *Land der unbegrenzten Möglichkeiten* (land of unlimited possibilities), as the United States was called. To justify that moniker, the shows focused on feats that ranged from the absurd or ludicrous to the outright insane, such as the crowning of a Miss America, an acrobat's tightrope walk at a dizzying altitude between two skyscrapers without the benefit of a safety net, a daredevil's plunge down Niagara Falls in a steel drum, or someone trying to set an endurance record perching on top of a flagpole. The American newsreels' preoccupation with offbeat feats gave me an early impression of the United States as a country peopled largely by an assortment of trifling oddballs who took nothing very seriously except their unending pursuit of the sensational. An occasional sighting of President Franklin D. Roosevelt served only to deepen that impression. I felt that FDR, with his jutting chin, jaunty cigarette holder, and broad movie-star smile, was the personification of the devil-may-care spirit of America. Only now and then would there be a hard news account that let me know that not all was fun and games in the United States. Newsreel coverage of the sensational kidnapping and murder of international folk hero Charles Lindbergh's two-year-old son in 1932 and the equally sensational trial that four years later resulted in the execution of Bruno Hauptmann, a German immigrant, for the crime were cases in point.

Even if the make-believe world to which I was introduced at the Europa Palast differed markedly from reality, I still cherish the memories of those Sunday afternoons when during two enchanted hours I would leave Stückenstrasse and Barmbek far behind and enter a magical realm populated with villains and heroes, gangsters and cops, cowboys and Indians, knights and knaves, and where the boundaries of time and space were as limitless as the human imagination.

JEWS

It wasn't long after Hitler came to power that the words *die Juden* started cropping up around me with increasing frequency. As far as I knew, I had never seen a Jew, but on occasion I had heard my mother speak of Jews in hushed tones. Once, I overheard her and a friend discuss the firing of a doctor at the hospital because he was a Jew. "What a shame," my mother had said. "He was such a fine person and such a good doctor." This gave me the idea that Jews were nice people who, for some inexplicable reason, were being persecuted and thus deserved my sympathy. This view changed fairly quickly as my impressionable mind began to absorb more and more of the ideological poison that poured forth from the *Ministerium für Volksaufklärung und Propaganda* (Ministry for Public Enlightenment and Propaganda), headed by Dr. Joseph Goebbels, via our teachers. To assure that we children got the right message, the Nazis ordered the summary dismissal of all teachers who were deemed "politically unreliable" and, therefore, unfit to teach. This included teachers with Jewish backgrounds, teachers who had been active in political parties that were hostile to the Nazis, such as the Communist and Social Democrat parties, and those teachers who openly refused to join the *N.S. Lehrerbund* (National Socialist Teachers Association). Among the first apparent victims of the purge was our kindly homeroom teacher, Fräulein Beyle. At the end of my second school year, we were simply told that she had been transferred to another school and that another teacher, Herr Grimmelshäuser, would take her place. I never found out what happened to her or whether she was indeed allowed to continue her teaching career. I sorely missed her, since she had been the first educator who had encouraged me to make the most of my potential.

Although we children were never told what went on, we sensed that there was something in the air by the mysterious disappearance of several additional teachers. Those who remained outdid one another in demonstrating their zeal for Hitler in hopes of saving their jobs. Not a day went by without our teachers making derogatory references to Jews, and since—to my knowledge—we had no Jewish schoolmates with whom we could have formed friendships, we easily believed the scurrilous propaganda. "Had it not been for the Jews," insisted Herr Grimmelshäuser, "Germany could have easily won the World War." Herr Grimmelshäuser, a tall, gangling man with dark wavy hair and black horn-rimmed glasses, was leading up to explaining the "stab in the back" notion that had been widely accepted by Germans as the real reason for Germany's massive defeat in World War I. According to Herr Grimmelshäuser's version, Jews spread lies among the German civilian population about German military setbacks and defeats until they had convinced the people that any further war efforts were futile. Thus deprived of the people's moral and material backing, the up-to-that-point victorious German troops collapsed—beaten not in combat, but by a treacherous, Jewish-engineered "stab in the back" at home.

Herr Grimmelshäuser delighted in reading to us articles from *Der Stürmer (The Stormer), Der Völkische Beobachter (The People's Observer),* and *Der Angriff (The Attack),* three prominent Nazi Party newspapers, which were chock-full of Jew-baiting articles. A typical Nazi "news story" would report the eviction at Christmastime of a fine German family by a Scrooge-like Jewish landlord because they had fallen behind in their rent payments due to the father's illness. Such journalistic gems read to us by Grimmelshäuser had the cumulative effect of making us children dislike Jews from the bottom of our innocent little hearts. But much worse was yet to come. One day, Herr Grimmelshäuser announced that we were to view an important film that, he promised, would give us a far better idea of what Jews were really like than he could. The short film depicted Jews as deceitful, gesticulating, morally and physically unclean beings. It was a much milder version of the "documentary" entitled *The Eternal Jew* that hit the screens a few years later and has been rated as the most vicious anti-Semitic propaganda film ever conceived. It purported to show Jews in an overcrowded ghetto, scurrying about furtively in their various disreputable pursuits. Next, the camera switched to a colony of loathsome-looking rats, scurrying about furtively, like the Jews, in their beastly scavenging. To make sure that the point was not lost on the audience, the announcer explained that Jews, like rats, constituted *Ungeziefer* (vermin) that spread diseases and caused plagues, and therefore had to be excised from society if society was to regain its health.

Both films left deep impressions on us kids. Weeks after the screening of the first film, we would still shudder with disgust at the thought of coming into physical contact with Jews, whom we now viewed as physically repulsive, morally corrupt, cowardly, blatantly dishonest, intellectually mediocre, but extremely cunning—and, therefore, extremely dangerous—creatures. Jews' avowed objective, we were made to believe, was the total destruction of the noble race of German people and their noble culture. This, we were told, Jews tried to accomplish either by trickery or violence or, if that didn't work, by defiling noble Aryan blood by mixing it with their own inferior blood.

"Why don't the police arrest them and put them in jail?" one of my classmates demanded to know after one of Herr Grimmelshäuser's anti-Jewish lectures.

"Just be patient, my boy," Herr Grimmelshäuser counseled the outraged boy. "I'm sure that in due time the Führer will come up with a solution."

HITLER STRIKES HOME

Usually my mother came home from work looking cheerful, ready to spend another pleasant evening with me. But one night, instead of greeting me with her customary smile, she seemed on the verge of tears. When I asked her what was wrong, she blurted the devastating news that she had been fired from her job.

While I couldn't fully grasp the enormity of the impact of her dismissal on our economic well-being, I found it impossible to imagine her no longer being a part of the hospital. The *Krankenhaus* had been the center not only of my mother's professional life but of her—no, our—social life. All of her closest friends were hospital coworkers whose children were my playmates and friends, and most of our outings involved them.

To spare my feelings, my mother carefully avoided letting me know that her firing was in any way related to me. Instead, she offered a vague explanation about having been let go as part of a sweeping reduction of hospital staff. Actually, she lost her job as a result of a new Nazi policy that barred Jews and other "politically unreliable persons" from government employment. It wasn't until many years later that Mutti told me the real reason for her dismissal—the fact that she had conceived a child by an African—and some of the details of the ordeal she suffered while fighting to keep her job.

The politically and racially motivated purges, which were carried out nationwide throughout governmental agencies and facilities, amounted to a massive shake-up of the entire St. Georg Hospital staff, from the lowest manual laborers to the highest-level medical professionals. Anyone unable to produce a clean bill of "racial health" was forced to leave. My mother's immediate superior, a male head nurse by the name of Craemeyer, had for years bragged about his Jewish ancestry. When the hospital administration ran a racial background check on him, he squeaked by, but just barely, thanks to the fact that his last recorded Jewish ancestor had been born before the Nazis' crucial turn-of-the-century cutoff date. After that, Herr Craemeyer never mentioned his Jewish ancestors again.

Immediately after being fired, as Mutti years later recounted to me, she went up the hospital administration chain of command to plead with various officials for a rescinding of the dismissal order. Each told her the same thing, that the order was irrevocable and that absolutely nothing could be done. Finally, she requested in writing, and was granted, an appointment with one of the hospital's higher-ups. When, on the morning of the appointment, she followed a receptionist into the administrator's spacious office, my mother was in for a huge surprise. Seated behind a giant desk was a short, squat man in a brown Nazi uniform. She immediately recognized him as someone who had until recently worked in the hospital's laundry and whose obnoxious sexual passes she had on several occasions turned down. Like so many Nazi functionaries of that period, he had obviously been rewarded for his political activities with an instant promotion to a high-level job.

Jumping to his feet, he greeted my mother effusively, as if they had always been the closest of friends. "Come in, Bertha. Have a seat. It's so good to see you again. Now what can I do for you?"

When she had sufficiently recovered from her initial shock, she told him that, in spite of the fact that she had never been politically active, she had been let go "for political reasons." She also explained how she had appealed to anyone she could think of who might be able to help, but to no avail.

"You've come to the right person. Your case is not nearly as hopeless as it seems," he responded encouragingly after hearing her out. "I am positive that I can arrange for you to get your job back," he added with an encouraging smile. "You do understand, however, that I can't go out on a limb for a person with your—let's say—past without you showing me some cooperation. *Eine Hand wäscht die Andere.* (One hand washes the other)."

When my mother, who was beginning to smell a rat about the size of the administrator, demanded to know what he had in mind by "cooperation," the squat man suddenly dropped his pleasant mask. "Let's not try to play the naive one," he fumed. "You know exactly what I am talking about."

At this point my mother had heard enough and prepared to leave the office, but like an enraged pit bull, the administrator threw himself between her and the door, and before she could fully comprehend what was happening, slapped her several times hard across the face. "A woman like you ought to be grateful that a German man still wants to have anything to do with her," he shouted. "Now get out and don't you ever let me see you again."

Later, my mother shared this experience with some of her close friends and told them of her determination to pursue the matter in court. They strongly counseled her against taking legal steps by pointing out that suing the Nazi official was tantamount to suing the government, an absurdity under the present regime. They warned her that this would only call unwanted attention to her situation and could result in bringing the full brunt of the Nazi regime down upon us. "You're in a no-win situation," they told her, "and if you know what's good for you and your boy, you'll forget the whole thing." Reluctantly, but no doubt wisely, my mother took their advice.

MY FRIEND KLAUS

Having been brought up by a widowed mother who had reared nine children by her own hard labor, my mother found it unthinkable to apply for welfare aid. To tide us over until she was able to find another job, she gladly accepted housecleaning work from several former colleagues at the hospital who had heard of her plight and wanted to help. One of them was a Jewish doctor who had himself been fired from his position during an earlier Nazi purge. He was still allowed to maintain his private practice, but was restricted to the treatment of non-Aryans.

He, his wife, and their seven-year-old son, Klaus, lived in a large, luxurious apartment on Grindelalle, a main thoroughfare that led through Hamburg's upper-middle-class, predominantly Jewish community. Although my mother was now their once-a-week cleaning woman, her new employers regarded her primarily as a friend and encouraged her to visit them after work and on weekends, and to bring me along as well. As a result, Klaus and I became good friends.

One day, as my mother and I were on our way to her cleaning job, we noticed groups of SA and SS troopers lining the downtown streets. Many of them were carrying signs that read *DEUTSCHE, KAUFT NICHT BEI JUDEN* (Germans, do not buy from Jews). Inspired by the signs, I confided to my mother that I, too, hated Jews because my teachers had taught us that Jews were repulsive. My mother looked at me for a long time with sad eyes, and finally asked me whether I liked Klaus. I couldn't see what Klaus had to do with my dislike of Jews but told her that I liked Klaus a lot. Still scrutinizing me with that sad look, my mother said, "Klaus is a Jew, and so are his father and mother."

I was stunned. How could my dear friend Klaus or his kind parents be the despicable people I had seen in the movie? All of a sudden, nothing seemed to make sense to me anymore.

When my mother saw my confusion, she tried to reassure me. "The only thing that's different about Jews is that they go to a different church, which is called a synagogue," she explained, "but that doesn't make them bad people. The Nazis don't like Africans either, and they are just as wrong about Jews as they are about Africans."

"But why don't the Nazis like Africans and Jews?" I kept probing.

"Because the Nazis feel they are better than everybody else," she explained. "They believe that all non-Nordic people, particularly Jews, are inferior. Unfortunately, they're in charge and there is nothing we can do about it."

"Does the Führer believe the same thing?" I demanded to know.

"I'm sure he does," replied my mother, obviously uncomfortable with the direction the conversation had taken.

I could accept, with some reservations, that there might be a few bad people in the government, but to believe that Hitler, the man whom I had been taught to worship as Germany's savior, should be capable of even the slightest mean act was beyond my comprehension.

My mother, noticing my inner turmoil, cautioned me never to talk to anyone about what she had just told me lest both of us get into serious trouble. I gave her my *Ehrenwort* (word of honor) and sealed my promise with a solemn handshake. German boys, it had been drilled into me from as far back as I could remember, never break their *Ehrenwort,* no matter what. My mother took another long, serious look at me that told me she knew her secret was safe with me.

When we arrived at our destination, Klaus's father opened the door. "Did you see those *Dreckschweine* (dirty pigs) out there, Bertha?" he asked my mother, with obvious reference to the placard-carrying storm troopers. While he, his wife, and my mother talked in hushed tones in the living room, Klaus and I went into his room, where we were soon engrossed in our favorite pastime of arranging his toy soldiers into marching formations in preparation for war. That evening, I said goodbye to Klaus as usual and promised to return the following week. But a week later my mother told me that we wouldn't be returning after all, because Klaus's father had accepted a staff appointment from another hospital and the family had moved to Berlin. What my mother kept from me at the time in order not to frighten me was that Klaus's parents had advised her to discontinue her contact with them. They had explained that, like all German Jews, they were under close scrutiny by the much feared *Geheime Staatspolizei*—the Gestapo—and that by associating with Jews, she ran the risk of making our already precarious situation even worse. They also told her that at one time they had intended to leave Germany but now thought they had waited too long and let the opportunity pass.

I didn't hear any more about Klaus and his parents until several years later, after the infamous Kristallnacht (Crystal Night) of November 9, 1938. That was the night of the Nazis' first major nationwide terror attack on German Jews, during which practically all synagogues were destroyed, including 267 prominent temples, but that number rose to more than one thousand if one includes smaller, unofficial places of worship; more than seven thousand shops were plundered; ninety-one Jews were killed and some thirty thousand Jews were arrested. The government ordered this pogrom, which derived its name from the massive destruction of store windows that left the sidewalks covered with broken glass, in retaliation for the assassination of the German diplomat Ernst von Rath in Paris by a seventeen-year-old Jewish youth named Herschel Grynszpan. Kristallnacht also coincided with the fifteenth anniversary of the Nazis' ill-fated 1923 putsch in Munich, during which eighteen Nazis were killed.

After school, following the widely reported terror attacks of the previous night, I took a stroll with several of my classmates through Hamburger Strasse, Barmbek's main shopping artery, to see for ourselves the damage we had heard so much about. The reports had not been exaggerated. Sidewalks on both sides of the major thoroughfare were covered for miles with broken glass. All of the windowless stores, we were told, belonged to Jews. "Had you been here last night," one boy boasted, "you could have 'bought' anything you wanted without money." I could readily see what he meant, for the shop windows that were normally filled with merchandise were completely bare, as were the shelves inside the stores. Several of my classmates expressed satisfaction that the Jews were finally getting their well-deserved punishment for all the wicked things they had done to Germany. I wanted to tell them that not all Jews were wicked, but remembered that I had promised my mother never to talk about that.

By the time I arrived home, I found my mother crying. When I asked her what was the matter, she confessed to me that the story she had told me years before about Klaus and his parents leaving Hamburg was not true, and that she had just heard that all three had been found dead in their apartment, the apparent victims of a drug overdose administered by the doctor. It took my mother many months to recover from her grief. But for me, the idea of death was still too abstract to have any real meaning. To this day, I can still see Klaus standing at the door as I told him I would see him again next week.

TANTE FATIMA

A periodic but unavoidable embarrassment, as far as I was concerned, were the occasional visits of my Tante Fatima, my father's oldest sister, who had returned from Switzerland to complete her studies for her *Abitur* (high school diploma) at the Helen Lange Oberrealschule. A petite woman in her early twenties, she was, by anyone's account—including her own—a genius who was conversant in English, German, French, Spanish, Italian, and her native Vai. In addition, she was a whiz at math, chemistry, and biology and played the violin well enough to give recitals despite a badly crippled right hand.

The reason Tante Fatima's visits got on my last raw nerve was not that I disliked her, but that we two had diametrically opposed agendas. My constant endeavor was to remain as inconspicuous as possible in order to avoid unnecessary attention or humiliating ridicule. Tante Fatima, on the other hand, loved nothing more than being the center of attention, and deliberately dressed and acted in a way that made it impossible for her to be overlooked. Long before I made the discovery that black was beautiful, she wore an Afro so huge it would have aroused the envy of a Fiji Islander. And to make doubly sure that she was noticed, just in case her enormous Afro failed to do the trick, she never went anywhere without her well-worn bright yellow leopard-skin coat, a most unusual piece of clothing in my staunchly provincial neighborhood. Each time Tante Fatima came around, she insisted on taking me out to some nearby *Konditorei* for a pastry and whipped cream treat. Invariably, our appearance would trigger stares, giggles, and insulting *Neger* remarks that made me wish the earth would open up and swallow me. Neither of us was amused when at one *Konditorei* the waitress snidely suggested that we try some of the establishment's delicious

Negerküsse (Negro kisses) or *Mohrenkopfe* (Moors' heads), two popular chocolate-coated pastries.

It irked me beyond words when people assumed that Fatima was my mother. More than once I had to fight some of my cronies who, after seeing me with Fatima, insisted that she was my real mother since we looked so much alike, and that the white woman I called my mother had merely adopted me. The latter idea was particularly annoying to me since, when I was much smaller, I entertained the same suspicion until my mother convinced me, by pointing out some examples in the animal kingdom, that mothers with white skin could have babies with brown skin as long as the father had dark skin.

Occasionally, Tante Fatima would take me to Blankenese, the beautiful Hamburg suburb overlooking the Elbe River, where ostensibly she would visit Pastor Heydorn, the rector of Hamburg's historic St. Katharinen *Kirche* (church). A longtime friend of my grandfather Momolu, Pastor Heydorn was a prominent German liberal and the founder of the *Menschheits* (Humanity) Party, one of the early opposition parties in Nazi Germany. Actually, Fatima came to see the pastor's handsome oldest son, Richard, with whom she carried on what to my uninitiated eyes seemed like a rather intense relationship. I would tag along bored as the two walked hand in hand through the wooded park of the huge Heydorn estate. Most of the things they talked about were way over my seven-year-old head, but they would also talk about their future in Liberia, where Richard intended to become a missionary.

Later that evening, after we had returned to Hamburg, I heard Fatima tell my mother about the frequent insults she and Richard drew from indignant Nazis whenever they were seen in public together. At the time I attributed those insults to Fatima's exaggerated exotic looks, and felt that she could easily reduce her problem by simply getting rid of that oversized Afro and that hideous leopard coat. Several years would pass before I understood the larger picture, the unbridled hatred of interracial romance in Nazi Germany.

Without realizing it, I once caused Fatima at least as much embarrassment as she had ever caused me. Christmas was approaching and she asked me what she could get me as a gift. At the time, among the more popular toys that season were little—about three-and-a-half-inch—plastic SA and SS men in their painted-on brown and black uniforms. I already owned a platoon's worth and had spent many hours staging my own mini-parades. All I needed now to make my life complete, I explained to Tante Fatima, was a matching miniature set of Nazi leaders consisting of Hitler, Göring, and Goebbels that could be purchased in toy stores throughout the city. They not only bore a striking resemblance to their living models, I explained, but their right arms could be raised and lowered for an authentic Hitler salute.

On Christmas Eve, as I had hoped, the three figurines of Hitler, Göring, and Goebbels were standing beneath our Christmas tree. It wasn't until weeks later that Tante Fatima told us what she had to endure to make my Christmas gift possible. She said that when she was about to leave the toy store with her purchase, the salesman hollered for everyone to hear, "Don't get any ideas of sticking needles into the toys the way you people do back home, because if anything happens to the Führer, Göring, or Goebbels, we'll find you and hold you responsible."

Fatima said her first impulse was to throw the package at the salesman and leave the store. Only after she thought about the money she had already spent and my disappointment if I didn't get my wish did she change her mind.

One day, Fatima, who after completing her *Abitur* had enrolled at the University of Hamburg as a medical student, arrived with a fat letter from Momolu. The news was that he had been cleared of the embezzlement charges and freed from jail and that President Barclay's vendetta against the Massaquois, while still stifling the family's progress, had become less intense. Except for Nat, who was still in jail, all the Massaquoi men had come out of hiding and lived in various parts of Liberia. My father had temporarily gone into exile in Lagos, Nigeria, where his mother lived with her second husband, but now he had moved back to Monrovia.

Momolu apologized for being unable to be of more financial assistance to Fatima and advised her to continue to make use of her linguistic talents to supplement the small allowance he had been sending her. Without going into details, he told her that he was extremely worried about the "political developments" in Germany, and was working on arrangements to have her go as soon as possible to the United States, where, with the help of friends like W. E. B. Du Bois, the black civil-rights activist, she would be able to continue her studies. By "political developments," he undoubtedly was referring to Hitler's incessant saber-rattling and the mounting prospect of war. If he read Hitler's *Mein Kampf*, which is more than likely, he may also have realized the precariousness of Fatima's status at the University of Hamburg. In Hitler's revealing blueprint for the Third Reich, which he penned while incarcerated at Landsberg prison for his aborted putsch in Munich, the future dictator left no doubt what he thought of university-trained blacks. "From time to time," he wrote, "illustrated papers bring it to the attention of the German petty-bourgeois that some place or other a Negro has for the first time become a lawyer, teacher, even a pastor, in fact a heroic tenor, or something of the sort. While the idiotic bourgeoisie looks with amazement at such miracles of education, full of respect for this marvelous result of modern educational skill, the Jew shrewdly draws from it a new proof of the soundness of his theory about the *equality of men* that he is trying to funnel into the minds of the nations. It doesn't dawn on this depraved bourgeois world that this is positively a sin against all reason; that it is criminal lunacy to keep on drilling a born half-ape until people think they have made a lawyer out of him, while millions of members of the highest culture-race must remain in entirely unworthy positions; that it is a sin against the will of the Eternal Creator if His most gifted beings by the hundreds and hundreds of thousands are allowed to degenerate in the present proletarian morass, while Hottentots and Zulu Kaffirs are trained for intellectual professions. For this is training exactly like that of the poodle, and not scientific 'education.' The same pains and care employed on intelligent races would a thousand times sooner make every single individual capable of the same achievements. . . ."

It was not until 1937 that Momolu was able to make good on his promise to get Fatima out of Germany and enrolled at Fisk University in Nashville, Tennessee. When she paid us one last visit to say goodbye, I sensed that she would be gone for a long time and suddenly realized that I would miss her a lot since she had been my only tangible link to Momolu as well as to my father, who hadn't written a single letter to my mother and me since he left Germany. Now eleven years old, I had outgrown being embarrassed by her exotic presence—super Afro, leopard coat, and all—and proudly, yet sadly, walked her to the train station to start her long journey, via Switzerland, to the U. S. A.

SUMMER FUN IN SALZA

A long-standing and extremely popular government-sponsored social program in Hamburg was the annual summer *Ferienzug* (vacation train), which gave thousands of city kids a chance to spend their four-week summer vacation with relatives in various rural parts of Germany. Each year, beginning at age six, I looked forward to making the six-hour train ride to visit Onkel Karl, my mother's brother, Tante Grete, and my four-years-older cousin, Trudchen, who lived in the tiny village of Salza near Nordhausen at the edge of the scenic Harz Mountains.

Following registration several weeks in advance of the trip, my mother would take me to Hamburg's *Hauptbahnhof* (main train station) where I would be assigned to a counselor, usually a female social worker, who would fit me and the suitcase I carried with all-important tags. The tag, which I was admonished to wear around my neck throughout the trip, listed my name and address and the name and address of Onkel Karl. Since neither we nor my relatives had a telephone, my mother had written Onkel Karl the exact time of my arrival.

After several hours of riding southward, the train, which had been packed with kids in Hamburg, emptied as more and more children reached their destination. One stop before Salza, my counselor alerted me that the next stop would be mine. When the train pulled into Salza, I immediately spotted Onkel Karl, a rather portly gentleman, Tante Grete, a thin-as-a-reed woman, and Trudchen, a rather chubby girl. The counselor turned me and my suitcase over to their care, wished me an enjoyable vacation, and reminded Onkel Karl that she would be back for me in exactly four weeks.

Compared with the hustle-bustle of Hamburg, life in the tiny village of Salza was idyllic, tranquil, and eventless. Automobiles were a rarity, while cattle and sheep on cobblestoned Hauptstrasse, the village's only thoroughfare, were commonplace. In Salza, people from the next village, a few miles away, were almost regarded as foreigners. The arrival of someone from as far a place as Hamburg and as exotic looking as I caused quite a stir. Prior to my first visit, Tante Grete had seen to it that everybody in the village knew that her nephew from Hamburg was the son and grandson of African big shots, information that added considerably to my status as a rare attraction. Despite vast differences of our respective worlds, or because of them, I was an instant hit with the village boys, who never failed to be impressed with my only mildly exaggerated accounts of big-city life. They were awestruck when I told them about buildings that were ten stories tall, so tall that one needed a *Fahrstuhl* (elevator) to get to the top; ferryboats that transported people throughout the city along a vast network of canals; ships that were bigger than buildings; and a carnival ground many times the size of Salza that was packed with merry-go-rounds, magic shows, hot dog stands, and shows featuring the world's tallest man, fattest woman, and an "Ape Woman" supposedly captured in the Borneo jungles who was covered from neck to toe with long monkey hair.

If hailing from the big city made me feel sophisticated by comparison with Salza's simple country folks and their countrified ways, nothing made me more aware of the huge gulf that existed between my world and theirs than a strange contraption in the backyard of my relatives' three-story apartment building. It took several days and a near internal explosion before I was able to overcome my revulsion and use the outhouse for the purpose it was intended for. There simply wasn't any way to shield my nostrils against the foul stench that emanated from the round, head-size hole in the wooden plank that constituted the seat. Through it I could see a round, nearly filled metal receptacle buzzing with flies and around which chickens were merrily pecking away in a disgusting search for food. Fittingly, the amenities of the facility—such as they were—consisted of newspaper pages cut into neat little squares skewered on a large nail protruding from the wall. It was during those moments when I smelled the stench and felt the unyielding, sand paper–like newspaper on my pampered behind that I missed Hamburg the most. But there were far too many things I enjoyed in Salza to keep me from feeling homesick.

Onkel Karl, Tante Grete, and Trudchen treated me like the son and brother, respectively, they never had. A master tailor, Onkel Karl enjoyed having me around when he fashioned men's suits from bolts of cloth while seated cross-legged on his worktable. In Salza, as elsewhere in Germany, money was in short supply. Onkel Karl had worked out barter arrangements with some of his customers, either local farmers or tradesmen like himself, whereby they would pay with their produce or skills instead of currency.

Three times a week, Onkel Karl's barber would make a house call to give him an expert shave and, whenever necessary, a haircut. In return, the barber received a new high-quality suit each year.

The only thing that dimmed my otherwise idyllic vacations in Salza was Tante Grete's conviction that I needed fattening up. Obviously equating Onkel Karl's and Trudchen's chubbiness with health, she was determined to put some additional pounds on me. No matter how much I protested that my stomach couldn't handle the mountains of food she piled in front of me, she sternly insisted that I eat every bit. The result was that each supper, I would put in overtime at the kitchen table gagging on humongous sandwiches, since I was not allowed to play again until I had eaten everything on my plate.

Each Sunday, largely for my benefit, the entire family went hiking or by rail to some of the Harz Mountains' most scenic spots, including old mountain-top fortresses and castles. Following each of these weekend hikes, I returned filled with, and deeply moved by, Germany's history and old legends, which my lively imagination weaved into an enchanted realm that made me long for bygone days of chivalrous knights and magical feats.

By the time my four weeks in Salza were up, I had finally had my fill of country life and longed once again for the big city. On the day of my departure, Tante Grete made sure that all of us were standing on the station platform well ahead of the train's arrival, that my shoelaces were tied, and that I and my suitcase were properly tagged. As promised, my counselor and the vacation train arrived on time to take me back. After a seemingly never-ending exchange of goodbyes, and a big hug and kiss from Tante Grete that I hoped none of the kids on the train had noticed, I boarded and was soon part of a boisterous bunch of kids who were wildly debating who had done and seen more. I had no doubt that none of them could top the places I had visited and the sights I had seen.

It was dark when our train finally pulled into the brightly lit, cavernous dome of Hamburg *Hauptbahnhof*. Seeing my mother's face in a sea of parents' faces after what seemed like an eternity gave me a feeling of inde-scribable joy and complete happiness. Although I had become extremely sensitive about displaying affection or emotions in public since I entered school, I made an exception when I let my mother hug and kiss me to her heart's content. It was at that point that I discovered the old verity that absence makes the heart grow fonder.

WRIEDE ARRIVES

Looking back, I can recall quite a few people who caused me grief when I was a child, but not one of them was quite as relentless, as consistently mean-spirited and cruel in his effort to make my life miserable as Herr Heinrich Wriede, our new school principal. Unlike his predecessor, who during my first school year kept such a low profile that I can recall neither his name nor the way he looked, Wriede was not a man to be ignored or forgotten. A strapping, reddish-blond six-footer in his mid-forties, Wriede was a cousin of the writer Gorch Fock, and reputedly a poet in his own right. In addition, he was a fanatic follower of Hitler, a fact he emphasized by affecting a square, albeit reddish-blond, Hitler-type mustache.

Herr Wriede came into my life—and I into his—sometime during my second school year, on the day he became our new principal. To introduce himself to us, he had the entire student body and faculty assemble in the schoolyard, where, resplendently attired in the brown uniform of an *Amtswalter,* a mid-level Nazi functionary, he strutted around in high boots and riding breeches like a general inspecting his troops. His stated purpose was to impress upon us—teachers and pupils alike—that a new wind was blowing at Kätnerkampschule and that henceforth, things would be done the Wriede way—if we knew what he meant. Of course we boys didn't know what he meant, but from the tone of his voice we got a pretty good idea that "the Wriede way" was nothing we'd be particularly crazy about.

As he paraded in front of us, he suddenly spotted me among the ranks of boys, and, like a snake trying to mesmerize its prey, fixed his hateful gaze on me.

"What I intend to instill in this school is pride in being German boys in a National Socialist German state," he intoned without taking his eyes off me.

I had grown quite uncomfortable under the principal's stare, but just as I was about to avert my eyes, he moved on, continuing to elaborate on his theme. After Wriede had finished and we returned to class, I couldn't rid myself of the unfamiliar and quite unsettling feeling of having just met a personal enemy, someone who wished me ill. It didn't take very long before I found my suspicion confirmed.

The first time Wriede gave me tangible evidence of how he felt about me was when he filled in for our sick gym teacher. The principal announced that he would conduct a *Mutprobe* (test of courage) to separate the cowards from the boys with guts. I had no problem with that; in fact, I welcomed the opportunity to show off my prowess, because I had always believed—and repeatedly proven—that I had at least as much guts as the next boy in my class.

After Wriede marched us to the *Turnhalle* (gym), he had us build an obstacle course by arranging various pieces of equipment—parallel bars, pommel horses, balance beams, and so on—in a wide circle. They had to be spaced widely enough so that leaping from one piece of equipment to another could not be done without a certain degree of difficulty. One gap he wanted left so wide that the only way it could be traversed was by jumping into the air and grabbing on to a thick rope that dangled from the ceiling and then, Tarzanlike, swinging to the other side. To add to the difficulty of the maneuver, Wriede positioned one boy beside the big gap with the instruction to keep the rope in constant motion with the aid of a long stick.

Surveying the course, I anticipated no problems and confidently awaited my turn. By the time it came, most boys had successfully completed the course, though a few had washed out and, on Wriede's orders, been sent to the "cowards' corner." I got through the major part of the course quite easily and was headed for the big gap when I saw that Wriede himself had taken the place of the boy with the stick. Rather than letting the rope swing to and fro, he held it back in such a way that it remained totally out of my reach. As I waited for him to release the rope, ready to leap as soon as it swung toward me, Wriede shouted, "*Feigling* (Coward)! *Kein Mut* (No courage)! Get out of the way!" Not quite believing that he could be this unfair, I waited another moment to see if perhaps he would relent and send the rope my way. But he became only more enraged, shouting at me, "Out of the way! Give somebody with courage a chance. Get over there with the other cowards!" Reluctantly I complied and joined the small group of washouts. I felt as if I had just been whipped. In fact, a beating would not have hurt me nearly as much as being unjustly branded a coward.

Up to that moment, I had craved Wriede's approval despite his pointed rejection of me. I had even felt pangs of jealousy when I observed how kind and caring he could be with other children in my class, especially those whose blond hair and blue eyes projected the Nazi physical ideal. But quite suddenly, my almost perverse need to be liked by this man vanished and gave way to unadulterated—albeit impotent—hate.

I did not tell my mother about the incident, afraid that in her anger she would confront Wriede and thereby make matters worse. Instead, I decided not to let anything Wriede said or did bother me. But that was easier said than done, as I was soon to find out.

One day, several months before our homeroom teacher Fräulein Beyle was "transferred" out of our school, she announced that it was time for us to prepare for our traditional annual *Elternabend* (parents' night), during which pupils from each grade would entertain parents with skits, small plays, poems, and musical renditions. After picking a simple play written in Hamburger *Platt* (Low German) about a boy's excitement over the first snowfall of the year, Fräulein Beyle held auditions to determine who would get which of the play's three parts. After reading each part, I was awarded the lead role and told that I had exactly two weeks to memorize my part. I could hardly wait to tell my mother. Mutti, in her new role as a proud stage mother, spread the word of my pending starring debut to Tante Möller and some of her closest friends. About a dozen or so said they would be delighted to come, and asked me to get them the required thirty-pfennig tickets while the getting was still good.

Leaving nothing to chance, Fräulein Beyle had assigned an understudy for each part and had us rehearse over and over until we knew every word of the play backward. The day before the big event, while we were in the midst of rehearsals, Herr Wriede entered the classroom. Motioning Fräulein Beyle not to interrupt us, he seated himself directly in front of me. Until that moment, I had been completely free of stage fright. But now that I looked into Wriede's cold, unsmiling eyes, a strange sensation of panic took hold of me. After telling myself that I had nothing to be afraid of since I had my lines down pat, I quickly regained my composure and went through the rehearsal without a hitch.

Before Wriede left the class, he asked Fräulein Beyle to accompany him out to the corridor. When she returned to the classroom, she looked perturbed, but didn't say anything. Somehow, I couldn't escape the uneasy feeling that her changed demeanor had something to do with Wriede's visit and me. I couldn't have been more correct. When the class ended, she asked me to stay. "I don't know how to tell you this," she started apologetically after a long pause, "but Herr Wriede wants me to give the lead part to Gerd [my blond, blue-eyed understudy]. He thinks Gerd would be better for the part."

"How does he know Gerd would be better for the part if he didn't even watch him rehearse?" I interjected meekly in a futile attempt to sway an unreasonable judgment against me with reason.

"I didn't agree, or else I wouldn't have given you the part to begin with," responded Fräulein Beyle, "but there is nothing I can do. Herr Wriede is the *Schulleiter* and I must follow his orders."

When I told Mutti what happened, she became livid with anger but cautioned me not to let Wriede's cruelty get to me and, above all, not to let my dislike for Wriede cause me to dislike school. "School is a wonderful place and most teachers are decent men and women, like Fräulein Beyle," she assured me. "You can take my word," she added, "that sooner or later, Wriede will get his punishment."

She then contacted Tante Möller and her other friends who had planned to attend the parents' night and offered to make restitution for the tickets since my performance had been canceled. They wouldn't hear of it, especially after they learned the apparent reason why I had been given the boot. Tante Möller, who never minced her words, put her thoughts exceedingly graphically when she told my mother that since her little Hans-Jürgen wasn't allowed in the play, they could keep her thirty pfennig and "stick them up their Nazi behinds."

The next time Wriede went out of his way to pick on me was when he stopped me in the hall and, in front of several of my classmates, jabbed a long index finger into my chest. "You are not to wear this shirt in school anymore," he snarled at me without further explanation. The khaki-colored shirt, a birthday gift from Tante Möller, was similar to those worn by the Hitler Youth, and the principal was obviously under the impression that I was wearing part of a Nazi uniform.

When my mother showed up at the principal's office the next day to have a word with him about the incident, he immediately launched an attack. "The Hitler Youth uniform," he shouted at her, "symbolizes our proud young Aryan generation. By letting your son wear that uniform you are making a mockery of everything that uniform stands for. I must therefore advise you to see to it that he doesn't wear that shirt to school ever again."

When the principal had ended his tirade, my mother reached into her bag, pulled out the freshly laundered item in question and calmly put it on the principal's desk. At close inspection, it was easy to see that the shirt was not part of a regulation uniform but simply an ordinary, khaki-colored shirt. Unwilling to apologize for his mistake, Wriede tried to hide his embarrassment by insisting that the potential for confusion made it unwise for me to wear the shirt, even if it was not official Nazi garb.

At this point my mother exploded. "I said to him," she recounted later, "that until a law was passed that expressly forbade the wearing of khaki-colored shirts by unauthorized persons, you were going to wear that shirt in school as often as you felt like it, whether he liked it or not." Knowing Mutti, I have no doubt that she told Wriede exactly that and probably a great deal more. At the time, she merely told me that she'd leave it up to me to decide what I wanted to do about the shirt. Since I knew that my wearing it was a sure way of getting Wriede's goat, I chose to wear it often— so often, in fact, that within a few months its khaki color had faded to off-white from frequent laundering and it got so threadbare that Mutti decided it was time to retire it.

EMPEROR HEINRICH AT CANOSSA

As a dyed-in-the-wool arch-Nazi, Wriede was on a constant alert to weed out anything that conflicted with his deeply entrenched conviction of German superiority. On one such occasion, he was pinch-hitting for another teacher who was teaching us medieval German history. We had been studying the trials and tribulations of the German emperor Heinrich IV (1050–1106), who, according to our text, had been excommunicated by

Pope Gregory VII in some jurisdictional dispute. The ban caused many of the emperor's vassals to withdraw their support from him. In order to regain their allegiance and his imperial clout, Heinrich was obliged to throw himself at the mercy of the pope and beg for lifting of the ban. This he did by journeying as a simple penitent to the temporary papal residence at the castle of Canossa in northern Italy.

Prior to Wriede's arrival, a student orderly had, on instruction from our regular history teacher, put up a large illustration that depicted a wretched-looking Emperor Heinrich, dressed only in a thin pilgrim's shirt, standing barefoot in deep snow next to a castle. In the foreground a resplendently robed and mitered Pope Gregory looked down on the emperor from one of the castle's turrets. The artist's rendering of the historic event was a typical visual aid in use in German public schools, but one that apparently had been overlooked by the censors of the Nazis' Ministry of Education.

Entering our classroom, Wriede spotted the illustration and immediately flew into a rage. Ripping it from its stand and throwing it to the floor, he shouted, "*Lügen, Lügen, nichts als Lügen* (Lies, lies, nothing but lies)!" The rest of the hour he denounced the entire historic episode as "a fabrication by a bunch of lying monks." No German emperor, he ranted, would have humiliated himself like that before an Italian pope. The only reason we were reading such nonsense in our history books, he explained, was that Catholic monks were among the relatively few literate people at the time and, therefore, were the only ones who recorded "history." Consequently, he told us, they wrote "history" not the way it was but the way they wished it had been.

Despite my personal dislike of Wriede, his view of recorded history, which caused him to reject any historical data he found inconsistent with his ideas of German superiority, made a great deal of sense to me at the time. It was quite comforting to me and my budding sense of patriotism to be reassured that "our" emperor did not behave like a wimp.

Wriede's attempts to demoralize and wear me down with his frequent verbal attacks achieved just the opposite. The more he picked on me, the tougher I became, until I felt that I could take just about anything he was able to dish out. Fortunately, Wriede was not typical of the teachers I encountered during my eight years in Hamburg's public schools. Most were professional educators who treated me like everybody else. And there were a few, like Fräulein Beyle, who—sensitive to my particular plight—went out of their way to make my life a little easier.

Among the latter was Herr Schneider, a goateed man with erect, military bearing who taught us zoology, biology, botany, and, in a roundabout way, about the birds and the bees. Despite his being a bona fide World War I hero who had distinguished himself as an infantry first lieutenant on the western front, he was a most gentle soul as he introduced us kids to the flora and fauna of the earth. He won my undying affection when, while trying to explain what the people of India looked like, he said, "They have the same beautiful, smooth brown skin as your classmate Hans-Jürgen." After that, he couldn't do any wrong as far as I was concerned, even when he kept us several hours after school just to watch a couple of birds feed their new-born chicks.

HERR GOSAU

Another teacher who made no secret of his fondness for me was Herr Gosau, our school choir director, a handsome, mild-mannered gnome of a man with impeccably groomed gray hair and mustache. His only concession to Nazi regimentation was his rendering of the mandatory *Heil Hitler* salute at the beginning and end of each class. Without asking for Wriede's approval, he had made me a member of the choir, insisting that I had not only a good singing voice but above average musical ability. In addition to music, Herr Gosau instructed us in a course called "Religion," but which was really a course in biblical history.

He never brought up the subject of race, but I instinctively felt that he was on my side. This was especially apparent after an incident during a weekend school outing at the sprawling *Jugend Park* (Youth Park) in sub-urban Langenhorn, during which we pupils entertained our parents with a variety show in an open-air theater. Following our choir's rendition of several songs, I took my seat beside my mother in the audience. The finale of the show was announced by Wriede as a "humorous song-and-dance number" by the senior class choreographed by none other than Herr Wriede himself.

The act started with a chorus line of eighth graders walking rhythmically toward the audience while mumbling an unintelligible chant. Suddenly, the line opened in the center and a short boy, totally covered with black paint and clad only in a grass skirt over swim trunks, leaped out. To the beat of tom-toms, the *Ersatz* African put on a frenzied performance jumping and gyrating while the chorus line droned on wildly in gibberish that was obviously meant to sound African.

As soon as the *Negertanz* started, many eyes in the packed outdoor auditorium turned to me and my mother. At first my mother wanted us to walk out, but she changed her mind, perhaps realizing that our leaving would draw even more attention. So we sat through the whole thing, which, it seemed to us, would never end. When it finally did end, the performers and Herr Wriede received a rousing ovation.

Still devastated by the demeaning spectacle, my mother and I rode quietly home on the city train, each deep in thought, when she was approached by Herr Gosau, who had witnessed the show. After introducing himself as my music teacher, he said, "Your son is musically very gifted," without making any reference to the racist show we had just seen.

Herr Gosau's words were just what my mother needed to hear. "I'm glad to hear an expert say that," she replied, "because I have always felt that Hans-Jürgen has musical talent."

In the course of their conversation, Herr Gosau offered to give me violin lessons in his spare time, free of charge, provided my mother would buy me a violin. Without discussing it with me, my mother assured Herr Gosau that I would have a violin and would be ready for my first lesson no later than a couple of months hence.

I hated the very idea of learning to play the violin. Among my peers in the street, a violin was for sissies. The mere thought of being seen in the street with a violin case—that we kids contemptuously called a *Kindersarg* (children's coffin)—gave me the creeps. But the matter was out of my hands. My mother was determined that I take violin lessons and that was it.

The hardest part was accumulating enough money to buy a violin, since violins, even secondhand ones, weren't cheap. Although Mutti had found a permanent job as a factory worker at the nearby Hamburg–New York Gummiwaren Fabrik, a hard rubber factory, she barely made enough money to make ends meet. Under the piecework system, called *Akkord,* she was paid according to her daily output, and the only way she could earn more money was to force herself to work at the highest speed her nerves could endure. By driving herself to her limits at work and after considerable scrimping and saving, she proudly handed me a violin—a rather handsome instrument, I had to admit—replete with bow and *Kindersarg,* which she had bought on a layaway plan from a neighborhood secondhand shop. Since I didn't have the heart to hurt her feelings or to turn down Herr Gosau's generous offer, I made *gute Miene zum bosen Spiel* (smiled in the face of adversity), to quote Mutti, and resigned myself to the inevitable. Once a week after school for nearly a year, I joined three other "lucky" students for two hours of intense violin studies under Herr Gosau's tutelage. While I genuinely loved music, I detested the marrow-jarring sounds I produced. Finally, after a particularly gut-wrenching session during which I tried unsuccessfully to bend my stubborn fingers to the uncooperative instrument as Herr Gosau instructed, he took me aside and, without any sign of annoyance, announced that he was throwing in the towel. "You are musically extremely gifted," he assured me, "and I urge you to continue your musical development in some form or another, but the violin simply doesn't seem to be your instrument."

Amen. I couldn't have agreed with him more. I felt badly, though, for disappointing the old gentleman and especially my mother, who had to give up her secret dream of one day having a violin virtuoso for a son. That evening I told her that my violin lessons had come to a halt; she was clearly saddened, but accepted the inevitable without any recriminations. "Be sure to thank Herr Gosau for his kindness" was all she said.

HERR HARDEN

And then there was Herr Harden, my first English teacher. An equal opportunity tyrant, he was in a class all by himself. The most positive thing I remember of him is that he hated all the other boys as much as he hated me. Harden was an obese, bull-necked man who, except for thick glasses that made his eyes appear like a series of concentric rings, bore an amazing resemblance to a caricature of John Bull. Herr Harden was a fanatic practitioner of the "spare the rod and spoil the child" philosophy, and—backed by a system that condoned, if not encouraged, corporal punishment—literally made the rod the centerpiece of his pedagogy. As a result, he was the most despised and feared teacher on the Kätnerkamp faculty. He was also the first teacher who got a piece of my hide during my eventful eight-year elementary school career.

Actually, I had nobody but myself to blame for meeting up with Herr Harden's lethal weapon. Taking lessons in English, French, or Spanish was entirely voluntary and a special privilege reserved for pupils with top marks in German rhetoric. Had I not signed up for English classes, our paths would never have crossed and I would have been spared much grief. But once we signed up, we were not allowed to drop the course.

It wasn't long before I realized I had made a catastrophic mistake. With each of Herr Harden's violent outbursts at the slightest provocation, my initial enthusiasm for learning English diminished rapidly until I wished the language didn't even exist. Whenever we mispronounced a word while reading aloud in class, Herr Harden would immediately go into one of his choleric seizures and correct us at the top of his voice as if he were teaching a class of the severely hearing impaired. Poking his thumb at us, he would bellow over and over, "This is the thumb! This is the thumb! and not, Zis is ze sumb!" If a pupil, for whatever reason, failed to do his homework and got caught, Herr Harden without exception would call him to the front of the class, order him to bend down and touch his toes, and administer three slashing licks with a wicked-looking yard-long switch. The sound of that switch and the screams of the hapless victim made me determined never to give Harden any reason to try his switch on me. But the odds were against me.

In order to attend English classes, we pupils were obliged—much to our regret—to rise an hour earlier twice a week, since all foreign-language classes were scheduled before regular classes so as not to interfere with the regular curriculum. During the winter months it was still dark when we arrived at school, where we had to wait for Herr Harden to let us into the building. Usually, he would arrive a few minutes before class began at 7 A.M., after a rather lengthy bicycle trip from his suburban home.

It had long been our fervent hope that one morning Harden would get run over by a truck or at least oversleep. According to school policy, if a teacher did not show within twenty minutes after the beginning of class, early class was automatically canceled. Several times we thought we might get our wish when Harden hadn't shown up by the time the nearby church bell struck 7 A.M. But each time we were disappointed when, just in the nick of time, Harden's bulky silhouette rounded the corner on his bicycle.

One fateful morning, however, our time had come. It was fifteen minutes past seven and no Harden in sight. Since none of us had a watch and it was still too dark to see the church clock, we had to rely on our instincts to gauge the passage of five minutes. Finally, when all of us agreed that at least five minutes had elapsed and there was still no sign of him, we dispersed like rats leaving the sinking ship.

Our joy over our successful coup was considerable but short-lived. Two days later, as we faced Harden in class, following his arrival at 7 A.M. on the dot, he went into an apoplectic rage that made us fear for his sanity and our lives. With veins bulging at his forehead, he shouted that his patience with us had finally come to an end and that if we thought we could make a fool of him, we were sadly mistaken. He then insisted that we had left that morning well ahead of his arrival "before 7:20 A.M." With that, he ordered all twenty or so of us to come forward, row by row, and reap our well-deserved reward.

I'm sure that even the less quick-witted among my classmates knew immediately what Harden had in mind. With growing terror, I watched while Harden whacked away with his switch—three licks per pupil—until the class was filled with howling boys holding their aching behinds. Like a condemned man at a mass execution, I watched my comrades fall, one by one, under the cruel hand of the executioner. Finally, it was my turn to pay for my part in the "conspiracy." Before I knew it, it was all over. At first, I only felt three sharp stings, which, I thought, I could manage. But within seconds, the pain grew steadily until my entire posterior seemed on fire. I instantly realized what the howling and crying around me was all about, but I was determined and managed not to cry.

Unfortunately, my run-in with Harden wasn't my only acquaintance with corporal punishment. The events that led to my second brush with this barbaric aspect of German education came as a result of an old Hamburg street custom called *Kloppe* (rumble) in which fighting between boys from adjacent neighborhoods erupts like instantaneous combustion. No one among the warring factions knows, or cares, what the fight is all about or who started it, other than experiencing the joy of kicking butt. It all begins with someone out of nowhere hollering *"Kloppe!"* This sets off a rush to arms—wooden handles, broomsticks, bats—anything that lends itself to inflicting minor cuts and bruises. We younger boys would take our marching orders from the older boys and usually would be assigned as lookouts to report advancing enemies or—God forbid—the approach of a *Schako*, which is Hamburg street talk for cop.

On this particular occasion, two classmates of mine and I were entrusted with an especially dangerous mission. After each of us was handed two water-filled pop bottles, we were told to wait in ambush until the enemy "soldiers" had come within throwing distance, then hurl the bottles at the pavement directly in front of them.

Eager to demonstrate our courage, we did exactly as told, with amazing results. As our bottles exploded on the pavement, the advancing attackers were caught in a hail of glass shrapnel that caused them to beat a hasty retreat.

The next morning in school, still basking in the new status to which my bravery had elevated me, I was unceremoniously summoned to the class of Herr Siegel where, to my dismay, something akin to a war-crimes trial was in session. After several witnesses, including some of our street enemies, testified that they had seen me—no one else, mind you—throwing pop bottles filled with water like hand grenades, Herr Siegel gave me a stern lecture on the gravity of my action and how fortunate I was that no one had lost an eye or was otherwise seriously hurt.

In retrospect, Herr Siegel's comments made a great deal of sense to me, except that I was being singled out for punishment—the usual three lashes. When he asked me whether I had anything to say in my defense, I didn't think that snitching on my partners in crime would have been ethical or get me off the hook, but I questioned Siegel's jurisdiction in this case—his right to punish me for something that had happened after school and outside the school building. But Herr Siegel waved my objections aside. I had always considered him a decent sort of guy, too civilized to stoop to Herr Harden's level, but as he whacked away at my rear end, I painfully concluded that I had been wrong.

As so often, my mother had been right. She had often warned me not to get involved in mischief, even if other boys were doing the same thing. "Afterwards," she said, "the only one people will remember is you."

BOOKS TO THE RESCUE

If the relentless barrage of Nazi propaganda to which we were constantly exposed failed to close my mind permanently, it was because of a childhood habit of mine that had reached compulsive proportions. As soon as I had learned to read, my mother fostered my interest in books, and by the time I was eight years old, I had become hopelessly addicted to reading books— any books. Since I grew up in the pre-television age, books became my primary source of diversion, escapism, and information, and every pfennig I earned running errands or that was handed me by well-meaning adults for the purchase of candy, I saved up to buy books. A compulsive reader in her own right, my mother made sure that I had a public library card and that at Christmas, Easter, and birthdays, most of the presents I received were books.

Thanks to my truly eclectic literary taste that didn't distinguish between good and bad books, appropriate- or inappropriate-for-my-age books, I read anything I could get my hands on with equal enthusiasm. Consequently— and in spite of the Nazis' restrictive, one-dimensional totalitarianism—I became part of a vast, multifaceted, and multicolored world long before I was able to physically escape the mental prison that was Nazi Germany. If it had been Dr. Goebbels's intention to keep our young minds nationalis- tically inward-directed, he had missed the boat as far as I was concerned. The genie of knowledge in the form of dozens of dog-eared books was out of the bottle and filled my mind with wondrous images that made me yearn for adventures far beyond the narrow boundaries of Germany.

Through the pages of my books, I could traverse time as well as space, reality as well as fantasy. Before I was fourteen years old, and decades before nuclear-powered submarines and space travel ceased to be science fiction, I had traveled into outer space and twenty thousand leagues beneath the sea with Jules Verne. James Fenimore Cooper had me smoking the peace pipe in a wigwam of a Native American chieftain years before I laid eyes on a real Native American. Long before I would actually behold the Coliseum and other remnants of Roman antiquity, with Henryk Sienkiewicz I watched Christians being fed to hungry lions and Nero fiddle while ancient Rome was burning. Harriet Beecher Stowe let me feel the pain of slaves in the South of far-off America, evoking in me a strange sense of empathy that at the time I refused to recognize as having been brought on by a feeling of kinship. Miguel de Cervantes had me root for deranged Don Quixote in his quest for knightly honors. Charles Dickens brought me face-to-face with the horrors of institutionalized child abuse during the Industrial Revolution in merry old England. Sir Arthur Conan Doyle had me follow Sherlock Holmes, accompanied by his sidekick Dr. Watson, through the narrow cobblestone streets of foggy nineteenth-century London as the master sleuth searched for clues to a mysterious crime. Mark Twain had me rafting down the Mississippi with Huckleberry Finn and Jim, the slave, long before I saw North America's mightiest stream. Victor Hugo made me shudder as the guillotine did its grisly work on behalf of French liberty. And long before I had the opportunity to visit tropical island paradises on plush cruise ships, Robert Louis Stevenson let me sail the seven seas with buccaneer scoundrels and swashbuckling heroes in pursuit of hidden treasures.

Ironically, among my favorite books during my formative years were those that dealt with the old Germanic legends of Siegfried, the fairest of fair knights, which provided much of the National Socialists' racial mythology. What fascinated me most about the chivalrous knights of yore was their iron-clad code of honor, to which they adhered even in the face of certain death. By far my favorite and—by no coincidence—the most macho of the Teutonic deities was Thor, god of war, who when angered cruised the heavens wielding a magic hammer that dispensed lightning and thunder.

Thanks to my books, I was able to escape at will from some of the more painful situations in my daily existence into worlds that, however perilous, were fair, where good was rewarded and evil punished. Reading provided me with an effective buffer against the constant racial attacks by the likes of Herr Wriede and helped to blunt their impact on my immediate consciousness. Without my being fully aware of it, reading became my indispensable survival tool.

WORDS OF WISDOM

Of the many characteristics that defined my mother, one of the more pronounced ones was her incurable optimism. This was most apparent in her high expectations for me in spite of the dim outlook imposed by Nazi racial laws. Nothing could shake her conviction that, quite apart from race, I had exceptional potential and that some day—Nazis or no Nazis—I would make something of myself. After she learned from Tante Fatima that Liberia had a shortage of university-trained engineers, she decided that I should become an engineer and one day help Liberians build urgently needed bridges and roads. Never mind that my math grades were the lowest on my report card. She convinced me that an engineering career would be within my reach, if only I reached hard enough. To encourage me to do just that, she would say, "If you want to become a hook, you'll have to start bending early."

Imbued with a strong aversion toward religiosity—an aversion that has resurfaced in me—she was convinced that you could go to church and pray until you were blue in the face and know the Bible backwards in five languages and still not be a good person. The only way to accomplish that, she believed, was by treating your fellow human beings, and animals, right. She didn't attend church regularly until, well into middle age, she married a devout member of the Serbian Orthodox Church and actively participated in her husband's observances of his church's rituals. Instead of religious dogma, she had at her command an inexhaustible supply of proverbs, rhymes, and maxims to which she adhered. There was one for every occasion a person might possibly encounter in a lifetime—advice on how to manage money, how to treat friends, why it pays to be punctual, and on and on. It was a legacy from her mother, one she was determined to pass on to me. By the time I started first grade, I already knew that "lies have short legs," especially after having been caught in a lie. When she tried to teach me the benefits of a righteous life, she'd say, "A good conscience is a soothing pillow." To instill modesty and politeness in me, she'd say, "With hat in hand, you can travel through the entire land." To keep me from treating a school chum meanly, she'd warn, "If you dig a hole for others, you'll fall into it yourself." When I seemed unappreciative of a money gift because it was smaller than I expected, she would remind me that "he who doesn't honor the penny doesn't deserve the dollar." Although, unlike the Ten Commandments, they lacked divine endorsement, these little morsels of German folk wisdom have lost nothing of their validity since I became a man, something I've tried to impress upon my two sons. Today, nothing pleases me more than to hear them quote their *Omi* (granny) or me when making a point.

Endowed with a great sense of humor, she genuinely enjoyed a funny story even when the joke was on her. Thus, she delighted in telling and retelling stories like the one in which a Freudian slip made her address a professor with an exceedingly generous proboscis as Professor *Nase* (Nose).

Mutti loved to sing—anything from operatic arias to tunes from movies and operettas, folk songs and hit tunes from her youth. One of her frequent laments was that she didn't have a beautiful voice. That realization, while perhaps true, did not make her any less inclined to fill our apartment with songs, whether she was knitting, crocheting, or doing the laundry. "Where there's music, settle down," she would say, "for evil people have no songs."

Generous to a fault, Mutti would spare no effort to help a needy friend in distress. More than once she gave up her own bed and slept on the couch in order to provide temporary shelter for one of her friends who had marriage problems. Any friend who asked her for a favor could consider it done. On the other hand, she was a courageous, stubborn, and combative woman who didn't mind confronting anyone, high or low, who she felt had done her or me wrong. But if ever someone she had trusted crossed her in a major way, she would put that person out of her life for good with no possibility of reconciliation. She was of the opinion that "trash fights and trash makes up."

Unbounded resiliency enabled her to get through the many ups and downs of her long life. Strong and determined, she used to quip, "Weeds don't perish," whenever someone noted her remarkable ability to bounce back from adversity.

Despite her outspokenness that spared no one, Mutti was well liked and, in turn, liked people. Frequently on weekends, our tiny attic was packed with her friends, mostly fellow hospital and factory workers, who gathered for a *gemütlichen Abend* (cozy evening) of talking, singing, laughing, eating, and coffee drinking, all of which were her favorite pastimes. During cold winter evenings, she would warm and enliven her social gatherings even more by serving her guests a glass of *Glühwein,* a hot beverage of wine, hot water, lemon juice, sugar, and nutmeg, that soon had everyone singing. That's about as lively as things would get, and shortly after my bedtime, everyone thanked her for a great evening and went home.

MUTTI'S INNER CIRCLE

In spite of Mutti's professed anti-Catholic bias, which her own mother had instilled in her when she was a small child, her closest friend and confidante was Rosel Genseder, a statuesque, buxom redhead and a staunch Catholic. This indicated to me that her occasional talk about the not-to-be-trusted Catholics was just that—talk—and wasn't to be taken too seriously. Rosel, who spoke an unreconstructed Bavarian dialect that I had difficulty understanding, had newly arrived from the Bavarian countryside when she and my mother were hired as unskilled workers by the hard rubber factory in Barmbek.

And then there was Liesbeth Schroeder. Liesbeth had only one major objective in life, which was to find a husband, and this perennial quest had become an all-consuming obsession that frequently stood between her and common sense. Although by no means a close friend or even a well-liked companion, needy Liesbeth, a former fellow nurse's aide, had over the years attached herself to my mother in such a way that my mother found it impossible to shake her off. Never one to take no for an answer, Liesbeth just kept coming until she, too, became part of Mutti's regular social group.

In Mutti's circle of closest friends was Erna Schmedemann, the mother of little Erika of striptease fame. "Tante Erna," as I called her, was among those who persuaded my mother not to make unnecessary enemies by fighting her dismissal from the hospital. She knew what she was talking about. Her husband, Walter, my mother's former coworker at the hospital, had been a functionary in the outlawed German Social Democrat Party (SPD) before Hitler's rise to power. Just a few months earlier, he had been arrested by the Gestapo, the new regime's secret police, and incarcerated without a trial. I always knew when my mother and Tante Erna were discussing Onkel Walter's fate. Tante Erna would be sobbing quietly and they would talk in hushed tones in an obvious attempt to keep me from hearing what was being said. That only heightened my curiosity and, pretending that I wasn't interested in their conversation, I picked up enough little bits here and there to get a pretty good idea of what had happened to Onkel Walter. I learned that Onkel Walter had been picked up in the middle of the night by two plainclothesmen and taken to a prison in suburban Fuhlsbuttel, ostensibly for having distributed anti-Nazi pamphlets. "I know they beat him," I heard Tante Erna tell my mother, "because he had bruises on his face the last time they let me visit him." She also suspected that they kept Onkel Walter chained at his wrists and ankles because she noticed that his shirtsleeves and trouser bottoms were covered with rust stains when she picked up his personal clothes after he had been issued a prison uniform.

I still couldn't understand why Onkel Walter was being punished if, as Tante Erna insisted many times, he hadn't done anything wrong. When I couldn't contain my curiosity any longer and asked my mother, she tried as best she could to explain that the reason for his imprisonment was not that he had committed a crime but that he had disagreed with the government.

That explanation left me more confused than enlightened, since everybody knew that the government—meaning Hitler—was always right. Bewildered, I asked, why would Onkel Walter disagree with him? My mother promised to explain it to me when I got a little older and could better understand. Meanwhile, she asked me not to discuss Onkel Walter with anyone, especially at my school.

On numerous occasions, Erna would tell my mother of her many futile attempts to win her husband's freedom. Eventually, she hit on the idea to have Erika join the *Bund Deutscher Mädchen* (League of German Girls, or BDM), the distaff side of the Hitler Youth, so that after attaining a leadership position, she could put in a good word on behalf of her dad. As far-fetched as her plan appeared at the time, it eventually met with partial success. Following more than four years of incarceration, her father was released in 1938 after Erika—by then a model BDM girl—bombarded the *Reichskanzlei* with letters in which she explained her exemplary Nazi lifestyle as a dedicated BDM leader and begged for her father's release. Ultimately, the future Hamburg senator Walter Schmedemann was rearrested at the outset of the war and was forced to spend the war years in a concentration camp. More letters by Erika in behalf of her father, this time addressed to SS *Reichsführer* Heinrich Himmler, were ignored.

ONKEL MAX

Since my mother, with her dark hair, brown eyes, and rosy cheeks, was an extremely good-looking woman, she attracted more than her share of men. I had gotten quite used to them buzzing around her like bees around a flower whenever we went out, and I felt flattered when they talked about "your pretty mother." Once in a while, a lucky fellow would be invited over for Sunday afternoon *Kaffee und Kuchen* with us, but unless he received my unreserved approval, he rarely got a second chance.

Enter Max Walz, a divorcé ten years my mother's senior who worked on the hospital's kitchen staff. From the moment she brought "Onkel Max" home and introduced him to me when I was about five years old, I took a liking to the gentle giant of a man with the brown wavy hair and huge, sensitive hands that seemed to be able to do everything. The fact that he walked with a limp because one of his legs was shorter than the other, a defect he was born with, as Mutti explained to me, was something I soon accepted as quite normal, as I felt he accepted my brown skin.

Multitalented Onkel Max played the bandoneon, a square accordion-type instrument, as well as the lute and the guitar. He could also paint and draw portraits like a professional artist and, to top it all, rode a motorcycle on which he took my mother and me for long weekend hikes. In the evenings, he filled our home with music, read to us, or taught me how to sketch or build a model plane.

One day Onkel Max announced that with the help of his carpenter brother he was going to build himself a thirty-foot sailboat. Having become used to the idea that there was nothing Onkel Max couldn't do, my mother and I spent many weekends watching how, plank after plank, he turned his dream into reality. After about a year's work we helped launch the sleek vessel, which he had named *Kuddel* (*Platt* for Karl) after his brother, then went along on its maiden voyage to watch Onkel Max sail and navigate the craft up and down the Alster with expert skill. After that, we went sailing practically every summer day, ending each sail with a social hour with friends at the Alster yacht club Onkel Max had joined.

To me, Onkel Max and my mother seemed the ideal couple, and I looked forward to the day when my two favorite people would get hitched and Onkel Max would become my dad. But that wasn't meant to be. Even in my wildest dreams I never suspected that I was the reason Onkel Max wouldn't consider marrying Mutti.

I had always known that Onkel Max, while not a member of the Nazi Party, was an avid Hitler supporter who approved of practically everything the Nazis did. That was all right with me since, in my immaturity and ignorance, I was as brainwashed as he. Mutti, knowing of his infatuation with Hitler, studiously avoided discussing politics with him, except once when she told him, after one of the Nazis' customary fake elections, that she had not voted for Hitler.

"You mean to tell me that you didn't vote for the man who has done more for Germany than any other living soul!" he shouted incredulously in an agitated voice that I had never heard before.

"The only thing your Hitler has ever done for me is get me fired from my job," my mother shot back, equally agitated.

That brief exchange was the beginning of the end. Gradually, as Hitler's influence grew, Onkel Max's presence in our lives began to shrink, to the point where he no longer took us sailing or, for that matter, anywhere else in public. Finally my mother had had enough. One night, after I had gone to bed, I was awakened by the sound of Mutti's angry voice in the living room. "I know what your problem is," she shouted. "You are ashamed to be seen with us when your Nazi cronies are around. Well, you don't have to be ashamed anymore. I want you to get out and never come back!"

I never saw Onkel Max again. Losing my hero—the man who taught me all I knew of what it might be like to have a father—left a painful void, coupled with a deep sense of betrayal, which took several years to subside. What hurt me even more than his leaving was his reason for leaving. No matter how much my mother tried to convince me that I was not to blame, deep in my heart I knew that the man I loved like a father, and who I thought loved me like a son, left because he felt he could no longer afford to be seen with me.

CRIME AND PUNISHMENT

Growing up nondelinquent was not one of several options I had, but an ironclad, immutable mandate laid down by my mother. Having been reared in a large family by a hardworking, no-nonsense matriarch, she was not one to put up with bratty behavior. As a result, she never had a problem telling me "No!" and making it stick when she thought it was necessary to accomplish the main goal she had set for herself, which was to make a decent man out of me.

Sometimes her methods of instilling values in me and indelibly impressing upon my young mind that crime doesn't pay were as creative as they were effective. It didn't take me long to realize that her wheels of justice turned swiftly and inexorably. I especially remember an incident that happened when I was a little tyke of about five years.

We had visited one of her fellow nurses whose son, Kurt, was about my age. While our mothers talked, we played quietly in a corner with Kurt's toy soldiers until it was time for us to go home. We had walked about five minutes when my mother noticed a small bulge in one of my pockets. "What's that in your pocket?" she demanded to know.

"Nothing," I replied in a voice that didn't carry much conviction.

"Let me take a look," my mother insisted, and reached into my pocket.

"You call that nothing?" she asked while holding up a little toy soldier. "How did that soldier get into your pocket?"

"I don't know," I replied feebly.

"You are a thief, and I shall see to it that you'll go where thieves belong— to jail. But before I do that, we'll go back to Kurt and you'll apologize to him for stealing his soldier."

Deeply humiliated by having been exposed as a thief and a liar, I followed her back to her friend's apartment where I returned the toy soldier to Kurt and apologized sheepishly. But the worst was yet to come. After we were back in the street, my mother marched me straight into a nearby police station and addressed the desk sergeant.

"Officer, what do you suggest we do with this boy who has stolen a toy soldier from his friend?"

The officer looked down on me from his desk with a long, menacing stare that sent chills along my spine. "I think we should lock him up with the rest of the criminals," he said finally.

By this time I was so horrified that I burst out in loud screams while begging the policeman and my mother to spare me. In return, I promised them never to steal again.

"I tell you what, lady," the officer suggested, "let's give him one more chance, but if you ever catch him stealing again, just give me a call and I'll have him picked up right away."

With a wink at my mother that I was unable to interpret, the officer told me that, at least for the time being, I was free to go. The ordeal conjured up by my mother's creative intervention has remained etched in my memory as though it happened yesterday. I never again gave my mother cause to take the cop up on his offer.

MAKING ENDS MEET

Having watched her mother successfully rear nine children (another two died in infancy) by herself, my mother never regarded our situation as a particular hardship case or considered us as poor folks. Through prudent management of what little money she made on her job, and aided by a keen nose for bargains, she was able to provide us with all the necessities of life, including quality clothing, nourishing food, and even an occasional luxury, such as a visit to a movie matinee.

Like most German women of her generation, she avoided going into debt, convinced like her mother that *borgen macht Sorgen* (to borrow makes sorrow). Consequently, she categorically never bought anything on credit. Instead, she was a great believer in layaway plans. All major household items in our home she acquired through this method, including her pride and joy, a foot-driven Singer sewing machine that converted into a handsome small wooden table when not in use. It was a source of immense pleasure and pride to her to know that there wasn't a single item in our home that wasn't paid for.

By example, my mother taught me the discipline of delaying gratification of my wishes, of which the biggest at the time was to own a bike. After she surprised me one day with the news that she had made a down payment on a secondhand but mint-condition bike she had watched me admire in the window of a downtown bicycle shop, she took me along whenever she made her weekly payments to give me a chance to look at and touch the bike that one day would be mine. Having already learned to ride on some of my buddies' bikes, I was more than ready for the big event. Each successive visit to the shop stretched my patience to the breaking point, but didn't diminish my joy of anticipation. On the day my mother made the final payment, she brought her own bike along so that we could celebrate my new acquisition with a joint ride home. I had imagined that first ride on my own bicycle countless times, but the actual experience surpassed my fantasy by miles. For weeks, I felt I was riding on clouds instead of two balloon tires, until it gradually sank in that this gorgeous contrivance was really mine.

Ownership of a bike opened up an entirely new life for me. Whereas before I had been largely confined to my immediate neighborhood, barring an occasional streetcar ride downtown, I suddenly had the means to transport myself to any part of the city and beyond. Consequently, each day after finishing my homework, I would set out with one or several bike-owning pals and explore the city. On Sundays, weather permitting, my mother and I would bicycle to one of the picturesque *Walddörfer* (forest villages) that surround much of Hamburg and pick a cozy clearing in the forest where we would picnic on sandwiches and read to our hearts' content. For Mutti and me, those quiet hours at the bosom of mother nature constituted the epitome of *Gemütlichkeit*. As we pedaled through the small towns with their handsome homes and neat flower and vegetable gardens, we engaged in one of our favorite pastimes, daydreaming of one day living in our own little house. With the exception of some upper-middle-class types, we knew of no one who had realized that impossible dream of homeownership.

SALZA REVISITED

I continued to spend my summer school vacations in Salza, but like every-thing else in Germany, Salza had undergone a noticeable change for the worse since the Nazis came to power. It certainly was no longer the friendly, idyllic little village I had learned to love. The boys I used to play with had become members of the Hitler Youth and, unlike my peers in Hamburg, pointedly avoided me. Their peasant fathers, who on weekdays wore dung-splattered coveralls, were strutting around on Sundays in brown SA uniforms and polished riding boots and were acting important. It was quite obvious that Hitler's singling out farming as the nation's most honorable occupation had gone to their heads. In addition, they had been told—and believed—that they were of superior stock because of their unsullied Aryan blood. Each was busy trying to outdo the other in demonstrating his blind devotion to Hitler and his policies.

Since Salza was a tiny community with only a few hundred inhabitants, it meant that meddling in other people's political business was the order of the day. Thus, Tante Grete received dozens of discreet inquiries as to why each summer she and her family harbored a boy who she claimed was a relative but who looked like a fugitive from Africa. Once I overheard her tell Onkel Karl about the duplicity of a neighbor woman who, before Hitler came to power, had often let me sample her home-baked cake and other treats. The woman, whose husband had risen from lowly chewing-tobacco factory worker to weekend Nazi big shot, had taken Tante Grete aside and told her "confidentially" that she had it on good authority that having me stay with her family during the summer was definitely not in her best in-terest. Tante Grete responded that I was her husband's blood relative and that she would never deny her husband's own flesh and blood, no matter who didn't like it.

On the evening before my return to Hamburg, we were treated to a strange spectacle. Dozens of young men carrying small swastika streamers marched up and down Salza's Hauptstrasse, shouting and rabble-rousing and singing *"Muss i denn zum Städtele hinaus,"* the traditional German fare-well song. Obviously high on beer, some were stumbling in and out of taverns while others banged indiscriminately with their fists on shop windows and doors. When I asked Onkel Karl what the ruckus was all about, he explained that the young men had just passed their muster for induction into the *Arbeitsdienst* (Labor Service), a compulsory year of mostly *Reichsautobahn* construction work, followed by a period of military service in the *Wehrmacht* (armed forces). Since it was possibly their last night as civilians, Onkel Karl explained, the police traditionally looked the other way and let them have one last fling.

"Why are they so happy when they have to leave and become soldiers?" I wanted to know.

"Because it is an honor to wear the uniform of your country," responded Onkel Karl, an anti-Nazi but patriotic World War I veteran. "One day, when you're grown, you, too, will become a soldier."

Onkel Karl was right, but neither he nor I could have known at the time that when that time came, I would wear the olive drab of the U.S. Army instead of the gray of the *Deutsche Heer* (German Army).

I had already decided not to return to Salza the following summer, but that decision was purely academic, because the next time my mother tried to sign me up for the vacation program, she was told that only members of the Hitler Youth qualified for free transportation on the vacation train. Onkel Karl and Tante Grete insisted that I come anyway at their expense, but my mother wouldn't hear of it. Thus ended one of the most delightful phases of my childhood. The next time I returned to Salza a few years later, it was under totally unexpected and quite different circumstances.

MIRROR, MIRROR ON THE WALL

It would still take years before I fully understood, and was able to permit myself to believe, that Hitler was an infinitely evil, morally corrupt psychopath. Desperately, I kept clinging to the government-promoted image of a benevolent demigod and savior of the German people. After each psychologically crushing blow dealt me by one of Hitler's minions, I rationalized that I had been victimized by an overzealous Nazi underling who had overstepped his authority and perverted the Führer's grand scheme. I simply could not get myself to blame the architect of the racist policies himself. Only after years of maturing and of being rejected, humiliated, and psychologically brutalized was I able to see Hitler himself for what he really was and as the ultimate source of my mounting problems. It was not until I reached my teens that the awful truth struck home. Until then, instead of putting the blame for my problems with racists where it belonged, I blamed myself. More than anything, I blamed my appearance—especially my African hair, which I had come to loathe. Although I had vowed not to let Wriede get the better of me, his and other teachers' all-out psychological warfare against me had taken its toll. Under the steady barrage of the hated word *Neger* and the equally offensive *Mischling,* my self-esteem had plunged to a frightening low.

After a girl I had been playing with told me that I looked better with my cap on, I rushed home and did what I had avoided doing for some time, namely taking a long, probing look in the mirror. To say I didn't like what I saw would be putting it mildly. The boy who looked back at me, I decided with brutal objectivity, was plain ugly. His nose was much shorter and wider than that of "normal" boys, and his skin, although smoother-looking than the skin of other boys, was several shades too dark to pass for a tan. Worst of all was the kinky hair. From my perspective, every day was a bad hair day. After experimenting for a while with my cap, I concluded that the girl had been right; covering my hair definitely minimized my African appearance and, therefore, improved my looks.

Convinced that if my hair were straight, half of my problems would be solved, I was ecstatic when I came across some information that seemed to have the potential of forever changing my life. I had read in one of my adventure books that members of an African tribe ceremoniously straightened their hair by dipping it in a concoction made from a sugarlike substance dissolved in hot water. So one day after school, I embarked on a strange, ever-so-secret mission, aimed at surprising my mother with my new straight hair. First I emptied my mother's sugar jar into a small pot filled with water. Then, while stirring the mixture with a spoon, I brought it to a boil on our gas stove. After letting the syrupy concoction cool off, I massaged it into my hair as if it were shampoo, wiped off the excess with a towel, then waited impatiently for the transformation to take place. While waiting, I fantasized what my new life with straight hair would be like. Having just seen the movie *The Elephant Boy,* I envisioned my future looks to approach those of Sabu, the appealing Indian youth whose jungle epic had made him the darling of German moviegoers. I decided that once my hair was straight, I definitely would wear it longer, but under no circumstances as long as Sabu's. Between daydreaming, I'd run my fingers through my hair to find out whether there was any change. There was a change, all right. The colder the concoction got, the stickier and messier my hair became, until it was one impenetrable, gooey mess. After waiting more than an hour for more promising results, I concluded that the experiment was a dismal flop and literally threw in the towel.

Fortunately, a few rinses in hot water restored my hair to its original kinky condition. But the emotional damage caused by my disappointment was much more difficult to repair. At first I decided not to tell my mother about the "incident," but when she came home and demanded an explanation for my still wet hair and the empty sugar jar, I changed my mind and confessed.

Instead of getting angry about the wasted sugar, she told me how very sorry she felt for me that I didn't like my hair. "Whether you know it or not, your hair is beautiful," she tried to assure me.

"It's easy for you to talk," I told her, pointing to her lustrous, wavy dark brown hair. "You've got straight hair like everybody else."

"I would give it to you if I could. I so much wish I could, if that's what would make you happy," she said, "but I can't. So you just have to learn to like the hair you've got. One day, when you are older, you'll understand and agree with me when I say that your hair is beautiful."

There was nothing my mother could have said at the time to make me feel good about my hair and the way I looked. How could there be? The last time I had heard an impartial person make a flattering comment about my appearance had been what seemed to me a lifetime ago, while the last time I heard a disparaging remark was only that afternoon.

There were two aspects of my appearance, however, that I not only appreciated but was actually rather proud of, despite the fact that they were probably racial traits. One was my physique. Although I was of average height, I had a well-proportioned, athletic body with well-muscled legs and arms. The other was my teeth, which earned me many compliments, espe-

cially during annual dental examinations in school. Invariably, the exam-
ining dentist would invite the entire class, including the teacher, to line up
and take a peek into my mouth in order to "get an idea of what absolutely
perfect teeth looked like." To me, this procession past my open mouth was
my annual moment of glory. But nothing lasts forever. My annual teeth-
modeling stint came to a gnashing halt one day when, to my utter disap-
pointment, the dentist discovered two cavities on a molar that ended my
claim to having "absolutely perfect teeth."

I ONCE HAD A COMRADE

Among my least favorite classmates was Egon Faber, the ranking class clown
and son of a Nazi functionary. Since I had not yet developed my anti-Nazi
bias, his father's affiliation had nothing to do with my dislike for him. The
reason I held Egon in such low esteem was that he simply got on my nerves.
Incessantly showing off, Egon would stop at nothing to get attention or a
few laughs. Extremely creative when it came to thinking up new ways of
being obnoxious, he once regaled the class by taking a leak out of the second-
floor classroom window into the schoolyard.

That performance, which was climaxed by Herr Grimmelshäuser's un-
heralded entrance, would have undoubtedly resulted in immediate corporal
punishment had it not been for his father's clout. All of us kids resented his
virtual immunity from punishment.

For the most part, I avoided Egon like the plague and, since the antipa-
thetic feelings seemed mutual, he avoided me, too, until one day when he
literally bumped into me, leaving an impact that lasted throughout my life.
At the time we were nine years old and in the fourth grade. It happened at
the end of recess in the schoolyard. In keeping with school regulations, we
had been standing at attention in formation and were awaiting the teacher's
orders to march back to class. Egon, who stood directly in front of me, was
clowning as usual by tickling the boy in front of him. When the boy spun
around to face his tormentor, Egon reared suddenly, causing the back of his
hard, crew-cut blond head to crash into my left eye. The impact was so

severe that my eye immediately swelled shut. Wincing with pain, I was ready to deal Egon a retaliatory blow but was deterred by the stern look of a teacher who had come to check on the commotion. All I could do for the moment was to hiss menacingly, "I'll get you for this," to Egon who was barely aware of the damage he had caused. My anger at Egon kept growing and growing throughout the rest of the school day as my eye turned a conspicuous shade between violet and black that seemed to amuse everybody but me. It was my firm intention to make good on my vow to get even with Egon the next day in school. But it turned out to be a vow I not only couldn't keep, but that I later wished I had never made.

The following morning I arrived in class, ready to settle the score with my fists at the first opportunity that presented itself. I immediately looked for Egon, but without success. He apparently had taken my warning seriously, I figured, and decided to keep out of my reach by staying home. When Herr Grimmelshäuser was about to call roll, the door opened and an upper-class student entered. He and the teacher exchanged a few words that we couldn't understand. Suddenly, Herr Grimmelshäuser bolted out of his seat, visibly shaken by what the boy had told him. After regaining his composure, he addressed the class with, "Boys, I have a sad announcement. I've just learned that our classmate Egon Faber is dead. He shot himself accidentally yesterday after school." Following his announcement, Herr Grimmelshäuser dismissed the class for the day.

News of Egon's death left the class torn between grief and speechless disbelief. The teacher's words hit me in a very personal way. I became convinced that, although I wasn't the one who pulled the trigger, somehow I was responsible for Egon's death because of the blind hatred I had felt for him following the previous day's schoolyard incident. In my anguish, I was prepared to tell him not to worry about my black eye, that I knew he didn't hurt me intentionally, and that all was forgiven. But then I realized that I would never get another chance to tell him that, and that I had to go on living with the thought that the last words he heard coming out of my mouth were a hateful threat. All of a sudden, my long-harbored dislike for Egon evaporated as if it had never existed, to be replaced by an overpowering need to mourn him as a dear friend.

When details of Egon's death made the rounds through the street grapevine, we learned that the shooting occurred around 4 P.M. in the entrance hall to his apartment building, only a five-minute walk from my home. It seemed that after returning home from school, Egon had accidentally come upon his father's service pistol in a drawer. Carefully hiding his find from his mother, he had taken the weapon and gone downstairs to the street, where he summoned some of his playmates with the announcement that he was about to give a special performance. Several kids, lured by the promise of excitement, followed him into the hallway. For several minutes, he brandished the weapon in various "Stick 'em up!" poses, aimed it at some of the kids, and even pulled the trigger several times. Yet nothing happened, apparently because the weapon's safety was on.

Around that time, his mother discovered that her husband's pistol was missing and, suspecting her son, came running down the stairs shouting, "Egon, Egon, give me the pistol!" Seeing his mother approach, Egon was ready to surrender the weapon—but not without one last look into the barrel and a simultaneous squeeze of the trigger. This time, for some reason, the safety was off and the weapon discharged. Shot through his right eye, Egon died within seconds in the arms of his grief-crazed mother while his non-comprehending playmates looked on in horror. The boy who stopped at nothing to get some attention had paid the ultimate price for his compulsive showing off.

When school resumed, Herr Grimmelshäuser informed us that Egon's parents had requested that the class attend the burial service and that, on that occasion, we would sing "*Das Lied vom Guten Kamerad* (The Song of the Good Comrade)," Germany's traditional military burial song. For three days, hours on end, we rehearsed the song until Herr Grimmelshäuser was satisfied that we got it right.

On the day of the funeral—my very first—we were bused to Ohlsdorf Cemetery at the outskirts of Hamburg, reputedly the largest burial ground in Europe. There, we took up position beside the newly dug grave and the closed coffin that looked much too small, I thought, to contain the remains of our classmate. Facing us, on the other side of the coffin, were Egon's stern-faced father, his uncontrollably crying mother, and his teary-eyed sister. The mere thought that the weapon that had claimed Egon's life belonged to his father made me shudder.

After a few words from Herr Grimmelshäuser and a short burial service by a Lutheran minister, the coffin was lowered into the grave while we pupils sang with subdued voices our well-rehearsed farewell song.

Several days following the funeral, I still had a black eye. But instead of being a source of ridicule, it had changed into a mark of distinction that all my classmates beheld with reverence and that I displayed proudly, like a badge of honor. For all of us kids, the impact of Egon's death was tremendous, since he was the very first contemporary dead in our young lives. My black eye took on special significance, since it represented the last tangible evidence of Egon's life among us. I fervently wished that this eerie link with the boy we had just buried would never go away, but as the days passed, it kept fading until one morning I noticed that it had totally disappeared. It was at that moment that I realized with unbearable sadness that Egon Faber, the class clown I used to despise, had left my life forever.

QUEST FOR CONVERTS

Not long after his rise to power, Hitler let it be known that those diehards who refused to embrace his Nazi ideology were part of the old order that was on the way out. Regardless of the parents' political persuasion, he boasted, he would make sure to have the undying devotion and loyalty of their sons and daughters. "Germany's youth," he bragged, "will belong to me."

To make good on his boast, schools throughout Germany were ordered to mount elaborate drives aimed at recruiting pupils for the *Hitlerjugend* (HJ)—the Hitler Youth movement. The schools were aided in their efforts by a formidable arsenal of visual aids—charts, slides, documentary and feature films—churned out by Goebbels's propaganda ministry, which spared no effort when it came to winning converts among the young. One such film, *Hitlerjunge Quecks,* left a lasting impression on me when it was screened in my school during *Volkskunde* (folklore) class. It was the tragic story of a handsome, blond teenage boy nicknamed Quecks, who grows up in a predominantly Communist Berlin slum. His father, an alcoholic Communist sympathizer, who divides his time between getting drunk and mistreating his wife, was played convincingly by Heinrich George, at the time Germany's premier character actor and an avowed Hitler fan.

Escaping temporarily from his seamy surroundings, Quecks secretly attends a Hitler Youth outing where, within an idyllic Boy Scout–like setting, he experiences for the first time in his life wholesome camaraderie and bonding around a campfire. When he returns to his bleak neighborhood, he does so as a converted *Hitlerjunge* and active worker for the Nazi cause. While distributing Nazi leaflets, Quecks is cornered by one of his father's Communist cronies, who, after branding him a traitor, knifes him to death. As Quecks lies dying in the arms of his new Nazi comrades to the strains of the Hitler Youth's anthem, "*Vorwärts, Vorwärts* (Forward, Forward)," composed by no less a Nazi honcho than HJ leader Baldur von Schirach himself, he becomes the youngest martyr of the movement.

The film left as deep an impression on my ten-year-old, impressionable, non-Aryan mind as it did on the minds of my Aryan peers. I know, because when after the movie the window shades were raised, there was a suspicious rash of nose-blowing and sniffles throughout the auditorium.

It would be years before I discovered that the film's message of Nazi virtue and Communist evil had been a brazen distortion of the facts. The truth was that during their many bloody clashes for dominance in Germany, the Nazis and Commies were virtually indistinguishable. Both were totalitarians, ever ready to brutalize in order to crush resistance to their respective ideologies.

With arch-Nazi Wriede at the helm, Kätnerkampschule aggressively pursued the indoctrination and recruitment of young souls for the *Jungvolk,* the HJ's junior league for ten- to thirteen-year-olds, whose members were known as *Pimpfe* (cubs). Hardly a day went by without our being reminded by our teachers or Wriede himself that for a German boy, life outside the movement was no life at all. Pursuing his objective with characteristic single-mindedness, Wriede was tireless in thinking up new gimmicks to further his goal. One day, he announced his latest brainchild, a schoolwide contest in which the first class to reach 100 percent *Jungvolk* membership would be rewarded with a holiday.

The immediate effect of the announcement was that my new homeroom teacher, Herr Schürmann, became obsessed with the idea of winning the coveted prize for our class and some brownie points for himself. Toward that end, he became a veritable pitchman, who spent much of his—and our—time trying to persuade, cajole, or otherwise induce our class to join the Nazi fold. The centerpiece of his recruitment drive was a large chart he had carefully drawn on the blackboard with white chalk. It consisted of a large box divided into as many squares as there were boys in the class. Each morning, Herr Schürmann would inquire who had joined the Hitler Youth. After a show of hands, he would count them, then gleefully add the new enlistees' names to his chart. Gradually the squares with names increased until they outnumbered the blank ones.

Up to that point I had followed the contest with a certain degree of emotional detachment because quite a few of my classmates, including some of my closest pals, had let it be known that they had no interest in anything the HJ did and would not join, no matter what Wriede or Schürmann had to say. That suited me fine since I, too, had no intention of joining. But under the relentless pressure from Schürmann, one resister after another caved in and joined.

One morning, when the empty squares had dwindled to just a few, Herr Schürmann started querying the holdouts as to the reasons for their "lack of love for Führer and *Vaterland*." Some explained that they had nothing against Führer and *Vaterland* but weren't particularly interested in the kinds of things the *Jungvolk* were doing, such as camping, marching, blowing bugles and fanfares, and beating on medieval-style drums. Others said they didn't have their parents' permission, whereupon Herr Schürmann instructed them to bring their parents in for a conference. When it came to what I thought was my turn to explain, I opened my mouth, but Herr Schürmann cut me off. "That's all right; you are exempted from the contest since you are ineligible to join the *Jungvolk*."

The teacher's words struck me like a bolt of lightning. Not eligible to join? What was he talking about? I had been prepared to tell him that I hadn't quite made up my mind whether I wanted to join or not. Now he was telling me that, even if I wanted to, I couldn't. Noticing my bewildered expression, Herr Schürmann told me to see him immediately after class.

Until the bell rang, I remained in a state of shock, unable to follow anything that was said. I felt betrayed and abandoned by my friends and terrified at the prospect of being the only person in class whose name would not appear on the chart. At age ten, I was as tough as any of my peers, able to take just about anything they dished out in the course of rough-and-tumble schoolboy play. What I couldn't take, however, was feeling that I didn't belong—being treated like an outcast, being told, in effect, that I was not only different but inferior.

Schürmann invited me to take a seat beside his desk. "I always thought you knew that you could not join the *Jungvolk* because you are non-Aryan," he began. "You know your father is an African. Under the Nuremberg Laws, non-Aryans are not allowed to become members of the Hitler Youth movement." Charitably, perhaps to spare at least some of my feelings, he omitted the much maligned and despised Jews from his roster of ineligibles.

"But I am a German," I sobbed, my eyes filling with tears. "My mother says I'm German just like anybody else."

"You *are* a German boy," Herr Schürmann conceded with unusual compassion, "but unfortunately not quite like anybody else."

Having gotten his point only too well, I made no further plea.

"I'm very sorry, my boy," Schürmann concluded the conference. "I wish I could help you, but there's nothing I can do; it's the law."

That evening, when I saw my mother, I didn't tell her what had transpired in school. Instead, I asked her to come with me to the nearest *Jungvolk Heim,* the neighborhood *Jungvolk* den just one block up the street, so I could join. Since I had never expressed the slightest interest in joining the HJ, she had never felt it necessary to burden me with the thought that I would be rejected. Thus, my sudden decision to join took her completely by surprise. When she tried to talk me out of it, even hinting that there was a possibility of my not being accepted, I grew frantic. I told her that I simply had to join since I could not be the only one in my class who was not an HJ member. But she still didn't think it was a good idea. "Please take me," I pleaded, almost hysterically. "Maybe they'll make an exception. Please!"

Against her better judgment, my mother finally relented and agreed to do whatever she could to help me join. When we arrived at the HJ *Heim,* a long, solidly built, one-story stone structure, the place was buzzing with activities and paramilitary commandos. Through the open door of a class-roomlike meeting room, I could see a group of boys, most of them about my age, huddled around a long table, apparently listening to a troop leader's lecture. They wore neat uniforms, black shorts, black tunics over khaki shirts, and black scarfs that were held together at the neck by braided leather knots. Most of them, I noticed with envy, wore the small black *Dolch* (dagger) with the rhombus-shaped swastika emblem of the Hitler Youth. Ever since seeing it displayed in the window of a neighborhood uniform store, I had secretly coveted this largely ceremonial weapon. Even the words *Blut und Ehre* (blood and honor) that were engraved on its shiny blade, and whose symbolic meaning had totally eluded me, stirred my soul. I knew that once my membership in the HJ had been approved, nothing would stand in the way of my becoming a proud owner of a Hitler Youth *Dolch.* I wanted it so much, I could almost feel it in my hand.

After one *Pimpf* spotted me, I immediately became the subject of snickers and giggles until the troop leader, annoyed by the distraction, shouted "*Ruhe* (Quiet)!" and closed the door. When my mother asked a passing *Pimpf* to show us to the person in charge, he clicked his heels, then pointed to a door with the sign HEIMFÜHRER. Upon my mother's knock, a penetrating male voice shouted, "Enter!"

"*Heil Hitler!* What can I do for you?" asked the handsome, roughly twenty-year-old man in the uniform of a mid-level Hitler Youth leader who was seated behind a desk. He reminded me of an older version of my erstwhile bodyguard, Wolfgang, tall, athletic, blond, and blue eyed—in short, Hitler's ideal Aryan man.

My mother returned the mandatory Nazi salute, then asked, "Is this the right place to apply for membership?"

The young man looked incredulous. "Membership for whom? For *him?*" he inquired, his eyes studying me as if they had spied a repulsive worm.

"Yes, for my son," my mother responded without flinching.

The Nazi recoiled. "I must ask you to leave at once," he commanded. "Since it hasn't occurred to you by now, I have to tell you that there is no place for your son in this organization or in the Germany we are about to build. *Heil Hitler!*" Having said that, he rose and pointedly opened the door.

For a moment I thought my mother would strike the man with her fist. She was trembling and glaring at him with an anger I had never before seen in her eyes. But she quickly regained her composure, took me by the hand, and calmly said, "Let's go." Neither she nor I spoke a word on the way back home. I felt guilty for having been the cause of her anguish and humiliation, and I was afraid she would be angry. Instead, when we reached our apartment, she just hugged me and cried. "I'm so sorry, I'm so sorry" was all she could say.

Seeing my mother like this was more than I could bear. "Please don't cry, Mutti," I pleaded while tears were streaming down my cheeks. It was a rare occurrence, since usually we outdid each other in keeping our hurt to ourselves. We were Germans, after all.

Two days later, the moment I had dreaded with ever-mounting anguish arrived. Herr Schürmann, with a joyfulness bordering on ecstasy, chalked in the final two names on his chart. He then took a wet sponge and carefully erased the last remaining empty square, the one that represented me, thereby graphically emphasizing my non-person status. "Congratulations, class! We have just reached our goal of one hundred percent HJ membership," he rejoiced. "I am extremely proud of you and grateful that you have brought honor to your class and to me. I think we should let the principal in on the good news." With that, he left the classroom, only to return a few minutes later with Wriede in tow.

The principal praised the class for having "dedicated your lives to Adolf Hitler and his vision of the Third Reich." Since it was a Saturday and therefore only a half school day, he explained, the class would get the promised day off the following Monday. The news was greeted with a deafening roar of approval that lasted until Wriede restored decorum by reminding us that we were not in a *Judenschule* where lack of discipline was the order of the day. Since none of us had ever attended a *Judenschule*, we were obliged to take the principal's word.

I had followed the morning's proceedings with growing embarrassment, since I was painfully aware that none of the praise heaped on the class by Schürmann and Wriede included me. The only thing that helped somewhat to restore my morale was the thought of not having to return to school until Tuesday. Thus, by the time school let out at noon, I had bounced back and was chatting and laughing with several classmates as we crossed the lobby on our way out. Just before leaving the building, I heard a familiar voice shout, "You, come here!"

When I turned around, I saw the principal standing in the door of his office. I knew at once that he meant me, since he had never addressed me by my name.

"Come in a minute; I have to talk to you," he announced.

Suddenly, a sinking feeling got hold of me. I had no idea of what the principal wanted to discuss with me, but I was convinced that it was nothing I wanted to hear. My instincts proved only too right.

"I am a fair man," Wriede started, "and I hope you are fair, too. Are you?"

I assured him that I was fair, indeed.

"That's good," he continued, "because then you'll agree that it would be very unfair to give you a day off when you have done nothing to earn it. You wouldn't want that, would you—to get something you didn't earn?"

Now the cat was out of the bag and I realized how Wriede had been setting me up.

"Well, would you?" the principal insisted.

"No," I finally replied, "but—"

"That's good," Wriede cut me off, "because I have already spoken with Herr Dutke, and he's told me that it is all right with him if you spend a day in his class. So on Monday morning you report to Herr Dutke. Do you understand?"

"I understand," I answered, although at that time, at age ten, I really hadn't been able to figure out why Wriede treated me so meanly.

"That's all. *Heil Hitler!*" Wriede dismissed me.

"*Heil Hitler!*" I saluted and walked out of his office and home.

I never told my mother what had happened. I was certain that had I done so, she would have defied Wriede by keeping me out of school on Monday, regardless of the consequences to her. So to keep her from getting upset and to avoid trouble, I went to school on Monday as if nothing had happened, as a special "guest" in Herr Dutke's class, where, after being welcomed with a sneer, I had to put up for an entire day with Dutke's snide racist remarks.

THE MORELLS

The fact that all of my classmates had become card-carrying members of the *Hitlerjugend* had in no way affected our relationship. Those who were close to me before they joined the *Jungvolk* remained so afterward. We continued to play and have fun together and visit each other's homes as if nothing had changed. Since we were too young and naive to see the big picture, we remained totally oblivious to the visual irony we created—a boy with an obviously generous amount of African genes playing in brotherly harmony with a bunch of blond boys in Nazi uniforms. Although my classmates were bona fide *Jungvolk Pimpfe,* few were true converts to Nazi ideology. Some had joined merely to get Schürmann and Wriede off their backs, while others had been pressured by their fathers, who feared that not having their sons join could hurt them on their jobs. The rest had merely jumped on the bandwagon in order not to be left out, a feeling I understood only too well. Whatever their reasons for joining, most of them stopped being active members after just a few short months when the novelty of going to meetings, on hikes, and to demonstrations had worn off, and dropped out altogether within a year or two. It became quite obvious to me that to most of my classmates, the *Jungvolk* was no more than a fad whose time had run out.

A typical example of the fleeting interest the boys had for the Hitler Youth was Eugen Braun, the blacksmith's son. One of the first on our block to join and wear the organization's uniform, he even played in his troop's drum-and-fanfare corps, which—to some people's delight and others' chagrin—made the windows rattle as it strutted through the neighborhood. But within a few months, before I had a chance to turn completely green with envy, Eugen had quit the *Jungvolk,* hung up his uniform, and turned to other interests.

This relatively quick disillusionment with the HJ—which, as a matter of sour grapes, I welcomed from the bottom of my heart—did not occur in my class alone but was manifest throughout my school and, I suspect, throughout the city and beyond. I suspect that despite the massive, and much publicized, presence of Hitler Youth at Nazi rallies, the percentage of German boys and girls who were active participants in Hitler Youth activities on a regular basis was relatively small. In theory, the Nazis had intended to forge the Hitler Youth into a tool that would get hold of German youngsters from the moment they were ten years old and mold them until they were adults and ready to join the Nazi Party. Except for a few hard-core Hitler Youth members who followed the prescribed course, the plan remained a Nazi utopia. There was talk at the time that the Nazis wanted to boost the embarrassingly low HJ membership by establishing the *Pflicht* (compulsory) HJ for reluctant joiners. Fortunately, when the plan was inaugurated at the beginning of the war it was never vigorously enforced and, as a result, was mainly ignored.

There were other aspects of the Hitler Youth movement that never quite caught on. Very few girls, for instance, followed the fashion dictates of the Nazi Party, which championed hair—preferably blond—braided and coiled in *Schnecken* (snails) above the ears, or tied into a bun. No girl in my school or neighborhood would have wanted to be seen dead with that kind of Nazi poster girl look. Instead, they wore their hair any which way from sleek pageboys to fashionable perms.

I suspect that the vast majority of the men in my neighborhood became involved with the Nazis for reasons that had little to do with ideology. Like most German men, they were better craftsmen, mechanics, tailors, and butchers than students of politics. The German school system, which had reserved secondary and higher education for an intellectual elite, simply didn't prepare them for political and philosophical thinking. Under Hitler, most of them had prospered beyond their wildest dreams; they had steady employment, tax deductions for multiple children, free health care, and many other formerly unheard-of benefits. They were convinced that a political party that had made good on its promise to wipe out unemployment, the scourge of the working class, deserved their support. Their monstrous guilt, however, one that will never be erased, is that they let the perks they enjoyed under the Nazis make them blind and deaf to the suffering and annihilation of countless fellow citizens whom the Nazis had branded as undesirable.

Among the highly ballyhooed perks that helped make the Nazis attractive to "the man in the street" were the all-pervasive *Kraft Durch Freude* (Strength Through Joy) programs of the *Deutsche Arbeitsfront*, which were designed to keep working people fit by giving them affordable recreation that ranged from visits to the opera and the theater to Mediterranean cruises on a fleet of specially built luxury liners. Some joined the party because they liked the way they looked in a uniform and enjoyed participating in parades and the paramilitary spectaculars for which the Nazis were famous. In addition to giving them ranks of authority and a wide range of new activities, the Nazi Party brought excitement and a sense of being macho, even heroic, into their humdrum proletarian lives. Above all, it provided them with a framework that made respectable their favorite pastime of carousing and hanging out with the boys.

Typical of the men in my neighborhood whom the Nazi Party had given an entirely new lifestyle and identity was Herr Wilhelm Morell, a bald blue-collar type. A mechanic at Hamburg's largest department store chain, he was a devoted husband to his rather corpulent wife and a doting father to my buddy Karl and his two brothers, Hans and Gerd. All the Morell boys had inherited their father's broad, Slavic-looking face. The Morells lived around the corner from me in a tiny first-floor apartment at the end of an alley of two-story row houses that linked Stückenstrasse with Haferkamp, the location of Eugen Braun's blacksmith shop.

Before my very eyes, Herr Morell underwent a most amazing transformation that, to some extent, explains the curious attraction the Nazi Party held for the average German man. Within only a few short months of joining the party, Herr Morell acquired an entirely new persona. From a drab, quiet, and unassuming working stiff whose idea of a rip-roaring time was an occasional couple of beers with the boys from the shop at the neighborhood pub, he turned into a dashingly uniformed small-time official who, with the single-mindedness of a beaver building a dam, strutted purposefully about the neighborhood in the never-ending pursuit of his new duties. The fact that his new position as a bottom-level *Blockleiter* (block warden) was part time and unsalaried did nothing to diminish his zeal. Considering himself the eyes and ears of his party on our block, Morell ministered to a vast portfolio of concerns that ranged from keeping tabs on anti-Nazi utterances to arranging for the awarding of *Mutter Kreuze* (mother crosses) to mothers who had given birth to four or more Aryan kids, to spying on welfare recipients to make sure they were not living above their means. In addition, he attended meetings, marched in parades, stood for hours in any kind of weather shaking a metal can while collecting money for various Nazi charities, including the vaunted *Winterhilfswerk* (winter aid project), whose motto was *Keiner soll hungern, keiner soll frieren* (No one shall starve, no one shall freeze). He also went from door to door passing out copies of virulently anti-Semitic Nazi literature. *Parteigenosse* (party comrade) Morell accepted unquestioningly his party's doctrine that Jews are the root of all evil, although I doubt seriously that in our blue-collar environment he ever knowingly met a Jew face-to-face, let alone was harmed by one. At the same time, he was totally color blind and exhibited a curious case of schizophrenia where I was concerned. For some inexplicable reason, his bigoted thinking did not extend to me. On the contrary, as the closest buddy of Karl, I was included in most of the Morells' activities and treated almost like a member of the family. To the dismay of my mother, who had come by her loathing of Nazis honestly, I had become a virtual fixture in the home of the biggest Nazi on the block—in the lion's den, so to speak. But since she liked Karl and didn't want to interfere with our friendship, she reluctantly looked the other way while keeping her fingers crossed.

As his party's loyal lookout man, it hadn't escaped Herr Morell's notice that we didn't fly a Nazi swastika flag from our window on national holidays, as had become the unwritten law. When he asked my mother the reason for this serious nonfeasance, she told him that she simply couldn't afford to buy a flag, which I knew was only half of the truth. He told her not to worry and the next day presented us with a brand-new swastika flag, replete with mast, compliments of his Nazi Party chapter. Herr Morell even came to our apartment and personally installed a mast base outside one of our windows. Thus deprived of any excuse, my mother decided to fly a Nazi flag on every national holiday henceforth to avoid unnecessary trouble.

Strangely enough, and contrary to what one might expect from the sons of the biggest Nazi in the neighborhood, only one of the Morell boys was an active member of the *Jungvolk*. Hans, the oldest, was an eager *Pimpf* who regularly attended functions, while Karl, with the tacit approval of his dad, joined on paper only and never took part in a single *Jungvolk* meeting. Gerd was too young to join. When I asked Karl why his father let him get away without participating, Karl told me that his father had tried at first to get him to go to meetings but had finally gotten tired of nagging. "As long as I keep my membership so he can tell anyone who wants to know that I'm in the Hitler Youth, it's okay with him," Karl explained.

Through my intimate contact with the Morells throughout the years, I was well informed about the private goings-on in various households on our block, especially who was considered a reliable *Genosse* (comrade) and who needed watching, for despite his slavish devotion to his duties, Father Morell could not resist gossiping with his family and friends about what he had learned as a result of his various investigations. By keeping my mouth shut and my ears open, I learned, for instance, that one of our neighbors had been sentenced to a prison term for violating Paragraph 175 of Germany's penal code, which outlawed homosexual conduct. Herr Morell seemed to have the goods on everybody in the community who had strayed—or was suspected of having strayed—from the narrow path of righteousness, including some of his own Nazi cronies. "He's been warned two times already," I once overheard him saying. "If we catch him doing it again, he'll be kicked out of the party." Although much of what I heard while playing mouse during Morell's discussions with his inner circle was way over my head at the time, by letting it sink in and putting two and two together, I usually came up with four.

HERR DUTKE

I would be hard pressed to decide which of the two biggest bigots among my teachers was the meanest, Herr Wriede or horn-rimmed Herr Dutke. Dutke used to delight in wearing his Nazi uniform in the classroom to lend an especially festive note to his courses of *Volkskunde* (folklore), which he used mainly to vent his racist hostility. "Stop that *negerhafte Grinsen* (negrified grinning)," he once hissed at me when he caught me joining the class in innocent laughter. "Negroes don't have a thing to grin about in National Socialist Germany." To drive home his point, he frequently picked pupils who came closest to what he and his fellow Nazis considered the ideal Aryan type by having them stand in front of the class and pointing out their blond hair, blue eyes, "nobly formed skull," and other "desirable" physical features. Ironically, behind his back, my classmates referred to arch-Nazi Dutke by a term my mother had taught me never to use in a derogatory context. They called him "the Jew," partly because of his large hook nose and partly because of his exaggerated entrepreneurial spirit, both of which the Nazis had identified as unmistakably Jewish traits. Dutke, a little party wheel who also taught music and physics, was known throughout the school to use every imaginable opportunity to augment his teacher's salary with some rather suspect business deals. Although his deals were highly unethical, if not illegal, he operated with impunity, most likely because of his Nazi Party affiliation.

Dutke hated my ten-year-old guts not only as a matter of Nazi principle but also because on two occasions I had, quite unintentionally, obstructed his ceaseless effort to combine the business of education with his habitual need to hustle students. While wearing his music teacher's hat, he announced one day that he would teach the class how to play the harmonica, something I had already accomplished on my own. To do that, he said, everybody needed to buy a harmonica. It so happened, he explained, that because of his special connections, he was able to offer every student a real bargain on the purchase of a small Hohner instrument.

As it turned out, all of my classmates went for it and, after consulting their parents, placed their orders. The only person in the class who didn't order a harmonica was, you guessed it—not because I wanted to thwart Dutke's scheme to make a little money on the side but because I already had a harmonica, and quite a superior instrument at that. After I had taught myself to play the harmonica on a cheap instrument about a year earlier, my mother had rewarded me by buying me a rather expensive, chromatic deluxe Hohner harmonica. Dutke, however, regarded my refusal to buy a harmonica from him as a personal affront. He retaliated by forbidding me to bring my harmonica to his class or to participate in any way, although my instrument was in the same key as the harmonicas he had ordered.

A similar scenario unfolded in physics class, where Dutke tried to teach us the workings of a crystal detector radio set. After several lectures on the subject, he showed up in class with a single earphone in which he had soldered—quite ingeniously, I thought—the miniature circuitry of a crystal detector set. He then demonstrated to us that all one had to do with his "invention" was to attach one of the two wires coming out of the earphone to a water faucet for grounding while holding one up into the air as antenna and, presto, one could listen to the *Norddeutscher Rundfunk,* Hamburg's state-owned and -operated radio station.

He then told the class that for only a few *Reichsmark*s, they, too, could become the proud owners of a "pocket detector radio." With television still on the drawing board and radio the undisputed mass communications king, we kids were duly impressed with Dutke's gizmo, which seemed to fore-shadow the advent of the transistor radio. The idea of being able to listen to radio wherever one happened to be had tremendous appeal, and many of my classmates were ready to talk their parents out of the necessary cash to acquire the intriguing toy.

I was so impressed with the idea of a truly portable miniature radio set that required no batteries or electric input that I went straight home and started some tinkering of my own. After working an entire Sunday, I came up with a small, three-by-four-by-two-inch wooden box into which I had fitted the circuitry and earphone of a crystal set. In principle, my little radio box worked just like Dutke's boxless earphone.

When I took my gadget to school and demonstrated it to my classmates, they were full of praise and admiration. But when I expected similar approval of my handiwork from Herr Dutke, I was in for a big surprise. Disregarding the fact that I had been the only pupil in his class who had been inspired enough by him to make the effort of putting his teachings to work, he berated me for coming up with a clumsy imitation of his own creation and told me not to bring such *Murks* (Hamburg slang for poor workmanship) into his class.

I was devastated, and so were some of my classmates, who tried to console me after class by telling me that the only thing that made Dutke mad at me was that he couldn't sell me one of his earphones. I was certain that they were partially right but I also knew that there was another, even more important reason for Dutke's rejection of me—the color of my skin.

My suspicion was soon confirmed. When a pupil referred to my scholastic and athletic abilities to refute Dutke's contention that people of other than "Aryan blood" were both intellectually and physically inferior, Dutke dressed down the pupil for daring to disagree with him. He then lectured the class that my case was merely the exception that proved the rule, and suggested that whatever "normal characteristics" I displayed I had definitely inherited from my Aryan parent. Without the slightest consideration of my feelings, he suggested that in my case the last word had not yet been spoken, and that there was still a very good chance that my inferior blood would surface in one form or another. "There are many ways of being racially inferior," he argued. "I wouldn't be at all surprised if your *Klassenkamerad* one day winds up as an antisocial element, such as a criminal or an alcoholic, or if he isn't already susceptible to a host of debilitating diseases."

After passing on that piece of information, Dutke ordered me not to leave the room when the bell signaled the end of class. "What I have to tell you won't take long," he announced after making sure that all the children had left the room. Looking at me with undisguised loathing through his thick horn-rimmed glasses, Dutke chided me for trying to turn the class against him and for showing my disrespect of him with my constant *"negerhaftes Grinsen."* "Let me tell you something, young man. Don't feel so smug, because after we have finished with the Jews, people like you will be next. That's all I have to say. *Heil Hitler.*"

Although I couldn't grasp the full significance of what he had meant by "finished with the Jews," I had learned that Jews were the most hated group of people in the country and, as a result, at extreme risk. For a while I debated with myself whether or not to tell my mother what Dutke had told me, but decided against it. What was the use? It only would get my mother into a fight she couldn't possibly win. So I left things alone in the hope that Dutke and his prophecy would simply go away.

THE SHAME OF THE RHINELAND

One morning in early March 1936 when I arrived at school, the entire building was abuzz with excitement that emanated from the teachers and soon spilled over to us pupils. We were told that the Führer had just scored a major coup. In defiance of the Treaty of Versailles, which Germany signed at the end of World War I, he had ordered his troops to march into the demilitarized Rhineland, on Germany's border with France. For the moment, the whole country was holding its collective breath in anticipation of a hostile response from the Western powers, a response that never came.

After summoning the entire school to the auditorium, Herr Wriede, his chest stuck out in a visible display of pride, announced that, thanks to the courage of our beloved Führer, "one of the most shameful chapters in Germany's history has come to a close." He then went on to tell us about the terrible humiliation Germany had suffered at the hands of the victorious Western allies when it was forced to permanently withdraw its military forces from the Rhineland to lessen the likelihood of German military aggression. "Thanks to our Führer," Wriede declared, "you German boys can again walk with your heads held high."

Just as I was about to share in the pride and hold my head a little higher, Wriede put a damper on my lifted spirits by explaining that the forced withdrawal of German troops after World War I had paved the way for the "ultimate insult" to the German people—the illegal occupation of the coal-rich Ruhr area by some forty thousand "uncivilized French *Neger*" troops. These savages out of the African jungle, he explained with an expression of utter disgust, were permitted by their French officers to freely mingle and fraternize with the German people, with the catastrophic result that the Rhineland was being saddled with thousands of physically and mentally inferior bastard children. Today's courageous action by our Führer, Wriede continued, would forever prevent a recurrence of such humiliating infringement on Germany's sovereignty.

What the principal didn't mention was the fact that Hitler had already put into motion a sweeping program that provided for the forced sterilization and eventual extermination of the "Rhineland Bastards." The plan was openly advocated in the writings of his minister of agriculture, *Reichsbauernführer* Richard-Walther Darre, who as early as 1933 wrote for everyone to read:

It is essential to exterminate the leftovers from the black Shame on the Rhine. These mulatto children were created either through rape or by white mothers who were whores. In any case, there exists not the slightest moral obligation toward these racially foreign offspring. About fourteen years have elapsed in the meantime; those of the mulattoes who are still alive will now enter the age of puberty, meaning that there isn't much time left for long discussions. Let France and other states deal with their race question the way they want; for us there is only one solution: extermination of all that is foreign, especially in the case of these that through violence and amorality created damages. Thus, as a Rhinelander I demand: sterilization of all mulattoes with whom we were saddled by the black Shame at the Rhine.

This measure has to be carried out within the next two years. Otherwise it is too late, with the result that hundreds of years later this racial deterioration will still be felt. Legal prevention of marriages with race-foreign elements is ineffective, since what is not possible legally usually happens illegally.

Because of its racial policies, Hitler targeted France as "by far the most terrible enemy." "This [French] people," he wrote in *Mein Kampf,*

... which is basically becoming more and more negrified, constitutes in its tie with the aims of Jewish world domination an enduring danger for the existence of the white race in Europe. For the contamination by Negro blood on the Rhine in the heart of Europe is just as much in keeping with the perverted sadistic thirst for vengeance of this hereditary enemy of our people as is the ice-cold calculation of the Jews thus to begin bastardizing the European continent at its core and to deprive the white race of the foundations for a sovereign existence through infection with lower humanity.

What France, spurred by her own thirst for vengeance and systematically led by the Jew, is doing in Europe today is a sin against the existence of white humanity and some day will incite against this people all the avenging spirit of a race which has recognized racial pollution as the original sin of humanity. . . .

Hitler then goes on to predict that

if the development of France in the present style were to be continued for three hundred years, the last remnants of Frankish blood would be submerged in the developing European-African mulatto state. An immense self-contained area of settlement from the Rhine to the Congo, filled with a lower race gradually produced from continuous bastardization. . . .

Hitler's malevolent plan to sterilize, then murder mixed-race children in the "liberated" Rhineland was far too close for comfort. But luckily, I did not learn of the fate of these unfortunates until after the war, and thus was spared years of agonizing over when their tragic lot might catch up with me.

JOE AND JESSE, MY NEW HEROES

In the summer of 1936, my frequently bruised ego received a huge boost from a totally unexpected source. It came in the persons of two young black American athletes, one a professional boxer and the other an amateur track-and-field man. Their names were Joe Louis and Jesse Owens. Although I was not to meet either of them in person until I was well into adulthood, both men had a profound and lasting effect on my life, since they instilled me with genuine pride in my African heritage at a time when such pride was extremely difficult to come by.

By spring 1936, word reached Germany that a young black American was to fight Max Schmeling, the Nazis' version of the Great White Hope. Joe Louis, we learned, was a twenty-two-year-old fighting machine from the cotton fields of Alabama and the auto factories of Detroit whose uninterrupted string of knockouts had earned him the nickname "The Brown Bomber" and made him the top contender for the world heavyweight title, held at the time by James J. Braddock, his white countryman.

From the moment the news hit the neighborhood, all eyes were again on me. Confirming that the tendency to insist that "all blacks look alike" is not confined to American whites, most of my buddies insisted, "You look exactly like Joe Louis." Never mind that there was at least a 150-pound difference between the American fighter and me, everybody on the block agreed that I came as close to being the *Braune Bomber* as anyone in the neighborhood had ever come. I could hardly disagree with that.

It occurred to my pals that I and the man who had been predicted to defeat the best fighter on the European continent were veritable brothers under the skin, that we shared not only the same complexion, the same hair, and the same white teeth, but, more important, that in our veins ran the same mysterious, all-powerful African blood. The more the German press touted the Brown Bomber's phenomenal punching power, the higher rose my stock among my peers. I never let on that, like any dyed-in-the-wool Hamburger *Junge,* I had rooted for Schmeling, our hometown hero, for as long as I had followed his career. But since my peers hailed me as the Brown Bomber's successor, I became obliged to forgo my local patriotism and come out for my black brother from the States. This took a great deal of psychological wrestling with myself, since my loyalty to Schmeling was as deep as any ten-year-old boy was capable of feeling. Then something happened that made it quite easy for me to decide. Reading a prefight interview with Schmeling in a local newspaper, I came across an alleged quote by my hero in which he promised to "turn the *Neger* boxer from a Brown Bomber into a green-and-blue bomber." This remark (which, along with more racist remarks attributed to him, Schmeling was to emphatically deny after the collapse of the Third Reich) hurt me to the quick. I felt betrayed by the man who had been an idol to me, and decided then and there that henceforth, my loyalty would belong to Joe Louis, the man everybody said looked exactly like me.

While the Nazi-controlled press presented Louis as a formidable puncher, it also stressed that he was mostly brawn and little brain, and predicted that Schmeling's superior intelligence, coupled with his superb fighting skill and experience, would prevail.

The Nazi regime's interest in boxing in general and Schmeling in particular was no accident. Hitler, while nurturing his grandiose dreams of world conquest, had proclaimed that he expected German boys to grow up "tough as leather, swift as greyhounds and hard as Kruppsteel." Toward that end, he ordered that physical fitness of German youths and boys in particular become a chief objective of Nazi education. Max Schmeling, the man picked by Goebbels's propaganda machine to symbolize Germans' manly virtues of physical strength, precision reflexes, endurance, sportsmanship, courage, and squeaky-clean living, seemed an unlikely choice for the job. For one thing, the black-haired, pug-nosed, beetle-browed fighter with the chronic five-o'clock shadow lacked the fair skin and blue eyes favored by the Aryan mythmakers, and at age thirty-one, he was considered by many fight buffs as being over the hill. But beggars can't be choosers, and ex-heavyweight-boxing-champion Max Schmeling was the closest thing to a German super-athlete the Nazis could get their hands on.

In 1930, he had become the first and only German to win the world heavyweight title when he was fouled by a low blow from American Jack Sharkey and Sharkey was disqualified. Two years later, he lost the title in a rematch. But thanks to a tremendous Goebbels's press buildup, which made him the idol of my generation, he was put on the comeback trail.

On June 19, the day of the fight, men and boys in my neighborhood talked about nothing else but the upcoming match. While most were rooting for Schmeling, many had grave doubts that their man would be able to withstand the awesome punching power of the black American. Whenever I joined the discussions, the boys on the block immediately deferred to me as the authority on Joe Louis. Sensing my new position of importance, I eagerly obliged them with details on how Joe would put an end to Max's world title ambitions. Since I had read and memorized everything on Joe Louis that I could get my hands on, I was able to rattle off interesting facts about my hero, from his awesome vital statistics to his ability to knock out opponents with a single punch of either hand. While my cronies listened in awe, I savored every moment of my new elevated status. It felt wonderful to note the respect accorded to a black man by people who normally felt superior to blacks, and have some of that respect rub off on me. I hadn't enjoyed that feeling of pride in my African ancestry since my grandfather left Germany six years earlier. To me, that seemed like a lifetime away.

I could hardly wait for the day to end so that the fight, which was scheduled for around 9 P.M. (U.S. EST) in New York City's Yankee Stadium, could get under way. Since that would make it about 3 A.M. in Germany, I asked my mother to set the alarm clock for 2 A.M. (just to be on the safe side) so I could get up and listen to the fight transmission on my trusty crystal earphone set. At 2 sharp I was awakened by the shrill bell of the alarm clock. After waiting an unbearably slow hour, during which the German announcer described the tense atmosphere among the nearly forty thousand spectators in Yankee Stadium, I finally heard the gong signal the beginning of round one. For the first three rounds I was buoyed by the superior performance of the Brown Bomber, whose hooks and jabs had already closed Schmeling's left eye. Then, in the fourth round, the totally unexpected—no, the impossible—happened. Two successive crashing rights by my countryman to the chin of Joe Louis put my hero on the canvas for the count of four. I was screaming my head off for Joe to get up, but the only person who could hear me was my mother, who came running into my bedroom to find out what was going on.

"Joe's been knocked down!" I screamed. "Joe's in trouble!"

Not fully comprehending the significance of what I had just told her, and not too pleased about having been awakened again, my mother asked me to keep my voice down.

"It's nothing but a boxing match," she tried to console me. "You can't take that sort of thing too seriously."

There was no way I could explain to her that the black man who was fighting some four thousand miles away was not only fighting for himself but also for me, that his victory would be my victory and his loss—heaven forbid—a major catastrophe for me.

Until that point, the possibility of Joe Louis's losing the fight had never entered my mind. Now there was a distinct possibility that Schmeling, the ten-to-one underdog, would defy the odds and emerge as the winner. If that happened, what would I tell the kids on the block who had believed me when I told them that Joe would beat the stuffing out of Max? How could I ever face them again? These and similar thoughts tortured me as the news from Yankee Stadium that came through my headset turned from bad to worse to excruciatingly intolerable. Obviously hurt seriously by one of Schmeling's crashing rights to the chin in the early rounds, Louis took blow after punishing blow as the rounds went by, but stayed on his feet, bolstered only by the power of his will. In the twelfth round of the fifteen-round match, my worst nightmare became reality when Schmeling ended the fight by landing a solid right to Louis's jaw that sent him to the canvas for the count of ten. The man I believed was invincible, who had been my ticket to prestige and respect among my peers, had been destroyed.

Although it was still pitch black outside, I was unable to go back to sleep. Instead, I was lying awake, reliving every agonizing moment of the past hour until finally a leaden sleep put a temporary end to my ordeal.

But the worst was yet to come. The next day—a Sunday—I stayed inside all day to avoid running into any of the boys on the block. But I knew I couldn't hide forever. On Monday, whether I liked it or not, I had to go to school and face the music. As I entered my classroom, I was greeted by a barrage of ridicule from some of the same boys who only a few days earlier had looked at me in awe.

"What happened to your Brown Bomber?" someone asked contemptuously.

"The Brown Bomber turned out to be a *Flasche*," another boy chimed in, using the derisive street term for "weakling."

"I thought you said Louis could fight," sneered still another boy. "How come he let Max use him for a punching bag? I tell you why, because he's a *Neger* and a coward!"

The boy looked at me with an expression that I interpreted as saying, "If you don't like what I said, do something about it."

Without weighing the odds of fighting a boy who was a year older than I and accordingly bigger (since this was his second stab at fifth grade), I lunged at him and hit him in the face with a barrage of lefts and rights that would have done my idol Joe Louis proud.

The symbolism was not lost on my classmates, who had formed a circle around us and, instead of continuing with their ridicule, started to cheer me on.

"Hit him, Joe Louis!"

"Knock him out, Joe!"

"Another right, Joe!"

"Where's that left hook?"

My sudden, vicious attack had taken my opponent completely by surprise. Caught off balance, he fell backward while I was punching away, too agitated to stop hitting him. All of the anger, frustration, and shame I felt over the defeat of my hero came pouring out through my fists. Before I was able to inflict serious damage, I was grabbed from behind and pulled off my adversary.

"What in the world do you think you are doing?" a man's voice demanded to know. Herr Dutke, one of my least favorite teachers, had entered the classroom without anyone noticing him.

"He said Joe Louis lost the fight because he's a Negro and a coward," I said, trying to justify my attack.

"That's no reason to hit somebody," Herr Dutke shouted at me. "You can't go around hitting people just because they don't agree with you that *Hottentotten* make the best boxers. Max Schmeling has demonstrated in the most convincing way that a Negro's brute strength is no match for an Aryan boxer with superior intelligence. His victory was a great victory not only for Germany but for Aryan people throughout the world.

"Now apologize to your comrade for hitting him," Dutke ordered. I was determined to do no such thing, no matter what the consequences.

"Did you hear me? I told you to apologize!" Herr Dutke screamed.

I just glared at him defiantly without saying a word. But before Dutke had a chance to deal with my intransigence, Herr Schürmann, our home-room teacher, entered. Eagerly, Dutke briefed him on what allegedly had transpired. According to Dutke's version, I had gone berserk and beaten a boy because he had insisted that Schmeling was a better fighter than Joe Louis.

I was taken aback by Dutke's dishonesty, but remained silent. Before making his exit, Dutke recommended stiff punishment for "*diesen wilden Kerl* (this wild rascal)," meaning me, and Schürmann promised to take "appropriate action."

As soon as Herr Dutke had left, Schürmann listened to my version of the altercation, which my classmates corroborated. Herr Schürmann gave me a stern warning to keep my temper in check but suspended punishment. At the same time he issued an equally stern warning to my opponent, who had several facial cuts and bruises to show for our encounter, to refrain from making disparaging racial remarks aimed directly or indirectly at me. Then, Herr Schürmann told the class that he, too, had been listening to the fight, and that although Louis lost, he lost with honor by staying on his feet at least five rounds longer than anyone thought possible in view of the brutal punishment he absorbed.

I felt vindicated in the eyes of my classmates, and although I still had to listen occasionally to how a brilliant Max Schmeling beat a dimwitted Joe Louis, I heard just as many comments in praise of the American and his superhuman effort to remain on his feet. I never felt that in losing the fight, Joe Louis had let me down, but his defeat at the hands of Schmeling had nevertheless been a bitter disappointment to me. Now it felt good to know that many people still respected Joe Louis as the toughest fighter who ever stepped into a ring. Henceforth, when anyone called me Joe Louis, which happened quite frequently, I stuck out my chest and felt like a champ.

Shortly after the memorable fight in Yankee Stadium, a full-length doc-umentary film, entitled *Max Schmelings Sieg—Ein Deutscher Sieg (Max Schmeling's Victory—A German Victory)* ran in all of Hamburg's movie the-aters. Everybody in the neighborhood rushed to see this Goebbels-inspired propaganda film—everybody, that is, but me. I simply couldn't bring myself to relive my agony by watching my hero get beaten. Not until two years later did I overcome my aversion and watch the film, but only because by that time, Joe Louis had evened the score with a spectacular knockout of Schmeling in the first round.

While German sports fans were still debating the pros and cons of the first Louis–Schmeling fight, the approach of another sports spectacular, the 1936 Olympic Games in Berlin, was making headline news. Weeks before the opening of the games, the press reported that the U.S. Olympic team would include an appreciable number of black athletes. To avoid offending any of the fifty-one visitor nations, especially those that were fielding black and other non-Aryan athletes, the Goebbels-controlled press had refrained from the usual racist innuendoes and treated the news involving black athletes with uncharacteristic objectivity. Even the signs proclaiming JUDEN UNERWUNSCHT (Jews Not Wanted) that had proliferated throughout Hamburg in restaurants and other establishments of public accommodation disappeared for the duration of the festival to avoid stepping on sensitive foreign toes. The rather transparent idea behind this new modification of established racist practices was obviously to compound Hitler's coup of bringing the Olympics to Germany by casting the dictator in the image of a gracious and benign international host.

This temporarily revised national policy did not, however, prevent my neighborhood from receiving the news of blacks coming to Berlin with a great deal of condescension and ridicule that exposed the average German's abysmal ignorance of the United States. Many were amused by the idea that "a bunch of *Kanibalen*" were about to take on Germany's vaunted Olympic track team. The father of one of my classmates, a barber, told us in all seriousness that the blacks who were on their way to Berlin had been captured in the "American jungles" where, he explained, they used to roam free before being pressed against their will into Olympic servitude. He further had it on good authority that only those blacks who had been observed running the swiftest and jumping the highest in their pursuit of wildlife were captured and forced to train for the Olympics in order to hone their already formidable physical skills.

This man-in-the-street type of "knowledge" was not too far out of line from that of better-educated Germans. Herr Dutke preempted any possibility of a black Olympic triumph by telling us that blacks weren't athletes "in the true sense of the word" since they were "born runners and jumpers— like horses and other animals."

"For a German runner to lose to one of these half-civilized people from America," Herr Dutke assured the class, "is no more a disgrace than losing to a horse. Everybody knows that a horse is physically superior but mentally inferior to a man. The same is true for the *Hottentotten* from America."

Most of the derisive talk about inferior *Hottentotten, Kanibalen,* and *Buschneger,* which kept me in a continuous state of impotent rage, came to a sudden halt following the arrival of the American track-and-field team at the Olympic Village in Berlin. Even the most ignorant and prejudiced among my neighbors were quick to realize that the clean-cut young black men in the smart white uniforms who were smiling at us from the newspapers, magazines, and newsreels were anything but the primitive savages they had expected. Learning that the black athletes were college students made a deep impression on my education-worshipping countrymen, but what really made believers out of them was the blacks' gentlemanly and sportsmanlike comportment on and off the track.

A few days before the opening of the games, Karl Morell startled me with sensational news. His father was taking him, his older brother, Hans, and several neighborhood boys on a one-week trip to Berlin, and if my mother would give her permission—and come up with the train fare and a few extra marks spending money—I was welcome to come along. At first, my mother was dead set against letting me go. But when I convinced her by way of a two-hour hunger strike that my life might as well be over if I couldn't go to Berlin, she agreed to have a chat with Herr and Frau Morell to learn more about the trip. After a lengthy discussion with the Morells, during which they assured her that I would be in good hands and that there was no better way for a boy to spend part of the school summer holidays than to see the nation's capital and the Olympic Games, my mother relented.

On the morning of our departure, our group of about ten boys from the neighborhood, some in Hitler Youth uniforms, each loaded down with heavy backpacks and canteens, journeyed by *Hochbahn* to Hamburg's Central Station. Before boarding a *D-Zug* (express train) for Berlin, Herr Morell had us fall in and stand at attention like an SS honor guard for a snappy military briefing on what to do and what not to do on the trip. For the occasion, he, too, carried a backpack, but although he did not wear his

Amtswalter uniform, his polished brown riding boots and britches left no doubt about his Nazi Party membership.

The train was packed, mostly with schoolchildren who, like us, were venting their excitement by filling the air with deafening chatter and the occasional strains of a marching song. Listening to the cacophony and watching the landscape go by, I still found it difficult to believe that in a few hours I would be walking around our *Reichshauptstadt* (capital) Berlin, the city we kids had been taught to regard as the center of the universe.

When we arrived late at night at Berlin's famous *Anhalter Bahnhof,* we were hoarse from singing and dead tired. By the time we reached our youth hostel on the outskirts of the city, after a brief bus ride through Berlin's bustling night traffic and a quick look at the famous Brandenburg Gate and the *Funkturm,* Berlin's answer to Paris's Eiffel Tower, we were ready to hit the sack. But before we were allowed to go to sleep on the inviting mattresses that lined the walls of an attic dormitory, Herr Morell reminded us that we were breathing the same Berlin air as our beloved Führer, and made us render the Nazi salute. The very idea of the Führer's proximity gave me goose pimples that didn't go away until I was soundly asleep.

Unlike my original feelings toward Joe Louis and Max Schmeling, I never was torn by conflicting loyalties between the black Olympic athletes and the athletes of my motherland. From the very beginning of the games it was clear to me that the black athletes' victories were my victories, that their defeats were my defeats. I immediately felt a surge of pride over the very special kinship that linked me with these men from America, and before long, the names of Harrison Dillard, Dave Albritton, Archie Williams, John Woodruff, Cornelius Johnson, and Ralph Metcalf were as familiar to me as those of Germany's top Olympic entrants, like track ace Lutz Long. While all were accorded bona fide star treatment, none of the accolades showered on the black Americans compared with the ones the German fans reserved for their newly discovered Olympic darling—and my newest hero—Jesse Owens. Alabama-born, like Joe Louis, Owens was widely touted as the United States' leading prospect for track-and-field Olympic gold. But his actual performance surpassed even the most optimistic expectations of his newly won German fans. After an exhausting four days during which he made fourteen consecutive appearances, running four heats each in the 100 and 200 meters and jumping six times, Owens raced to victory in the 100-

and 200-meter sprints in 10.3 and 20.7 seconds, respectively, led off the winning 400-meter relay, and set an Olympic broad jump record of 26 feet, 5 5/16 inches. The fact that Herr Morell was able to get us admitted to only a fraction of the events and that from our seats way up in the packed stadium's bleachers we could barely see the action on the field did nothing to dampen our enthusiasm for the games.

An alleged snub of the black quadruple gold-medal winner by Hitler, which was widely reported at the time in the United States, was predictably overlooked by the Nazi-controlled German press. Whether the dictator deviated from his earlier practice of congratulating the winners personally in order to avoid shaking hands with a *Neger* is largely a matter of conjecture, since no gold-medal winner after Owens was "honored" in this way. It is a fact, however, that the dictator left the Olympic Stadium before Cornelius Johnson, the black high-jump gold-medal winner, had a chance to ascend the victor's stand, and that he discontinued greeting winners from then on. When I asked him years later what he thought of the infamous "snub," Jesse Owens told me that he was not sure that Hitler meant to snub him or the other black athletes by not receiving them in his private box. "He was obviously a very, very busy man who had better things to do with his time than shake hands with jocks" was the way Jesse dismissed the non-incident. "But even if he meant to snub us," Jesse added, "I couldn't have cared less."

It wasn't until several weeks after our small group's return to Hamburg that I could let a day go by without my recapitulating the feats of the Olympic heroes and the fact that I had been there. With all the publicity showered on Jesse Owens, some of my playmates could not resist calling me Jesse, the way a short while earlier they had called me Joe. Again I took it for the compliment it was intended to be. There was no doubt that as Jesse's star had ascended in Berlin, so had mine among my peers.

As in the case of the Schmeling victory, the Nazis did not let the opportunity go by to give the widest possible publicity to another major sports coup (Germany had won the lion's share of gold medals) and prepared a full-length documentary propaganda film of the Olympic Games, *Olympia*. Divided in two parts entitled *Fest der Völker (Festival of the People)* and *Fest der Schönheit (Festival of Beauty)*, the film was directed by Germany's cinematographic genius (and rumored Hitler mistress) Leni Riefenstahl, who produced a masterpiece that still draws raves from movie buffs.

This time, I eagerly went to see the film. Only too aware of the prevailing racist attitudes, I had resigned myself to seeing Jesse relegated to a few cameo appearances, but was pleasantly surprised to find that the film focused more on Jesse than on any other Olympic star. I didn't believe my eyes when time and again the Riefenstahl cameras zeroed in on Jesse with close-up after close-up that left little doubt about the director's profound preoccupation with her subject. There were numerous shots taken from various angles of Jesse's well-muscled, ebony-hued body, glistening with perspiration, each capturing the grace and power of his movements. At other times, the cameras focused on his expressive face as he concentrated in preparation for action, and on his guileless, open smile following each victory. There also was plenty of footage that recorded the outbreak of pandemonium as the Berlin stadium erupted with deafening chants of "Jesse! Jesse! Jesse!" aimed at spurring the black American to victory. The film, obviously intended to bolster the Nazi concept of Aryan supremacy, ironically turned out to be a monument to the superiority of one non-Aryan superstar.

When at the end of the film the lights went on in the movie theater, people who spotted me were looking at me not with the usual ill-disguised expressions of ridicule, condescension, or contempt, but with obvious admiration and approval. "There's Jesse's little brother," I heard one man point me out to his children. I felt a surge of pride that I found extremely difficult to conceal. That feeling of pride recurred whenever someone mentioned the names Jesse Owens or Joe Louis and sustained me throughout my childhood years.

Many years later, when, in the course of my work as *Ebony* managing editor, I met my two heroes in person—Joe Louis in Las Vegas, where he was a greeter at Caesars Palace, and Jesse Owens in Chicago, where he ran his own PR firm—I had the chance to personally thank them for what they had done for me. Looking puzzled at first, both accepted my gratitude with characteristic modesty when I told them that as a ten-year-old black kid in Nazi Germany, I was able to walk a bit taller because of them.

THE *HINDENBURG*

Many of the Nazis' high-priority projects were designed to impress upon the German people and the rest of the world that Germany was flourishing and on the road to becoming a respected world power again. Foremost among them was the construction and operation of the largest airship ever built, the monstrous dirigible LZ-129 *Hindenburg,* which dwarfed its behemoth sister ship, the *Graf Zeppelin.*

For months before the *Hindenburg* inaugurated the first regular transatlantic dirigible passenger service, Dr. Goebbels's press had ballyhooed "this great technological marvel of National Socialism" and hailed it as living proof of Germany's world leadership in "the most important technology of the twentieth century." Having seen the *Hindenburg* in numerous newsreels and in the newspapers, we kids were easily impressed with Germany's "bold leap into the future" via this lighter-than-air marvel and never got tired of discussing its daunting capabilities. But although I had become quite familiar with the LZ-129's awesome dimensions, nothing had prepared me for my first and only encounter with this monster of the skies.

The day the *Hindenburg* was scheduled to visit Hamburg in a low overflight turned out to be a beautiful sunny day. About an hour before the event, the denizens of Stückenstrasse No. 3, minus Tante Möller, who said she was too old and too scared to participate, climbed a small ladder through a narrow hatch onto the roof of our three-story building. With eager anticipation I searched the sky for a sign of the familiar cigar-shaped colossus, my sense of excitement heightened by the rooftop perspective, since my mother had never before allowed me to go up there. All the roofs around us were packed with people who had come to witness the historic event. Among them I recognized some of my playmates and soon we were killing time by waving and shouting back and forth.

Finally, somebody pointed southward and hollered, "There it is!" Looking up, I saw the airship at a considerable distance, heading directly toward us. At first, I was disappointed, since it didn't seem nearly as large as I had imagined. But slowly and surely, the *Hindenburg* grew bigger and bigger and the droning of its engines became louder and louder until it loomed menacingly directly before us. For a moment I found its gargantuan size so oppressive that I had difficulty breathing. I was convinced that if the monster came any closer, it would crush me and everyone else on the roof. Before I knew it, the monster was directly above us, casting its vast shadow over our street. I could clearly make out the word *Hindenburg* on its hull and, extending from its aluminum underbelly, its passenger gondola and its four external diesel-powered turbines that were filling the air with a window-rattling drone. Within seconds, as quickly as it had come, the *Hindenburg* had passed over us. Rapidly, it shrank until the black, white, and red swastika emblem on each of its four gigantic tailfins disappeared from view.

For days after the *Hindenburg*'s Hamburg visit, we kids talked about nothing else. We felt as if that unique experience had forged a special link between us and the giant airship and eagerly followed its triumphant Atlantic crossings in the news. Yet, less than a year later, on May 7, 1937 (May 6, U.S. time), our hopes and dreams for our technological marvel were shattered with the news that the *Hindenburg* had exploded shortly after its arrival at Lakehurst, New Jersey, and that thirty-six persons had lost their lives.

Germany was stunned. A week later I watched the dramatic newsreel footage of the *Hindenburg* disaster and people trying to save themselves by jumping from the exploding wreck. I found it difficult to reconcile the stately airship that had so proudly flown over my house with the crumbling hull that was being consumed by fire.

Although the Nazi press went along with the American official version of the suspected cause of the catastrophe—static electricity caused by atmospheric conditions likely set off the spark that triggered the explosion—most Germans, including me, believed foul play was involved. The story made the rounds that the United States, envious of Germany's preeminence in airship construction and operation, barred German access to helium gas, thereby forcing Germans to make do with the more buoyant, but also more volatile, hydrogen. Thus set up by Americans, Germans reasoned, a well-aimed bullet may have set the *Hindenburg* aflame. After the war I heard that Germany was barred from using helium to prevent the *Hindenburg,* with its global range, from becoming a formidable weapon, capable of bombing U.S. cities in the event of war.

While the eulogies for the fallen airship contained much talk about the construction of an even bigger and better *Hindenburg,* the catastrophe at

Lakehurst put an end to Nazi ambitions to establish Germany as the leader in lighter-than-air technology and to dirigible passenger service in general. It also put forever to rest my childhood dream of one day traversing the skies in the *Hindenburg*.

WAR CLOUDS ON THE HORIZON

Headlines about the *Hindenburg* catastrophe were soon replaced by a series of pivotal events heralded by the Nazis. "Today," Principal Wriede proudly told us, "the Führer has forever freed us from the humiliating shackles of the Treaty of Versailles." He was referring to Hitler's latest speech, in which he spelled out Germany's need for *Lebensraum* (living space) and his determination to expand, peacefully, if possible, but by force, if necessary, in clear contravention of the treaty.

Next, we were told that a villainous fellow by the name of Kurt von Schuschnigg, chancellor of neighboring Austria, was stirring up trouble for Nazi Party members in Austria whose only crime was their persistent demonstrations aimed at reuniting Austria with Germany. When, under pressure from Berlin, Schuschnigg resigned, the leader of the Austrian Nazi Party, Dr. Arthur Seyss-Inquart, took his place. His first act of office was to ask Hitler to send German troops, ostensibly to prevent bloodshed. On March 12, 1938, at dawn, German troops crossed into Austria where, according to the newsreels we watched, they were received by the Austrian people with open arms. That same day, Hitler, a born Austrian, arrived at his childhood home in Linz and announced the accomplishment of his mission "to restore my dear homeland to the German Reich."

We kids were thrilled to learn that Germany had overnight grown by nine million people, 32,375 square miles, and vast industrial, agricultural, and natural resources. To drive the point home, our teachers had us study the newly acquired territory with the help of huge display maps. We also were taught that since *Anschluss* (union) with the German Reich, Austria was henceforth to be known as *die Ostmark* (the eastern territory). By the time new maps that reflected the boundary changes were delivered to our school, another event made them obsolete before we had a chance to study them. On October 1, German troops invaded Czechoslovakia and claimed the ethnically German Sudetenland. The uncontested conquest added ten thousand square miles of new territory with a population of 3.5 million (including 700,000 Czechs) to the German Reich.

Our teachers were ecstatic in praising the virtues of the Führer whose genius had added vast territories to the *Vaterland* "without firing a single shot." It didn't take much on the part of our teachers to convince us of the Führer's omnipotence and to instill in us an unshakable belief in his leadership. The ubiquitous slogan, "*Führer befiehl, wir folgen* (Führer, command, we follow)," was more than a slogan to us ten-year-olds. It was a promise that many of us intended to keep, even at the risk of our lives.

WRIEDE'S REVENGE

In the midst of these major historical events, our school was rocked by an unexpected announcement that affected us even more profoundly. Kätner-kampschule, we were told, had to be vacated forthwith to be converted into a special institution for children with learning disabilities, or what we kids cruelly called a *Dofenschule* (dunce school). This meant that classes would be completely broken up, and pupils and teachers would be reassigned to other schools in the district. "Those of you who don't like to move," Herr Schürmann had joked, "are welcome to stay." He then read off the roster of our new assignments. I was assigned to a school at Schleidenstrasse 11, on the bank of the Osterbek Canal, more than twice the distance from my home than Kätnerkamp. Luckily, about twenty of my classmates, including some of my closest cronies, were assigned to the same school.

At first I reacted to the news with mixed emotions. On the one hand, I was excited about the pending change and the prospect of being rid of Wriede and Dutke; on the other, I felt anxious about leaving the familiar environment and facing an entirely new world with different people and different problems. Eventually, however, my curiosity won out and I began to look forward with eager anticipation to whatever new challenges were in

store for me. Finally, the anxiously awaited day arrived. On the morning of
the last day, the entire school marched into the auditorium on the top floor.
While we stirred impatiently in our seats, several teachers took turns giving
flowery speeches that were packed with flattering pro-Hitler clichés but void
of content. Then came the highlight of the event, a farewell address by
Schulleiter Wriede. As usual, he took the opportunity to wear his beloved
Nazi uniform. There were muffled giggles from us boys as the principal
assumed a pose similar to that of Hitler in the life-size portrait of the dictator
on the wall behind the speaker's podium. His obvious attempt to give his
voice a more guttural, Hitlerian quality promptly provoked further giggles.

Visibly annoyed by his young detractors, Wriede told us that the time
for fun and games would soon be over and that very soon we would no
longer be boys but men who had to take our designated places in Germany's
economic and political life. Abruptly, his voice derailed and climbed out of
control into the falsetto range. The resulting squeak was met with uproarious
laughter from the pupils.

From the start of the principal's address, I had shifted uneasily in my
seat. While the humor of the ridiculous, erect figure on the podium was not
lost on me, I had learned the hard way to control my boyish urge to giggle
along with my peers. On more than one occasion, Wriede had singled me
out and made me pay for the collective sins of the class. Although this was
my last school day at Kätnerkamp, I resolved to play it safe up to the very
last minute I was under Wriede's jurisdiction in order to give the mean-
spirited principal no excuse to retaliate.

He told his young audience that they were facing an enviable future, and
that in a few years they would be old enough to volunteer for military service
in the best military organization the world had ever known. The *Deutsche
Wehrmacht,* he explained, offered unlimited opportunities for young men
who had grown up the way the Führer wanted them to grow up. "Should
you ever be called upon to fight for your Führer and your *Vaterland,* I know
that I can depend on you to do your level best to make Kätnerkampschule
proud of you," he added.

Then, after suggesting that in every barrel of apples, there are a few rotten
ones, he continued, with a withering stare in my direction, that there would
be some boys who, for one reason or another, would be found unworthy of
the honor of wearing the uniform of a German soldier. For them, he said,

he had only one piece of advice: to get out of Germany while they could, because the future Germany would be a Germany of soldiers, not of cowards and shirkers of duty. Thanks to the Führer, he concluded, Germany would never again become a haven for treasonous non-Aryan scum—Jews, Negroes, and other misfits. Hitler would not allow them to defile noble German blood and to cheat the German people of the rewards of their hard-won victories.

At Wriede's mention of the world "Negroes," I tried in vain to find cover behind the back of a shorter classmate. As if on command, all eyes shifted to me as everyone tried to get a better look at the boy whom the principal had just branded an enemy of the German people. My heart started pounding so hard that I feared it could be heard throughout the auditorium. My knees began to tremble and my body became drenched in sweat. I wished that the floor would open and swallow me to remove me from the humiliating stares of my peers. But the floor did not swallow me and I had to endure the stares. In my agony I recalled, as so often in the past, the old admonition that "German boys don't cry," no matter what. It helped me to suppress the tears of shame and humiliation that were welling up in my eyes. Through my tear-blurred vision, I could see Wriede sneer at me from the podium with a smug, malicious grin that signaled the principal's satisfaction with having hit his favorite target where it hurt the most. As so often in the past, I had been made a convenient scapegoat for Wriede's chagrin over having been ridiculed by the class.

Building to a climax of his diatribe, Wriede continued to extoll the blessings of a military career, praising those among us who would be chosen by divine providence and found worthy of giving their lives for our beloved Führer and for the future of our beloved *Vaterland*. With those sentiments, he bid the school farewell.

Less inspired by the principal's speech than by euphoria over their temporary freedom from school authority, the kids let go with a wild teacher-defying howl, then stampeded down the steps and into the street. Unlike a few minutes earlier, nobody paid any attention to me. Who had time for other people's problems at a time like this? School was out for a week and the future, thanks to Adolf Hitler, looked brighter than ever—or so they thought. Slowly, I followed the throng into the street.

By the time my mother returned home from work, she found me lying on my bed, my eyes fixed at the ceiling in an empty stare.

"What's the matter?" she asked, sensing that something was wrong.

"Nothing. I just have a headache," I replied without convincing her.

"How did school go?" my mother kept probing.

"Okay, I guess. Nothing special. Just a few speeches and things."

Having seen that same empty stare on my face before, my mother knew exactly how I felt.

"I bet it was that stupid Wriede again," she guessed with uncanny accuracy. "You promised me not to let that ignorant man upset you anymore. Just think that today was the last day you had to put up with him, and you'll feel better right away."

My mother was right. As long as I lived, Wriede would never have another chance to humiliate me and play his sadistic games with me. For all practical purposes, Wriede—the bane of my short existence—was dead. I felt as if a heavy weight had been lifted off me. All of a sudden life looked bright again, and the fact that school was out for at least a week made it even better.

SCHLEIDENSTRASSE II

Following the week's hiatus, I, along with some twenty Kätnerkamp classmates, reported for reassignment to Schleidenstrasse 11. Unlike the shy kid who had arrived for the first school day at Kätnerkamp six years earlier, I now was a preadolescent with an attitude. Instead of the panic that had gripped me on my first school day at that time, I felt almost cocky and looked forward to whatever the future held in store for me. For one thing, I knew that scholastically I had nothing to worry about, and as far as the possibility of running into racist teachers was concerned, I was determined not to let them get the best of me. Having survived the likes of Wriede and Dutke, I felt I could cope with just about anything that crawled from under the rock of Nazi pedagogy.

After being divided into two groups, we were assigned to two different classes. My group, which by a stroke of luck included my two closest buddies Karl Morell and Fiffi Peters, wound up in Class 7B. Our new teacher was Herr Henry Herbst, a young man with black hair, bushy eyebrows, a permanent five o'clock shadow, a jutting jaw, and keen, chiseled features. Because of a striking resemblance to the fictitious Sherlock Holmes–type hero of prewar Germany's best-selling whodunit paperbacks, his pupils called him Tom Shark behind his back. The nickname was meant more as a compliment than as a putdown for, like the paperback sleuth, Herr Herbst had acquired the reputation of being an extremely fair, no-nonsense fellow who knew his stuff.

After welcoming us *Neulinge* (newcomers), he ticked off a long list of particular no-nos that he said he would not tolerate in his class. "If anyone ever told you that learning should be fun," he continued, "forget it! In my class, gentlemen, learning is work—hard work, as a matter of fact. Those of you *Neulinge* who think they can rest on their lazy hides are making a serious mistake."

When the bell signaled the end of the first class, Herr Herbst asked me to stay. I braced myself for some Wriede-type shenanigans. After the other boys left the classroom, Herr Herbst asked me to sit down.

"I don't intend to talk about this ever again," he opened the discussion, "but I thought you should know that your skin color is of absolutely no importance to me. In my class, you will be treated like anybody else. I've seen your report cards and know that you are an excellent student. If you are willing to work hard and behave in my class, I see no reason why we shouldn't get along. Do you?"

Pleasantly surprised, I assured him that I didn't see any reason either; he shook my hand and dismissed me. For the nearly two years he was my teacher, he kept his word. He never mentioned my race again or gave me the slightest indication that it mattered to him.

Adjustment to my new classmates was similarly frictionless. As usual, my appearance generated a great deal of curiosity, especially during recess on the schoolyard, yet no one seemed inclined to provoke me. For a few weeks we Kätnerkamp boys kept mostly to ourselves. But soon we started making new friends and the lines between *Neulinge* and old-timers became more and more blurred until the only person who was still referring to us as *Neulinge* was Tom Shark. I soon figured out the basis for his hangup. For whatever reason, he was fiercely competitive with us *Neulinge* and tried hard to prove that his old pupils were more advanced than we. That turned out to be a rather frustrating task since we were usually as good as his old students and occasionally even better. Fortunately, Tom Shark was impeccably fair, so he never cheated when grading our papers in order to help the members of his old class come out on top. Yet nothing seemed to please him more than when, on a rare occasion, one of us *Neulinge* admitted that we hadn't yet covered a certain subject that his old pupils had mastered.

There was only one boy who showed resentment toward me. He was Arne Arnholdt, the school's swimming ace. But his hostility was short-lived and before long we became good friends. When I asked him later why he had acted so hostile, he confessed that when I first arrived, word had gotten around that I could outswim Tarzan. Fearful that I would soon topple him from his first place swimming spot, he said he acted out his jealousy. All his negative feelings evaporated when he saw me swim for the first time and discovered that the rumor about my swimming prowess had been highly exaggerated and that I was nowhere near his league.

Even though I breezed through most subjects with customary ease, there were two subjects that gave me a run for my money—English and math. In math, I at least managed—by hook or by crook—to get a passing grade, mainly by convincing Tom Shark that I really tried. In English, on the other hand, I was completely over my head. Since I had joined the class of Frau Dr. Fink, the only teacher in the entire grade school with a doctorate, my progress in English had ground to a complete halt. While my previous English teacher, Herr Neumann (who had replaced bulldog Harden), had made the language come alive by having us converse and write themes in English, Frau Dr. Fink had us conjugating verbs until we were ready to collapse. The more boring her classes became, the less interested I became, until I reached the point where I no longer cared whether I ever spoke another English word. My frustration was shared by Frau Dr. Fink, who gave vent to it at the end of the school year when, instead of giving me a grade, she wrote on my report card, "Hans-Jürgen has absolutely no talent for learning English." During nearly four decades of laboring as an English-language journalist and trying to put together sentences that make sense, I have occasionally been haunted by the notion that, perhaps, the old gal had a point.

Shortly after enrolling at Schleidenstrasse, I made an important discovery, or rather rediscovery—girls. From the time I started school, girls had been practically invisible to me. They just happened to be on the other side of the schoolyard, and neither I nor any of my peers paid them much attention. All of a sudden that changed. Without any particular triggering event, girls our age almost overnight became ever present in our thoughts, speech, and action. Although still separated from them physically by a gender-segregated school system, we boys in seventh grade had suddenly become keenly aware of and attracted to our counterparts in the school's female wing. Judging by the way they giggled and flashed their eyes at us provocatively, there could be no doubt that the feeling was mutual.

Communicating our newly awakened interest in girls during recess took a variety of forms that ranged from loud, boisterous behavior to showing off with various physical stunts to actual fights, not unlike the fights of two male lions over the affection of a lioness. The big difference was that our fights weren't over the affections of anyone, but merely a device for showing off and attracting attention. A more subtle and far more effective method of signaling interest in a member of the opposite sex was by starting an exchange of notes, which were surreptitiously passed back and forth by couriers like me. Because the likes of Wriede and Dutke had made me only too aware of the Nazi-imposed taboo of my becoming involved with German girls, I was definitely not a player, but contented myself with deriving vicarious romantic gratification by serving as go-between and confidant to various pairs of lovers. Like Cyrano de Bergerac, I would coach a friend on how to win the affections of a girl, never letting on that I, too, was smitten with her. While a far cry from the normal one-on-one relationships my classmates enjoyed, my approach to puppy love was the best I could muster under the circumstances. It gave me a legitimate reason for being near and communicating with my secret love without having to risk rejection or worse, being told by an adult—perhaps the girl's parents—that I was out of line.

A NEW HOBBY

To the generation of boys who grew up with me in Hamburg there was nothing more important, more compelling, and more absorbing than *Fussball* (soccer), Germany's national pastime. All the boys in my class were crazy about *Fussball*, and those who weren't good at playing the game made up for it by being enthusiastic spectators and fans. For some strange reason, I was neither. Somehow, I never felt the slightest inclination to chase, kick, or butt a ball, or to sit in the bleachers and watch others do it. In a city that breathed, ate, and slept soccer, my indifference toward the sport made me almost as much an aberration as did my skin color. My indifference to whether HSV, Hamburg's vaunted amateur soccer team, won or lost was tantamount to high treason. Consequently, when it came to *Fussball*, my classmates justifiably thought of me as a *Flasche* and strenuously avoided having me on their teams. Only my prowess in track and field kept my peers from dismissing me as a total physical dud.

It hurt my pride to be regarded as a soccer nonentity, but not enough to put forth a serious effort to become a respectable player. At the same time, I felt a strong need to participate in some sport that I could be as enthusiastic about as my soccer-playing buddies, one that would give me the recognition I craved.

Coincidence soon came to my aid. One day—I was about twelve at the time—several friends and I were walking home from school when a young, athletic-looking blond man stopped us, introducing himself as Rudi, the coach of an amateur boxing club in suburban Bramfeld. Rudi wanted to know whether we had any interest in boxing, since his club had a pre-junior division. He suggested we check it out and, if we liked it, join.

I was certain that the coach's invitation did not include me, since by that time it was clear to me that all organized sports activities in Germany were regulated by the Nazi Ministry of Sports. The disastrous outcome of my quest to join the Hilter Youth had ended my hope of ever being admitted to an organization that would receive me without reservations as an equal and welcome me with open arms. But before I could walk away in anticipation of being told that the club did not accept non-Aryans, the coach turned directly to me.

"If you'd join, I could make a real good boxer out of you," he told me.

I could hardly believe my ears, but that was all I needed to hear to make up my mind to join.

"Just come to the the Old Gun Club," Rudi said. "We're training every Tuesday and Friday night and every Sunday morning."

All five of us promised him that we'd be there, pending permission from our parents of course.

As I had expected, my mother was less than ecstatic about the idea of my joining a boxing club. Surprisingly, she gave her blessing anyway. "I know the first time you get hit hard enough that it hurts, you're going to quit," she predicted.

Mutti knew me well, but not that well.

The gym, which was located in the rundown converted beer hall of the defunct gun club, was a fifteen-minute bicycle ride away. When we boys arrived, it was bustling with the activities of about thirty men and boys, several of them our own age. Amid the whirring sound of rope skipping, we could hear the rapid-fire impact of leather gloves as two men sparred in the ring, while others whacked away at an arsenal of heavy bags and punching balls that hung suspended from the ceiling.

Within a few months, this all-male underworld of blood, grunts, and pungent stale sweat had become my world. Three times a week, I would mount my bicycle, dressed in a gym suit, a pair of boxing gloves slung around my neck, and head for Bramfeld. Soon I was obliged to make the trip alone, since my four buddies dropped out, one by one, as soon as they learned the hard way that boxing was a two-way street. You give some and take some.

Rudi, a former amateur national lightweight champion and an electrician by trade, turned out to be a hard taskmaster when it came to teaching us the fine points of the sport and honing our bodies and minds to a fighting edge. Yet he was a kind and sensitive friend who, with infinite patience, instilled in us a love for boxing and the meaning of true sportsmanship. From him I learned that there's nothing lower than a low blow, a kidney punch, or hitting a man who's down. He never let us start a round of sparring without shaking hands, or leave the ring without a comradely hug.

Rudi was convinced that I had great potential as a fighter because of what he termed my "natural ability"—fast legs, fast hands, and fast reflexes, assets he felt were well worth cultivating. Since under prevailing amateur boxing rules I could not enter into formal competition in the junior league until I reached the age of fourteen, Rudi figured that in two years he would have me ready to take on anyone in my weight class. "I'll make you a German junior champion," Rudi promised. "Just do your part and keep working as hard as you have been working, and leave everything else to me."

There was nothing I wanted to believe more than that I could become a champ—especially since Joe Louis, the new heavyweight champion of the world, my hero and role model, had just redeemed himself after his defeat by Max Schmeling two years earlier. With a sensational first-round knock-out, he had destroyed Nazi Germany's great white hope and put the lie to Aryan supremacy, as far as I was concerned. Even though I was a staunch Joe Louis fan, I agreed with Rudi and most Germans who felt that the American boxing establishment had cheated Schmeling out of the world championship after his decisive victory over Louis by denying him a title fight with Jim Braddock, the champ. Instead, the Americans finagled to give the title fight to Louis, who—quite predictably—put Braddock away. To think that one day I might be a boxing champion like the Brown Bomber from America was mind-boggling, yet, if I could believe Rudi, not necessarily too far-fetched.

But even without such long-range dreams to inspire me, my time at the boxing club was enormously rewarding and well spent. Besides channeling some of the aggression I'd begun to display in response to the repeated slights I received, it improved my physique and immeasurably enhanced my standing among my peers. My prestige soared to an all-time high. Even the older and bigger boys were beginning to take me seriously and treat me with respect. As word spread around school and my neighborhood that I had become a bona fide exponent of the manly art, so did the conventional wisdom that to mess with me was definitely not a good idea.

By an odd coincidence, shortly after I joined the boxing club, Hitler made boxing lessons an integral part of all schools' athletic curricula, since he was convinced that boxing built character and bolstered self-confidence. By the time the first boxing classes were taught in my school by a teacher who had to take a crash course in the sport's fundamentals, I was already an accomplished amateur boxer. Since in the land of the blind, the one-eyed man is king, I was hailed immediately as a boxing phenom. As a result, the teacher frequently asked me to demonstrate various boxing techniques, from proper footwork to the correct way of throwing a punch to skipping rope at a speed that made the rope all but invisible to the eye. He even had me put on exhibition bouts with a string of opponents. Since they were all inexperienced, sparring with them gave me a chance to demonstrate my expertise without having to worry about getting hurt. But after a couple of weeks of basking in my new-won glory, I was informed by the teacher that he had to stop the exhibition matches, since they were not part of the required curriculum. I was certain that the real reason he called off the bouts was the fear of some of his colleagues that my continuous display of non-Aryan dominance in a sport as popular as boxing sent the wrong message. But the damage had already been done. My reputation as the school's best boxer had been firmly established and, in fact, remained intact for the rest of my school days.

Meanwhile, back at the club, I had to earn my reputation as a creditable contender the hard way—by facing ring-savvy opponents. Rudi made sure that I saw plenty of action, often pairing me with boys who had both weight and reach advantage over me. In doing so, he taught me how to take advantage of my superior speed and trigger-sharp reflexes, which enabled me to duck or step aside a split second before a punch could land. Sometimes, my reflexes would let me down and I had to pay the penalty in the form of a bloody nose, a cut lip, a swollen eye, or an unhinged jaw that made chewing excruciatingly painful for weeks. There were many times when I seriously considered hanging up my gloves rather than risk taking another punishing blow. But each time I changed my mind when I thought of how my quitting would play at school and in my neighborhood. Besides, I really didn't have the guts to look Rudi in the eye and tell him that I couldn't take it anymore. So instead of quitting, I chose the only other way out of the pressure cooker into which I had put myself. I got serious. With Rudi's constant encouragement, I trained harder and harder to work out the kinks in my boxing style. Between grueling hours on the punching bag, running, and jumping rope, I would spar with each of the dozen or so kids in the junior league. Gradually, ever so gradually, I transformed myself into such an elusive target that I was able to step into the ring with any of my peers without having to worry about getting hit. I could see a punch coming and take evasive action long before it could land and do any damage.

Fear of being called a quitter wasn't the only reason I stuck it out. Another was that life at the Bramfeld Boxing Club was strangely detached from the Nazi politics that seemed to pervade everything else. It was an apolitical island in a sea of rabid Hitlerism. What it lacked in amenities, such as shower facilities and up-to-date equipment, it made up in esprit de corps. The members were plain, working-class people who genuinely liked and accepted each other, including me. The few times my race was mentioned, it was in the context of an enviable plus. Most of my teammates agreed with Rudi that my father's African genes were a decided asset in the ring. Even though their view reflected a certain degree of stereotypical thinking, I didn't feel offended, since I subscribed to it myself. I had no idea whether my father was athletic or not, but I was convinced that my unusual aptitude for boxing had everything to do with him.

Neither Rudi nor I ever doubted that my hard training would pay off eventually in garnering for me and the club a junior amateur boxing championship. By the time I reached my fourteenth birthday, Rudi felt I was ready to enter the national tournament. It was therefore as devastating for him as it was for me when the application he submitted to the *Reichssport-verband* (Reich Sports Association) in my behalf was rejected because of the old bugaboo: *"Nichtarier."* I'd heard that often enough to know there was no hope, but Rudi was not a man to give up easily. Without hesitation, he composed a letter to the highest sports authority in the country, *Reichssport-führer* Hans von Tschammer und Osten. He said he knew someone with connections who would make sure that the *Reichssportführer* would read the letter himself. In his letter, which Rudi read to me, he explained how I excelled both in sportsmanship and boxing skill. If given the opportunity to compete, Rudi pleaded, I would not only win the title *Deutscher Jugend-meister* (German junior champion) in the junior featherweight division but also be a credit to my club and the sport of boxing in general. In closing, he appealed to the *Reichssportführer's* own sense of sportsmanship and fair play.

I thanked Rudi for sticking out his neck for me, but knew that the very points Rudi had made were sufficient reason for a Nazi racist not to let me fight. My instincts proved correct. While I'll never know whether von

Tschammer und Osten ever saw Rudi's letter, I know Rudi never received a reply. So when the deadline for registering for the championship tournament drew near, another boy, one I had chased around the ring many times during training, was entered instead of me.

A few weeks later, to my chagrin, my replacement received a hero's welcome as he returned to the club with his newly won junior-division title. While I realized my having been barred was not his fault, I couldn't help feeling deep resentment toward him. As far as I was concerned, he had something that rightfully belonged to me. I couldn't wait, therefore, to meet the new *Box Meister* in the ring again—if only during training—to demonstrate to him that he was champion in name only. I could well understand why he avoided a ring encounter with me as long as he could by staying away from training or by claiming to feel indisposed. Eventually, however, he ran out of dodges and I got my wish. With a ferocity I hadn't felt since I had taken up boxing, I unleashed a barrage of punches that soon had blood spurting from the champ's nose as he staggered into the ropes. Even after Rudi shouted for me to break, I kept hitting him as if he were my mortal enemy. Finally, Rudi had to step into the ring and pull me off the badly shaken champ. "I'm sorry I wrote what I did about your sportsmanship," Rudi shouted at me in obvious disgust.

"Don't tell me about sportsmanship!" I shouted back at him, then pulled off my gloves, dressed, and walked out of the gym, my mind made up never to return.

THE WAR COMES TO HAMBURG

The news on September 1, 1939, that Hitler had ordered German troops to cross the Polish border and attack Poland was received with open enthusiasm by me and my eighth-grade classmates. In our youthful patriotism, which had been carefully nurtured by Goebbels's insidious propaganda machine with daily reports of escalating Polish provocations against German nationals living in Poland, we felt that it was high time that Germany let the Poles know that you couldn't push Germans around. Our only regret was that at age thirteen, we were much too young to get a piece of the action and worried that the war would long be forgotten by the time we were old enough to bear arms. That's why we felt jealous when one day Herr Herbst announced that he had to give up his teaching post to report for military service. A few weeks later, following completion of basic training, he visited us to show off his brand-new crew cut and army private's uniform. As he regaled us with humorous accounts about his adjustment to military life, none of us imagined that neither Herr Herbst nor the majority of our classmates would survive the war.

To our great disappointment, life in Hamburg went on pretty much as if we were still at peace. The only reminders that we were actually at war were the daily accounts in the press, the *Sondermeldungen* (special reports) on radio, and the expanded weekly newsreels. The latter were one of the most potent weapons in Goebbels's propaganda arsenal. Vivid frontline footage brought home to us the German military juggernaut's crushing of the vastly outclassed Polish army in eighteen days. Valiant attempts by the Poles to charge advancing German tanks with lance-toting cavalry from a bygone era were presented as one big Polish joke. There was much rejoicing over the German victory among us kids, but Poland and the war seemed far away to us—too far, we felt, to change our lives. So for the time being, we had to content ourselves with "doing our share" of the war effort by going from door to door after school to collect leftover bones from housewives' kitchens and taking them to our schoolyard, where they formed a huge stinking pile before being hauled away to be processed into strategically important lubricants. Otherwise, except for the increasing presence of men in military uniforms and the stringently enforced blackout that was aimed at preventing enemy aircraft from locating ground targets and also to save electricity, life in Hamburg remained deceptively normal and—as far as we youngsters were concerned—intolerably dull. But all that was soon to change.

With the broadening of the war through the entry of Britain and France into the fray, there was plenty of action we kids could enjoy vicariously. Soon, our sports heroes were replaced by military heroes, such as submarine commander Günther Prien, who with his U-47 sneaked into Britain's heavily fortified, "impenetrable" naval harbor of Scapa Flow and sank the British battleship *Royal Oak* and 833 crewmen. Unscathed, he and his men returned to their home base and a hero's welcome by Hitler in the *Reichskanzlei*, the Nazi equivalent of the White House. Other military heroes Dr. Goebbels touted successfully as role models for German youths were fighter aces Werner Mölders and Adolf Galland, whose records of enemy aircraft knockouts were reported daily by the press like soccer scores.

Yet not all accounts of German victories in the newsreels were joyous occasions for me. Some I found outright embarrassing. After the massive defeat of the French army by German troops in early June 1940, Goebbels's cameramen delighted in showing thousands of battle-fatigued and demoralized French African soldiers in ragged uniforms being herded into German POW camps, with the sarcastic commentary, "Here come the defenders of Western civilization." The hapless prisoners were juxtaposed with footage of distinctly Aryan-looking fresh German troops marching confidently in disciplined formations. "And here," mocked the commentator, "come the barbarians."

Each special radio announcement of another German victory was accompanied by blaring fanfares and ended with a military choir's rendition of the popular fighting anthem *"Wir fahren gegen England,"* that was aimed at making fighting and dying in the "crusade against England" sound like a barrel of fun. The Goebbels press was jubilant when it reported the virtual destruction of the British city of Coventry by German bombs. It even coined a new adjective, *"coventriert"* (coventrized), which meant totally demolished. *Reichsmarschall* Göring, emboldened by his *Luftwaffe*'s early victories over enemy aircraft, boasted openly that if only a single Allied bomber would reach German air space, "you can call me Meier." The pronouncement was typical of Göring's brand of humor, since Meier was one of the most common, and thus least distinguished, German names. Göring's boast notwithstanding, the German Air Defense Command took no chances and launched a massive public air-raid shelter construction program. Soon, Hamburg was dotted with above-ground concrete bunkers, including two high-rise, fortresslike superbunkers on the Heiligengeistfeld, site of the city's popular winter carnival, the Hamburger Dom. The two superbunkers, which loomed on the horizon like hulking monsters, added a sinister touch to Hamburg's elegant skyline of slender church spires. In addition to providing air-raid shelters for thousands of civilians, they served as platforms for heavy *Flak* (antiaircraft artillery) batteries capable of doing head-on combat with low-

My maternal grandfather, Hermann
Baetz *(front row, second from right),*
as a worker in the German stone
quarry where he rose to quarry
master. Uftrungen, ca. 1890.
(H.J. Massaquoi Collection)

Wearing the crown and vestment
of the rank he inherited from his
father, King Lahai, Momolu IV, my
paternal grandfather, ruled as king of
the Vais until his abdication at age thirty
in a tribal dispute. Liberia, ca. 1905.
(H.J. Massaquoi Collection)

Wedding photo of my mother's
brother Karl Baetz and his bride,
Grete, includes my mother *(white
dress),* my mother Martha
Baetz *(seated),* two of my mother's
sisters, Frieda *(holding flowers)* and
Hedwig, and her brother Paul
(behind Karl). Nordhausen, ca.
1921. *(H.J. Massaquoi Collection)*

Liberian Consul-General Momolu
Massaquoi, my paternal grand-
father, in the official uniform of a
member of the diplomatic corps.
Hamburg, 1927.
(H.J. Massaquoi Collection)

My mother and I, at age two.
Hamburg, 1928.
(H. J. Massaquoi Collection)

Sporting the afro look at age
four. Hamburg, 1930.
(H. J. Massaquoi Collection)

With Hella Möller *(center),* my baby-sitter's grand-daughter, and two neighborhood playmates, Susi *(left)* and Irmgard Neuhoff in the Neuhoff family's backyard. Hamburg, 1931. *(H.J. Massaquoi Collection)*

With my baby-sitter Tante Möller *(second from right)* and my little playmate Erika Schmedemann, at the suburban weekend retreat of Erika's relatives. Hamburg-Ohlsdorf, 1931. *(H.J. Massaquoi Collection)*

Erika in the buff
and yours truly, at age
five. Hamburg, 1931.
(H.J. Massaquoi Collection)

Proudly displaying a
swastika emblem while
standing at attention, I am
flanked by other second-
grade school chums at the
end of recess while waiting
for the teacher's orders to
return to class.
Hamburg, 1933.
(H.J. Massaquoi Collection)

Helping my school chum Karl
Morell launch his sailboat in
City Park. Hamburg, ca. 1935.
(H.J. Massaquoi Collection)

My father, Al-Haj Massaquoi, at
age forty-five. Monrovia, Liberia,
1945. *(H.J. Massaquoi Collection)*

Pretending to be American seamen, my buddy Yankee Werner and I crash a British service club reserved for Allied personnel during the British occupation. Hamburg, 1946. *(H.J. Massaquoi Collection)*

The Three Ah-Yue Hon Lous: with my partners Ilse Hadje and Yue during our Hansa Theater stint. Hamburg, 1947. *(H.J. Massaquoi Collection)*

In the United States at last. Times Square, New York City, 1948.
(H.J. Massaquoi Collection)

During the Korean War with the vaunted 82nd Airborne Division. Fort Bragg, North Carolina, 1952.
(H.J. Massaquoi Collection)

flying enemy aircraft. They also were equipped with state-of-the-art *Horchgeräte* (listening devices), the precursors of radar, that looked like gigantic black metal ears of a futuristic monster. Not until after the war did the public learn that the soundproof basement of one of the bunkers also contained torture chambers for the Gestapo, which reportedly as late as April 6, 1945, used the facility to torture resistance fighters in order to force them to reveal the identities of their coconspirators.

To further discourage air attacks at low altitudes, which enhance the accuracy of bombing hits, the skies above Hamburg were dotted with *Sperrballons* (barrier blimps) that were tethered to the ground by strong cables capable of slicing through the wings of attacking airplanes. In addition, with the stringent dusk-to-dawn blackout rule in effect, we had to cover our windows with blankets in order to prevent even the tiniest light beam from reaching the streets. Throughout the night, antiaircraft units searched the sky with night-piercing columns of lights. To confuse enemy flyers and to protect the famous Lombards Bridge, which divides the city's scenic inner and outer Alster basins, the inner Alster was covered completely with camouflage nets while a phony Lombards Bridge was built parallel to the real one.

Other measures aimed at preparing for what Göring had promised would never happen included gas-mask and fire drills for civilians during which we were required to pass through a large, gas-filled tent while wearing a gas mask and to extinguish a small chemical fire with a fire extinguisher. To reduce the danger of fire following an incendiary bomb attack, Hamburg residents were ordered to participate in a massive program of *Entrümpelung* (junk disposal). As ordered, my mother and I, like thousands of Hamburgers, cleaned out our attic of unwanted old mattresses, furniture, toys, books, and so on, and deposited them on the sidewalks for removal by government trucks.

In spite of the massive anti-air-raid preparations, many people shared Göring's optimism regarding his *Luftwaffe*'s capability to keep us out of harm's way and regarded the measures as unnecessary. They soon learned that their trust had been misplaced. On May 18, 1940, an air attack on Hamburg by British Royal Air Force bombers killed thirty-four civilians and with them the credibility of Göring, who henceforth became the butt of many jokes about *Reichsmarschall* Meier.

For a while, bombings of Hamburg remained relatively rare occurrences, so rare, in fact, that whenever a building was hit, I and hundreds of other curiosity seekers would rush to the disaster scene to behold with awe the destructive power of an explosive bomb. It was during this lull before the storm that I was informed by Onkel Fritz that his mother, my beloved Tante Möller, who had looked after me when I was a little boy, had died at his home across the street from ours after a brief illness at age seventy-two. The news hurt me deeply, for Tante Möller was truly the grandmother I never had. It was she who, more than any other person, made a genuine Hamburger out of me and who instilled in me a love for the city that I know will endure as long as I live.

I consoled myself when Fritz Möller pointed out that his mother, who hadn't spent a single minute in an air-raid shelter, was lucky to have died peacefully in her sleep and thus avoided the escalation of the bombings and the resulting hardships that he felt were sure to come. Fritz was right of course but even he could not foresee the awful extent of his prediction.

As the aerial attacks and enemy overflights increased, so did the times we were awakened at night by howling sirens. Loaded down like mules with ready-packed suitcases that contained our most prized and essential possessions, my mother and I would join our neighbors and head for the nearest public air-raid shelter, half a block down the street. Unlike the above-ground bunker variety, "our" shelter, which could accommodate about one hundred people, consisted of a heavily reinforced, whitewashed basement beneath the old four-story waffle factory, once the dispenser of delicious waffle scraps, which had long since been closed. The basement was furnished with wooden benches and double-decker, mattressless cots along the walls. Each of its three rooms was equipped with a large air pump through which used-up air could be expelled and fresh filtered air sucked in by way of a manually operated broomsticklike lever.

As air-raid shelters went, ours wasn't exactly the most confidence-inspiring from a safety point of view. In fact, we had all but resigned ourselves to the certainty that in case of a direct hit, we'd all be wiped from the face of the earth. But our shelter was the most conveniently located and, we were told, offered "as much protection as we really would ever need." We were not convinced, but kept hoping for the best while expecting the worst.

LIFE GOES ON

Despite our increasingly precarious existence, life in Hamburg went on as close to normal as was possible under the circumstances. This included the observance of certain religious traditions, such as confirmation upon graduation from grammar school. As baptized Lutherans, all boys in my eighth-grade class were expected to participate in confirmation exercises. This was by no means an indication of our community's devoutness but merely proof of the durability of a local tradition. Spiritually speaking, we kids were impoverished cretins and proud of it. Our Nazi teachers, some of whom advocated a return to Teutonic paganism and the worship of a pantheon of Germanic deities, had conditioned us to regard churchgoing and praying as something strictly for sissies. As a result, most of us hadn't seen the inside of a church since we were baptized shortly after birth. Yet, in spite of the low esteem in which we held the church, we regarded our confirmation as the most important rite of passage in our lives.

To qualify for confirmation, our neighborhood *Heiligen Geist Kirche* (Holy Ghost Church) insisted that confirmands take weekly confirmation lessons in the church rectory after regular school hours and attend Sunday services for an entire year prior to the event. There were about seventy-five boys in my class and a similar number of girl confirmands who met on another day. Although we resented the infringement on our free time, we grudgingly went along with the program, if for no other reason than the fact that our parents left us no choice.

Unlike predominantly Catholic southern and western Germany, where observance of religious rituals had always played an important role in people's lives, mostly Protestant northern Germany was noticeably less devout, at least in terms of active participation. This was especially true in Hamburg, where most working-class people, although decent and law abiding, were largely content with a noninvolved, peaceful coexistence with God. *"Ich lasse den lieben Gott einen guten Mann sein* (I let God be a good man)" is how many Hamburgers summed up their aloofness from a divine creator. As a result, Hamburgers, for the most part, came into direct contact with the

church only four times in their lives—at their baptisms, at their confirma-
tions, at their weddings, and, finally, at their funerals. While not a native
Hamburger, my mother was no exception; she preferred sleeping late on
Sundays to sitting in church and taking care of her soul. After a week of
backbreaking work at the factory, she felt she deserved the rest. Yet in spite
of her lack of enthusiasm for going to church, she believed in God and
considered it a foregone conclusion that I should be properly confirmed.

The man on whose broad shoulders had fallen the improbable task of
making God-fearing young men out of us irreverent semi-heathens in twelve
short months was Pastor Ottmer, a barrel-chested bull of a man who had
no difficulty reconciling his professed belief in Jesus Christ, a Jew, with his
fanatical devotion to Hitler, the greatest anti-Semite of all time. An enthu-
siastic supporter of Hitler's military adventure in Poland, which he ap-
plauded as a justified step to correct old wrongs done to Germany, he never
ended a sermon without asking God for continued German victories and
the protection and blessing of "our beloved Führer." According to Ottmer's
theology, Jesus, by virtue of being the son of an "undoubtedly Aryan God,"
was only a half-Jew at worst, and demonstrably had inherited none of the
undesirable characteristics of his Jewish relatives on his mother's side. As
"proof," Pastor Ottmer pointed to two large paintings on the rectory class-
room wall, one depicting a blond, blue-eyed Jesus as an adult, and the other
a cuddly child Jesus who was even fairer and blonder.

Since confirmation lessons did not involve homework or grades, we con-
firmands brought an extremely cavalier attitude to our Bible studies and
paid only scant attention to Pastor Ottmer's teachings in class and from the
pulpit. That attitude reached its dramatic climax—or, more aptly, low
point—during one of the clergyman's Sunday morning sermons toward the
end of the year.

As usual, some of us had chosen to sit in the church's balcony, where we
were less exposed to the pastor's scrutiny and thus able to vent our boredom
by goofing off in a variety of ways. Some boys simply caught up on sleep,
while others played cards or some other game. I invariably read a whodunit
paperback. That particular Sunday, for lack of a better idea, a few fellows
were busy folding the day's programs that had been handed to us as we
entered the church into little paper gliders that we called *Schwalben* (swal-
lows). On a signal by one of the boys, they launched their paper missiles

from the balcony. It took all the self-control we could muster to keep from bursting out laughing as we watched a squadron of aerodynamically correct paper gliders descend slowly, silently, and in wide, graceful arcs toward the main floor of the church. Although some of the airborne paper missiles came frighteningly close to hitting Pastor Ottmer, the minister kept on preaching as if nothing was amiss. When he had ended his sermon with his usual request for divine protection for "our beloved Führer," he finally acknowledged the boys' prank. "I know who you are," he shouted at the sinners in the balcony with a voice that trembled with un-Christian anger, while the glare from his thick glasses was hitting us like laser beams. "I shall deal with you at the next confirmation class!"

We had no idea what plans Pastor Ottmer had for the perpetrators, but his display of rage did not suggest to me a Christian inclination to turn the other cheek. But since I had had nothing to do with the impromptu aerial extravaganza, I didn't give the matter much thought. When we showed up at the next class, Pastor Ottmer read off about half a dozen names, which, to my utmost surprise, indignation, and terror, included mine. Before I had a chance to protest my innocence, he ordered us to come to the front. He then informed us that he intended to make an example of us by barring us from participating in the confirmation exercises, which were only a few weeks away. When I finally spoke up and told him that I had merely been a more or less innocent bystander and had had absolutely nothing to do with the glider show, he told me to take my just punishment "like a man." Even the corroborating testimony of my story by several of the perpetrators could not sway him to let me off the hook. I remembered my mother's frequent admonition to stay clear of troublemakers with her favorite dictum, *Mitgefangen, mitgehangen* (caught together, hanged together). With 20/20 hindsight, I could see that she had been right. Even though I had not participated in the glider caper, I had put myself in the company of goof-offs on the balcony and thus gotten myself into a mess.

Had Pastor Ottmer told us that he was going to cut off our thumbs, we couldn't have been more shocked. What were we going to tell our parents, who had prepared for the upcoming event for almost a year? My mother had already bought my dark confirmation suit, the first suit I owned that boasted a pair of long pants. It also was the first suit she bought with newly introduced wartime rationing coupons. What would I tell our friends and neighbors whom my mother had invited to the confirmation feast? Simply that the confirmation was off because I was accused of misbehaving in church?

While I was desperately trying to think of ways to break the bad news to my mother between some desperate prayers for divine intervention, Pastor Ottmer gave us a stern lecture on the urgent need to rid ourselves of our childish ways, to assume responsibility for our actions and to grow up spiritually. "You may not realize it yet," he told us thirteen- and fourteen-year-olds, "but your childhood days are over." After letting us stew for a while in our own guilt and fear, he finally commuted our "excommunication" to an hour of hard labor each day after school, during which we had to keep the church grounds freshly raked and free of paper. He also told us that henceforth, the church balcony was off limits to us. "From now on, I want you right in front of me where I can see you," he barked. "That is all. *Heil Hitler!*"

Glad to have been spared the unthinkable, we walked out of the rectory in a state of euphoria, as though we had been given a second lease on life. Having come so close to the brink of disaster, I promised myself to heed Pastor Ottmer's advice and from now on stick a little closer to the straight and narrow path of righteousness.

A few weeks later on a bright Easter morning, following a long confirmation sermon by Pastor Ottmer, I was marching in a long procession of boys in brand-new dark suits and fresh haircuts who were approaching the altar from one side while a similar procession of girls in crisp dark confirmation dresses was approaching from the opposite side. Alternately, a boy and a girl received a blessing, a handshake, and a confirmation certificate from Pastor Ottmer. I knew that my mother was in the audience, but I was unable to locate her in the packed church. When it was my turn to step forward, I noticed that people in the audience, which was made up largely of relatives and friends of the confirmands, were craning their necks to get a better look at me. "Bless you," said Pastor Ottmer without any warmth, as he mechanically shook my hand. I had the distinct feeling that it had taken all of the Christian charity he could muster to treat me like any other boy.

APPRENTICESHIP

Four years earlier, when Herr Grimmelshäuser, my fourth-grade teacher, had informed me that—in spite of my excellent grades—I could be admitted to neither the *Realschule* nor the *Oberbau,* the German equivalents of high school, because I was a non-Aryan, he in effect told me that the door to a professional future for me was forever shut. Under Nazi rule, secondary and higher education, while free of charge, was restricted to those pupils who not only showed the greatest promise during their elementary education but who also were members of the Hitler Youth. For pupils who, for scholastic or other reasons, missed the boat, there were only two remaining alternatives: the skilled trades, by way of a three-year apprenticeship, or low-paying, unskilled labor for the rest of their lives.

Seeing me barred from a distinguished professional future hurt my mother more at the time than it did me. From the moment she had discerned in me a love for tinkering and using my hands while I was still a little boy, she had envisioned a future for me as a university-trained engineer. But after seeing that career path blocked, she resolved to help me become the next best thing to an engineer—an expert *Schlosser* (machinist), a trade open to me through the apprenticeship route. German apprentices at the time received no salary, only a token weekly allowance of *Taschengeld* (pocket money). This meant that my mother would have to support me financially for another three years. When I told her that I couldn't let her do that, she didn't want to hear a word I had to say. "You are going to apprentice, and that's that," she insisted. "But if it makes you feel any better," she added, "you can pay me back when you are rich."

Buoyed by youthful optimism, I told her that we had a deal.

Quite a few of my classmates were not as lucky as I. Although some of their parents were far better off financially than my mother, who was barely able to make ends meet on her meager factory pay, they refused to make further sacrifices after their kids left grammar school. Unlike my mother, they insisted that their sons go to work immediately and help earn their keep, thus condemning them to life as unskilled laborers.

A few months before eighth-grade graduation, we were sent to a down-

town office of the *Arbeitsamt* (Department of Labor) for vocational coun-
seling. This was one of the most crucial junctures in our young lives, since
failure to hit it off with an all-powerful counselor could mean having one's
career choice nixed or winding up in a backward sweatshop. Mindful of
that, I had considerable anxiety about my approaching meeting with my
assigned counselor, a Herr von Vett. By the time I knocked on the door to
his office, I was a nervous wreck. When a voice ordered me to come in, my
heart skipped a beat. Seated behind the desk was a blond, middle-aged man
of erect bearing, but all I could see at the moment was the telltale black SS
insignia of dual lightning bolts in the lapel of his civilian suit. This could
only mean that the man who held my future in his hands was a member of
the Nazis' fanatically racist elite organization. I immediately braced myself
for a humiliating, Wriede-type lecture on the necessity of keeping Jews and
other non-Aryans from infiltrating and subverting the trades. But the lecture
never came. To my great surprise and consternation, Herr von Vett gave
me a friendly wink and invited me to take a seat. After carefully perusing
my school records and nodding his approval, he asked me whether I had
brought with me something I had made, as we had been instructed. Appre-
hensively, I unwrapped a small ax I had forged at Eugen Braun's blacksmith
shop. "You made this ax all by yourself?" von Vett asked, noticeably im-
pressed.

"Yes, sir," I replied, and explained how for most of my childhood I
practically had the run of a neighborhood blacksmith shop.

"You can be of great service to Germany one day," von Vett suggested.

I thought I hadn't heard right or that von Vett had lost his last marble.
After all the putdowns I had endured in the past, his suggestion that I could
play a positive role in Nazi Germany seemed to border on the ludicrous.
But von Vett seemed serious. He predicted that one day, in the not-so-
distant future, Germany would reclaim its colonies in east and southwest
Africa. When that happened, he said, there would be a great demand for
technically trained Germans who would go to Africa and train and develop
an African workforce. "With your background and as an expert machinist,"
he explained, "you would be ideal for such an assignment."

Predicting that I would make an "outstanding machinist," von Vett con-
cluded the interview by promising me an excellent apprenticeship with a
first-rate firm. I thanked him, gave the mandatory *Heil Hitler* salute, and

prepared to leave. But he called me back. "Aren't you going to shake my hand?" the SS man wanted to know. I turned around, shook his hand. When I finally left the room, I was happy about the outcome of the interview, but very confused about von Vett's strange affinity for me.

I never saw or heard of the SS man again, but he kept his word. A few days after our meeting, I was notified by the Hamburg branch of Gottfried Lindner A. G., a highly regarded truck-trailer construction firm, to come in for an interview.

On a Monday in April 1940, dressed in brand-new, stiff blue coveralls, I began my three-year machinist apprenticeship with Lindner A. G., on Bramfelderstrasse, a ten-minute bicycle ride from my home. Besides me, there were three other new apprentices reporting for work: Heinz Scheel, an easygoing fellow with a weightlifter's physique; lanky Ingolf Dieter, the good-natured son of a midlevel police officer; and Lisa Röhling, a wholesome, girl-next-door type who was to learn the trade of bookkeeping in the front office. After Meister Neumann, the shop's technical boss, welcomed us in his office, he took us fellows out to the plant, where my unaccustomed senses were assaulted by the earsplitting noise that issued from various large machines, thick smoke that wafted throughout the shop and made breathing difficult, and arc welders' strobelike beams that attacked my eyes from every angle. "Don't look into the beams," Meister Neumann cautioned us, "or you'll injure your eyes."

My immediate reaction was deep regret over my choice of occupation. What had I gotten myself into? Why did I have to pick such a dangerous, hostile environment in which to make my living for the rest of my working days? Why hadn't I been smart like my buddy, Fiffi Peters, who on this same day was starting his apprenticeship as a waiter in Hamburg's elegant *Rathauskeller* at City Hall, dressed in an immaculate black tuxedo. But I realized that my regrets were far too late, and decided to quit my futile grousing and make the most of my situation.

Meister Neumann, a tall middle-aged man with a graying crew cut, a ruddy complexion, and an unmistakable Berlin accent, led us to a large wire cage that was equipped with a long workbench. On the wall above the workbench was a large poster with an illustration of a blond Siegfried-type worker with rolled-up sleeves and bulging muscles, holding a heavy hammer in his right hand. ARBEIT ADELT (Work ennobles)! the poster proclaimed in

large letters against the backdrop of a swastika flag. If the poster's intent was
to inspire us, it had totally missed its purpose with me. All I could see in
my immediate future was a lot of toil and drudgery and very little, if any,
nobility.

"This is your workstation," Herr Neumann announced. He explained
that the cage was there for our protection and that we were allowed to leave
it only to go to the washroom, on break, or when it was time to quit. "From
time to time," Meister Neumann continued, "you'll be assigned as helpers
to a journeyman in various phases of the trailer production. You will at all
times be courteous to the journeymen, always address them with *Herr* and
Sie, instead of by their first names and with the familiar *Du.* And you will
do without fail whatever they ask you to do. Is that understood?"

We all said yes, but I could tell by the miserable expressions on the faces
of my two compatriots that their hearts—like mine—weren't in it.

It took a while before I had resigned myself to the fact that, as Pastor
Ottmer had predicted, at age fourteen my childhood was irretrievably behind
me. Braced for a culture shock, I steeled myself to enter a coarse, frequently
cruel adult world. I found it difficult to dismiss from my mind an incident
in another Hamburg machine shop that had made the news several years
earlier. A machinist, attempting a practical joke, had sneaked up on a sleep-
ing coworker during noon break and inserted the hose of a pressurized
oxygen tank in the vicinity of the sleeping man's rectum in order to "pump
him up just a little." When he tried to gradually open the oxygen valve, the
oxygen escaped with such a force that it tore the intestines of the unsus-
pecting worker and killed him instantly. Keeping that grisly story in mind,
I decided never to be caught napping.

As first-year apprentices, we became the quintessential gofers who were
taught to regard our state of virtual indentured servitude to a bunch of vulgar
and often abusive journeymen and an unsympathetic *Meister* as part of the
natural order of the universe. Under the tutelage of these mostly foul-
mouthed and uncouth proletarians, all of whom—regardless of age—dis-
played a childish predilection for scatological and sexual "humor," we
apprentices had no choice but to grow up fast if we intended to survive in
this less than wholesome milieu. While the journeymen roared their ap-
proval, we demonstrated our newly found "manhood" by outgrossing each
other with a dedication that deserved a better cause. There was only one

boundary to our obnoxious behavior that none of us crossed. We never exposed our parents to the filth we were learning on our job. This meant that, as far as my mother was concerned, I was still her innocent son who wouldn't hurt a fly. By the same token, I was sure that even the more obnoxious journeymen at the shop were respectful and loving husbands to their wives, decent role models to their children, and good neighbors, like the journeymen I knew in Barmbek.

Journeymen seemed to regard it as their most sacred duty to impress upon us apprentices at every opportunity—and there were many—that we were a bunch of nitwits who were totally unfit for, and a disgrace to, our chosen trade. The only positive aspect in my new situation was that the low esteem in which journeymen held apprentices, especially the first-year variety, was universal and that, with the exception of one horrific incident, I was never singled out for demeaning treatment because of my race. While tolerating the status quo for the moment because I had no choice, I looked forward to the day when I added a few more inches to my height and a few more pounds to my frame to make a journeyman think twice before messing with me. Meanwhile, I took solace in the thought that three years hence, nobody, not even Meister Neumann, would be able to push me around.

Since we apprentices were to be seen only and not heard, initially communication between us and the journeymen was a pretty one-sided affair and largely confined to matters directly related to the job. Yet, by keeping my mouth shut and my eyes and ears open, I soon had a pretty good idea of what made the journeymen tick. Although they were too careful to openly say so, their sarcastic comments following each radio announcement left no doubt that they were no admirers of Hitler and the Nazi regime. Even their coworker Peter Schmidt, whom they had chosen as their *Obmann* (shop steward), and who was the official representative of the Nazi Party, frequently joined in the snickers at the government's expense. Schmidt, I learned, was the only man in the plant who had been singled out to take a cruise with his wife to Madeira, Portugal, under the auspices of the much vaunted *Kraft Durch Freude* program that supposedly was available to all German workers. On paydays, I frequently heard grumbling that since 1933, labor unions, along with pay raises, had disappeared, and that the only way workers could increase their pay was by working faster, more hours, and producing more.

As the journeymen got to know me better, they became less careful about what they said while I was around, with the result I heard a lot that wasn't meant for my ears, such as the most blatant gossip about Hitler and members of his top echelon. Propaganda Minister Joseph Goebbels, that married paragon of family values, was referred to as *der Bock von Babelsberg* (the he-goat from Babelsberg), after the German movie capital in Berlin, because of his alleged excessive use of the casting couch and his numerous dalliances with various movie stars. Through the same unimpeachable sources I learned that supermacho SA chief Ernst Röhm, an Oliver Hardy look-alike, had actually been sleeping with his young SA troopers before he was branded a traitor and murdered on Hitler's orders. Another juicy tidbit was that Luftwaffe chief Hermann Göring's mother had had a rich Jewish lover who supported Göring during his youth. Because of his inability to resist stuffing his immense girth into ever-fancier medal-bedecked uniforms, Göring was the butt of most of the political jokes in the plant. The workers still snickered about his much ballyhooed "Wedding of the Decade" in 1935, when he married an obscure actress named Emmy Sonnemann, and the subsequent birth of their daughter, despite rumors that injuries he had sustained during the abortive 1923 Nazi putsch in Munich had left him sterile or impotent or both. The girl's name, Edda, the jokesters claimed, was an acronym that stood for *Emmy dankt dem Adjutanten* (Emmy thanks the adjutant), implying that Göring achieved fatherhood only with a little assist from his aide. Also in for regular ribbings came labor czar Robert Ley, who, it was alleged, was actually a Jew who had dropped the letter *v* from his original name, Levy, and who, it was alleged, was a certified alcoholic. Plumpish Hitler Youth leader Baldur von Schirach, according to my older colleagues, hid his homosexual tendencies behind the respectability of marriage and fatherhood; and Luftwaffe General Field Marshal Erhard Milch, another Aryanized Jew, had his Jewish mother remove his racial stigma by claiming that he was not her biological son but his late Aryan father's out-of-wedlock child. As far as my coworkers were concerned, nothing was sacred, which meant that even the Führer himself was not immune to their scrutiny and ridicule. Thus I learned that contrary to the official version, which held that Hitler had no romantic interest in women because he had dedicated his entire existence to the German people, he once had carried on a sizzling, incestuous love affair with his teenage niece Geli Raubal, who killed herself when the affair went sour. I also heard persistent rumors that the Führer and film actress-director Leni Riefenstahl were an item.

All this reckless talk, which, if overheard by the wrong person could have landed the purveyors in a concentration camp, was normal everyday conversation fare, indicating to what degree mass support for Hitler and his henchmen had eroded and what little respect they enjoyed with the working class.

HANS VOLLMER

It had been my intention to say goodbye to boxing for good, but I soon changed my mind. Somehow, boxing had gotten into my blood. I needed the physical exertion, the feeling that my body was performing at its peak, and I also enjoyed the camaraderie, the esprit de corps inside and outside the ring. Rudi convinced me that even without a championship belt, amateur boxing had its own rewards, and persuaded me to keep training. But shortly thereafter, he and several of the older club members were drafted by the *Wehrmacht,* and the Bramfeld Boxing Club collapsed. What was left of its membership was taken over by *Box Verein Polizei,* a much larger organization sponsored by the Hamburg Police. Strangely enough, nobody objected when I, along with several of my old Bramfeld teammates, showed up for training at the downtown *Polizei Kaserne* (police barracks) gym, although the gym was crawling with cops whose top commander was none other than archracist SS *Reichsführer* Heinrich Himmler. To this day I wonder why I was allowed to mingle freely with Hamburg's Finest without stirring a ripple and what possessed me to take the chance of regularly putting myself in harm's way, since coming to the attention of just one SS-connected policeman who took exception to the presence of a non-Aryan could have sealed my fate.

While training regularly at the *Polizei Kaserne* and at the club's local branch on Bachstrasse, I met a young middleweight junior division champ, Hans Vollmer, an extremely savvy boxer three years older and nearly a head taller than I, who, despite his youth, had the uncanny ability to send opponents to dreamland with one single punch of his right. Soon he became my best friend and the vicarious outlet for my frustrated boxing ambitions. Each time he prepared for a fight, I experienced the tension and the excitement just like he did, and when he won a boxing contest, I felt as if it was my victory as well.

Despite our preoccupation with boxing, our friendship was not confined to the boxing ring, but extended to our spare time. A third-year vulcanizer apprentice, a trade in which he learned to process rubber, Hans frequently joined me in our off hours to check out the various nightspots. Since Hans lived in Barmbek's neighboring district of Hamm, which was notoriously devoid of places for young people to hang out, we either dropped in at Café König in my neighborhood or at one of the many dives on St. Pauli's Reeperbahn.

Frequenting places crowded with feisty young men provided countless opportunities for getting into trouble. Hans and I usually avoided confrontation by simply walking away from challenges, especially since our boxing coach had impressed upon us that outside the ring a boxer's fists are lethal weapons that he must use with the utmost discretion. But on one occasion, Hans decided to ignore the coach's advice. We had walked past a group of men in their early twenties who were standing in front of a nightclub when one of them, a beefy six-footer, seemed to be bothered by my presence. "What's the *Neger* doing here?" he inquired, loud enough for us to hear.

As if stung by a hornet, Hans spun around and faced the man. "What was it you just said?" Hans demanded.

"I asked what the *Neger* is doing here," the man repeated, then stretched himself to his full six feet and added menacingly, "And what's that to you?"

At that moment the other men began to encircle us in an obvious move to join the fracas.

I had hoped that the man who had insulted me would take a better look at Hans and notice the flattened nose, the scar over his left eyebrow, the broad shoulders and narrow hips, and conclude that he was facing a seasoned boxer and call the whole thing off. But instead he raised his fists in an awkward boxing stance and advanced toward Hans. Before he could take another step, Hans's lightning-quick right fist had landed on his jaw with a sickening crunch that sounded like breaking bones. As if felled by a bullet, the six-footer collapsed as his knees buckled beneath him, then crashed backward to the ground where he remained mumbling unintelligibly while tiny rivers of blood oozed from both corners of his mouth.

As soon as they had witnessed Hans's handiwork, the other three men ran in every direction, eager to spare themselves a similar fate. No matter how much Hans invited them to return and even the score, they kept their distance, visibly drained of their belligerence. A firm believer in quitting while ahead, I told Hans to forget about extending challenges and to get the hell out of the place. I was particularly concerned that if Hans had broken his opponent's jaw or worse, there could be extremely unpleasant repercussions, especially if his victim was a Nazi. Fortunately, we were able to leave the scene without incident and never heard another word about Hans's swift action on my behalf.

I had been at Hans's modest apartment in Hamm many times and met his father, also a vulcanizer, and his mother, a Red Cross nurse, both of whom were immensely proud of their only child's achievements in the boxing ring. From the few times I had met Hans's parents, I had always assumed that they were just an ordinary working couple whose biggest adventure in life was watching their only child achieve victories in the boxing ring. But I soon learned never to judge a book by its cover. One day when Hans and I stopped by his apartment, I heard his mother and several men talking in a foreign language I couldn't identify. When I asked Hans, he told me that his mother was Russian and that she would often meet with Russian workers to help them with their problems if she could. The people his mother was entertaining were Russian *Fremdarbeiter* (foreign workers) who had been captured by German forces in Russia and forced to work in the German war industry.

I found it hard to believe that Frau Vollmer, who looked and sounded like a bona fide Hamburg *Hausfrau,* and who even spoke unadulterated Hamburg *Platt,* was a Russian. When I asked how she got to Hamburg, she told me a touching love story that would have made Dr. Zhivago turn green with envy. During World War I, her future husband was a wounded German soldier captured by the Russians and moved deep into Russia to a military hospital where she was a young nurse. While she nursed the German soldier back to health, they fell in love, but when the war ended, the soldier was shipped back home to Germany. Before leaving, he vowed to return to Russia as soon as possible and come for his beloved nurse. She said three years passed during which she saw neither hide nor hair of her lover, but she never gave up her belief that he would make good on his promise and return to her. Then one wintry night, she said, there was a knock on her door and a near-frozen Hans Vollmer, Sr., stood outside, ready to take her back to his homeland and marry her.

From the moment I heard that story, I looked at Hans and his parents with different eyes. It made me wonder why, when some people will go to the end of the world to be united with their loved ones, my own father didn't take a single step to be reunited with my mother and me.

A few days later, Hans dropped in unexpectedly with the horrifying news that his home had been totally destroyed by a direct hit during the previous night's bombing attack. Like many Hamburgers, he and his parents had become lax about going to an air-raid shelter each time the alarm sounded, but this time, inexplicably, they heeded the warning. Some of his neighbors who had ignored the sirens were later recovered from the rubble as corpses.

Within a few weeks, the Vollmers were provided with a much more spacious apartment in an upscale neighborhood and lavishly compensated for their losses in a widely publicized government display of generosity toward early bombing victims. When Hans proudly showed me around his newly decorated and furnished apartment that, unlike their old hole in the wall, boasted such luxury features as a full-size, tiled bathroom and a modern electric kitchen, I secretly wished that my home would be next on the RAF's demolition list. Eventually, my wish would come true, but not in the way I had hoped.

With the RAF stepping up its retaliatory air attacks on German cities, bombed-out buildings became a common sight in Hamburg. Not so common, however, was the sight of prominent Nazis at the scenes of bombing disasters. I heard much grumbling among the people over the fact that Hitler himself was never seen at bombing sites where his mere presence might have done much to boost the people's shattered morale.

SWINGBOYS

By the time I reached my second apprenticeship year, I no longer considered working as hard and as long as a full-grown man such a harsh reality. It had simply become reality. Yet, even under those trying conditions, my life was not all work and no play. Each day after quitting time, I and thousands of Hamburg's teenage boys underwent a remarkable metamorphosis. After much scrubbing, primping, and brushing, we would change from grease- and grime-splattered blue-collar workers into meticulously coiffed, manicured, and dressed men of the world—or so we thought. With each metamorphosis, we would temporarily leave the world of machines, grit, and toil behind and enter the fantasy realm of the "swingboys," an unchartered, unorganized, and leaderless, yet highly visible fraternity whose membership dwarfed that of the vaunted Hitler Youth. The swingboy movement, if one could call it that, had neither dues-paying members nor elected leaders, only devotees. While mostly a working-class phenomenon, since there were more of us blue-collar types than members of the upper class, the swingboy cult cut across economic and social classes and included youths from every walk of life. Not unlike the American punkers of the eighties, German swingboys were acting out an adolescent need to rebel against conformity, in our case against Nazi regimentation. Like the punkers, we had neither a political creed nor a political agenda. But unlike the grungy-looking punkers, we were exaggeratedly neat and dressed like men-about-town. Our unstated aims were to express our antiestablishment mind-set, short of getting into serious trouble with the Gestapo; to listen whenever possible to jazz, which we had adopted as our favorite music because it was banned by the Nazis as *Negermusik;* to impress the girls with our macho and sophistication; and last—but by no means least—to get laid. In my particular case, this last objective was based more on wishful fantasy than on realistic expectations, since I considered my chances of finding a willing partner and the necessary privacy to achieve my goal as absolutely nil.

Swingboys went to great lengths to become the direct antithesis of Nazi youths. This meant wearing our hair long and with sideburns in contrast to the short, military-style haircuts and clean-cut look prescribed by the Hitler

Youth leadership. Unfortunately, thanks to my African ancestors, my hair refused to cooperate. Only after continued "conditioning" with gobs of pomade did it reluctantly submit to the prescribed over-the-collar swingboy style. When it came to growing sideburns, I fared even worse. No matter how often I shaved in front of my ears to encourage hair to grow, the area remained as hairless as a baby's butt. This obvious shortcoming, however, was amply offset by my precocious, much-envied ability to grow a mustache. While a bit on the sparse side, it could nevertheless be seen with the naked eye. Thus, I was never tempted to consider the ultimate "remedy" for upper-lip nudity. The procedure, which was highly recommended by our journey-men, consisted of treating the area under the nose with a series of nightly applications of dog feces. Many of my peers were as skeptical as I about the remedy's effectiveness, but I knew for a fact that some who were ridiculing the procedure publicly were using it privately—just in case it might work. To them, looking authentically swingboy was worth a little inconvenience.

Our well-established swingboy trademark was a dandylike facade that belied the fact that most of us were rough-and-ready guys who were as handy with a wrench and a hammer as we were with our fists. As a total putdown of the "wholesome," outdoors lifestyle advocated by the Hitler Youth lead-ership, we chose as our main role model and idol an ever-so-suave musical film star by the name of Johannes Heesters, a smooth lady-killer who, with his pale complexion and carefully coiffed long black hair, epitomized the indoor type. Like the debonair, Dutch-born Heesters, we wore knee-length double-breasted jackets, wide-bottom pants that nearly covered our shoes, starched shirt collars, waist-fitting navy blue overcoats, matching homburg hats, and—as a touch of ultimate elegance—white silk scarfs. The thought that we pimple-faced, fuzz-cheeked adolescents didn't look like Heesters but like Heesters's caricatures never entered our minds.

Since dance band musicians were high on the swingboy prestige scale, second only to movie stars, I decided to give my image and ego a much-needed boost by taking a second stab at a musical instrument, after my abortive brush with the violin. One day, I noticed a gleaming silver trumpet in the window of a downtown music shop, and it was love at first sight. Within hours, I returned to the store with the necessary cash from my savings and the instrument changed owners. Shopping around for a trumpet teacher, I settled on a conservatory that offered trumpet lessons on hourly terms I could afford. Unlike my halfhearted attempt at becoming a violinist, I threw myself body and soul into mastering the complexities of the trumpet. But no matter how hard I tried, I failed to develop a satisfactory embouchure. After carefully inspecting my trumpet and finding it in good order, my trumpet teacher decided that the fault must lie with my lips. "I think your lips are too full for playing the trumpet," he ventured, then showed off his Aryan lips, which, while playing, he would compress into a razor-thin vertical slit. "Perhaps you should switch to another wind instrument, like the clarinet, which requires a different embouchure where lip size is of no consequence," he suggested.

When I pointed out that world-famous jazz trumpeter Louis Armstrong was not exactly noted for thin lips, he argued that what came out of Satchmo's horn wasn't exactly music either. On that sour note, I terminated my trumpet lessons at the Vermeeren Conservatory, unshaken in my belief that if Satchmo's lips weren't too big to play trumpet, neither were mine.

Rather than give up my dream of learning to play the trumpet, I decided to teach myself as best I could. To the annoyance of our neighbors who were my captive audience, I never got tired of practicing. The result of my efforts didn't turn me into a budding Louis Armstrong, but my playing improved to a point where some of the fellows in the neighborhood told me that I sounded real good.

The hub of swingboy activity in my neighborhood was Café König, an expansive nightclub that featured a lively combo consisting of a tenor saxophonist, a pianist, a drummer, and a bassman, each of them a swingboy in his own right. Despite the fact that alcohol-free "beer" was the only beverage served, the joint was packed and jumping seven nights a week. "Jumping," however, did not include dancing. By a recent order of the government, public dancing had been suspended. Dance prohibition was aimed at curbing the opportunities for hanky-panky between frontline soldiers' lonely wives and prowling civilian and military males on the home front. The German military high command had deemed such liaisons a threat to the morale of the fighting men. From what I observed, I had reason to believe that the ban on dancing did nothing to stem the tide of married women finding romance in the arms of men they weren't married to.

Getting in on the Café König action as a fifteen-year-old was easier said than done. Youths under the age of eighteen were barred from nightclubs by law, and violators, if caught, could count on stiff punishment. Since I and some of my buddies had no intention of waiting three years for our turn, we threw caution to the wind and became regular crashers. Each time we visited our hangout, we faced an element of danger and suspense. To get inside, we not only had to get past a sign that stated YOUTHS UNDER 18 NOT ALLOWED, but more important, past the chief enforcer of that policy, Herr Wilhelm König, the owner of the joint. König was a Nazi Party member in good standing with a swastika button in his lapel to prove it. A short but enormous ex-wrestler who bore an uncanny resemblance to his boxer dog, which never left his side, König doubled as greeter and bouncer, depending on which of his talents was needed at any given time. Having once seen him charge like a tank into a dozen or so unruly patrons while single-handedly breaking up a brawl, I was convinced that he was not a man to be trifled with. But although he regularly turned back dozens of boys and girls after checking their IDs, he never stopped me once or gave me a hard time. He also turned deaf whenever the band got carried away and, at the urging of the crowd, squeezed a few forbidden jazz tunes into their normal repertoire of foxtrots. Getting caught by the wrong person or persons in the act of playing jazz could get band members arrested, fined, suspended, or—in the case of incorrigible recidivists—sent to the Russian front.

Part of the excitement of being a swingboy was the harassment by the Hitler Youth that came with the territory. Rarely did a week go by without a Hitler Youth *Streife* (patrol), consisting of from ten to twenty uniformed young men, showing up at our popular hangout. They would quietly block the exits, then fan out and systematically go from table to table in order to check—of all things—the length of the male patrons' hair. Swingboys with the longest hair were ordered outside and marched under guard to a facility where several barbers stood ready to give them the clipping of their lives. Since there was an implied correlation between long hair and anti-Nazi attitude, those who had their locks forcibly sheared "wore" their baldness like a badge of courage. They were regarded by us as the martyrs of the movement, young men who had paid the ultimate price for their conviction.

The closest I ever came to getting my compulsory haircut was when I was ordered outside by a junior member of a patrol. Happy to have finally been chosen for this distinction, I stuck out my chest and prepared to leave the club. But before I had reached the door, the leader of the patrol intervened. "You may wear your hair as long as you like, *Kamerad,*" he said, in an exaggeratedly polite tone. "We really don't care what you do with your hair." When I returned to my table under the humiliating stares of the entire club, I realized that the spirit of Heinrich Wriede that had made my life miserable during my school years was still very much alive.

Although the swingboy fad in Hamburg was for the most part harmless and more a nuisance than a threat to the security of the Nazi state, the Gestapo was not amused by the ubiquitous dandylike youths. Toward the end of the war, it reportedly arrested some four hundred of the city's swingboys and sent about seventy to concentration camps.

REINGRUBER

Since changing employment was all but impossible during the war, we were surprised when one day a new machinist journeyman by the name of Reingruber showed up at our plant. All we learned about this white-haired toothpick of a guy in his mid-fifties was that he was from Bavaria and, like most Bavarians, a Catholic. In predominantly Protestant Hamburg, that combination made him a member of the much-maligned minority referred to as *Saubayern* (Sow-Bavarians), a "compliment" the Bavarians returned by calling all non-Bavarians *Saupreussen* (Sow-Prussians).

I couldn't have cared less about Reingruber's church affiliation and geographic origins, and never participated in the contemptuous scuttlebutt that abounded behind his back. As far as I was concerned, Reingruber was an all-right guy, especially since he went out of his way to befriend me. But Hannes Mauer, one of the journeymen who had become a close buddy of mine, kept warning me. "Watch your steps, boy," he cautioned me. "I don't know what it is, but there's something about this Reingruber fellow that isn't quite right."

None of Mauer's warnings made sense to me, since Reingruber had never said or done anything I considered suspicious. I therefore was not displeased when Reingruber informed me one day that he and I had been assigned to air-raid watch together. Throughout the war, all plant employees were re-

quired periodically to spend a night at the plant on air-raid watch duty. In
the event of an incendiary-bomb fire, we were expected to attack the blaze
with fire extinguishers and thereby save the plant.

It was in the autumn of 1942. Air attacks on Hamburg were still a rel-
atively rare occurrence, so Reingruber and I could reasonably expect an
eventless night. Before bedding down on cots, we killed time reading and
listening to front-line radio reports from the Führer's headquarters. Things
were still going pretty much according to Hitler's plans. Poland, France,
Belgium, and Holland had fallen. German troops were deep inside the Soviet
Union in the suburbs of Stalingrad. British naval forces had been badly
mauled in an attack on Tobruk in North Africa, while the Japanese were
beating the hell out of the Americans in the Pacific.

In spite of all the "good news," Reingruber was pessimistic. Referring to
the day's newspaper headlines that announced another Japanese victory at
sea, Reingruber informed me that the Japanese were now unstoppable.

"Don't think that they'll be satisfied with being the rulers in Asia," he
lectured me. "As soon as this war is over, the Japanese will send a special
hit squad to Berlin and assassinate Hitler. After that, they will take over the
entire world. In any event, whether they'll be beaten by the Allies or by the
Japanese, the Nazis will soon be through."

Although Reingruber's scenario of the war's outcome seemed a bit far-
fetched to me, who was I to argue with as mature a journeyman as the
Bavarian? But remembering Hannes Mauer's warning about that "funny
feeling" he had about Reingruber, I decided against adding my two cents'
worth and intentionally withheld whatever opinions I had on the matter.

Having thus run out of things to discuss, we turned off the lights and
went to sleep. The next morning, after a siren-free, eventless night, we got
up and went back to work.

I had all but forgotten about Reingruber's dire predictions regarding the
outcome of the war when a secretary summoned me to the plant manager's
office. There, my memory received a most unwelcome, jolting assist. Already
assembled were the plant manager, Herr Habicht; Meister Neumann; and,
inexplicably, my fellow air-raid guard, Reingruber. All three looked at me
with grave expressions that together signaled bad news. To me, the whole
thing smacked of a major ass-chewing in the making, but I couldn't figure

out for what. Least of all could I explain to myself what Reingruber had to do with all this.

"Herr Reingruber here tells us," said Herr Habicht, coming right to the point, "that you made some treasonous remarks last night. Specifically, you told him that it was only a matter of time until Germany would lose the war. You do realize the seriousness of such talk, don't you?"

I was stunned, unable to speak. For a moment my vision blurred from anger and fear—anger at Reingruber, who stood there fixing me with an inscrutable smirk, and fear because of the dangerous predicament into which his bald-faced lie had put me. I had often heard that making "treasonous remarks," like treason itself, was punishable by death. At the thought of execution, my knees began to shake and I felt like throwing up. I realized that I had been set up, that I had been shamefully betrayed by a man who had given me the impression that he liked me. But why? Why did Reingruber hate me so much that he wanted to destroy me? What had I ever done to him? These and similar questions raced through my head, but no answer emerged.

"Well, what do you have to say for yourself?" The voice of Herr Habicht yanked me back into the nightmarish reality.

"It's not true," I stammered. "It's all a lie. He's the one who said it, not I." Fully aware how unconvincing my voice sounded, I looked helplessly from Habicht to Meister Neumann, and then, with unconcealed contempt, at Reingruber, who was still regarding me with that inscrutable smirk.

I felt a growing urge to hit him in his face, to hit him and hit him and hit him until his face was nothing but an unrecognizable bloody mess. I had to force myself not to look at that insolent smirk, because I felt that the urge to destroy Reingruber right then and there was becoming stronger than my ability to control myself.

"You may go back to the shop now, Herr Reingruber." Herr Habicht, seemingly sensing what went on in my mind, dismissed the journeyman.

After Reingruber had closed the door behind him, Herr Habicht resumed the conversation in what seemed a somewhat less unfriendly tone.

"I don't know who is lying," he said. "It is obvious that somebody here isn't telling the truth. I don't have to tell you, my boy, that this kind of talk can get you into the most serious trouble.

"We have always been pleased with your performance here as an apprentice," he continued. Therefore, we would really hate to see anything bad happen to you. For that reason, we shall refrain from referring this matter to the authorities for further investigation."

There was no doubt in my mind what he meant by "authorities."

"You do realize that if Germany were to lose the war," he continued, "all of us would be finished—you, I, everybody. You do realize that, don't you?"

"Yes," I stammered, while trying unsuccessfully to impart a ring of sincerity to my quivering voice.

The truth, which I could not admit, was that I had never believed the widely accepted Goebbels's propaganda that all Germans would be liquidated, tortured, raped, imprisoned, or enslaved should the Allies win the war.

On the advice of Herr Habicht and Herr Neumann, I avoided Reingruber like the plague, but I could not help staring at him with all the hate I felt for him whenever our paths crossed. When I told Hannes Mauer about what had happened, he felt vindicated in his initial judgment of the Bavarian, but even he was unable to come up with a plausible explanation for Reingruber's motive to denounce me after initially pretending to be my friend.

Less than a year after this memorable interlude, in the July 1943 raids that destroyed most of the city, the plant was leveled. I and other Lindner A.G. workers who survived the raids moved to other cities and other jobs. Although I had every intention to get to the bottom of Reingruber's treachery and, if possible, to even the score after the war, I never got the chance. No matter how hard I looked for him, I never saw or heard of Reingruber again.

GRETCHEN

In spite of a few rather promising contacts with members of the opposite sex during my early childhood years, my relations with young women grew increasingly tenuous as I got older. By the time I reached the age of fourteen, my contact with girls had largely fizzled and been replaced by wishful thinking and secret fantasies. The event that set the stage for this frustrating state of affairs occurred four years earlier. At that time, one of my teachers, Herr Dutke, told the class that non-Aryans, "like your classmate Hans-Jürgen," were prohibited by the Nuremberg racial laws from marrying or associating with German women. The purpose for the prohibition, Dutke explained with ill-concealed relish, was to prevent *Rassenschande,* the most cardinal of cardinal sins under the Nazi regime, by which superior Aryan blood was diluted with inferior non-Aryan blood. Such dilution, he elaborated, if allowed, would ultimately lead to the destruction of the German people. Accordingly, *Rassenschande* was considered worse than murder.

At the time, I was much more upset about having again been used as the class's resident "contemptible non-Aryan," than over the news that I wasn't allowed to marry German women. At age ten, getting married did not rank high on my list of priorities. But as I reached adolescence and girls began to become increasingly important in my thinking, Dutke's words started to take on a new, frightening meaning.

Yet my fear of running afoul of the law was only part of the problem that kept me from enjoying a normal relationship with girls. As far as the opposite sex was concerned, I had long considered myself an ugly duckling. The occasional *"I gittigit,"* the German expression of extreme disgust, with which some girls reacted to my looks, did not exactly bolster my self-esteem. Even if there hadn't been laws that prohibited *Rassenschande,* what girl in her right mind, I reasoned, would want someone like me? Thoroughly convinced that no girl could possibly be interested in me except, perhaps, in a platonic way, I never let on when I liked a girl, no matter how much I yearned for her. In this way, I hoped to spare myself the humiliation of what I believed would be certain rejection. Unlike most of my pals, who were beginning to pair off with the girls in the neighborhood, I had no girlfriend and seemingly no prospect of ever having one.

All that was to change with the arrival of a tall, slender, and exceedingly haughty girl my age. Her name was Gretchen Jahn. The moment I saw her, as she, her younger brother, and their mother moved into an apartment a few houses up the street, I was smitten. But getting to know her better was more than I dared to hope.

The Jahns, I learned later through the neighborhood grapevine, had lived in a better part of Hamburg, but following the breakup of Frau Jahn's marriage to a well-off police official, were forced to settle for a less affluent lifestyle. That did not keep Frau Jahn from acting quite superior. On the contrary, she kept her contact with neighbors to an absolute minimum and apparently encouraged her children to do the same. In that she was quite successful. Neither Gretchen nor her brother paid any attention to the kids on the block, and they in turn repaid the Jahns in the same coin. Most of my buddies hated the mere sight of Gretchen, whom they considered stuck up and much too skinny, and thus utterly lacking in sex appeal. That suited me just fine, since competition, I felt, would have made my already hopeless situation only more so. As far as her looks and demeanor were concerned, I felt she was the most elegant and aristocratic creature I'd ever laid eyes on. Next to her, I felt, the other girls on the block looked like plump peasants. But as always, I kept my real feelings to myself.

By a fortuitous coincidence, the center of social activities for the boys on my street was a broad concrete stoop directly below the Jahns' second-floor apartment. There, to the chagrin of the building's occupants, we congregated regularly and noisily in groups ranging from five to fifteen or more. I frequently caught precious glimpses of Gretchen at the window, a fact that made me considerably more reticent in manner and speech than my freewheeling peers.

I would have remained Gretchen's secret admirer till the end of time had it not been for another coincidence. Walking home one fall afternoon, I couldn't believe my eyes when just as I was about to pass our greengrocer's store, I saw Gretchen leaving with a huge net filled with potatoes. The load was obviously more than she could easily handle, but before I had been able to make up my mind as to whether or not to offer her my assistance, she asked me if I would be kind enough to help. Would I?

When I started to introduce myself while relieving her of her burden, she said, "I already know your name; it's Hans-Jürgen."

"How did you know?" I asked.

"I know a lot about you," she replied, then proceeded to tell me what school I went to and that my father lived in Africa, that my mother and I lived on the third floor of Stückenstrasse 3, that I was an amateur boxer, and on and on. She certainly had done her homework.

To her amazement, and amusement, I then turned the tables on her by telling her all I knew about her, that her name was Gretchen and her brother's name Ingmar, that her father was a big shot in the police, and that, before they moved to Barmbek, they used to live in Uhlenhorst, where she and her brother had attended the *gymnasium* (high school).

Within minutes we had arrived at her house where, fortunately, the stoop was deserted, sparing us the inevitable wisecracks from my pals.

"Can you help me carry those stupid potatoes upstairs?" she asked. Again I was only too happy to oblige. When we reached her apartment and I prepared to beat a hasty retreat, she told me to wait. "I want you to meet my mother."

From what I had heard about Frau Jahn, I was none too eager to make her personal acquaintance. But it was already too late for me to take a rain check, because Gretchen had knocked and Frau Jahn had opened the door.

"Thanks, Hans-Jürgen, for helping Gretchen with the potatoes," she said with a friendly smile, without waiting for her daughter to introduce us. Apparently, she, too, had heard about me before. A stately woman with visible traces of former beauty, she was much nicer than I had imagined her.

"It's nothing, Frau Jahn," I replied. When she had disappeared inside the apartment and I prepared to leave, Gretchen thanked me for being so chivalrous, then—catching me totally by surprise—asked me what my plans were for the rest of the evening. I really hadn't any plans, and when I told her so, she asked me whether I wanted to go for a walk with her "around seven." Without giving it a moment's thought, I said fine and we agreed to meet in front of the church two blocks from our street.

I arrived almost half an hour early, and with every elapsing minute I grew more apprehensive. "Panicky" is actually a better word. What was I going to talk about? Why did she want to be with me in the first place? I knew enough about the Nazis' preoccupation with *Rassenschande* to realize that our rendezvous, however innocent, would be severely disapproved of. What if people saw us together and didn't like what they saw? What were we letting ourselves in for? I suddenly realized how complicated my life was becoming and how woefully unprepared I was to cope with it.

Although it was getting dark, I could clearly see Gretchen's lithe figure approaching. The moment she reached me, the bells in the clock tower above tolled, first four, then seven times. It seemed like a fitting beginning of the first date in my young life.

Somehow, the panic vanished as she came into sight, and before long, we were merrily chatting about anything that popped into our minds—the recent German invasion of Poland, our interests, our likes and dislikes, our teachers, and the people in the neighborhood. She told me that she didn't care for the boys in my crowd because they acted crude and uncultured. I, on the other hand, was different, she insisted, which is why she became attracted to me. I didn't see where, except for my obvious racial traits, I was all that different. I certainly did not consider myself cultured and refined, but she got no argument from me.

From the first moment of our meeting it was quite obvious to us that our interest in each other was everything but platonic, although neither Gretchen nor I said so or even broached the subject of romance. We didn't have to. I didn't have the slightest idea what she saw in me—by most prevailing standards a freak. But who was I to argue with her taste? The important thing was we both could feel the chemistry. As far as my own emotions were concerned, I felt like an entire chemical plant that was ready to explode. At the same time, there was nothing overtly sexual about our feelings. We were innocent in the true sense of the word—two young people who, without knowing why, were attracted to each other, trusted each other, and needed each other.

When I told her about my concerns about being seen in public with her, she surprised me by telling me that she had thought about it and knew we were taking chances, but that she was willing to take the risk. "We just have to be careful," she said, resigned to the problems that were facing us. I still wasn't convinced. The last thing I wanted was to get her into trouble. "What about your mother?" I asked. "What does she think about our meeting like this?"

"My mother doesn't mind. She likes you. She's been watching you for some time and thinks you are a gentleman. She'd rather see me go with you than with any of the other boys in the street."

She conceded that her father, the police official, was a different matter altogether, but she said that he had been transferred to another city and therefore we didn't have to worry about him. When I asked her whether she missed her father, she bluntly told me, "No." Then she confided that her father had been physically abusive to her and her mother and that, as a result, she and her mother had broken off all contact with him. She said he had made her join the BDM (*Bund Deutscher Mädel,* the League of German Girls), but that after her parents separated, she no longer went to BDM meetings. As a member of the police and SS, he even tried to bolster his standing by trying to interest her in participating in the *Lebensborn* (Fountain of Life) program, which, she explained, was a pet project of SS *Reichsführer* Heinrich Himmler aimed at producing superior Aryan offspring through selective breeding of "women of good blood" with SS men.

It was mainly her father's oppressive behavior that led her to question his National Socialist beliefs and, in the process, become a real rebel and anti-Nazi. At the moment, she said, her biggest frustration was with the type of education she received in school, which, she insisted, treated girls like prospective "breeding cows" by preparing them exclusively for motherhood and wifely duties instead of future careers. Unlike boys, who were encouraged to aspire to a wide variety of interesting careers, she said, girls were taught nothing but domestic skills such as cooking, knitting, and how to care for babies, in addition to "racial hygiene," folk studies, and gymnastics. It wasn't until Gretchen called my attention to it and pointed out the unfairness of it all that I considered the unequal treatment of girls as something other than a normal and proper fact of life. It had been drummed into our heads by our teachers that, in the Führer's National Socialist state, men ran the show with women as their helpmates.

We had hardly noticed the passing of time as we chatted and walked through the dark streets until we passed the church again and the bells tolled nine. Throughout the evening, we had not touched once. Emboldened by the blackout that mercifully cloaked our secret meeting from public scrutiny, I reached for her hand, squeezed it gently, and held it until we had arrived at her house. When we said good night, we did so without making plans to meet again, but we both knew that it would be soon.

Gradually, our secret relationship blossomed and our meetings after dark increased both in frequency and intensity. For a while, I didn't know what to do with my nonplatonic feelings for Gretchen and how to express the romantic urges inside, until one evening she broke the ice. I was just about to say goodbye in front of her house, as I had done many times before, when, without warning, she put her arms around me, held me tightly, and kissed me squarely on the mouth. From that moment, our relationship was never the same. Within a few additional meetings (mostly on park benches), and after extensive practice in kissing and fondling, Gretchen and I were transformed from shy and hapless novices into the most passionate secret lovers since a star-crossed couple met clandestinely on a balcony in Renaissance Verona, Italy. Gretchen even introduced me to kissing French-style, a skill she insisted she had picked up by reading about it in a book. At first I found the very idea utterly repulsive. However, after several intense practice sessions with Gretchen, I became an enthusiastic practitioner of this weird but ever so delightful form of socializing. But all our passion notwithstanding, Gretchen had laid down an ironclad rule that, as a boxer, I had been taught to respect and obey: no action below the belt. It was a tough rule for both of us, but Gretchen was determined to resist temptation and remain a virgin for years to come.

It was inevitable that sooner or later the neighborhood would get wise to the fact that something was going on between Gretchen and me. But except for some teasing from the fellows about my making out with a "stuck-up sack of bones," and a girl's warning to Gretchen that she'd "wind up with a checkered or plaid baby one day," there were no serious repercussions. In spite of that, we never considered ourselves out of the woods, and continued making our meetings as inconspicuous as possible. When we ventured outside our immediate neighborhood, to movies, carnivals, or on daytime outings, I always made sure to bring a buddy along as decoy. I reasoned that a threesome appeared like a more ambiguous, therefore less suspicious, relationship than a twosome. To make the deception work, I would always position myself in such a way as to lead the uninitiated observer to believe that I, not the decoy, was our trio's "fifth wheel."

It wasn't long before it became obvious to me that I had lucked out with Gretchen in a bigger way than I had realized. I had always liked the way she looked, but within a few months after we became an "item," she started to fill out in all the right places until she had turned into a curvaceous beauty. All of a sudden, the fellows were not only noticing her but hitting on her. But the groundwork I had laid apparently paid off. Gretchen continued to look at the other boys as *primitive Proleten,"* and had eyes only for me. Even when girls of our age group started to date older fellows, Gretchen, for some strange reason, remained loyal to me. Her undisguised affection for me did much to restore my self-esteem, which had been at an all-time low after years of racial taunts, ridicule, and hostility. But my newfound romantic bliss was soon to receive a devastating blow.

I had just taken Gretchen home after one of our long nightly walks through the dark streets of Barmbek when my eyes were temporarily blinded by the piercing beam of a flashlight. *"Sicherheits Dienst* (Security Service)!" a man's voice behind the flashlight snarled. The words sent shudders of unmitigated terror down my spine, since I was only too familiar with the reputation of the SD as the most ruthless, and most feared, intelligence branch of the SS.

"What are you doing walking the streets at night during blackout?" a man in a black leather coat and wide-brim hat demanded to know after flashing an ID that I was unable to read.

"I was just taking a walk," I answered feebly. "I live on this street, just a block away."

Apparently not satisfied with my reply, the man ordered me to accompany him to the nearest police precinct. For a moment I considered running away and disappearing into the night, but thought better of it. Where could I go? And even if I escaped, how long could I elude my captor once he had given the police a physical description of me?

When we arrived at the police precinct, the man identified himself to the officer on duty, then grabbed my arm and pushed me toward the officer's desk. "I caught this man loitering a few blocks from here," the SD man reported. "It looked to me as if he was on the prowl for defenseless women or looking for an opportunity to steal."

Before the policeman had a chance to respond, the SD man asked, "Have you ever seen this man before? He claims to live somewhere around here."

The police officer took a long look at me, then shook his head. "No, I can't say that I have," he replied, "but I've been in this precinct only a short while. Let me ask one of my colleagues who has been here a bit longer than I." Just then, one of the veteran police officers whom I had known practically all my life walked by. When the desk officer asked him whether he knew me, he said that he didn't know me by name but that he had seen me around the precinct since I was a little boy. "What is he supposed to have done?" he asked.

The SD man repeated his accusation, but this time with less conviction.

"You've got the wrong man," the police officer asserted. "This young man is an apprentice at Lindner A. G., where he works much too hard to have enough energy left to prowl the streets at night looking for trouble. I happen to know that because the son of one of my colleagues apprentices with him."

"Well, in that case, I shall consider this matter closed," the SD man said. "But in these times, one can never be too careful."

Without offering an apology to me, he gave the Hitler salute and left.

I could have hugged the policeman for coming to my rescue, and thanked the coincidences that caused him to know my apprentice buddy and to show up just in the nick of time.

But the incident also drove home the point that Gretchen and I had been walking on thin ice. I was convinced that had the SD man caught us together, both of us would have been in for a rough time. I decided then and there that our regular nightly meetings would have to come to an immediate halt, no matter how painful our forced separation would prove to be.

When I told Gretchen the following day what had happened to me, and explained to her that we couldn't go on meeting the way we had without courting disaster, she said she understood, but that she had no intention of giving up on our relationship. "We just have to be patient and wait for things to change," she suggested without much conviction in her voice.

Realizing that before things could change in our favor, Germany would have to lose the war and the Nazi government would have to be driven from power, we knew that our hopes and dreams rested on an extremely long shot.

ON THE HOME FRONT

As the war went on and our visits to the shelter became more frequent, the dank and cold basement below the old waffle factory assumed an increasingly important role in our lives. It literally became our home away from home, a veritable social center where neighbors who had only known one another by sight, or not at all, became friends, and where daily concerns about the children, the men at the front, and other war-related problems were shared. While my mother and most adults bemoaned the nightly shelter visits as a frightening ordeal, I looked forward to them because they provided Gretchen and me with the only opportunity to enjoy some sort of a relationship while meeting surreptitiously in one of the shelter's two pitch-black *Gasschleusen* (gas lock chambers).

When I wasn't with Gretchen, I would shoot the breeze with my new pal Karl-Heinz Bülow, a dark-haired fellow about my age who had a few months earlier moved with his parents a few houses down the street from where I lived. Karl-Heinz was a telephone lineman apprentice employed by the *Reichspost* (post office). His father, a projectionist at the Europa Palast cinema, was among the first men in the neighborhood drafted by the army. Within a few months of his arrival, Karl-Heinz had acquired a reputation as one of the biggest skirt chasers on the block and, according to persistent rumors that he was happy to confirm to me, he had been looking after the needs of a front-line soldier's wife until she gave him the boot when she caught him trying to seduce her best friend. Since I was still "innocent," so to speak, I couldn't help but be impressed with Karl-Heinz's precociousness. That's why, when he suggested that we should get together sometime, I eagerly agreed. Soon we became inseparable, as Karl-Heinz kept me entertained with the freewheeling daring with which he pursued women in particular and life in general. Like many teenagers at the time, he was staunchly anti-Nazi but fanatically partial to military uniforms, which, he insisted, women found irresistible.

The best vantage point from which to observe the validity of his hypothesis was our air-raid shelter on weekends before dancing was outlawed. In addition to us regulars, the shelter would be packed with uniformed members of the *Wehrmacht* and their dates. They were the patrons of Café Classen, a nearby club, whose dance revels had been interrupted by the air-raid alert. No sooner had they entered the shelter than the café's combo would set up and the partying would start all over again. Some of the couples would foxtrot, while others would repair to the darkest corners of the shelter where, to the impotent indignation of the older folks and the envy of Karl-Heinz and me, they would engage in the most explicit kind of behavior short of sexual intercourse. While watching as the young women literally threw themselves at the men in dashing uniforms, we concluded that the fringe benefits of joining the military were well worth it.

With not much else to look forward to than working seemingly endless shifts and spending the nights in a dank air-raid shelter, we were constantly seeking action—any action—to keep boredom at bay. It wasn't long before Karl-Heinz came up with an idea. Showing me a bunch of keys he had found among his father's things, he explained that they were the keys to the Europa Palast and suggested that if I had the guts, he would treat me to my very own private performance.

After considerable misgivings and, as usual, in disregard of my better judgment, I reluctantly agreed to come along, mainly because I didn't want to admit to Karl-Heinz that I lacked the courage. In keeping with his plan, we waited until the movie personnel had locked up and left shortly after the last show, at about 10 P.M. We then sneaked up a fire escape that led to the projection booth and Karl-Heinz let us in, after trying out several of the keys. After making sure that my earphones were properly adjusted and that I was comfortably seated in front of one of the large square peepholes that offered a view of the screen on the opposite side of the theater, he inserted a reel into one of several huge projectors and, flipping an assortment of switches, started the film rolling as if he had done nothing else in his life. At the movie's mid-point, Karl-Heinz climaxed his performance by expertly blending in a second reel on another projector.

I was impressed but too scared to appreciate his efforts or the film, which I had difficulty enjoying because of a growing sense of foreboding. As a result, the film's title and content have totally slipped my mind. When the movie was over, Karl-Heinz calmly returned everything to its proper place and, after turning off the lights and locking the door, we left as if nothing had happened.

It was not until I was safely lying in my bed and reflecting on our adventure that the full impact of what I had just done struck my consciousness. No matter how innocent and innocuous our intent, the fact remained that I had illegally entered a place of business while taking advantage of the blackout. In wartime Nazi Germany that was a capital offense.

Mulling over the possible consequences of our misdeed—not the least of which would have been my mother's monumental disappointment in me—I broke out in cold sweat and vowed never to get involved in a stupid thing like that again. My resolve would be tested soon enough.

The following evening after returning from work, Karl-Heinz asked me whether I'd be interested in another "private performance." I couldn't believe my ears. We had just pulled off one of the most daring capers in the annals of juvenile stupidity, hardly a day had passed, and my pal was hankering for more.

"I'm sorry," I told him, "but I've already made other plans."

But as far as my impulsive friend was concerned, that didn't fly.

"I know what's the matter with you; you're chicken!" he groused, and walked away in a huff.

I knew he was right, but I hadn't the slightest intention of convincing him otherwise. For once I had acted smart, as I was soon to find out.

That same night, my mother and I were awakened by a commotion across the street. As we looked out of the window, we saw several policemen with flashlights on the same fire escape I had climbed only twenty-four hours earlier. It was too dark for us to make out any details, but I had a good idea of what was going on; Karl-Heinz had been back at his little game and this time he had gotten caught.

My suspicion was confirmed the next day by Karl-Heinz himself. He told me that after I had turned him down, he asked another pal to come along, and that they were surprised by police who arrested them and locked them up for the night. Luckily, he said, the theater's owner, a kind old lady, who was summoned in the morning, recognized him as the son of one of her drafted employees and put in a good word for them. The result, he said, was that charges of criminal trespassing were dropped.

I was happy for Karl-Heinz, but I was not so sure that had I been the one who got caught in the act, I would have been equally lucky and treated with leniency. I promised myself to watch my step more carefully than ever.

LAST TANGO IN HAMBURG

Since dancing was the name of the game as far as we swingboys were concerned, the government lashed back by outlawing swing dancing in all public places. Because most young people in Germany didn't have the foggiest idea what was meant by swing dancing other than that it entailed "wild, *Neger*-like, sexually explicit contortions and gyrations," the ban was largely academic. But soon that was to change when dancing of any kind was prohibited. There was, however, a legal way of getting around the rigidly enforced prohibition. Since the *Verbot* did not include dance lessons, many swingboys and -girls signed up for them whether they knew how to dance or not. After taking one beginner's course, which entailed formal instruction, "advanced students" could sign up for a course without lessons that merely provided an opportunity to practice what they had learned—in other words, an opportunity to dance to their hearts' content.

I knew about this loophole in the law and would have liked, like so many of my peers, to take advantage of it, but I didn't dare, since I was more than certain that I'd be turned down. I could already hear the sneers if I tried to enroll. "You want to dance with our pure-blooded, blond and blue-eyed Aryan women? You must be mad!"

I convinced myself that I'd be laughed out of the place the way I had been laughed out of other places before, and decided to spare myself the humiliation—until one day my boxing buddy Hans Vollmer suggested that we sign up for dancing lessons. Without giving him my reason, I told him that I wasn't interested but agreed to come along to take a look at the place.

The studio we went to was the Arthur Lucas *Tanzschule,* just a few blocks from my home. When we entered the studio office, a few swingboys and -girls were waiting their turn to register. The bald man with the rimless glasses seated behind the desk, we learned, was Herr Lucas, the dance teacher and studio proprietor. When it was Hans's turn, I was about to step aside, but Herr Lucas invited both of us to take a seat in front of him and handed each of us a registration form. Here it comes, I thought while carefully perusing the form for some embarrassing trip-up questions, such as "Are you Aryan? If not, specify." But all that was asked was the name, age, address and whether the applicant wanted to take the beginner's or advanced course. After we returned the completed forms to Herr Lucas and paid a modest fee, he told us that we were duly enrolled students at the Arthur Lucas *Tanzschule.* There was nothing in Herr Lucas's demeanor that indicated to me that he considered my enrollment in his course as something out of the ordinary.

The beginner's course for which Hans and I had signed up was for three months of two-hour lessons each Sunday afternoon and Wednesday evening.

Our class, which was held in a huge hall, consisted of about two dozen young fellows and an equal number of girls ages eighteen to twenty-five. I had been prepared for some giggles from the females, but to my surprise, not one of them paid me any undue attention, thus relieving me of my greatest fear. If any of the fellows had acted uncouth toward me, I would have been prepared to respond in kind, but had a girl started ridiculing me, I would have been helpless.

Before starting his first class of instruction, Herr Lucas had us take seats on two facing rows of chairs, girls on one side and boys on the other, then lectured us on dance-floor etiquette. Most of his tips for proper gentlemanly comportment, with which he tried to impart a touch of class to us mostly blue-collar types, were pearls thrown before swine. They barely went into one ear before they had exited the other. We especially ignored, and frequently violated, behind Herr Lucas's back, his stern instruction as to where not to put our hands and what not to do with our knees and thighs while dancing. It seemed to us that Herr Lucas had entirely missed the point of what dancing was all about. Another of his cardinal rules of which we frequently ran afoul required that we walk, instead of stampede like a thundering herd of elephants, across the dance floor in order to ask the girls to dance. There was method behind our madness. It hadn't taken us hopeless male chauvinists very long to learn one important verity: those who arrive last must take what's left; and what's left invariably were the girls with the least sex appeal. Since class rules required the girls to accept male partners on a first-come-first-served basis, they did not enjoy the freedom of picking and choosing, or altogether avoiding an undesirable partner.

Herr Lucas, it turned out, was an excellent instructor and I caught on fast. Before I knew it, I had mastered the first dance on the lesson plan, the English waltz, and in quick succession became proficient in dancing the tango, the polka, and, finally, the foxtrot, which became my favorite. Being among the better dancers in the class kept me from being reduced to wallflower status whenever Herr Lucas announced "*Damenwahl* (Ladies' choice)!" It was years before I heard of the stereotypical notion that all blacks have rhythm and can dance. But my experience seemed to bear out the stereotype. Hans Vollmer, having not a single drop of African blood to call his own, had a considerably harder time than I making his feet move according to the beat of the music. It took near-superhuman effort on both Herr Lucas's and Hans's parts before he managed to get the hang of the most basic steps.

While some of us swingboys had heard that the jitterbug was the number-one dance craze in the States and were anxious to incorporate it in our own repertoires, we had never seen it danced because of the wartime ban on American films. Consequently, we used our imagination and put our own spin on the foxtrot in hopes of recreating what we thought was the jitterbug. The result was a bewildering hodgepodge of movements and steps that, as I realized years later while watching authentic jitterbugging, resembled the jitterbug about as much as the minuet did. But since we had no role models by which to judge our performance, we "jitterbugged" to our hearts' content behind Herr Lucas's back, and in the process proved beyond a shadow of doubt that ignorance is truly bliss.

One Sunday, just as Herr Lucas was demonstrating some new steps, the main door to the dance hall opened and in poured a contingent of about twenty Hitler Youths. After ordering to stop the recorded music, their leader took the floor and announced that there would be a brief haircut check. While his people checked the emergency exits and the men's washroom for would-be escapees, he and a subordinate marched slowly along our row of chairs. I wasn't particularly worried about flunking the haircut inspection. Instinctively I felt that this time far more was at stake.

Judging by previous run-ins with these uniformed zealots, I feared that they would challenge my very presence in a place that provided me, a non-Aryan, with physical contact with Aryan girls. I had gotten to know my enemies only too well. Not letting the HJ leader out of my sight as he moved closer and closer, I noticed that when I had come within the scope of his peripheral vision, he did a double-take, then zeroed in on me. "What do we have here?" he demanded, as if confronted by a rare species from the animal kingdom. "What in heaven's name are *you* doing here?"

At this point, the usually mild-mannered Herr Lucas stepped forward and demanded that whatever the HJ leader had to say, he should say it in the studio office next door. When the HJ leader complied and we three were alone, Herr Lucas produced several documents, which he handed to the brownshirt.

Identifying himself as a member of the NSDAP (Nazi Party) and of the *N.S. Kulturkammer* (Nazi Chamber of Culture), he told the HJ leader that he was a veteran of World War I, during which he had attained the rank of captain and was wounded and awarded the Iron Cross, first and second class, for valor. "I deeply resent having my competence questioned by your inferences that this young gentleman does not belong in my class," he bristled. "In case you don't know, this young man's father was an officer in General Lettow-Vorbeck's colonial forces in East Africa and served with highest distinction.

"I want you to know that you will hear about this when I get through talking with certain people who are very interested in learning about your kind of irresponsible and intrusive behavior."

Duly impressed and humbled by what he had just learned, the HJ leader apologized profusely to both Herr Lucas and me. *"Nichts für ungut* (No offense meant)," he repeated several times before clicking his heels and rendering the *Heil Hitler* salute. By the time we returned to the dance hall, some of the HJ had rounded up several swingboys they had targeted for free haircuts. "Let those comrades go," the leader countermanded his subordinates, then assembled his troop and beat a hasty retreat.

Following the incident with the Hitler Youth patrol, I looked at Herr Lucas with different eyes. Instead of the slightly comical figure I had seen before, a man who with his rimless glasses and pudgy face could have been Soviet Foreign Secretary Molotov's twin, I now saw a man who fearlessly stood up against racial intolerance. Except for a brief moment after the incident, when I thanked him for coming to my aid, we never discussed again what had happened on that Sunday afternoon. As a result, I never found out whether he had knowingly made up the story of my father's serving in General Lettow-Vorbeck's army or whether he had heard that story somewhere and believed it to be true. All I know is that the story and the way he presented it did the trick of keeping that obnoxious Nazi off my back. During subsequent months, when Hans Vollmer and I were enjoying advanced dancing courses, we never saw another Hitler Youth patrol.

A FAREWELL TO VIRGINITY

The fact that we were fellow sufferers forged a tight bond between us apprentices at Lindner A. G. While I was on very good terms with all of them, I was especially close to one, a lanky blond second-year *Stift* (tack), as apprentices were nicknamed, by the name of Walter Bauer. Walter lived on a small farm in a rural part of suburban Langenhorn, where his family raised chickens and pigs. With war food rations becoming smaller and smaller, he would often slip me a huge, homemade sandwich to ease my insatiable appetite. In turn, I would help him with some difficult task whenever his machinist skills left him in the lurch. The fact that he was a Hitler Youth member never seemed to hurt our friendship.

One day Walter arrived at work visibly upset. When I asked him what had happened, he swore me to secrecy, then confided in me that he had gotten himself into a pickle. He said that he and a friend from a neighboring farm had been literally caught with their pants down by a policeman as they were masturbating each other in the countryside. After taking them both to their respective homes, the cop told their embarrassed fathers that he could have their boys prosecuted under Germany's antihomosexual law, but that he would give them a break. He then lectured the fathers on what, according to prevailing conventional wisdom, he felt they should do to make "real men" out of their wayward boys and to prevent them from becoming permanently *schwul* (gay).

The upshot of all this, Walter explained, was that his father, after raising holy hell with him, ordered him never to get near the other boy again. Then, following the cop's advice, his father had given him ten marks with the instruction that the next time he felt his sap rising, so to speak, he should go to a *Puff* (bordello) and get himself squared away. Walter said that, as far as his sap level was concerned, he was way overdue for a squaring away and that his homosexual encounter happened merely because he didn't know any cooperative women, not because he was gay. Since he had never before been with a hooker or, for that matter, with any woman, he wondered whether I would mind coming along for moral support and, maybe, have my own sap level adjusted.

For a moment I wavered. As much as I had looked forward to the time when I would "become a man," I wondered whether I'd be up to the task, since I had had virtually no other sex education than that provided by the foul-mouthed bunch of journeymen. In addition, I felt slight pangs of guilt because of Gretchen, although she had told me that sex was definitely out until she was at least twenty-one and married. But my biggest worry was that I wasn't sure whether the Nazis' law against non-Aryans having sex with Aryans applied to hookers as well. After taking everything into consideration, I threw caution to the wind and agreed to come along, but only to take a look.

Of Hamburg's three well-known districts of ill repute at the time—Kalkhof, Herbertstrasse, and Winkelstrasse—Walter and I picked the latter. Kalkhof, in the city center near the elegant Jungfernstieg, had the reputation of having the best-looking hookers, but because their patronage consisted largely of well-heeled downtown businessmen, they also charged an arm and a leg. Herbertstrasse, in St. Pauli, catered largely to sailors. While it was more modestly priced, we decided that it was too far out of our way. Before setting out on our venture, Walter and I consulted some of the younger, more trustworthy journeymen at the plant. They were only too glad to fill us in on the finer points of brothel patronage and on what two beginners on a *Stift*'s budget could expect. Whatever you do, we were warned, don't ever leave your jacket containing your wallet in another room if you don't want your wallet lifted by one of the hooker's pals while you are "busy." We also learned that the going rate at Winkelstrasse was five marks for a quickie, which normally lasted from three to fifteen minutes, depending on how quickly a customer completed his business. We were also told not to let on that we were virgins lest we be charged an additional breaking-in fee.

Thus loaded with invaluable advice, Walter and I met on a Sunday afternoon at one of the two entrances to Winkelstrasse, a narrow, L-shaped alley flanked by old row houses. The two entrances at either end of the alley were designed to permit ready access without exposing the street to the general public's view. We cringed when we read a sign that plainly stated that the premises were off limits to youths under the age of eighteen. Since sixteen-year-old Walter was virtually under orders from his father to get himself a hooker, he wasn't too worried about breaking the law. Barely fifteen, I found it more difficult to rationalize since I had no such mandate from my mother.

"Let's just go in and take a look," Walter suggested when he noticed that I was on the verge of changing my mind. "What's wrong with that?"

At the time I hadn't heard of peer pressure, but it certainly worked with me. Without giving the sign another thought, I followed Walter into the forbidden zone. The place was bustling with men of all ages and descriptions, but mostly middle-aged, respectable-looking family men. Like window shoppers downtown, they were slowly walking up and down the alley and appraising the merchandise.

In the ground-floor display windows of each row house, seated women offered their wares. There were girl-next-door types in prim blouses and skirts; shapely vamps in clinging evening dresses and plunging necklines; slender hard-buns types in skimpy lingerie; overweight, over-the-hill matrons trying to recapture long-gone youth and beauty with makeup, and dim red lights; and chain-smoking peroxide blondes with hard faces. All were vying for the attention of the passing men, mostly by rapping on the window with a key or coin.

Although I had on me at least fifteen marks, which constituted more than two weeks' apprentice wages, I had not yet made up my mind whether to take the plunge into non-virginhood. When one of the younger women tried to summon us to her window with a particularly enthusiastic rap of her keys, Walter mistook her eagerness for a compliment and listened to what she had to say. "Do you want to come in and have a nice time?"

"How much?" asked my pal, in a voice that told me his sap had passed the dangerous "full" mark.

"Five marks," she replied.

Walter asked me to wait, then disappeared through the door she had opened for him.

When he returned about ten minutes later and I asked whether he had really done "it," he nodded. Except for his ear-to-ear grin, he looked no different to me. Somehow, I had always assumed that this rather important rite of passage in a man's life left a more noticeable mark.

"How did you make out?" I asked, fishing for details. He told me that "it" really wasn't as difficult as some people made it out to be and that once he got started, it all came to him naturally. In fact, he bragged, he did so well that the girl invited him to come back real soon.

Duly impressed, I decided right then and there to try my own luck, a resolve that Walter enthusiastically endorsed. Momentary scruples about being unfaithful to Gretchen quickly diminished as I reasoned that my relationship with Gretchen—at her own insistence—had nothing to do with sex, and that sex with a hooker had nothing to do with love.

Afraid of being seen walking into a brothel, especially by some Nazi who might object, and also because I was exceedingly bashful, I decided to delay my move until after it got dark. Walter and I agreed to kill time by doing some more window shopping. Learning that nearby was a special brothel for foreign workers that contained only foreign hookers and was off limits to Germans, we decided to take a look for curiosity's sake. Among the added "attractions" of the foreign prostitutes, someone informed us, was that they did not insist on the use of condoms like their German counterparts.

Undeterred by a sign that ordered German nationals to keep out, we mingled with the clientele made up of an assortment of non-German Europeans. It was immediately clear that the foreign women, who, like their customers, represented a cross-section of Nazi-occupied territories, were far less inhibited in their methods of attracting customers than their German colleagues. Instead of sitting behind windows and waiting for customers to make their move, the foreign hookers were aggressively recruiting in the yard in front of the four-story building in which they were housed. Some gave prospective customers a preview of things to come by lifting their skirts; others went even farther and grabbed men by their crotches in order to whet their sexual appetites.

When a frisky mademoiselle from France grabbed Walter in this manner and started to kiss him in the ear, he immediately caught his second wind and was ready to spend his remaining five marks. But before he could enter into the necessary negotiations with her, two plainclothesmen flashed IDs and ordered Teutonic-looking Walter to leave the area at once. Although I was sure they had seen me, the two officials ignored me, apparently thinking that I was a foreigner.

After I caught up with Walter, we returned to the German bordello, which now seemed almost wholesome by comparison. Since it had gotten dark, I felt less inhibited and intensified my search for a suitable partner with whom to consummate my transition into manhood. My choice fell on a pretty, short-skirted brunette whose ample bosom and voluptuous thighs seemed ideal for what I had in mind.

Noticing my interest, she responded with a rap on the window. When I told her that five marks was all I had, she swore that she was courting financial ruin by accepting welfare cases like me, but that she'd make an exception, "just this once." Seconds later, I was following her up what seemed to me one of the steepest stairs I had ever climbed. With each step I felt more like a condemned man on his way to the gallows. That feeling deepened when I looked up and noticed that my date's partially exposed behind was nearly twice as wide as it had appeared to me in the window. Having dealt only with sleek Gretchen, I felt thoroughly intimidated in the presence of so much woman.

When we reached the top of the stairs, my hostess opened the door to a tiny room, which, although cold weather was still months away, was stiflingly overheated by a small cast-iron oven in the corner. A sickening odor from a mixture of cheap perfume and burned rubber filled the room, most of which was taken up by a large, overstuffed bed.

Without making small talk of any kind, she held out her hand. "Aren't you forgetting something?" was all she said.

I couldn't think of anything I might have forgotten until I remembered that the inviolable rule of prostitutes, according to my journeymen mentors, was to collect their pay before they went to work. Embarrassed over my lack of sophistication, I handed her a five-mark bill, which quickly disappeared in her already overloaded bra.

Had I been able to think of an excuse that provided me with a graceful way of getting out of the place, I surely would have done so, even if it meant that I had paid my hard-earned money for nothing. But as much as I racked my brain, I couldn't think of a thing.

After telling me to drop my pants and undershorts, my hostess—with the expertise of a high priestess performing some sacred ritual—poured water from a kettle on the stove into an enamel face bowl, dipped a washrag into it, and started giving me a below-the-belt minibath. She then explained that she had to be extremely careful with customers because if her biweekly compulsory medical inspection by the *Sittenpolizei* (morals police) revealed that she had caught VD, she would lose her license to "work." Following a brief "short-arm inspection" and rubdown with a dry towel, she pulled out a fresh condom and, before I could say *Danke schön,* had me all suited up and ready to go. Without further ado she flung herself backward on the bed, spread her ample thighs, and reminded me in a querulous voice that time was money and that five marks didn't entitle me to spend all night.

To my own surprise, I did not wilt under fire and make a fool of myself as I had feared. Instead, guided by instincts that had been handed down to me through the ages, and with only minimal cooperation from my business-minded, unromantic partner, I did what came naturally until I reached the point of no return.

With an expertise that was obviously acquired during years of practice, the hooker retrieved the condom, flung it into the oven, and gave me another perfunctory rubdown with the towel. After I had dressed, she led me down the steep stairs and bid me an unemotional farewell.

My mission had been accomplished. By the standards of my peers, I had concluded an important rite of passage and joined the ranks of "real men." But the experience of sex for money left me not only emotionally unfulfilled but thoroughly disgusted with myself and this thriving industry. Unlike Walter, who wasn't interested in an emotional experience and who had already made plans to become one of Winkelstrasse's regulars, I decided right then and there never again to go the hooker route.

FORBIDDEN FRUIT

Among the more pleasant memories of my apprenticeship at Lindner A. G. were those of Gerda Schmidt, one of the secretaries in the company's front office. Gerda was a petite thirty-something brunette whose pleasing smile and hourglass figure endeared her to all the fellows in the shop. Each Friday, about an hour before quitting time, Gerda would enter the shop with a large cardboard box containing our pay envelopes and go from station to station to hand us our wages. Invariably, her arrival would set off a burst of lascivious howls, wolf whistles, and indecent proposals that among contemporary women would rank as blatant sexual harassment, but that Gerda accepted as her due with a big smile and a provocative swivel of her hips.

Over the years, half of the fellows in the shop had tried to score with Gerda, but all had struck out. Eventually, several rumors made the rounds, one claiming that Gerda was secretly seeing an "important" married man, another that she was a lesbian, and still another that she thought it beneath her to go to bed with a blue-collar worker.

I had heard all of these rumors, but none could keep me from developing a monstrous crush on her. I could hardly wait for Friday to come, not because I would get my measly seven marks' apprentice pay, but because I would get another close glimpse at the woman of my dreams. The minute she stepped into the shop, my heightened senses picked up the sweet scent of her perfume as it mingled with the acrid industrial odors of the plant. Ironically, when the moment I had awaited with such longing arrived and the object of my lust stood in front of me, all I could do was count my money and stammer a barely audible *Danke* while averting my eyes in order not to reveal my true feelings. Each time after she had left, I could have kicked myself for not having handled myself with a bit more savoir faire, and promised to do better the next time.

I was thoroughly convinced of the hopelessness of my case. To assume that a sexy, experienced woman like Gerda, who could have any man she wanted, would be interested in a teenager who had only one miserable sexual encounter in a whorehouse to his credit, and who was racially tainted to boot, would have been sheer megalomania. If I was wrong—and I was as sure as one could be that I was not—I was in big, big trouble, for I knew that I didn't have the strength to turn her down.

I again thought of Herr Dutke's admonitions. Only after I reached puberty had the fiendish truth hit me: I, a perfectly healthy male, had been condemned to suppress all human urges and to live in preordained celibacy, not as a matter of choice but as a matter of immutable law. If I entertained any notions of simply ignoring that law, they were countered by chilling accounts I had heard, detailing how Jews who had been caught committing *Rassenschande* with German women had paid for their "crime" with castration or even their lives. By a strange coincidence, I frequently would find our daily newspaper left lying around our home unfolded in such a way as to make it all but impossible for me to miss an article that dealt with this distasteful subject. It was my mother's way of warning me, since she could never bring herself to discuss sex with me. Yet, despite all the warnings and danger signals I had received, I reached the decision that, in due time, I had to do what I had to do.

One afternoon, shortly before quitting time, I literally bumped into Gerda in the workshop's *Gemeinschaftsraum* (community room). She was posting a notice on the bulletin board. After uttering what was supposed to be a greeting, but came out as an unintelligible mumble, I prepared to walk past her and return to the shop.

"Let me ask you something," she said, stopping me. "Are you scared of me?"

"No, I'm not scared of you," I responded, totally caught off guard.

"Then why do you act as if you are every time you see me?" she kept digging.

"What makes you think I act like I'm scared of you?" I countered, embarrassed, although I knew exactly what she was talking about. What she didn't seem to know was that my insecure behavior around her had absolutely nothing to do with fear of her. The only thing I was afraid—no, terrified—of was the prospect of making a fool of myself.

"Well, if you aren't afraid of me, why don't you come closer?" I took a few steps toward her to prove that she was wrong, but she was still unconvinced. "Come closer, real close," she teased.

I took another step until our bodies almost touched.

"Be careful, you'll get me all dirty," she warned, pointing at my grimy coveralls. Then she tilted her head upward and kissed me on the lips.

"Maybe you're not afraid after all," she observed. "If you like, we can meet tonight and watch a movie." At Am Zoll Theater, they are playing *Hallo Janine* with Marikka Rokk and Johannes Heesters."

Although the two popular dance-and-singing stars were among my favorites, I couldn't have cared less what or who was playing, and without giving it another thought, agreed to meet her at eight o'clock. At that particular moment, I was completely without a will of my own, and had she asked me to meet her that night on the dark side of the moon, I would have agreed.

Suddenly, it occurred to me that she might not be fully aware of all the implications of a tryst with me and I decided that it was my duty to warn her, even at the risk of her chickening out.

"You know that the Nazis won't like our going to the movies together," I tested the water.

"Of course I know, but the Nazis can kiss my behind," was her treasonous reply.

That evening, I scrubbed and dressed with extra care in preparation for the adventure ahead. Whatever second thoughts cropped up in my mind, they were quickly dispelled by my hopeless state of anticipation. With near-fatalistic resignation, I invoked the old popular German proverb that holds—quite illogically, I think—that *Wer A sagt muss auch B sagen* (he who says A must also say B). I certainly had taken step A, and nothing could stop me from taking a crack at step B. If everything worked out according to my plan, today—July 31, 1941—would go down in history as the day when I learned the true meaning of making love. Much later I discovered that it was also the day on which *Reichsmarschall* Hermann Göring issued the first known written order for the murder of all Jews living under Nazi rule, an action he referred to as the *Endlösung* (Final Solution).

Gerda was already standing at the entrance to the theater when I arrived. After spotting me, she bought her ticket and I bought mine. To the un-initiated eye, we were perfect strangers who, like hundreds of other strangers, happened to sit in adjacent seats. Soon the lights went out and the *Wochenschau* (weekly newsreel) started. Since the beginning of the war, the former newsclips from around the world had been replaced by a format of front-line action consisting of predictable scenes of German victories on land, at sea, and in the air.

After making absolutely sure that the man who sat to my left was deeply engrossed in the action on the big screen, I slowly, ever so slowly, moved my right hand toward Gerda's left thigh. Emboldened by the absence of resistance to my advance, I began to gently move my hand up and down her thigh while gradually increasing the pressure. Luckily, because of the thunderous gunfire on the screen, only I could hear Gerda's heavy breathing and the occasional moans that escaped from her mouth. During the brief intermission between the newsreel and the evening's main feature, she leaned toward me and whispered, "Meet me outside."

By the time I caught up with her, the sun had gone down and it was pitch black outside. "What were you trying to do to me—drive me mad?" she teased. She then suggested that we'd take a walk to nearby Wiesendamm, a two-lane street whose long center footpath with its trees, shrubbery, and wooden benches made it an ideal lovers' lane. We found the place deserted and selected a strategically located bench that was flanked by two trees.

Flying strictly by the seat of my pants, I literally put myself in Gerda's experienced hands. When we heard approaching footsteps, ecstasy mingled with fear as we held each other tightly while holding our breath. As the steps came closer and closer, my anxiety grew. Any moment I expected to hear a voice shout *"Sicherheits Dienst!"* But the footsteps went by and kept on going. When they were completely out of hearing range, we came alive again until we both had our fill. In addition to worrying about getting caught, I had been afraid I would make a complete fool of myself. But perhaps my youthful ardor and energy had compensated for my inexperience, for Gerda assured me that I showed a great deal of promise for a fifteen-year-old boy.

She was adamant in refusing my offer to let me take her home. "Let's not stretch our luck too far," she said. That remark brought me back to reality. Reality for me was that, unlike my Aryan friends who were dating to their hearts' content, I had to sneak around like a thief in the night and risk the Gestapo's brutality.

When I finally showed up at home, I still could smell Gerda's penetrating perfume. Knowing that my mother had an extremely keen sense of smell, I was convinced that she would notice the perfume the moment I set foot in the door. But tactfully, she never mentioned it. Instead, she asked me how I liked the movie. At first I wanted to tell her that I liked it okay, but somehow the lie refused to come out of my mouth. "I ran into some girl I know and we decided to leave the movie early and go for a walk," I told her, sticking as close to the truth as I could.

"Is she a nice girl?" my mother inquired with typical motherly nosiness.

"Yes, very nice," I responded.

"Just be careful, Hans-Jürgen. You know what I mean," she warned, with that troubled look on her face that weighed on my conscience like a ton of bricks.

THAT OLD GANG OF MINE
GOES TO WAR

One after another, my boyhood cronies were disappearing from the neighborhood. Most had been drafted for military service and a few—for reasons that had nothing to do with love for Hitler or *Vaterland*—had volunteered. Karl-Heinz Bülow, the avowed anti-Nazi, joined the navy for the sole purpose of improving his chances of scoring with girls. He was counting on the widely known fact that girls were partial to men in navy uniforms. According to a censored letter he sent me, he had already seen plenty of action on a submarine in the Atlantic, yet none so far with the girls in port. So had most of my other pals: Eugen Braun, the brothers Hans and Karl Morell, and Fiffi Peters, the former waiter apprentice. Jack Spederski joined the army to escape the humdrum life of an unskilled laborer. He wound up in the Soviet Union as a tank driver in the celebrated Panzer Division Gross-Deutschland. Walter Brauer, my red-light-district coconspirator, had become a motorcyclist in one of the army's famed KRAD units. Only Wolfgang Neumann, the ex–Hitler Youth leader and my one-time bodyguard, had volunteered for the vaunted *Waffen*-SS because of his unshakable belief in Hitler's cause. For his trouble, he made all the hometown papers when he received a battlefield commission for bravery somewhere in Belgium, and again when—to no one's surprise—his name was among the first to appear on the daily newspapers' steadily growing military obituary pages.

In spite of the mounting German casualties at the various fronts, I rather looked forward to doing my share of fighting, if for no other reason than to prove that I was as good as everybody else. Yet I dared not volunteer lest I be turned down—as so often in my life—for being non-Aryan. That's why I rejoiced when one day an official-looking letter—the equivalent of Uncle Sam's "Greetings"—summoned me to report for my physical examination, called *Musterung*, to determine fitness for the one-year paramilitary *Arbeitsdienst* (Labor Service), which all seventeen-year-old German boys were required to join prior to serving in the *Wehrmacht*. If they had no use for me,

I reasoned hopefully, they wouldn't bother to have me take the physical. Feeling more and more optimistic, I decided that there was no better way for me to erase the racial difference that had always set me apart from even my closest friends than to wear the much-respected uniform of a German soldier. Once in that uniform, I was certain that I would prove beyond a doubt that I was as good as anyone else.

The morning of the *Musterung*, I and several hundred youths also born in 1926—including a fair number of long-haired and dapper swingboys—were herded into the huge gym of a downtown public school. Since many of the young men present made no secret of their hope to be rejected by the draft board, I thought it wise to keep my military ambitions to myself.

The gym's walls were lined with tables manned by *Wehrmacht* and *Arbeitsdienst* officers in their respective uniforms. The booming voice of one officer ordering us to shut up ended the din of our conversations. After characterizing us as a miserable bunch that was badly in need of straightening out, the voice ordered us to have our pictures taken, then to strip completely, shoes, socks, and all, and to leave our clothes in neat piles on the floor. We then were ordered to walk in a single file in front of the tables where officers were busy checking us out from scalp to toes while writing down their findings on stacks of forms. From the remarks I overheard while passing the various inspection stations, I concluded that I was in perfect general health, that my eyesight, hearing, and teeth were above normal, but that I was several pounds underweight, due, likely, to the stringent rationing of food.

"Too bad we can't draft you," a sympathetic *Arbeitsdienst* officer told me. "All you need is a year of our good food and regular work in fresh air to put some meat on your bones." The officer's words, however well meant, jolted me back into Nazi reality and crushed my hopes of ever escaping the cursed stigma of race. I suspected that if I wasn't even considered good enough to dig holes and build *Autobahnen* for the Labor Service, I certainly wasn't considered good enough to fire a rifle for the army. My suspicion was confirmed when, at the last table, an officer handed me my brand-new *Wehrpass* (military pass), which detailed my military status and which all male civilians were required to show on demand by authorized persons. Near my photo someone had written in ink the lowercase initials "n.z.v." When

I asked an officer to explain what that meant, his laconic response was *"Nicht zu verwenden* (not usable)."

With all of my buddies having left for military service, my life at the home front became pure drudgery—all work and no play. Even at the shop, all of the younger men had either been drafted or had volunteered for one of the armed forces' branches. That left me virtually without any contact with men near my own age. But boredom was the least of my problems. As one of a tiny, rapidly dwindling group of able-bodied young men who were not yet in uniform, I became more conspicuous—and subsequently more self-conscious—because of my civilian attire than because of my race. Amid the constant praise of "our men in uniform who are giving their all for Führer and *Vaterland*," I developed a stifling sense of inferiority and of total isolation that grew and grew until it threatened to overpower me. That feeling reached a peak when a wounded *Waffen*-SS officer on crutches accosted me in the street and loudly questioned my right to walk around in safety while "brave German men" had to risk life and limb in combat. I realized then that my situation as a non-Aryan civilian was fraught with grave potential danger. Remembering Herr Dutke's prophecy that after the Nazis were done with the Jews, I would be next, I felt I was sitting on a time bomb that was ready to explode. The only thing I felt that could save me was to become a member of the armed forces and wear that uniform, since nobody was respected more in Germany than a German soldier.

Even the prospect of becoming one of the mounting front-line casualties—which by mid-1942 was a strong possibility—and my growing suspicion that Hitler's war was wrong and headed for disaster, could not diminish my determination to join the military. I reasoned that I'd rather take my chance of getting hurt or killed on the battlefield than fall into the hands of the SS. In effect, I was willing to climb aboard a sinking ship when I was still relatively safe ashore. Looking back today, I can readily see how foolish my thinking was, but at the time, it made all the sense in the world to me.

The crucial question was how I could get the military to accept me. It dawned on me that perhaps I might have better luck going the volunteer route. The idea seemed at least worth a try. Although declared ineligible for the draft, I hoped that the heavy casualties suffered by all branches of the *Wehrmacht* had created enough vacancies to literally give me a fighting chance.

I had no problem getting a day off from work after I explained to Meister Neumann what I intended to do. Volunteering for military service was high on the list of national priorities. I took an early train to suburban Rahlstedt, the location of Hamburg's *Wehrbezirkskommando* (regional military command). When I arrived, the suburb buzzed like a beehive with military activities. Soldiers of all branches were scurrying around, on foot and in camouflage-gray vehicles that bore the familiar open-ended cross logo of the German *Wehrmacht*. Most of the soldiers I passed were too busy to notice me, but the few who did invariably did a double take, obviously surprised to see an able-bodied young man in civilian clothes, and a black one at that. I wasn't sure whether they were startled by my civilian status, my "unusual" looks, or both. But I didn't care, figuring that once I wore a uniform, too, they wouldn't think of making fun of a comrade-in-arms.

My thoughts were interrupted by the screeching brakes of an open staff car that had pulled up beside me. *"Sie da! Wer sind Sie und was machen Sie hier?* (You there! Who are you and what are you doing here?)," an army lieutenant colonel in the rear seat demanded to know in a voice that betrayed a mixture of contempt and suspicion.

Glad to oblige, I pulled out my *Wehrpass* and handed it to him. After leafing through the document, the officer carefully studied my photograph, then compared it with me. "So what is it you want?" he continued his interrogation.

"I want to enlist in the army, *Herr Oberstleutnant,*" I replied, hopeful that my ability to recognize his rank would make him more favorably disposed toward me. But no such luck.

"You *what?*" he asked, in utter disbelief that couldn't have been greater had I asked him for his daughter's hand in marriage. "Enlist in the army? You must be mad. Don't you know that non-Aryans are barred from service in the German *Wehrmacht*? Even your *Wehrpass* states that you are *untauglich* (unfit)."

"Yes," I admitted, "but I had hoped that because of the army's great manpower need it might make an exception."

The officer was visibly getting angry. "Let me tell you something," he snarled, his steel-blue eyes narrowing to slits, "Germany is not, and never will be, so hard-up as to need the likes of you to win the war. My advice to you is to get back to your job as fast as possible and not waste any more valuable production time with your foolish notions. *Verstanden* (Understood)?" Not waiting for my reply, he threw my *Wehrpass* at me and ordered his driver to drive on.

The verbal attack from the army officer had taken me completely by surprise. It was so unexpected that it sent me into a state of utter dejection. I had been prepared for the possibility of having my enlistment request turned down, but I was not prepared for gratuitous insults.

Without bothering to get a second opinion at the recruitment office, I dragged myself back to the station and caught the next Hamburg-bound train. As I sat on the train, still numb from the dressing-down I had just received, I kept hearing the officer's voice: "Germany is not, and never will be, so hard-up as to need the likes of you to win the war." I remembered that I had heard similar sentiments when I was only ten years old and my mother tried to have me accepted by the Hitler Youth.

Remembering, my numbness vanished and gave way to rage. I resolved in that instant that if I couldn't join them, and I couldn't fight them, I would do the next best thing and hate them from the bottom of my heart. It was my hatred for the Nazis that sustained me during the remaining war years that were still lying ahead.

THE BEGINNING OF THE END

After the German army's massive defeat at Stalingrad in the winter of 1942, it became clear to even the most optimistic Germans that the war was not going as smoothly as they had hoped. One indication that German troops were unprepared for the subzero temperatures in the Soviet Union was an emergency appeal by the government for German women to donate their fur coats, muffs, and hats to the war effort so that the garments could be retailored to provide warm clothing for front-line soldiers who were literally freezing to death.

To keep up morale at the front and at home and to minimize the damage inflicted by the Allied forces, Dr. Goebbels's propaganda machine went into overdrive to turn defeats into victories. In the process, an entirely new vocabulary was invented that included such euphemisms as a *strategische Absetzung* (strategic distancing) for a German retreat. One key tool in Goebbels's propaganda war to maintain the fighting spirit of the German people was the movie industry. In rapid succession it churned out films that either romanticized the war, depicted Jews as the root of all evil, or simply provided an emotional relief. Undoubtedly the most anti-Semitic movie ever produced by the Nazis during the war was director Veit Harlan's notorious *Jud Süss,* with Ferdinand Marian, one of Germany's most distinguished actors of the time, in the title role. Marian, who put his heart and soul into his role as a despicable Jew every moviegoer loved to hate, committed suicide after the war, apparently because of shame and guilt. Some propaganda films designed to lift the rapidly sinking morale featured the romantic adventures of dashing military officers, such as *Die Grosse Liebe (The Great Love)* in which popular star Zarah Leander leaves the audience with the upbeat message, *"Ich weiss es wird einmal ein Wunder geschehn* (I know a miracle is going to happen)." Soon, millions of anxious Germans were singing the hit song, hoping against hope that a miracle would happen that would turn their misfortunes around and put an end to the war. Other typical propaganda fare included Hollywood-type song-and-dance musicals aimed at letting people forget, if only for a couple of hours, about hunger, bombs, casualties, and a host of other war-related calamities.

Goebbels's determination to bolster morale was felt even at the workplace. On several occasions our shop was visited by "Strength Through Joy" teams of entertainers—usually two or three—who, for an hour or so, tried to cheer us up with humor and accordion tunes. While we were appreciative of even the smallest diversion from the relentless pressure of war production, we realized that we were only receiving crumbs. All of us had seen newsreels of workers at major defense plants being visited by Germany's most prestigious symphony orchestras, such as the Berlin Philharmonic.

Another tool aimed at boosting morale by intentionally misleading Germans about the progress of the war was the state-controlled *Deutsche Rundfunk* (German [Radio] Broadcast). Even some of the more gullible citizens began to regard with increasing skepticism its distortions and lies. To offset the predictably one-sided news accounts, I risked severe consequences by listening to the German-language news broadcasts by the BBC, an act the Nazis considered treasonous and dealt with accordingly. Punishment for breaking that law ranged from incarceration in a concentration camp to death. Although I had no specific knowledge of what went on in them, word had gotten out that concentration camps were hell on earth.

Ironically, my source of Allied news was our small, battery-powered *Volksempfänger* (people's receiver), an inexpensive, government-built and -marketed appliance that had been intended to give every German a chance to own a radio and be propagandized. Notwithstanding my mother's laments about the danger involved in my illegal activity, I became addicted to BBC news, whose integrity I trusted more than the obvious lies churned out by Goebbels' propaganda mill. To keep from getting caught in the act, I would put the radio on my bed, then cover it and my head with a heavy blanket while my mother would listen at the door to make sure nobody was standing outside. During this clandestine operation, our squeaky stairs served as a primitive yet highly effective alarm system. Thanks to the BBC, I had a fairly accurate picture of the disastrous defeat that Hitler's war machine was headed for, long before Germans who relied entirely on Goebbels's fabrications had a clue.

Unfortunately, my superior source of military information exposed me to the constant temptation of sharing what I had heard with other, less-informed friends and to contradict information disseminated by the Goebbels press. In one instance, I narrowly missed blowing my cover when, on May 10, 1941, the Nazi press broadcast the sensational news that Rudolf Hess, Hitler's deputy, had flown to England in order to negotiate a peace settlement. Eager to learn more details, I kept tuning in to the BBC. A few days after the incident, the German-language broadcast from London confirmed the German report, stating that Hess had landed somewhere in Scotland. When, in a subsequent discussion of the Hess caper with some of my fellow workers, I repeated the word *Scotland*, one of them corrected me, insisting that Hess had landed in England, as all the early German reports indicated. Fortunately, he wasn't the suspicious kind and didn't press me to find out where I had gotten my information. Had my coworker put two and two together and wished me harm, he would have been able to prove that I had engaged in "highly treasonous activity" by listening to and disseminating enemy propaganda.

The seeming defection of as high-placed a Nazi as Rudolf Hess proved a gigantic embarrassment to the Nazi government, and no pains were spared by the Goebbels propaganda machine to put a benign spin on the entire affair. Part of that effort was the official explanation on the air and in the press that Hess had been under a severe mental strain and acted while not really himself. This gave rise to hundreds of jokes about "crazy Hess," including the one in which a down-on-his-luck man enters a Nazi employment office and asks for a job.

"What kind of a job do you have in mind?" the Nazi official wants to know.

"I hear there's a vacancy for deputy Führer," the man replies.

"Are you crazy?" the indignant official shouts at him.

"No," the job-seeker replies. "Is that a requirement?"

To compare the BBC broadcasts with their German counterpart, I also listened, quite legally, to the nightly reports of William Joyce, also known as Lord Haw-Haw, an American-born, Irish-reared radio personality who was beaming Goebbels's propaganda in English from Berlin. Unfortunately, my English at the time wasn't advanced enough for me to understand everything Lord Haw-Haw had to say, but I did catch his threats of pending doom and dire consequences for the British people if they didn't surrender posthaste. He made these threats in spite of the fact that Hermann Göring's *Luftwaffe* had already been handed a crushing defeat in the Battle of Britain, with which Hitler had intended to establish German air supremacy as a prelude to his planned invasion of the British Isles. As it turned out, the British never forgave Lord Haw-Haw for his attempts to undermine their fighting spirit and unceremoniously hanged him as a traitor in London after the war.

In addition to British radio reports, there were other, more tangible signs that indicated to me that Hitler's war effort was in serious trouble. From the time I had begun my apprenticeship, Meister Neumann had always held my coworkers and me to the highest standards of German workmanship in our production of ammunition trailers. To assure that only flawless vehicles were certified for front-line duty, a small army of military inspectors were constantly going over every welding seam, every rivet, and every screw. The slightest deviation from specifications resulted in immediate rejection of the vehicle by the inspectors and a chewing out of the person responsible by Meister Neumann. Literally overnight that procedure was changed. Explaining that the draft had produced a serious manpower shortage at the plant

and that, as a result, we were running dangerously behind production sched-
ule, Meister Neumann instructed us that henceforth our main objective
would be to turn out as many vehicles as we could in the shortest amount
of time. Then he shocked everyone with words we thought we'd never hear
coming from the mouth of the plant's most obsessive perfectionist and arch-
enemy of *Murks* (sloppy workmanship). "Never mind if the trailers aren't
perfect," he said. "Perfect ammunition trailers that don't reach the front
line in time are useless in our effort to win the war." Also gone with the
high production standards were the military inspectors, who, we were told,
had been reassigned to the front, where the army high command felt they
were needed more urgently.

Being swept up, like everyone else, by the swiftly moving events of the
war, I had hardly noticed that the three years of my apprenticeship were up
and that it was time for me to take my *Gesellenprufung* (journeyman exam),
consisting of two days of practical and theoretical tests. Although I had
looked forward to the day when I would move up and join the ranks of
skilled machinists, the thrill was gone by the time I was told that I had
passed the exam and was handed my *Gesellenbrief* (journeyman's diploma).
Under restrictive war regulations I was unable to follow the tradition of my
trade and move to another job. That meant that I would have to stay at my
old job, where, regardless of my new official status, I would never be given
the proper respect by my former superiors and frequent tormentors. Besides,
I was sick and tired of making ammunition trailers whose assembly-line
manufacture no longer offered any challenges to me. Even the thought of
receiving full journeyman's pay instead of the puny weekly apprentice al-
lowance did little to boost my morale.

I wished that something would happen that would put an end to the
drudgery and boredom I felt, something that would bring change and per-
haps some excitement into my humdrum life. Nobody warned me at the
time to be careful what I wished for because I might get it. Little did I know
that a disaster of monstrous proportions would soon provide me with
enough change and excitement to last me for the rest of my life.

OPERATION GOMORRAH

"Imagine more than fifty percent of metropolitan Boston smashed into ruin and filled with decaying bodies. Take every single building in the corporate limits of Boston proper, and pound it to wreckage; burn everything that can be consumed by fire; kill tens of thousands of people. Imagine Boston destroyed in this manner, left in ruins and ash and pestilential stench. Imagine all this in its worst—and you understand Hamburg in its reality." Thus wrote military aviation writer Martin Caidin in his 1960 book *The Night Hamburg Died,* in which he chronicles the horrors wrought by "Operation Gomorrah," the code name for ten days of relentless attacks by heavy British Lancaster and Halifax bombers in the summer of 1943. It was my good fortune to be among those who survived without a scratch the "utter hell of sustained fire" that, Caidin wrote, "not even Hiroshima and Nagasaki, suffering the smashing blows of nuclear explosions, could match."

For me and my mother, "the utter hell" started on hot, sweltering July 29, 1943, a Thursday, sometime around 9 P.M. At that time, the sirens howled their familiar pre-warning, indicating that enemy aircraft had once again crossed the British Channel and were headed in the direction of Hamburg. As more than a hundred times in the past, my mother and I had each grabbed two suitcases that contained our most essential belongings and headed for the public air-raid shelter half a block down the street. For us, as for the rest of the city's population, nightly shelter visits had become a way of life. But this night was different. Vast portions of the city had been leveled and thousands of people had been killed by enemy bombs during the preceding two nights, and so the sound of the sirens had acquired a new, more ominous significance.

Some of our neighbors, frightened by the prospect of additional air attacks, had grabbed as many of their belongings as they could carry and left the city to stay with friends or relatives. Gretchen, her mother, and her brother were among them. The previous night, Gretchen had told me in the shelter that they were already packed and would leave at daybreak for Göttingen, in lower Saxony, where they had relatives. My mother and I had considered the option of leaving the city also, but decided against it since rail transportation out of Hamburg was in virtual chaos because of the sudden mass migration of panic-stricken people. Getting hit by strafing aircraft while stuck in an overcrowded train, we knew, was as likely as getting hit in an air-raid shelter. We decided to take our chances in the city.

For the first couple of hours following the sounding of the alarm, things were deceptively calm. I had gone to the main entrance gas-sluice, a tiny foyer, where about a dozen men had gathered to smoke and to look at the starry sky through the open hatch. To my delight I discovered among the mostly older men a former neighborhood chum of mine, Jack Spederski, whom I hadn't seen for a couple of years. Smartly dressed in the uniform of the vaunted *Panzer Division Gross-Deutschland,* Jack explained that he had the dubious pleasure of being home on furlough from the eastern front. The impressive collection of medals and combat badges on his tunic let me know that he had had more than his share of front-line action. When I complimented him on being a bona fide hero, he scoffed, "I'm fed up with the war, but I've learned to make the best of a bad situation."

Jack told me that, contrary to conventional wisdom, his "elite" division was not made up entirely of eager volunteers but included a sizable number of reluctant draftees like himself. He said that his unit's reputation as one of the most formidable German combat teams was well deserved and due, in part, to its frequent refusal to take prisoners. At first, Jack said, he felt squeamish when ordered to shoot unarmed Soviet soldiers who had surrendered, but after seeing so many of his own comrades killed or maimed, killing became easier and easier until he could do it without giving it another thought. "It's either them or us," he rationalized, "so you do your best to make sure it's them. You do what you have to do."

Jack conceded that his unit's ask-no-mercy, give-no-mercy reputation had a down side. It not only struck fear in the hearts of the enemy, he explained, it also made the enemy fight harder and resist longer in order to escape certain death.

I had a difficult time imagining that the soft-spoken, gentle, and somewhat withdrawn Jack I had known as a boy had become a tough, unfeeling killer of unarmed fellow human beings. But looking at his medals, his firmly set jaw, and the glint in his blue eyes, I realized that the Jack Spederski I had known and the one who stood before me and casually talked about some of the liberties he and his comrades-in-arms had taken with Russian women were two entirely different persons.

Conveniently forgetting that it was the Germans who had invaded the Soviet Union and not the other way around, Jack assured me that the Russians really had it coming, since they refused to fight fair. As example, he recalled how some of his tank units had been decimated in battle by Russian kamikaze-type dogs. He explained that the dogs, which had explosives strapped to their bodies and were equipped with antennalike devices, had been trained to seek their food beneath tanks. The moment German tanks approached, the unleashed dogs would rush toward the tanks in anticipation of food. Once their antenna made contact with a tank, the explosives would detonate and dog, tank, and crew would be on their way to Valhalla. Jack, who seconds earlier had let me know that he saw nothing wrong with shooting Russian prisoners who had surrendered, waxed indignant about such "inhuman cruelty" to animals.

I was revolted by what I had just heard, but I felt it was pointless trying to make him see the flaws in his reasoning, with which he tried to justify his and his unit's atrocities.

Turning my attention from Jack to the conversations of the other men in the small room, I was in for some more horror stories, but this time they were much closer to home. Discussing the previous week's air attacks on Hamburg, one man said that he had been looking for his brother and sister-in-law who lived in the Hammerbrook district, but that he had given up all hope of ever seeing them alive again after he discovered that the entire district had been literally wiped out. Another man related how hundreds of people met with a slow, agonizing death after they had been set on fire by bombs containing a phosphorous liquid. He then gave a sickeningly graphic description of how the unfortunates had tried to save themselves by jumping into the canals, but that as soon as they would try to leave the water, the phosphorus would reignite in spontaneous combustion, forcing them to stay in the water until they became too weak to hold on or lost consciousness and drowned.

Although the mere voicing of doubt in a Nazi victory had officially been deemed a treasonous offense, the people openly speculated as to how long Germany could withstand this kind of massive destruction of its major industrial centers. One man, apparently indifferent to the presence of a soldier, gave the Nazi regime only "one more month, if that much." No one disagreed. It seemed that the more the German "man in the street" perceived the regime to be in trouble, the more emboldened he became to speak his mind. Unfortunately, his prediction of the Nazis' imminent demise was still two years premature.

One man suggested that there might not be another attack on Hamburg, because the British would probably want to capture the city as intact as possible. Little did he, or I, for that matter, know that months before the fate of Hamburg had already been sealed by the planners of Operation Gomorrah, which called for the total destruction of Hamburg, Germany's second-largest industrial city and its largest seaport. It didn't take long for us to find out.

I reentered the shelter to report to my mother that things were quiet outside and that, at least this night, we would probably be spared. Inside, the occupants—mostly women, children, and elderly men—who had been quiet and tense at the outset, had begun to relax and were chatting as usual. Suddenly, shortly after midnight, all hell—in the most vivid meaning of the term—broke loose. Amid the droning of what sounded like thousands of heavy bombers, we could hear the shrill crescendo of whining bombs threading their way downward before crashing with elemental force into the ground. With every explosion, the entire shelter shuddered as if rocked by a massive earthquake. Each explosion was followed by loud screams of frightened women and children. They became even louder when, within minutes of the initial attack, the lights went out and the *Dratfunk* (wire broadcast) went dead, apparently because of bomb damage. After that first pounding, there was a short moment of quiet followed by another pounding and another moment of silence. Gradually, the quiet intervals between the sound of detonating bombs became shorter and shorter until they had ceased altogether, giving way to a continuous hail of what sounded to us like exploding bombs of every size and description. Postmortem reports released by the Allies after the war confirmed that during Operation Gomorrah, the city had been struck by some twelve hundred land mines, thirty thousand heavy high-explosive bombs, more than three million stick incendiary bombs, eighty thousand hundred-pound liquid-phosphorus bombs, five hundred phosphorus canisters, and five hundred incendiary flares.

Reassessing the success of their bombing raids on Hamburg after the war, the British credited the effectiveness of their mission on their gambling on a new technology: metal strips they literally rained on the city. Released by the ton prior to the release of the bombs, the metal strips wreaked havoc on German antiaircraft artillery radar, making it virtually impossible for the *flak* to zero in on their targets. Whereas during all of their previous air attacks the British had suffered heavy losses, the metal strips permitted their bombers to maneuver above Hamburg with near impunity.

About an hour after the bombing started, the temperature in our shelter began to rise rapidly. We concluded that the factory above us had been hit by incendiary bombs and was on fire. Our suspicion was confirmed a few moments later, when thick smoke started oozing through several cracks in the ceiling. At this point, our neighborhood tailor–turned–air-raid warden made his presence known by shining a flashlight on himself. During less trying moments, he had often been the target of behind-the-back ridicule because of his officious pseudomilitary bearing. But this time, nobody felt inclined to snicker as he explained the gravity of our situation and, after setting up several battery-powered emergency lights, ordered all able-bodied men, including Jack and me, to man the manual air pumps and start pumping.

Jack and I started pumping away, but it soon became obvious that our efforts were counterproductive. Instead of fresh air, we were pumping in thick, acrid smoke from the outside and had to quit. Jack told me that facing Ivan in combat with frostbitten hands and feet was no fun, but that waiting like sitting ducks to be roasted alive or to choke to death in some "goddamn hole in the ground" like ours was worse.

Eventually, the bombing stopped. All we could hear outside was a loud hissing noise that we took for the sound of fire hoses in action, but which was actually caused, we learned later, by the firestorm that had been unleashed by the incendiary bombs, which had turned the streets above us into an inferno of up to fifteen hundred degrees Fahrenheit. Slowly but surely, the shelter filled with smoke and people began to cough and wheeze. Through the dim emergency lights that were getting dimmer as the batteries weakened, we could see thick smoke enveloping us. We were now faced with two alternatives, either stay in the shelter and suffocate or leave the shelter and become human torches. But with the sudden, thunderous collapse of the outside walls of the factory and the subsequent blocking of the exits, even those two horrifying options were cut down to one. That is, until we became aware of another threat to our lives. Someone touched the ceiling and discovered that it was burning hot, leaving us with the dismal prospect of its collapsing over our heads. With the news of another peril making the rounds, a wave of resignation settled over the shelter as people, huddling closely together in little family groups, seemed to give up hope of ever getting out alive. Except for continuous hacking coughs, there was silence. Even the children's crying had ceased.

I was sitting on the cement floor beside my mother, who, like me, was experiencing breathing difficulties and burning eyes. Although we had been told that our gas masks were no protection against smoke, we felt so desperate that we decided to put them on anyway, just in case they might do some good. We soon discovered that the gas masks were no help at all. If anything, they made breathing more difficult. But in our state of mind, we refused to admit their ineffectiveness and clung to them as if they were the only thing that stood between us and death.

While I fully grasped the seriousness of our predicament, I was unable to fathom that this was the end—that whatever my mission had been on this earth would end in this "goddamn hole in the ground." Even recalling the many corpses I had seen during the past few days in other parts of the city failed to convince me of the strong possibility that my luck, too, had finally run out. I felt neither optimism, pessimism, nor fear, just incredulity that this was going to be it. With my breathing under the gas mask becoming increasingly laborious, I became more and more detached from my surroundings, but without actually losing consciousness. I was still aware of the presence of my mother beside me and the fact that we were holding hands, but with her gas mask, she looked unreal to me, like a stranger from another planet.

How long I remained in this apathetic stupor, I don't know. The next thing I remember is that a man was pulling at my gas mask while shouting at me to take it off. At first, I believed that it was someone who wanted to save his own neck at my expense and I started holding on to my mask with all my might. Only after I noticed that he was wearing a Nazi uniform did I let go. Blindingly bright daylight was pouring through the front entrance of the shelter, and as soon as I took off the gas mask as I had been ordered, fresh air started pouring into my oxygen-famished lungs. My mother, too, took off her gas mask and was instantly revived. According to my wristwatch, it was 9 A.M. Our ordeal had lasted exactly twelve hours.

BOMBED OUT

Slowly, as if awakening from a nightmare, we filed out of the shelter—a long line of humans with a new lease on life. At the top of the stairs, we were greeted by the uniformed *Luftschutz* (Air Guard) rescue workers who had freed us. They told us to cover our heads with blankets or towels to protect ourselves against the thousands of flying sparks that filled the air.

The rescue workers cautioned us to remain calm, regardless of what we would see. Their advice hardly prepared us for what we saw. What awaited us was one of the saddest, most horrific sights in our lives. Stückenstrasse— no, all of Barmbek, our beloved community—was totally wiped out. As far as we could see, there was utter destruction. In stark contrast to last night's ear-shattering noise, a muffled silence had settled over the eerie scene. Occasionally, we encountered charred, mummylike corpses of people who apparently had decided too late to leave their homes and seek shelter. Most of the houses had been burned to the ground, others were still ablaze, and still others were only burned-out shells. One of them, now reduced to a smoldering pile of bricks, had been our home from the time I was a little boy. As we walked by, carrying the four suitcases and a few blankets that made up our worldly possessions, I watched my mother from the corner of my eye to see how she would take seeing everything lost that she had worked for so hard and for so many years. But to my surprise, she remained dry-eyed and composed. "The only thing that matters is that we are alive and unhurt," she reassured me and herself. "Everything else we can one day replace."

It was not until after the war ended that we learned the truth about the full extent of the casualties and destruction Hamburg had suffered as a result of Operation Gomorrah and thus could appreciate how truly blessed we had been to be among the survivors. More than forty-one thousand people had perished. Most of the victims died after facing the no-win dilemma of bar-

ricading themselves in their shelters and suffocating or confronting the in-
fernos that were raging in the streets. Some nine hundred thousand people
were made homeless. Nearly half of the city's buildings and some six hun-
dred major industrial plants, including its four biggest shipyards, were de-
stroyed. When the smoke had cleared, 277 schools, twenty-four hospitals,
and fifty-eight churches had been reduced to rubble.

Before my mother and I reached the el-train tracks where we expected
some protection from the airborne burning debris, my mother took off the
blanket with which she had covered her head. Suddenly I heard her scream,
"My hair!" Turning around, I saw that a piece of burning newspaper had
landed on her head and within seconds had singed a large hole in her thick
brown hair. Using my own blanket, I was able to quickly smother the flame,
which, fortunately, caused only a few minor burns to her scalp.

One after another, the survivors from our shelter arrived under the el-
train tracks, some grim faced, some jubilant, but all with the ordeal of the
previous night etched in their faces. There was hardly a dry eye as we walked
around, indiscriminately hugging each other—whether we were close neigh-
bors, casual acquaintances, or total strangers—sad to have lost everything,
yet happy to be still alive.

When I spotted my buddy Jack in the crowd, I asked him how he would
get back to his unit. "Don't tell anyone what I'm telling you," he whispered
conspiratorially, "but I'm not going back. After what happened here last
night, I'm sure the war can't last but a few more weeks, or maybe days.
Until then, I'll have myself evacuated with some of the other families."

Pointing to a suitcase he was carrying, he told me that as soon as the
opportunity presented itself, he was going to change into civilian clothes
and get rid of "*diese scheiss Uniform* (this shit uniform)."

While I shared his belief that the bombings certainly must have helped
hasten Germany's defeat, I wasn't nearly as optimistic as he. "What if the
war isn't over in a few weeks?" I asked.

"Don't worry about me," he said cockily. "I know what I'm doing."

"I hope you do," I said, and wished him well. After we shook hands and
he walked away, my eyes followed him until his stocky frame had disap-
peared in the crowd. I felt a strange sadness, as though I could sense that I
would never see Jack again.

By noon, several army trucks arrived that took us to the Moorweide, a huge parade ground in front of Dammtor train station, which had been designated as a major refugee aid station. There, we joined the huddled masses of thousands of survivors and waited our turn in endless lines to receive sandwiches and milk from the Red Cross workers. I couldn't help but marvel at the organizational skill and efficiency displayed by the emergency crews in bringing huge amounts of tasty food in such a short time to so many people.

Since all refugees could travel free of charge by train to any destination within Germany, my mother and I had decided that we would try to make it to Salza, at the edge of the Harz Mountains, where we were assured shelter at the home of our relatives. But there was a hitch. Several trains, jam-packed with refugees, were stuck in the station, unable to leave until a logjam of outbound trains had been resolved and the tracks had been cleared. Since that could take days, we decided to get on the first available emergency truck leaving the city and board a train later. That was easier said than done, because thousands of other refugees had the same idea. After several hours and numerous attempts, we finally succeeded in getting on one of the trucks that were ferrying refugees out of the city.

As we huddled with a truckload of fellow refugees among our meager belongings, all of us unbathed, disheveled, sweaty, and tired, it occurred to me how one major catastrophe had made us all equal—equally poor, equally filthy, and equally miserable. My "different" appearance, which used to turn heads wherever I went, suddenly had ceased to be of interest to anyone. People were far too preoccupied with their own tenuous toehold on civilization to worry about anybody's hair texture or shade of skin.

A young woman, who was seated on her battered suitcase next to my mother and me, kindly offered to share her last three cigarettes with us, which we confirmed nonsmokers gratefully declined. Major catastrophes, it seems, bring out the very best in people. Wherever I looked, I saw people eager to help alleviate the suffering of their *Volksgenossen* (fellow citizens). Unfortunately, that selfless concern for others that was so pervasive in the immediate aftermath of the catastrophe vanished as quickly as it had come with the first signs of a return to normalcy.

After several hours, our truck reached Lüneburg, where we were lucky to catch a southbound train, jammed beyond capacity with Hamburg refugees, just minutes before it pulled out of the station. Because all the compartments were filled, we had to make do with sitting on our suitcases in the packed aisle.

Midway between Lüneburg and Hannover, our train squealed to a shuddering stop amid wide open meadows. Hearing several shouts of *"Flieger-alarm,"* my mother and I followed the line of refugees headed toward the nearest exit. Leaping to the ground, we joined the stampede that was racing away from the train. I grabbed my mother's hand and pulled her along as fast as she could run toward a few clumps of bushes in the distance. Before we could reach them, a male voice shouted, "Everybody lie down!" We then heard the sputtering of an airplane engine above us. Dropping to the ground, we looked up and saw an RAF-marked fighter plane coming out of the blue sky and flying twice over the length of the train before disappearing.

After a while, our train engine's whistle signaled that the danger had passed, and a few minutes later we were once again on our way, filled with euphoric relief.

When we pulled into Hannover *Hauptbahnhof,* an army of Red Cross workers and other emergency personnel handed us sandwiches, milk, and apples through the train windows. When a Nazi *Amtswalter* in his brown uniform came in sight, one woman on the train started screaming, "You pigs got us into this mess!" and similar seditious remarks until someone gagged her by covering her mouth with a towel.

After an excruciating thirteen-hour train ride that under normal circumstances would have taken no more than five hours, we arrived at the tiny village of Salza am Harz, one stop before the thousand-year-old city of Nordhausen. It was way past midnight when we got off at the deserted whistle-stop.

For the first time since we escaped the inferno of Hamburg, we experienced complete silence. So "new" was the experience that it caused our voices to sound unfamiliar to us, as if they were the voices of strangers. To this day, none of the psychological and physical blows my mother and I endured during the war compare in my mind with the sense of total devastation we felt when the train pulled away and we were left standing on the dimly lighted platform, shivering from cold, weak with fatigue, and feeling utterly forsaken.

As tired as we were, we somehow managed the fifteen-minute walk down

Salza's dark and narrow Hauptstrasse until we reached Harzstrasse 6, our relatives' address.

We didn't have to explain anything. One look at us was all Tante Grete needed to realize what had happened to us. The next moment she and my mother embraced and cried. It was the first time since the cataclysmic events of the last forty-eight hours that I saw my mother break down.

The last time I had spent my summer school vacation in Salza was six years earlier, when I was eleven years old. Onkel Karl and Tante Grete looked exactly the way I had remembered them. Trudchen, now a chubby young lady of twenty-one, was engaged to an army corporal who was somewhere at the Russian front. All seemed genuinely glad to have us live with them.

It took some doing, but after a while my mother and I adjusted as best as we could to small-town life. Onkel Karl, Tante Grete, and Trudchen did everything possible to make us forget the horror we had gone through and make us feel at home. Accomplishing that was no easy task for any of us. Unlike Hamburg, where the people's disillusionment with the Nazis had become so palpable that the Nazis began to keep a lower and lower profile, Salza, like most small towns in central and southern Germany, was still the undisputed domain of Nazi functionaries. Since Salza was the kind of village where, it was said with only mild exaggeration, people made it their business to know the exact number of bedsheets each family owned, Onkel Karl and Tante Grete had learned to keep their political views to themselves, even from us. They didn't have to tell us to do the same.

On our arrival, the village was abuzz with the news of a few days earlier that Mussolini had been overthrown and captured by anti-German Italian troops commanded by Marshal Pietro Badoglio. The immediate effect of Il Duce's fall was massive defection of Italian troops and the near collapse of Italian resistance to Allied forces. The villagers, who had yet to get a real taste of war, took the news of the collapse of the vaunted Berlin-Rome Axis like a personal loss. Many vented their dismay through loud denunciations of the "cowardly Italians."

A few months after Mussolini's capture, the morale of the people in Salza received a much-needed boost. A news flash from the Führer's headquarters announced that Mussolini had been freed. Later we saw in the newsreel how a special, glider-borne commando of SS men, led by a strapping colonel named Otto Skorzeny, snatched Il Duce from the clutches of his captors in the Abruzzi Mountains and returned him, shaken but unharmed, to safety.

Like many World War I veterans, Onkel Karl had been redrafted by the army when the supply of younger recruits became increasingly scarce. Ostensibly, he was stationed in Erfurt, a short train ride away. In reality, he lived a near-normal civilian life at home. After learning that he was a master tailor, his commanding general had arranged for him to work out of his home in order to tailor fancy uniforms for him and his fellow senior officers. The few times my uncle donned his own corporal's uniform was when he traveled to his Erfurt garrison to take back finished uniforms and to pick up new work.

Occasionally, he pressed me into service by making me put on one of the gray gabardine, gold- or silver-braided tunics in order to apply the finishing touches. It gave me a sense of perverse satisfaction to imagine what General von So-and-So and Colonel von What's His Name would have thought had they known that their uniforms had been worn by someone who was considered unworthy of wearing even a private's uniform. Onkel Karl, on whom the irony of the situation seemed totally lost, never could understand my expression of amusement whenever I looked at my mirror image, resplendently uniformed as top Nazi military brass. "What's so funny?" he would ask. "Nothing," I would reply, without trying to explain.

Of all the losses I sustained during the conflagration in Hamburg, none had been as painful to me as the loss of my beloved hockey skates and my equally beloved trumpet. The shortage or total absence of "nonessential goods" rendered both irreplaceable. I especially missed being able to express myself musically. It was, therefore, a huge and most welcome surprise when Onkel Karl presented me one day with an old, beat-up B-flat clarinet that he had scrounged from one of his buddies. There was no doubt that it had seen better days. "I know it's not a trumpet, and it's not much to look at," my uncle said, "but it's the best I could do." With a great deal of intensive, tender love and care, I soon had the old licorice stick looking and performing almost like new. After many hours practicing, and after discovering that I had been playing with my mouthpiece upside down, I surprised everyone by being able to coax catchy modern tunes from the ancient instrument.

But with a war going on, my leisurely pursuit of my musical hobby was short-lived.

As required by law, my mother and I had registered with the local police precinct, thereby raising the number of several hundred Salza residents by two. In order to be eligible for food and clothing rationing cards, all able-bodied German males had to be employed in some phase of war production. I applied for a machinist job at a huge steel construction firm in nearby Nordhausen and was hired on the spot. Its size made my old plant in Hamburg look like a mom-and-pop shop. In its cavernous, deafeningly noisy hangar, I felt like an ant as gigantic steel objects passed precariously over my head, manipulated with precision by an invisible crane operator in a movable cabin high up under the ceiling. Although I had been hired as a certified machinist journeyman, I was clearly overqualified for the menial tasks I was assigned—grinding off burr left by cutting tools and moving loads with a forklift truck were among the more challenging ones.

THE SECRET OF THE KOHNSTEIN

As fall arrived, a troubling phenomenon caught my attention. A convoy of open military trucks passed daily by the window of my room at Harzstrasse 6. The trucks carried an unusual cargo—bald-shaven, emaciated-looking men in vertically striped convict garb, with hollow cheeks and huge, expressionless eyes that made their heads look like skulls. They stood jam-packed like cattle while several steel-helmeted armed SS guards seated on the tailgates faced them. The convoys of up to a dozen trucks were headed for the Kohnstein, a nearby pine-covered mountain to whose top Onkel Karl and I had hiked many times when I was a child. For the trucks' passengers, it was obviously a one-way journey, because whenever the convoys returned, they were empty.

The Kohnstein, my uncle told me, was now off limits to the public. It was totally fenced in and heavily patrolled. Another visible change was a huge gaping hole in the side of the mountain facing Salza, seemingly the entrance to a gigantic tunnel.

When I asked Onkel Karl what was going on in the Kohnstein, he merely put his index finger in front of his lips and whispered that whatever it was, it was a top government secret and none of our business.

"Don't go around asking questions about the Kohnstein," he warned me. "It'll only get you and all of us in trouble. The best thing to do is what everybody here is doing—forget what you have seen and act as if the Kohnstein doesn't exist."

That was easier said than done. I couldn't forget. The sight of the living dead in the SS convoy haunted me, especially at night when I would hear the trucks rumble past my window. Who were these wretched men? What were they doing in the mountain?

It wasn't until after the war had ended that I—and the rest of the world—learned the dark, horrible secret of the Kohnstein and its official name, Concentration Camp Dora-Mittelbau. In a diabolic scheme that could have been conceived only by fiends, the mountain served two major Nazi objectives: the production of the "miracle weapon," the V2 rocket, that was supposed to wrest an increasingly elusive German victory from the jaws of defeat, and the annihilation of literally thousands of men who, for one reason or another, had been branded enemies of the Hitler state.

While the expressionless faces of the men on the trucks betrayed utter despair, my wildest imagination was incapable of guessing the horror of torture, starvation, bone-crushing work, and—within a few months—death from exhaustion, undernourishment, and disease that awaited them once they entered the mountain.

I had no idea that only a fifteen-minute walk from where I lived in relative comfort, thousands of men were brutalized and literally worked to death, then cremated on the premises in ovens manufactured especially for that purpose. Neither did I guess that the black smoke that occasionally wafted from the mountain to Salza may well have originated from the crematorium. It didn't occur to me that the military staff cars that drove past the house might have contained some of the key people responsible for the mountain factory of death, including SS chief Heinrich Himmler, munitions chief Albert Speer, and the V-rocket mastermind, Wernher von Braun. Ironically, and shamefully, the latter would win laurels and VIP status in the United States only a few years later for spearheading the U.S. space program.

Spurred by curiosity and boredom, I decided one Sunday to take a walk in the direction of the Kohnstein to see how far I was still able to retrace my childhood steps. In retrospect, it wasn't one of my most brilliant ideas. Shortly after passing the last house of Salza on the Harzstrasse and the village's closed outdoor swimming pool, I reached a tall mesh-wire fence topped by barbed wire. There were several signs on the fence proclaiming that the area was off limits to unauthorized persons. From where I stood, I could clearly see the huge entrance to a tunnel but nothing more. There was no sign of life, with the exception of a solitary armed SS guard who, accompanied by a German shepherd dog, was slowly heading in my direction on the inside of the fence.

I had no desire to come face-to-face with the SS man and his dog. So before making eye contact with him, I turned around and headed back to Salza.

A few days later, when I returned from work, my aunt greeted me with an expression that spelled pending doom. Without a word, she handed me an official looking envelope from the office of Salza's mayor. The letter demanded my presence "on an urgent matter, as soon as possible." That, I knew, meant tomorrow. So before going to work the next morning, I went to the village hall, the only office building in "downtown" Salza. After waiting my turn while undergoing intense scrutiny from several villagers, all of whom, I was positive, knew already who I was, I was led into an adjoining office by a secretary, who told me that *Amtsleiter* Hirsch, the "mayor" of Salza, would attend to me personally. I had no illusion that this personal attention from the highest Nazi in the village was meant as a courtesy to me; rather, His Honor was short-staffed.

The big, brown-uniformed man seated behind a large desk in front of a huge swastika flag reminded me a little of Herr Wriede, my erstwhile school principal. I interpreted this as a bad omen. The mayor returned my *Heil Hitler* salute with a noncommittal expression, then asked for my ID. After carefully examining my *Wehrpass*, which indicated that I was ineligible for the draft, the mayor came straight to the point. "I have received a report that you have been seen spying at the Kohnstein. What do you have to say to that?"

At first I was unable to say anything. Being accused of spying at a top-secret military site was a matter of utmost gravity.

"I never spied at the Kohnstein or anywhere else," I finally told the mayor.

"Then what in heavens were you doing there?" Herr Hirsch demanded to know.

I told him about my hiking trips with my uncle as a child and how I was trying to relive that part of my childhood. Wisely, I left out my curiosity about the convoys and their strange cargo.

"As soon as I reached the wire fence and saw the 'Off Limits' signs," I assured Herr Hirsch, "I turned around."

The mayor seemed satisfied with my explanation, but warned me to stay away from that area in the future and to keep my nose clean in general.

"I have known *Schneidermeister* Baetz and Frau Baetz for many years," he told me. "They are fine people. So I don't want you to get them or yourself into trouble. Do you understand?"

After I assured the mayor that I understood perfectly, we exchanged *Heil Hitler*s and I was dismissed.

I never heard the end about my "foolishness" from Onkel Karl and Tante Grete after I told them what had transpired at the mayor's office.

"I told you to forget about the Kohnstein and not to worry about what's going on up there," Onkel Karl berated me, quite justifiably. "We are lucky the mayor is an old customer of mine for whom I've made many suits and uniforms. Otherwise, we could all be in deep trouble now."

I promised Onkel Karl, as I had promised the mayor, that henceforth I would watch my step.

BACK IN HAMBURG

At the time my mother and I were evacuated from Hamburg, we left in the belief that the city had been wiped out entirely, since we hadn't seen a single intact building on our way out. But during the ensuing months, we ran into several fellow refugees from Hamburg who assured us that substantial portions of the city had been spared.

The knowledge that not all of Hamburg had been reduced to rubble, as we had believed, triggered in us a longing to return that we found increasingly difficult to resist. It hadn't taken us long to discover that we simply weren't cut out for small-town life, no matter how idyllic. The mountains that surrounded us, and that we had once admired as beautiful tourist attractions, had in time become menacing prison walls to us that threatened to suffocate us. We both longed for the flat, unobstructed northern German landscape that surrounded Hamburg. No matter how much Onkel Karl and Tante Grete tried to make us feel at home and encouraged us to grow roots, we became more homesick by the day. Finally, we couldn't take it any longer, and decided to tell them that we were going back.

As we had expected, they all but hit the ceiling. Onkel Karl told us we were reckless and stupid for taking another chance to be killed by bombs when in rural Salza and Nordhausen we were safe from enemy attacks. Tante Grete played hardball by suggesting that we wanted to leave because we didn't think village life was good enough for us "city people." And Trudchen tried to change our minds by simply crying every time we brought up the subject. But after becoming convinced that nothing they could say would change our minds, they finally gave their blessing and wished us luck. A few days later, on a beautiful spring day, they saw us off with many hugs and tears, and the admonition that if things didn't turn out the way we expected, or if the air raids resumed, to come back on the next available train. The site was the same little whistle-stop where almost a year earlier we had arrived totally demoralized in the middle of the night, but this time our mood was upbeat, buoyed by anticipation of the old familiar sights and sounds.

With rail traffic restored to near normalcy, the trip back to Hamburg took only seven or so hours. Since it had gotten dark by the time we reached the city, we were mercifully spared the sight of the massive destruction that had almost claimed our lives. Although detonating bombs had turned the huge canopy over Hamburg's *Hauptbahnhof* into a glassless steel skeleton, the station, which was as busy as ever, was a most welcome sight to us. Without putting it into words, we both knew how deeply we felt about being back in the only city on earth where we felt at home.

At an information booth especially set up for returning refugees, we learned that the shelter for returnees nearest to where we used to live was a former elementary school on Brucknerstrasse which I used to pass daily on my way to school. A twenty-minute local subway train ride to Barmbek put us within walking distance of the shelter.

After checking our IDs, taking down our names, and handing each of us a clean, mothball-smelling blanket, a kindly warden briefed us on the amenities of his establishment, which consisted largely of two daily hot meals (lunch and supper) on the house, toilets, and cold water sinks for taking a "bath" in the basement, then led us to a classroom that had been converted to a dormitory. The room was filled with primitive wooden double bunks. The warden explained, with a telling wink, that since there were no lockers on the premises, it would be a good idea not to let our belongings out of our sight. He also told my mother that, since the place was co-ed, the only way women could assure themselves a measure of privacy while taking their baths was to get up in the morning before everybody else.

With privacy in mind, my mother and I chose two bottom bunks that were separated by a narrow aisle in the farthest corner of the room. On top of each bunk there were several stiff, porous sacks of some undefinable material filled with prickly straw and wood shavings—a far cry from the heavy mattresses, down-filled comforters, and fluffy pillows we had been used to all of our lives. But even the prospect of having to spend an entire night on these monstrosities could not dim our joy over having returned to our beloved city.

After storing our suitcases beneath our bunks, we joined our new roommates, about a dozen mostly elderly men and women, at a large table in front of the room for supper, which had been delivered in a huge, piping hot metal container by an emergency kitchen somewhere in the city. During the ensuing conversations, we learned that all were former Barmbekers who, like us, had lost virtually everything but their lives during the July 1943 bombing raids, and who, also like us, had returned because they found life away from Hamburg intolerable. All hoped to reestablish contact with family members and friends and to somehow rebuild their lives.

When the evening news came on the radio, everybody went silent. There were several sarcastic remarks when the announcer gave one of Dr. Goebbels's carefully worded reports of another "strategic withdrawal" of the German troops on the eastern front.

"Strategic withdrawal, my foot," sneered one of the men. "We are getting our ass whipped, that's what's happening. I wish they'd stop lying—" He abruptly stopped in midsentence as the warden poked his nose through the door to remind us that the lights would be turned off in half an hour, at 10 P.M.

"He seems like an okay fellow," the speaker resumed after the warden had closed the door, "but you never know about these Nazis."

I made sure not to voice my opinion, although I was in full agreement with him.

Two days later, two uniformed Nazi officials arrived at the shelter for a routine check of the residents. They carefully inspected and recorded our IDs and instructed us to either return immediately to our old jobs or, if that wasn't possible, to report to the employment office for reassignment to a new job. Each reminded us to do our share to help Germany win the war.

We knew that my mother's rubber factory had been largely bombed out and employed only a tiny skeleton crew, but decided to give it a try anyway. We were lucky. The personnel manager immediately put my mother to work in the kitchen and assigned her a bunk in a makeshift women's dorm. Since production at the plant had stopped, he said he had openings for machinists only in the company's intact branch plant in Harburg, Hamburg's neighbor city, south of the River Elbe. If I decided to take that job, he told me, I could stay at the Harburg plant's men's dorm rent-free. Without giving a great deal of thought to the consequences, I signed up, and the following morning, after a one-hour streetcar ride, I reported to my new boss, Meister Erdmann, the head of the Harburg plant's machine shop.

TALE OF TWO CITIES

When Herr Erdmann and I met, it was mutual dislike at first sight. Unable to conceal his feelings, Erdmann, a shriveled prune of a man with a permanent scowl, eyed me suspiciously as he briefed me on my future duties, which, he explained, consisted largely of troubleshooting. Housed in a dozen or so buildings throughout the plant were hundreds of steam presses used to mold hard rubber into various shapes under heat and pressure. Before the war, the company specialized in the manufacture of high-quality combs, smoking-pipe stems, and other useful household items. But like virtually all industrial plants in wartime Germany, the company had switched to the production of war-essential objects. Only the company's top brass, I was told, were privy to the military purpose, or purposes, of the various odd-shaped objects the presses were turning out at a record pace.

Among the machine shop's major responsibilities was the maintenance of a vast network of pipes that carried the steam from the boilers to the presses. Another was the tooling and replacement of worn-out machine parts. "You will be working quite a bit on your own in various departments all over the plant," Herr Erdmann concluded the briefing, "but just so we understand each other, there will be no goofing off on the job."

When I asked him what gave him the idea that I had come all the way to a miserable hick town like Harburg to goof off, he revealed the real source of his problem. "All you Hamburgers think you are so damn smart that nobody can tell you anything," he fumed. "Well, let me tell you something, my friend: I have already smelled in places where you have yet to shit."

Since I had no interest in hearing further details about his venturesome nose, I left his remark unchallenged, but decided right then and there that ours was not going to be a good relationship.

Later, several of the machinists who had been transferred to Harburg from the Hamburg plant told me not to take anything Erdmann said personally. Like many small-town Harburgers, they explained, he harbored an inbred suspicion and envy of all big-city Hamburgers.

In spite of Erdmann, I rather liked my new job, especially the virtual independence and mobility it afforded me. Since I was one of only a few machinists at the shop who were qualified gas (acetylene) and arc (electric) welders, I was soon in high demand for special welding assignments that earned me the respect of my machinist peers and even the grudging approval of Erdmann. I got along well with my coworkers, especially the Hamburg contingent, and I made new friends among the French foreign workers with whom I shared quarters at the company dorm. One in particular, a handsome Parisian in his early twenties by the name of Jean Heideiger, became a real close pal whose lasting legacy to me was the ability to tie a Windsor knot and all the French four-letter words I know.

One day, there was a big commotion in the factory yard when a convoy of army trucks discharged their load—a hundred or so Italian prisoners of war. They were part of several Italian divisions that, since the ouster of Mussolini and the subsequent surrender of the Italian army, had been captured by the German army and pressed into service in Germany's war industry. The newly arrived POWs were a pitiful, scared-looking bunch in tattered, dirty uniforms. All were unshaven, hollow-eyed, and near starvation. At every opportunity they were digging in garbage cans in hopes of finding scraps of food or stretching out their hands to us and pleading for *mangiare*. Without being asked, they hastened to assure us that they had always been loyal to Mussolini. "Mussolini *gut* (good); Badoglio *schlecht* (bad)," they insisted in an obvious attempt to ingratiate themselves to their captors. Since most Germans had never been too crazy about Mussolini and their Italian allies, whose fighting prowess they had always held in deep contempt, the German workers were not impressed. They nevertheless treated their new fellow workers with compassion, if not respect.

Within a few weeks, the Italians underwent a stunning transformation into reasonably well-fed and well-groomed hunks with glistening movie-star hairstyles and flamboyant personalities to match. Their initially obsequious demeanor had been replaced by a macho swagger and their straggly beards had given way to slick shaves and meticulously carved black mustaches. This dramatic change had not been lost on the plant's female workers, and before long I observed, with considerable envy, how some of the fairest maidens at the factory cavorted openly with their brand-new Latin lovers.

In addition to the Italian and French foreign workers there were also workers from the Soviet Union. The latter lived a far more restricted life and were kept in segregated camps. Since they were not allowed any social contact with Germans or other nationalities, I never became acquainted with any of them.

My life would have been reasonably bearable had it not been for the fact that I was obliged to live in Harburg, in those days an ugly, industrial town bereft of any type of diversion, except for a few movie theaters and a few neighborhood pubs. Consequently, I looked forward with eager anticipation to Saturdays, when the noon whistle signaled the end of the workweek and I would take the streetcar to Hamburg and visit my mother. With the permission of her roommate, a kindly old lady, I crashed Saturday and Sunday nights at her dorm and returned to Harburg on the streetcar on Monday morning.

One Saturday, a few minutes before plant closing, as I was rushing to catch the next Hamburg-bound streetcar, Meister Erdmann called me into his small, glass-enclosed office, from which he could overlook the entire shop. Handing me a work order, he informed me that a major steam pipe in one of the steam-press rooms had sprung a leak that needed repair. I carefully folded the piece of paper, shoved it in my pocket, and, promising Erdmann that I would take care of it first thing Monday morning, prepared to leave his office.

"Not so fast, my friend," he interrupted my getaway. He then explained that since the hole could not be welded shut while there was pressurized steam in the pipe, the job had to be done while the steam was shut off and the pipe had had a chance to drain, namely on Sunday. "This," he told me with a wicked grin, "is where you come in."

When I asked him, "Why me?" and pointed out that I had already made other plans that I couldn't change, he bluntly insisted that, since most of my fellow machinists had families and I didn't, the job was logically mine, whether I liked it or not.

I most emphatically begged to differ and stormed out of Erdmann's office, followed by shouts threatening dire consequences unless I changed my mind. Since I couldn't see myself skipping the weekly visit with my mother to which we both looked forward so much, changing my mind was out of the question. Besides, at age eighteen, I wasn't about to let a prune like Erdmann push me around. Without giving the matter another thought, I left the plant and within an hour was on my way to Hamburg.

I didn't resume thinking about Erdmann until I showed up at the shop the next Monday morning, still proud of myself that I hadn't let him intimidate me. To my surprise, he greeted me with a wide grin instead of his familiar scowl. I soon learned the reason for his uncharacteristic mirth. "Let's go for a little walk," he invited me, still grinning from ear to ear. After a few minutes, we entered a large hall filled with rows upon rows of steam presses. Usually, the hall was teeming with activity and filled with the hissing sound of escaping steam and the thumping sounds of presses. Now the hall was quiet, except for the chatter of fifty or so men and women who stood idly at their workstations.

"Put your hand here," Erdmann told me while pointing at the nearest press. When I did, I noticed that the normally scalding hot press surface was cold as ice.

"You're in big trouble, my friend," Erdmann said, grinning, "and it serves you right. I warned you, but you wouldn't listen. What you have done is sabotage, and I don't have to tell you what they do with saboteurs." He gleefully explained to me that my failure to fix the steam pipe on Sunday had resulted in a massive and irretrievable loss of valuable work hours and a subsequent loss of extremely vital war production.

After his lecture, Erdmann told me that the big boss wanted to have a word with me, then walked me to the administration building where he asked to see the plant's general manager. The prospect of facing the company's omnipotent, yet seldom visible, top executive caused all of the cockiness I had felt earlier that morning to evaporate and make room for feelings of unmitigated terror.

When we were admitted to the vast, wood-paneled executive office, the general manager, a corporate-type white-haired man with dark horn-rimmed glasses, was seated behind a desk. Seated in front of him was the plant's chief engineer, Erdmann's boss. The two men, apparently already well briefed by Erdmann regarding my act of "criminal nonfeasance," looked at me with grave expressions.

"What *um Himmels Willen* (in heaven's name) was on your mind when you decided not to show up for work as you had been ordered?" the general manager finally broke the silence. "Didn't it occur to you that willfully interfering with war production is sabotage?"

Trying to sound as convincing as I could, I told him that sabotage was the farthest thing from my mind, that the only reason I disobeyed Erdmann was that I felt I had been unfairly and arbitrarily singled out to give up my free Sunday, to which I felt I was entitled, since nobody had ever told me otherwise.

When I had finished, the general manager unleashed a tirade, pointing out that working a few hours on one Sunday was nothing compared to the sacrifices made day after day by our brave soldiers at the front. "What gives you the right to question an order from Meister Erdmann?" he shouted. "You have endangered the lives of our fighting men by depriving them of urgently needed weapons."

In my mind, I cursed my stupidity in not carrying out Erdmann's order to work on Sunday. I wholeheartedly agreed with his diagnosis of my predicament; I certainly was in big trouble. Just when the panic that gripped me was about to make me physically sick, the general manager calmed down. "Since your mother has been a valued, long-term employee with us, I have decided not to report the matter to the Gestapo this time in order to spare her any grief," he told me. "But," he continued, and his voice rose again, "I cannot let your flagrant disobedience go unpunished. So for the next five weeks, you will report for work every Sunday—or else! Is that understood?"

After I assured him that he could count on my compliance, I was dismissed, greatly relieved to have gotten away so cheap. There wasn't the slightest doubt in my mind that, had my "act of sabotage" been reported to the Gestapo, my fate would have been sealed.

Calling myself lucky, I silently endured five Sundays of backbreaking work and other punishments Erdmann had cooked up especially for me. Trained machinists were traditionally exempted from unskilled labor, but Erdmann ordered me to perform one of the most menial tasks he could find. "Let's see how good you are at cleaning the inside of boilers, my friend," he told me with a sneer that dared me to refuse. He was talking about the giant steel tanks that were used for generating steam. Unwilling to make Erdmann's day, I had no choice but to go along with his program. After entering through a narrow manhole, I spent hours attacking stubborn layer after stubborn layer of limestone deposits on the boiler's interior walls with an air chisel until the deafening staccato of the chisel and the thick choking dust it created forced me to come up gasping for air. At the end of a day spent inside a boiler without a mask or ear protection, I would be semi-deaf and coughing up dust for hours, only to return to the same job the next Sunday.

Yet even the physical hell I suffered inside the boilers didn't compare with the psychological torture I endured each time I encountered Erdmann's grinning face. It took all the willpower I could muster to keep from telling him how much I despised him, or worse, beating him to a pulp. By constantly reminding myself that Erdmann was hoping I would lose my composure and that the Gestapo was only a telephone call away, I managed to keep my cool.

One Saturday, again shortly before quitting time, Erdmann once more ordered me to weld a steam pipe that had sprung a leak. This time he got no argument out of me. But when I was about to start the repair, I noticed that the pipe and the ceiling to which it was attached were covered with a thick layer of a gluelike substance that I was unable to identify. When I reported this to Erdmann and suggested that the substance might present a fire hazard, he interrupted me. "Why don't you just for once do as you were told without opening your big mouth?" he hollered.

To avoid another incident, I closed my "big mouth," turned around, and started to do as I had been told. But as soon as the relatively small gas flame of my welding torch touched the pipe, it set off a gigantic column of fire that soon enveloped the entire ceiling. I was certain that the building would be destroyed and that this time there really would be a Gestapo inquiry into my "suspicious activities." Fortunately, somebody sounded the fire alarm and within a few minutes the plant's fire brigade was on the scene. A brief dousing with power hoses put out the fire.

As soon as Erdmann heard of the mishap, he nimbly tried to avoid blame by going on the offensive. "This time you've really done it!" he screamed. "I told you to weld the pipe, not to set the building on fire." Luckily I had already compared notes with a fellow machinist who had stood just a few feet away when Erdmann chewed me out for "opening my big mouth." So when Erdmann told me that on Monday we would have to see "the Big Man" again to make sure I'd get what was coming to me for my second act of sabotage, I was ready for him. "In that case," I replied calmly, "I shall bring along someone who heard you shut me up when I tried to warn you of a fire hazard." That was the last I heard from Erdmann regarding the incident.

But I soon discovered that I wasn't out of the woods just yet. I don't know what possessed me, but emboldened by adolescent insouciance—read "stupidity"—I had made it my habit each morning when arriving at our men's locker room to greet my coworkers with an exaggerated cheerful *Heil Hitler* salute. Foolishly assuming that everyone present was as fed up with the Nazis as I was, I intended my greetings to be a bit of clever sarcasm. But that's where I made my big mistake. One day, Carl Wedemayer, a veteran Harburg machinist who, it was rumored, had passed the Aryan test by the skin of his teeth, called me aside. "There have been complaints about you," he confided. "Some of the Harburgers, who can't stand you guys from

Hamburg anyway, have been taking exception to the way you come on with that '*Heil Hitler*' each morning. They know you are not sincere and they don't think it's funny."

I immediately realized that I had overplayed my hand and thanked him for tipping me off. If there's anything I should have learned by then, it was that the Nazis did not have a sense of humor when the joke was on them, and that if made fun of, they were known to strike back with unrelenting brutality. Hoping against hope that Wedemayer's warning hadn't come too late and that there wouldn't be any repercussions because of my stupidity, I promised myself to henceforth keep my big, smart-alecky mouth shut. Fortunately, my indescribable luck held up.

Two unforeseen developments helped lessen the ordeal of living and working in Harburg to a considerable degree. One was that my mother was being transferred to the Harburg plant's kitchen. The other was that she had found a place for us in Hamburg where we could live together under the same roof again. The place was the former public elementary school on von Essenstrasse, one of a handful of buildings in Hamburg's Eilbek district that had survived the July 1943 bombing. The school had been designated as a shelter for bombed-out homeless people like us. It had a house manager, a stern no-nonsense matron, who registered my mother and me and assigned us to classrooms that had been converted into dorms and were located on opposite ends of the school. She explained to us that up to 9 P.M., husbands and wives—like sons and mothers—were allowed to visit each other in their respective dorms. Although my mother and I had to rise as early as 5 A.M. six days each week and commute for at least an hour to Harburg by streetcar, and I usually didn't get back until 7 P.M., my mother and I were ecstatically happy for the first time in a long while. All that mattered to us was that we were together again. Nothing had worried us more than the thought of one of us being caught in an air raid while we were apart. As absurd as it seems now, we derived a strong sense of safety simply from being together.

Life for my mother and me was still hard, but it had assumed a certain rhythm of normalcy. We'd get up early in the morning and walk ten minutes through the ruins to catch a streetcar at Denhaide, where we would meet fellow workers from the rubber factory. Since my mother's kitchen job required fewer hours than my ten-hour daily schedule, she would catch an earlier streetcar back to Hamburg, and begin preparing our meager supper in the school's basement community kitchen.

In our daily preoccupation with surviving the war, my mother and I had almost forgotten about the racial problems that had plagued us in the past. But an incident that occurred when we least expected it jarred us back to reality. It happened on a streetcar on our way to work. Since seats were hard to come by, my mother and I had made it a habit to take turns sitting down if one of us was lucky enough to find a seat.

This particular morning, I was seated and half asleep while my mother was standing in front of me when a much-decorated, one-legged soldier on crutches grabbed me by the lapel of my coat and yanked me to my feet. "Get up, you *auslandisches Dreckschwein* (filthy foreign pig) and let this German woman sit down!" he shouted at the top of his lungs while pointing at my mother. "We didn't fight at the front so that *Dreck* like you can enjoy themselves at our expense."

Obviously, the good warrior had totally misjudged the situation in which he found himself, especially the German workers' growing disgust with everything that smacked of war, including its heroes. "Why don't you shut up and mind your own damn business," one of my fellow workers with whom I had only a casual acquaintance offered in response to the soldier's insulting remarks.

When the surprised infantryman challenged my colleague to a fight, the latter told him cruelly but truthfully, "You're not going to fight anybody. You may not realize it yet, but your fighting days are over, comrade. Now stop bothering our friend or I'll throw you off this streetcar."

Looking at several dozen pairs of hostile eyes and realizing too late that he had opened the wrong can of worms, the soldier let go of my lapel. Thoroughly humiliated, he awkwardly moved to the exit and quietly hobbled off the streetcar at the next stop. I watched him lean dejectedly on his crutches as the streetcar pulled away and tried—without quite succeeding—to rejoice over the well-deserved humiliation he had brought on himself.

Both my mother and I were moved by our fellow worker's display of solidarity. When I later thanked him for coming to my rescue in a moment of need, he told me to forget it. "It's high time these so-called war heroes realize that their glory days are over and that their medals and their missing arms and legs don't amount to much anymore."

His remarks, spoken quite openly for others to hear, made me realize how much the tide of war had shifted, but an incident a few days later served me as a grim reminder that at least for the time being, the evil forces of Nazidom still prevailed. It was on an icy cold winter day. Erdmann had sent me to a building to repair a broken metal window frame. From the first-floor window, I had a full view of the street that connected Harburg with Hamburg via the *Elbbrücken* (Elbe bridges). Suddenly, I noticed a strange procession of women, flanked by steel-helmeted, rifle-carrying SS men, headed slowly in my direction. As they came closer, I could see that they were mostly young women, some still in their teens, and that all of them were wearing the yellow star of David with the inscription JUDE, in keeping with Nazi law. While their guards kept watchful eyes on them and on passersby, the women cleaned the street with heavy brooms and shovels. The punishing cold notwithstanding, most wore only thin coats and some wore neither gloves nor hats, in contrast to the guards, who wore heavily padded winter gear. Despite their obvious misery, none of the women betrayed the agony they were suffering. Instead, they went about their task in absolute silence and without the slightest expression on their faces, like living dead.

Within a few minutes, they had disappeared around the bend of the street and I returned my attention to the task I had been assigned. But throughout the day and in the days that followed, I was haunted by the memory of that silent group of young women who had briefly crossed my path, wondering what horror they must have seen that had transformed them into mute and expressionless zombies, and what additional horrors their captors had in store for them, or for that matter, whether a similar fate was yet awaiting me.

The chilling news I received a few days later, when I accidentally ran into a former friend and neighbor of ours in downtown Hamburg, did nothing to lift my spirits. Gerda Bayer, a girl my age, and her parents had been with us in the air-raid shelter the night we were bombed out. Now living in Finkenwerder on the other side of the Elbe, she told me that when her family and other bombing victims were being evacuated from the burning city on that memorable morning, Jack Spederski, our friend who had been on furlough from the Russian front, changed into his civilian clothes and joined their group of refugees. She recalled that they wound up in a small village where they were given shelter and food, and eventually jobs. Jack, she said, lived an idyllic life, doing some farm work but mainly carrying on a hot romance with Ilse Kormann, a beautiful, dark-haired girl from our old neighborhood. But the idyll didn't last for very long. Perhaps on a tip from an informer, a uniformed Nazi from the village started making inquiries about Jack. When Jack got wind of this, he left in a hurry without leaving a forwarding address. Shortly thereafter, Gerda said, a detachment of soldiers from the *Gross-Deutschland Division* in Berlin arrived with bloodhounds and began to search the nearby woods. Within a few hours, Gerda said, they had found Jack and dragged him away in shackles. She said that since he had claimed her family as his relatives, the Bayers were informed a short while later that Jack Spederski had been shot by a firing squad after having been found guilty of desertion. While Jack and I had not been best buddies, the news of his death hit me hard.

TOTAL WAR

My dorm at the school on von Essenstrasse was sparsely furnished with a dozen or so steel bunks and as many lockers. Seated around a table in the middle of the room and listening intently to a small radio were five old-timers, typical Hamburg blue-collar types. Their advanced age had put them beyond the reach of the military draft; nevertheless, they worked in a variety of menial jobs around the city.

After eyeing me suspiciously in the beginning, they soon accepted me as one of them. To my continual amusement and entertainment, they turned out to be the most contentious bunch of people I had ever met. From the moment we got up in the wee hours of morning until the 10 P.M. lights out, they bickered and argued. Their perpetual quibbling notwithstanding, they were firmly united in their shared contempt of Hitler and the Nazi regime, a contempt they vented freely without regard for their safety. Their most scathing sarcasm they reserved for the daily radio reports from the OKW *(Oberkommando der Wehrmacht)*, the military headquarters, which informed the German people of the progress of Hitler's war. Disagreeing openly with everything the announcer said, they delighted in predicting that the *Schweinehund* Hitler and his fellow *Schweinehunde* would soon reap their just reward in front of an Allied firing squad.

Those words were music to my ears, but, remembering my close call with Reingruber, the treacherous journeyman from my apprentice days, I thought it wise not to contribute to their seditious discussions. I also made sure never to take sides in any of their numerous arguments.

On July 20, 1944, our dorm's radio crackled with the most sensational news of the war—a group of German army officers had tried to assassinate Hitler in a bomb plot at his Rastenburg headquarters. Miraculously, the Führer had escaped with minor injuries.

My dormmates could hardly contain their disappointment. They cursed and some of them threw themselves across their bunks in a show of mock despair over the fact that "the *Schweinehund* had gotten away." As more and more details of the failed plot and the identity of the main conspirator, Colonel Count Claus von Stauffenberg, were released, that sentiment was echoed among many workers throughout the Hamburg area, although with considerably more restraint.

My dormmates consoled themselves with the hope that another plot was just around the corner and that the next time, the plotters would not fail. I wasn't so sure. The swift and exceedingly brutal retribution against the plotters and their families seemed to me too strong a deterrent against another attempt to end the dictator's life.

The immediately noticeable effect of the failed coup was an order from the Führer's headquarters that all members of the *Wehrmacht* adopt the outstretched-arm *Heil Hitler* salute, previously used only by units of the *Waffen*-SS. The order was undoubtedly meant as a constant and grim reminder to the army, which had supplied the plotters, of who was boss.

With fighting morale sinking rapidly both at home and on the front, Hitler still had an ace up his sleeve in the form of a frail, club-footed man with thinning dark hair on an oversized head and huge, piercing dark eyes: Dr. Joseph Goebbels, *Reichsminister für Volksaufklärung und Propaganda*, the greatest spin doctor of all time. Within weeks of the failed coup, Dr. Goebbels was charged with the responsibility of mobilizing the country for the *Totalen Krieg* (total war), which he had proclaimed the year before. My dormmates and I listened incredulously as he appealed to the German people to dedicate their last ounces of energy toward the achievement of the "inevitable" *Endsieg* (final victory). Now he hinted at the deployment of secret *Wunderwaffen*, which, he promised, would turn the tide of the war in favor of Germany. Due to his relentless exaggerations, distortions of facts, and broken promises of victories just around the corner, his name had become a synonym for liar. It seemed ironically fitting, and had not escaped the masses, that he was an admirer of literature's greatest teller of tall tales, the legendary Baron von Münchhausen, so much so that he ordered an epic movie made about him that is still regarded as a cinematic masterpiece. Most people regarded the entire "total war" campaign as what it turned out to be, a criminal effort on the part of the doomed Nazi elite to prolong their lives by a few more months at the expense and peril of the people. But those who had been quick to dismiss "total war" as an empty PR slogan were proved woefully wrong.

Following on the heel of Goebbels's appointment came the introduction of the compulsory sixty-hour workweek, the suspension of all holidays, and the closing of all schools. In addition, so-called *Etappenschweine* (rear-echelon pigs) and *Drückeberger* (goldbrickers), soldiers who had managed to avoid front-line duty by serving in noncombat support units, were reassigned to combat units, regardless of their physical condition.

As part of the "total war" mobilization effort, the German military high command announced the forming of the *Volkssturm* (literally, People's Storm), a compulsory militia made up entirely of rejects—men who formerly had been considered too old, too decrepit, or, like me, otherwise unfit for military service. All men from age sixteen to sixty-five were ordered to report for *Volkssturm* duty regardless of previous military status classification.

In keeping with that order, on a nice fall Sunday morning, I trotted to a nearby army barracks that had been designated as *Volkssturm* induction station. Having long gotten my military ambitions out of my system, I expected to be sent home the moment the first recruiter laid eyes on me. But no such luck. Instead of being told to get lost because non-Aryans were too low on the evolutionary scale to deserve the honor of dying for Germany, an army corporal handed me a beat-up, obsolete-looking rifle and ordered me to join the ragtag-looking bunch of ancient men in civilian clothes who were shouldering ancient rifles like mine.

The officers and noncommissioned officers on duty were, without exception, much-decorated, seasoned combat veterans. Several wore black eye patches or carried their arms in slings. The senior officer in charge, a young major and wearer of the *Ritterkreuz* (Knight's Cross), saluted with his left hand because his right arm was missing. After welcoming us to the *Volkssturm,* he told us that in order to bring about the *Endsieg,* we had both the *Pflicht* (obligation) and *Ehre* (honor) to defend, if necessary with our lives, our *Vaterland,* which through treachery at home and abroad now found itself in its greatest hour of need. He then explained that the meeting was primarily an orientation session and that the following Sunday, we would be formally sworn in.

Much to my disappointment, none of the officers paid any attention to my exotic looks, which in the past had kept me out of military service. Instead, I was marched about the barracks ground like everybody else and given belated instruction on how to defend the *Vaterland* against the uninvited intruders who were closing in on Germany from every direction. Surveying my tottering comrades-in-arms, most of whom were cursing under their breath or ridiculing the attempt to turn them into combat soldiers, the ironic truth hit me that, my permanent tan notwithstanding, I was without a doubt the most physically fit in the entire group.

After an hour or so of perfunctory, out-of-step close-order drill, we were divided into small groups and assigned to cadres who gave demonstrations in the use of the *Panzerfaust* (armor fist), a hand-held grenade launcher that, we were told, was capable of knocking out a Sherman or Stalin tank. All we had to do, an instructor explained, was to wait in ambush until a tank came along and with one press on the trigger, *swoosh*—the tank and its crew would be history.

I recalled the remarks of the German army officer who only two years earlier had sneered at me when I told him that I wanted to enlist. Seething with racial arrogance, he had boasted, "Germany will never be so hard-up as to need the likes of you to win the war." If I needed any more tangible evidence that Germany was down on its ass and about to lose this war, I merely had to look into the mirror. Nazi Germany had clearly and incontrovertibly reached the point when it desperately needed "the likes of me," not to *win* the war, but merely to buy itself a few days of time before it would be crushed by the Allied juggernaut. The shoe, I decided, was clearly on the other foot.

After another pep talk from the major, we were dismissed and told to return the following Sunday for additional seasoning. I decided that I already knew all I ever wanted to know about the *Panzerfaust* and that coming for more instruction would be a waste of my valuable time. Since nobody had taken down my name or in any way recorded my presence, I surmised that nobody would miss me terribly in the event I didn't show up the following week. Momentary concerns about the possibility of being hauled before a military tribunal to answer to charges of desertion were swept aside with characteristic youthful bravado. "I'll cross that bridge when I get to it," I told myself. Fortunately, my luck held out again and the bridge remained uncrossed.

MISTAKEN IDENTITY

During the fall of 1944, more and more people in Harburg, which so far had been spared the fate of Hamburg, were plagued by fears that time was running out and were bracing for the worst. With most German industrial cities in ruins, I found it harder each day to believe that Harburg would be spared indefinitely. Before long, events justified my skepticism.

One bright afternoon while I was replacing a section of leaky steam pipe, the wailing of air-raid sirens interrupted my work. The warning sent me and everyone else in the factory to the underground air-raid shelter on the premises. There, welcoming any reprieve from the mandatory ten-hour daily work routine, the workers relaxed and chatted until a voice on the air-raid intercom system announced that a large contingent of heavy U.S. bombers was headed straight for Harburg-Wilhelmsburg. Soon, the conversations ended and tense silence pervaded the bunker. I reflected that, luckily, my mother should be safe and sound in Hamburg since the kitchen staff left early after cleaning up the kitchen and cafeteria following lunch.

Suddenly, through the droning of hundreds of bombers, the whining of the first bombs became audible. Next came a series of deafening explosions that were followed by violent, earthquakelike tremors. To me, the scene was only too familiar. Somehow, I felt strangely detached and calm, almost as if certain I would not be harmed. For most of my fellow workers, on the other hand, the massive day raid constituted their baptism of fire.

Contemptuously, I studied the cowering plant executives, all futilely trying to hide the mortal fear that had taken hold of them. What had happened, I wondered, to Hitler's arrogant master race of only a few years ago—especially their leaders? Meister Erdmann, normally all callousness and sarcasm, huddled pitifully in a corner, barely able to control the shaking of his limbs. Similarly, the plant's general manager, the haughty, white-haired arch-Nazi who not long ago had threatened to report me to the Gestapo unless I became more cooperative, was reduced to moans each time a bomb hit nearby.

Also seated among the group of cowering plant big shots was the plant *Pförtner* (gatekeeper) whose real name was Zervat or something like that, but whom everybody called Cerberus behind his back, after the mythical three-headed monster dog that guarded the gate of Hades. Zervat had come honestly by the contempt in which he was held by the rank and file. A fanatic Nazi, with an ever-present party button in the lapel of his neat black suit to prove it, he never smiled or mingled with any of the employees and delighted in literally lowering the boom on workers who were a split second late. When that happened to me once, he ordered me into his tiny station where he dressed me down for neglecting my duty to aid the war by being punctual, then threatened to report me to the personnel department for disciplinary action should I ever be late again.

Seeing some of my tormentors squirm with fear had a strangely modifying effect on whatever pangs of fear I experienced myself. For a moment, I had the perverse wish that a bomb should hit the plant above and put it out of commission, thus helping to hasten the end of the war.

I was not to be disappointed. Only moments later a deafening detonation and a bone-jarring quake that shook the shelter occupants out of their seats or off their feet left no doubt in my mind that my wish had been granted. The explosion knocked out the electricity, leaving the bunker in complete darkness. Once the earth stopped shaking as the bombings ceased, someone managed to open an exit door and the people, severely shaken but uninjured, scrambled up the stairs that led to the factory yard. I had difficulty hiding my glee over the sight that awaited me. The building that had housed the much-hated machine shop had been transformed into a huge mountain of smoldering rubble. I remembered that somewhere deep down under that vast pile of bricks, there was a locker containing a pair of shoes, a shirt, a jacket, and slacks that belonged to me. But my personal loss could not dampen the joy I felt over the U.S. airmen's work of destruction.

With the vitally important machine shop out of commission and most of the workers in a state of shock from the harrowing experience, management announced that everybody could go home and to report for work again the following day. In my case, going home was easier said than done. The destruction of the machine shop and nearby streetcar rails presented me with a big problem—how to get back to Hamburg? There was one immediate recourse. I decided to take my chance and walk to the Harburg *Hauptbahnhof,* in hopes of catching a Hamburg-bound commuter train.

The air attack had left a scene of widespread devastation and an eerie silence had settled over Harburg. Still deafened from the pounding of the bombs and choking from the dense smoke that covered the area, I stumbled over smoldering debris, past burning buildings, uprooted trees, and twisted streetcar rails. With the utmost care I avoided the many cables that the bombs had unearthed, which were coiled like angry snakes, ready at a touch to discharge their lethal voltage. I tried hard not to look too closely at the grotesquely charred and mangled corpses that were scattered all about. The thought struck me that only a couple of hours earlier these corpses had been living, breathing human beings, like myself. My thoughts about the fleeting nature of life were interrupted when a scream pierced the silence.

"There's one of them!" a female voice shrieked. Screaming hysterically at the top of her lungs, a woman of Valkyrian proportions pointed straight at me. "There's one of the murderers!" she continued. "Kill that American swine! Let him find out how it feels to burn alive!"

Summoned by the woman's screams, people came running from every direction to investigate. Within minutes, I was surrounded by an angry, cursing, and wildly gesticulating mob.

At first, I was at a total loss as to the meaning of the commotion. Then, looking down on the welding goggles around my neck, my grease-splattered blue coveralls, and—more to the point—my brown hands, the ironic truth hit me. They were mistaking me for a black U.S. pilot who, they believed, had bailed out after his plane had been shot down.

I felt like laughing and telling everybody what a bunch of jerks they were.

But I thought better of it, realizing that my situation was all but comical and that if there was a joke, the joke was definitely on me. Enraged over the destruction and casualties around them, the people were in no mood to listen to reason, certainly not when the facts, as they saw them, left no room for any other conclusion.

Fueled by the Valkyrie's constant screaming and urging "get it over with" by throwing me into one of the burning buildings, the mob's mood grew uglier. I sensed that the point had been reached where the slightest provocation on my part would trip my adversaries' collective hair-trigger nerves and turn them into an uncontrollable lynch mob. A look at their hate-distorted faces underscored the hopelessness of my predicament. I realized that to my captors, I represented a convenient scapegoat on which to vent their pent-up, impotent rage at their aerial tormentors. All that stood between me and a horrible death at the hands of my own countrymen now, I realized, was their deeply ingrained sense of obedience. At least for the moment, they still seemed reluctant to act without the command of a leader with authority. How long that reluctance would last, I did not dare to guess.

At the very height of my distress, I received a reprieve from quite an unexpected source. Just as the human wall around me grew more dense and more threatening, it parted and admitted a strapping police lieutenant. "Quiet, everybody, and back up to the other side of the street!" he shouted, his right hand suggestively resting on the holster of his huge service pistol. Conditioned to respecting uniforms, the people immediately obeyed. I breathed a sigh of temporary relief while wondering on whose side of the law the officer would turn out to be. After carefully examining my blue Kennkarte—an ID card all Germans were obliged to carry on their persons at all times—and finding it in order, the lieutenant relaxed his heretofore official demeanor and eyed me with unconcealed, almost fatherly kindness. "So what's the matter with you?" he demanded. When I told him what had happened to me at the plant, he soon became convinced that, my brown skin notwithstanding, my unadulterated Hamburger dialect was unmistakably homegrown.

"They're a bunch of hysterical idiots," the lieutenant said with a nod toward the crowd across the street. He got no argument from me.

"Now let's see if we can't get you home," the lieutenant said while flagging down an already overcrowded Hamburg-bound bus.

"How are you fixed for bus fare?" the lieutenant demanded.

When I told him that what little money I had carried that day had been left in the locker that was destroyed with the plant, the officer reached in his pocket and handed me the necessary change.

"I want you to make sure this young man gets safely to Hamburg. I am holding you responsible," the officer instructed the driver of the bus.

"Jawohl, Herr Leutnant," the bus driver replied. "Come aboard, young fellow."

Before complying, I thanked my good Samaritan who, in turn, wished me *"Hals und Beinbruch"* (neck and leg fracture)—a German expression for *Good luck.* As the bus pulled away, I heaved a sigh of relief, keenly aware of the hate-filled eyes of the crowd that followed me until I was out of sight.

It was not until quite a while after the war that I came to fully appreciate the mortal danger in which I found myself when the police officer came to my aid. Although they were never mentioned during the German war-crimes trials conducted by the Allies, there were hundreds of reliable reports about some of the most gruesome atrocities committed by German civilians and German military personnel, especially *Waffen*-SS, against black U.S. soldiers, including airmen who were forced to bail out over Germany or German-occupied territory. Efforts by some concerned eyewitnesses to bring the perpetrators to justice failed, partially because it became practically impossible to identify and locate the culprits and partially because of official apathy.

THE GIORDANOS

Early in January 1945, while returning late one night after watching a movie downtown, I got off the commuter train at Friedrichsberg station, then headed for the school that for more than a year had been my and my mother's home. I walked briskly along a footpath that wound gently through Eilbeckthal, a large, dark, and deserted park. Suddenly, I heard footsteps approaching from behind. While I had no particular reason to anticipate an attack, I was mentally prepared for one. In fact, I would have welcomed an opportunity to put my boxing skill to work in self-defense. As I looked over my shoulder and strained my eyes in the dim light cast by a thin sliver of moon, I could make out the outline of a man.

I slowed my pace to let the stranger catch up. As he walked beside me, I recognized a young fellow about my age, of stocky build and with thick horn-rimmed glasses. Immediately, I realized that I had seen that fellow many times among the swingboy crowd at Café König. The recognition was mutual.

"I know you," said the fellow. "You used to hang out at Café König. I'm Egon Giordano."

"I remember having seen you, too," I replied. I introduced myself and we shook hands.

"Want a cigarette?" Egon asked.

"No thanks, I don't smoke."

While Egon lighted a cigarette, we resumed our walk, nostalgically recalling the good times at our favorite neighborhood hangout before it was razed by bombs in 1943. Inevitably, our conversation turned to the war.

"It won't be long now and these goddamn Nazi swine will be finished," Egon announced wistfully.

I was struck by the hatred in his voice, but didn't respond. Although I harbored similar sentiments, experience had taught me to keep my opinions and my negative prognosis to myself when talking to people I had no particular reason to trust. When Egon noticed my reticence, he laughed.

"You don't have to be afraid of me," he assured me. "I thought you knew that I am a Jew."

On hearing the word *Jew,* I recoiled. I had all the sympathy in the world for Jews, but felt that because of my own precarious situation I needed being seen in a clandestine-looking meeting with a Jew like I needed a hole in my head.

"No, I had no idea you were a Jew," I finally replied. "What made you think I knew?"

"I thought everybody at Café König knew," he responded.

"Then how come you don't wear a star?" I probed suspiciously.

"Well, I'm actually only half Jewish. Half Jews don't have to wear the star of David as do full Jews," Egon explained. "My mother is a full Jew and my father is a German-born Italian."

Even a half Jew, I thought, was too close for comfort for me. What if some Gestapo patrol stopped us? They would never believe that our meeting had been a pure coincidence. I could already see the newspaper headlines: JEW AND NEGRO HANGED FOR TREASONOUS MEETING IN PARK DURING BLACKOUT.

Seemingly unaware of my discomfort, Egon continued the conversation. "I don't know whether you know it, but I have it on good authority that all of us non-Aryans, including you, are in imminent danger of getting wiped out," he confided. "The Nazis have known for some time that their game is up, that the war is lost, that they are finished, *kaput*. But they are determined not to go to their graves alone, but to take with them as many of us as they can get their hands on."

Then Egon told me that all across the country, wherever the German military was still in control, special Gestapo commandos were stepping up their efforts to round up non-Aryans they had missed so far. He said that his parents and two brothers and he had been lying low for some time, but if things got too hot, they were prepared to go into hiding at the drop of a hat and stay underground until the Allies arrived. "If you want to, you are very welcome to join us," he offered. "We have some trustworthy German friends who will hide us and supply us with food until this whole thing blows over. Just don't be naive and think that nothing will happen to you because the Gestapo hasn't come for you so far. Think! Why should the Nazis, who know that their time of reckoning has come, leave you and me unscathed to enjoy life and the peace that's just around the corner while many of them will go either to jail or to the gallows?"

I was stunned. Egon was making sense. Having been totally isolated from other non-Aryans, I had developed a false sense of security. Egon made me realize that we were all in the same boat, and that at any moment the boat could be sinking.

Despite my heightened awareness of pending danger, I suddenly felt good, almost euphoric. As long as I could remember, I had always had to face the Nazi menace alone. Except for my mother, I had no genuine allies with whom I could share my secret fears of living in a state whose avowed goal was to destroy me and my kind. Now, for the first time in my life, I had found a true brother, someone who knew from his own experience the terror of being regarded as a subhuman enemy by the highest authority of the state, someone who was as much at risk of being destroyed as I was. All of a sudden I felt a strong kinship with Egon, who only a few minutes earlier had been almost a stranger to me.

We had reached the end of the park and were entering a wasteland of massive destruction—row upon row of burned-out apartment buildings whose empty shells formed ghostly black silhouettes against the sky. We walked between mountains of rubble in the middle of the street, which, except for the sidewalks, had been meticulously cleared of debris. When we reached the school, which inexplicably was the only structure within miles that had been spared by the bombs, I prepared to turn in and call it a day. But Egon had other plans.

"You've got to come with me and meet my family," he implored. "We are living in a basement that we fixed up, not very far from here. You would make them very happy if you would meet with them."

Somehow, I just couldn't find the right words to turn my newfound compatriot down and, against my better judgment, agreed to come along.

We had walked another ten minutes or so through more ruins, past Barmbek's railway station, when we came to a side street where a narrow path, barely wide enough for one person, had been cleared. Soon, Egon stopped before a ruin that to the uninitiated eye looked no different from the rest. After standing still and listening for a while to make sure we hadn't been followed, he carefully tapped on a basement windowpane in what appeared to be a prearranged signal. Slowly, a blanket on the inside was moved aside for a few seconds to reveal the outline of a face. Immediately, the door next to the window opened and Egon led me into a totally dark, dank-smelling room that seemed full of people, although I could not make out a single one. After the door closed behind us, someone struck a match and lighted a kerosene lamp. In its dim light I suddenly could see several men and a woman staring at me.

"This is Mickey," Egon introduced me, using the nickname I had chosen for myself during my swingboy days. "I'm sure you've all seen him around in Barmbek at one time or another." Then, pointing toward a handsome middle-aged man with wavy, graying hair and an emaciated woman with sallow complexion and huge, dark-circled eyes, he said, "These are my parents, Alfons and Lilly Giordano," a pianist/accordion player and a piano teacher, respectively. The two young men, one about seventeen and the other twenty-two, he introduced as his brothers Rocco and Ralph. Ralph, whom I also recognized as a Café König regular, told me that he first saw me when we were children and our respective streets were "at war." He recalled that when we came face-to-face, something he couldn't explain made us turn around and walk away instead of beating each other up.

As soon as the introductions were over, the Giordanos literally fell over me, hugged me, and shook my hands as if I was their long-lost brother. It was obvious to me that they hadn't had any visitors for some time. They fussed over me and showered me with compliments until I blushed. Openly admiring my hair, my teeth, and my complexion, they all agreed that Africans were the real super-race. They bombarded me with questions, mainly about how the "Nazi *Schweine*" were treating me, what plans, if any, I had to assure my survival, how my mother was coping, and what I thought about the progress of the war. At that point they invited me to a small room in the back of the basement to listen to the latest news. I immediately knew what news they were talking about when I saw Ralph covering his head with a heavy blanket while fiddling with the knobs of a *Volksempfänger*, a small "people's receiver." After a few moments of whistling and crackling noises, I heard the familiar male voice of the BBC's German-language announcer. At Ralph's invitation, I shared the blanket with him. We could hardly contain our joy as we heard the announcer report that Soviet troops had freed nearly two thousand inmates in the Nazi concentration camp at Auschwitz, in Poland. Some Soviet troops, according to the announcer, had come within a few miles of Berlin. Following the broadcast, Ralph and I joined the others and told them the good news, which they received with mixed feelings.

The closer we came to the end, Herr Giordano theorized, the more dangerous the Nazis were getting and the more precarious our situation was becoming. He explained that the family kept their contact with the outside world to a bare minimum in order not to draw unnecessary attention to themselves. "You better act and go underground before it is too late," he warned, adding that he and his family would be delighted to have my mother and me join them. I thanked him and told him that I would think about it.

When I finally decided that it was high time for me to go home and get some sleep, the Giordanos implored me to keep in touch and to return soon and as often as possible. After an emotional send-off that matched their welcome, I walked home through the dark wasteland of ruins, filled with a welter of thoughts and emotions that made me oblivious of my desolate surroundings until I reached the school.

NO ROOM AT THE "INN"

Following the bombing raid on the Harburg plant and its partial destruction, the plant was closed and I was instructed to report to the *Arbeitsamt* (Labor Office) for immediate reassignment to another high-priority job. As a less essential worker, my mother was allowed to stay home until suitable work could be found. Under the prevailing Nazi emergency laws, no worker was allowed to quit or change jobs without special authorization from the government.

The *Arbeitsamt* directed me to report to a small auto-repair shop in downtown Harburg where, because of an acute and worsening gasoline shortage, government trucks and cars were being converted to wood-burning hydrocarbon gas-powered vehicles. This involved removing the vehicles' carburetors, installing huge wood burners that looked like six-foot-tall potbelly stoves in the back of the vehicles, then welding gas pipelines from the burners to the engines. The results were vehicles that could be fueled by throwing a few pieces of wood into the burner.

The shop, headed by a wizened little man who rarely left his tiny, cluttered "office," boasted a crew of eight, most of them Italian prisoners of war, and two German auto mechanic apprentices who somehow had escaped subscription by the *Wehrmacht*. The Italians, sensing that the end of the war, and thus their return to their homeland, was imminent, kept the shop reverberating with *O sole mio*s and all the familiar arias from Verdi and Puccini while turning out as little work as possible. There was an immediate affinity between the sons of sunny Italy and me. One of them, a handsome Sicilian with glistening jet-black hair and a complexion that was even a shade darker than mine, was instructed by the boss to show me the ropes.

Nino not only showed me the ropes, but before the day was up, he had added to my already substantial vocabulary of Russian, Polish, and French four-letter words and a fair number of Italian ones. While the work was not particularly challenging to me, I liked my new job a lot better than the old one. Its congenial and relaxed atmosphere compared favorably with Meister Erdmann's grumpy bullying.

On my second morning on the job, we heard a high-flying aircraft overhead. Sensitized about any activity in the air, we all looked up but did not see a plane. Instead, we saw what looked like a cloud of confetti descending toward earth. As the cloud came closer, the confetti grew larger and larger until it took on the form of thousands of leaflets that lazily floated toward us. Apparently, an enemy aircraft had penetrated Harburg's air space at an extremely high altitude without triggering the usual alarm.

It was widely known that the reading and disseminating of enemy propaganda leaflets by civilians was a capital offense. But impulsively throwing caution to the wind, several Italians and I dashed out of the shop and picked up some of the leaflets that had landed in the street. They were covered with small type on both sides. The only thing I could make out at a glance was the bold headline that proclaimed DER KRIEG IST VERLOREN (The War Is Lost).

I couldn't wait to read the rest of the good news, but as soon as I had stuffed the leaflet into my pocket, I was startled by the booming voice of a man who from about a block away was warning us not to touch the leaflets. Turning around, I saw a wildly gesticulating *Amtswalter* in his brown uniform running toward us.

Suddenly, panic gripped me as the gravity of what I had done began to sink in. I knew that I was in mortal danger if the Nazi caught me with the leaflet on my person. It occurred to me how utterly stupid I had been to hand the Nazis the rope with which to hang me. How did I always manage to get myself into such life-threatening situations? But it was much too late for self-incrimination or regrets. I knew I had to act fast or I was literally dead meat. Quickly returning to the shop, I raced to the washroom, where I locked myself in a stall. Without bothering to read the leaflet, I tore it into tiny pieces and flushed them down the toilet. No sooner had the last piece disappeared in the gurgling vortex of the commode than I heard the agitated voice of the Nazi ranting and raving in the shop. He was shouting at our boss that he had seen at least two of his *Makaronifresser* (macaroni eaters) pick up forbidden leaflets and insisted on conducting a search.

In the ensuing commotion, I slipped out of the washroom and, unnoticed by anyone, mingled with the rest of the crew. At the order of the Nazi, our boss had all of us line up and one after another step forward and empty our pockets. I was terribly worried that Nino, whom I had seen picking up a leaflet, might not have had a chance to get rid of it in time. When the Nazi ordered him to reveal the contents of his pockets, Nino stalled by telling him, *"Ich nix verstehen,"*—broken German for "I don't understand"— which was the standard reply used by POWs whenever they didn't want to cooperate.

"I'll make you *verstehen!"* the enraged Nazi shouted at Nino. But Nino continued to play stupid, thereby causing the Nazi to lose what little composure he had left. At that point, our boss intervened, telling Nino that refusing to cooperate would have the most serious consequences. When Nino finally complied, he did so with an insolent grin that grew wider and wider as each pocket he pulled inside out turned up empty. When Nino offered to drop his pants, the Nazi told him to shut up and to get out of his face.

I let out an inaudible sigh of relief. There was no doubt in my mind that Nino had picked up a leaflet, but I couldn't figure out how he had been able to fool the Nazi. When it was my turn to be searched, the Nazi looked at me intently while insisting that he was quite certain that I was "one of the Italians" he had seen picking up leaflets. Emboldened by my knowledge that I was "clean," as well as by Nino's brave performance, I looked straight into the *Amtswalter*'s eyes while pointing out to him that he was wrong on two counts. "I'm not an Italian, but a German," I told him in the best German at my command, "and I never touched a leaflet." With that, I pulled out all of my pockets to prove my point.

The Nazi looked at me incredulously, but offered no further challenge. Before leaving in visible frustration, he told our boss to keep an eye on his "lying and treasonous Italians."

Later that afternoon, long after the Nazi had left, I ran into Nino in the washroom. *"Du lesen Deutsch?"* he demanded to know in broken German.

"Of course I read German," I replied.

"Then you read to me." With that, he shoved a familiar-looking piece of paper into my hand that I immediately recognized as one of the leaflets that had almost gotten us into a world of trouble.

"Where did you hide it when the Nazi searched you?" I demanded to know. Nino pointed to his crotch.

"Right here." He laughed.

At first I couldn't make up my mind as to whether to laugh with him or chide him. "Suppose the Nazi had asked you to drop your pants as you had offered to do, what would you have done?" I asked.

"But he didn't" was Nino's laughing reply.

After making absolutely sure that we were alone, I read the leaflet to Nino. In substance, it stated that the war had moved into its final phase and that the inevitable Allied victory was imminent. It told Germans about the futility of their resistance, since it only prolonged their agony, and assured them that they had nothing to fear from the occupation forces.

I'm not too sure that Nino understood the fine points of the leaflet, but he was noticeably pleased with what I read to him. "Mussolini *kaput,*" he beamed. "Soon Hitler and Goebbels *kaput,* too, and soon Nino go home to Italia."

We concluded our conspiratorial meeting by my tearing the leaflet into tiny pieces and disposing them via burial "at sea" in the john.

Several days later, shortly after our lunch break, the familiar sound of sirens interrupted our work at the shop. As a precautionary measure, the boss instructed one of the apprentices to take the company truck and get the hell out of Harburg, while the boss drove his own sedan. We workers had the choice of either piling onto the back of the truck or taking our chance in a nearby public shelter. Remembering the last raid on Harburg, we opted for a ride on the truck.

We had barely reached the outskirts of Harburg when we heard the angry droning of what we later learned were American B-17s overhead. Within seconds, bombs were pounding the ground all around us. As soon as the truck came to a halt, we jumped off and threw ourselves on the shaking ground. When the first wave of planes had passed and I dared to raise my head and look around, I noticed several people hurrying along the street. "Where is the next public air-raid shelter?" I shouted.

The people looked at us and, without bothering to answer, continued on their way. After following them for several blocks, we came to a familiar public air-raid shelter sign. By the time we reached the shelter's entrance, we heard a second wave of planes overhead. Glad to have reached relative safety in the nick of time, we were about to scramble into the shelter behind the other people when the air-raid warden blocked our path. "Where do you think you are going?" he demanded rhetorically. "We don't have room for *Ausländer* (foreigners) in here," he informed the three Italians and me while letting the two Nordic-looking German apprentices pass. I was certain that the "rule" he cited was his very own invention, but nobody spoke up in our behalf. On the contrary. Behind the warden I saw the menacing faces of other Germans, obviously daring us to force our way inside. There were several German soldiers in the crowd. One look at their hate-filled faces and their pistols convinced me that it wasn't wise to challenge them.

With a terribly final-sounding clunk, the warden shut the heavy steel door of the shelter in my face, and as if that had been the signal, the bombing resumed. Under the circumstances, the best we could do was lie prone and tightly pressed against the wall of the shelter. As the ground began to shudder under the impact of bombs while bomb fragments whined and zinged all around us, I could see Nino next to me finger his ever-present rosary while mumbling over and over, *"Madonna vera! Madonna vera!"*

Like the first attack, the second raid lasted only a few minutes, but when it was over, we all felt that we had aged a few years. As soon as we had recovered a bit, we walked back to the truck, which, to our relief, was standing unharmed where we had left it. There, we waited for the return of the two apprentices. When, after many detours around massive destruction, we finally returned to the shop, we had another surprise—most of the shop was gone. Fortunately, this time the locker that contained my clothes had been spared. After changing and saying goodbye to Nino and his countrymen, I caught the next train to Hamburg, never to return.

Riding home and reflecting on the destruction of my two workplaces within three days, I was struck by the notion of possessing some weird kind of inverted Midas touch that turned everything I came in contact with to rubble. In a more serious vein, I could not help but ponder the pileup of narrow escapes during my relatively brief sojourn on earth. Should I be angry at fate for getting me into more than my share of tight spots, or should I be grateful for coming out of them essentially unscathed? After years of indecision, and with the benefit of hindsight, I now lean heavily toward gratitude.

MAX ROEPKE

The following day, I dutifully reported to the *Arbeitsamt* in Hamburg for reassignment to yet another job. After the official pulled my files and studied my qualifications, he told me to wait just a moment. "I think I have something that fits you to a T," he told me, then left the room. When he returned, he was followed by a tall, heavy-set man with a ruddy complexion and an even more ruddy nose that to me indicated an affinity for *Schnapps*. He was dressed in an expensive camel-hair coat, the kind that ordinary Germans hadn't been able to buy since the beginning of the war.

"I'm Max Roepke," the big man introduced himself while extending a ham-sized hand. "I own a trucking firm in Hoheluft and I could use an all-round machinist who can do just about anything."

I explained that I didn't know much about engines since I wasn't a mechanic, but that there was nothing a machinist was supposed to do that I couldn't do. Roepke studied my employment record, then nodded to the official and said, "I think he'll do fine." Then, turning to me, he said, "Well, then, that's settled. You'll start right away."

After signing a few papers, shaking the official's hand, and whispering something that sounded like "I'll take care of everything," Roepke became formally my master, whom I couldn't leave even if I wanted to. Suddenly, I had the distinct feeling of having just become the object of a deal, not unlike the slave trade in America. That impression deepened when, once outside, Roepke told me to get into his car, a sleek, canary-yellow BMW roadster. It became increasingly clear to me that my new boss was a man of considerable influence. The mere fact that he could still get his hands on critically scarce gasoline for use in his private automobile at a time when such use was largely restricted to the military indicated to me a man of formidable clout. In a matter of minutes, we arrived at his place of business, a two-story brick building that housed a small workshop, a garage, and several storage rooms inside a large fenced-in yard. Except for a young blond man in coveralls and an olive-drab Polish army cap, the place was deserted.

"This is Stanislaus, my yardman," Roepke explained. "He's going to be your helper whenever you need one. He'll show you where everything is and fill you in on the details. There isn't much work right now, but don't let that worry you. There'll be plenty for you to do."

With that, Roepke climbed back into his roadster and drove off.

Stanislaus assured me that my new job was a piece of cake, or, as he put it in half German, half Polish, *"kein Problema,"* and that I could count on him to show me the ropes.

In the weeks that followed, I saw very little of Roepke and had virtually nothing to do but polish up my Polish. One day, for no apparent reason, Stanislaus "filled me in on the details" all right—undoubtedly to a far greater extent than Roepke had intended. In his colorful, broken German, which he said he had learned during five years as a prisoner of war, he told me that Roepke was a big-time *Schieber* (black marketeer) who, in cahoots with high-ranking Nazi officials, operated a lucrative smuggling operation between German-occupied Holland and Germany. Roepke, he explained, ate better, drank better, and dressed better than Hitler. His trucks brought things, he said, that most Germans had forgotten existed.

To make his point, Stanislaus reached in his jacket pocket and pulled out a bar of chocolate. Breaking it in half in its wrapping paper and foil, he handed one half to me. I immediately saw what Stanislaus meant. I had almost forgotten what chocolate smelled and tasted like. "Where did you get this?" I asked.

"Come; I'll show you."

I followed him upstairs where, after telling me to keep an eye out for Roepke, he opened a door. What I saw inside the storage room made my eyes pop. Stanislaus was right. Many things I and most Germans had dismissed from our conscious minds because they had been unattainable for so long were staring at me in profusion from a number of piles that reached nearly to the ceiling. There were mounds of chocolate bars, cans of sardines, corned beef, ham, coffee, cocoa, cigarettes, cigars, pipe tobacco, quality soaps, hand lotions, perfumes, lipstick, and nylon stockings—you name it.

Before I could get over what I had just seen, Stanislaus told me that for a change there was a *grosses Problema,* or big problem. He then confessed that for some time, he had entered the room with a primitive skeleton key he had made and helped himself *"eine kleine Bischen"* to the goodies. This morning, he said, when he tried to lock the door after getting "us" a chocolate bar, his key broke off inside the lock. If Roepke found the door unlocked, he said, he'd be up the Polish equivalent of shit's creek. To keep that from happening, he begged me to put my machinist's mind to work and fix the damage.

All of a sudden I understood Stanislaus's sudden urge to share. My first inclination was to tell him, "No! Hell no," and leave it at that. The prospect of becoming an accessory to burglary seemed less than inviting. Then it occurred to me that, if pushed into a corner, Stanislaus might tell the boss that I, not he, had been breaking into the storage room and pilfering the goodies. Since Roepke didn't know me at all, whom would he believe, Stanislaus or me? I persuaded myself that I couldn't take a chance to find out. Keeping my thoughts to myself in order not to put ideas into Stanislaus's head in case they hadn't been there all along, I agreed to see what I could do about the door. Since time was of the essence, my plan was that he would make another skeleton key while I would work on extracting the broken key from the lock.

Once we had decided on a course of action, we proceeded with the efficiency of a *Mission: Impossible* team. Within a few minutes, I had removed the lock from the door, extracted the key portion, and reinstalled the lock. By the time my job was done, Stanislaus was putting the finishing touches on his skeleton key. But before we had a chance to put the two together and try locking the door, we heard Roepke's car drive into the yard. Trying not to look like cats that swallowed the canary, we busied ourselves with furiously sweeping the garage floor just as Roepke walked through the door. "Everything all right?" the boss wanted to know.

"Yes, *Pan; kein Problema,*" replied Stanislaus, while I, my heart pounding through my chest, nodded agreement. I almost had a cardiac arrest when Roepke walked toward the stairs.

"What do you want me to do with the broken tailgate one of the drivers dropped off yesterday?" I asked in a desperate attempt to stall him. The ruse worked. Roepke turned around and, trailed closely by me, walked out in the yard to inspect the badly damaged tailgate.

"Do you think you can fix it?" he asked.

"I know I can. It'll be as good as new," I replied.

"Good, see what you can do."

With a look at his wristwatch, Roepke climbed back into his BMW, waved at me, and drove off. Stanislaus's and my sighs of relief were more like yodels that could be heard nearly half a block away. As soon as Roepke was out of sight, we rushed upstairs and tried the key. After a few minor adjustments, the key turned smoothly in the lock, both closing and opening it.

Now that the crisis had been averted, we calmly deliberated on what to do about the cornucopia room upstairs. While we conceded that the ill-gotten contraband did not belong to us, we rationalized that neither did it belong to Roepke, to whom rationing of food and other scarce items should apply as much as it supposedly applied to all German citizens. Since Roepke hadn't shown the slightest inclination to share with us, we decided we were justified in giving justice a hand or two from time to time. This we thought to accomplish by an occasional raid of the room upstairs.

That evening, during my fifteen-minute train ride home, paranoia had me regard most of my fellow passengers as Gestapo agents in disguise who were out to get me. Any minute I expected someone in a long black leather coat to touch my arm and tell me that I was under arrest and order me to let him take a peek at the contents of the bulging briefcase I was clutching under my arm. But nothing of the sort happened. When I reached the school and saw my mother's eyes light up as I presented her with my treasures—a couple of chocolate bars, some sardine cans, and a few bars of soap—I felt like Robin Hood must have felt when he robbed the rich to give to the poor.

FREE AT LAST!

News of Hitler's death on April 30, 1945, did not reach Hamburg until the next day. But befitting the man who had lied to, betrayed, cheated, and finally all but destroyed the German people while wreaking worldwide havoc, the official announcement of the circumstances of his death was one preposterous lie. "The Führer Adolf Hitler," the terse announcement from the Führer's headquarters in Berlin claimed, "has this afternoon on his command post in the Reichchancellery, while fighting to his last breath against Bolshevism, died a soldier's death for Germany." No mention was made of the cowardly way in which this man for whom so many Germans had given their lives, voluntarily and otherwise, escaped accountability by committing suicide and leaving the German people holding the bag. But even the lie of a hero's death did little to restore the heroic image many Germans had once had of their Führer.

Many times during Hitler's heyday, I had wondered how Germans would react to the news of their leader's death. Giving my imagination full rein, I tried to conjure up the cataclysmic outburst of sorrow, the utter agony that I was certain Germans would exhibit at the death of the man they had elevated to near-godlike status. Thus, I was totally unprepared for the way my countrymen actually reacted to the announcement. When the news flashed repeatedly over the radio at our shelter, it was met with neither jubilation nor sorrow, just monumental, yawning indifference. Except for an occasional "good riddance," my roommates all but ignored the historic event during their inevitable daily arguments. Examining my own feelings, I was surprised to notice that I, too, did not react to the news of Hitler's death the way I had always imagined I would. Instead of the dancing-up-and-down kind of joyful relief—the kind I felt the morning after my mother and I survived Hamburg's firestorm—all I experienced was an apathetic sense of "so what?" I concluded that since I had lived with the prospect of my own death for so long, the death of a supervillain like Hitler, by whatever means, was too anticlimactic to arouse strong emotions.

More sensational than the news of Hitler's death itself was the revelation through Allied sources a short while later that the Führer had died in a suicide pact with his mistress, whom he had married the day before he blew out his brains with a pistol and she took her life by swallowing poison. Only when the name *Eva Braun* appeared in the news did Germans learn that this blonde, who was twenty years Hitler's junior, even existed. Now we learned that not only did Hitler have a bona fide romantic mistress, but that their close relationship had lasted almost the entire length of his twelve-year reign as chancellor. How was he able to carry on such an important affair for such a long time right under everybody's nose without anyone finding out? Most people had accepted the official explanation that the Führer lived a celibate existence in order to devote all his time and energies to his people. No one had an answer to explain how this exceedingly public man, whose every living minute seemed to be under the scrutiny of the national and international press, could keep Eva Braun hidden.

Prior to being informed of Hitler's death, and in open defiance of the Führer's orders to defend Hamburg to the last man, woman, and child, Karl Kaufmann, the city's Nazi governor, decided to surrender the city. He explained that he did this in order to save what was left of Hamburg and to spare its people further bloodshed and suffering. The news of Hamburg's pending surrender, which had been anxiously awaited by the war-weary citizenry, came to us via an extra-edition page of the *Hamburger Zeitung,* a joint venture of Hamburg's three major dailies, which read:

Hamburgers!

After heroic fighting, after untiring toil for a German victory, and under boundless sacrifices, our people have succumbed to a numerically and materially superior enemy. The enemy is preparing to occupy the country and is standing before the gate of our city. Units of the *Wehrmacht* and the *Volkssturm* have fought valiantly before our city against a vastly superior opponent. Undaunted, Hamburgers have discharged their obligation, at the front and at home; tough and unwavering you accepted what the war demanded of you.

The enemy is preparing to attack Hamburg from the air and on the ground with his enormous superior force. For the city and its people, for hundreds of thousands of women and children, this means death and destruction of the last means of survival. The outcome of the war can no longer be changed; however, combat in the city would mean its senseless and complete destruction. Those whom soldierly honor commands to continue the fight will have the opportunity to do so beyond city limits. Personally, I am guided by heart and conscience, in clear recognition of the conditions and with full awareness of my responsibility, to save Hamburg, its women and children, from senseless and irresponsible destruction.

I know what, in doing so, I take upon myself. I shall leave the judgment of my decision to history and you.

Hamburgers! All my work and concerns have always belonged to you and the city, and thusly, to our nation. That shall continue until fate recalls me. This war is a national catastrophe for us and a disaster for Europe. May all those who are responsible realize this.

God save our people and our country!

—KARL KAUFMANN

The news of Kaufmann's intention to surrender Hamburg came as a great relief to me and my mother, and, I am sure, to most of Hamburg's citizens. I was thoroughly convinced that the slightest German resistance would have resulted in an Allied military response of such magnitude that it would have ended all chances of survival. I suddenly felt that Mutti and I had passed the last hurdle that stood between us and liberation and that, barring any last-minute glitches, our survival seemed assured. Unlike many of my countrymen, who were uncertain as to what kind of treatment to expect from the conquering enemy, I looked forward to the day when the Allies were running the show, confident that I had nothing to fear from them. How ironic, I felt, that although I had never committed a single hostile or criminal act against the German state, I was forced to live for years in mortal fear of my own government and its henchmen.

The day before the scheduled takeover of Hamburg by the British on May 3, 1945, I had gone downtown to take one last look at the city while still under Nazi rule. Mainly, I had come to look for more visible signs of the pending collapse of German resistance. I was not to be disappointed. There was utter pandemonium as thousands of German soldiers poured into the city on trucks, cars, motorcycles, bicycles, and on foot. Some had deserted, while others had become separated from their units in the confusion caused by the total disintegration of the German military chain of command. Despite their uncertain futures, all appeared relieved to have escaped the fate of so many of their comrades, who had become eleventh-hour combat casualties in a war that they knew had already been lost.

Conspicuously absent from the milling throngs, I noticed, were members of the *Waffen*-SS and the heretofore ubiquitous Nazi functionaries in their beloved brown uniforms. Where had all the Nazis gone? It was a question that was to be asked by many with increasing frequency in the days, weeks, months, and even years ahead.

When I finally went to bed that night, it seemed sleep would never come. I heard the rumbling of the British artillery and, looking out of the window, saw lightninglike flashes illuminating the horizon in the south. No one insisted any longer that the lights and rumbles were caused by German, not enemy guns, as many Germans had still argued just a few days earlier. By this time, even the most die-hard believers in a German victory—people who had lived in total denial for the last couple of years—reluctantly conceded that the war was lost.

As much as I had waited for the moment, somehow I could not imagine that tomorrow the British would be here and that the Nazis would be gone for good. It was easier for me to imagine that the sun would no longer shine. After twelve years under Nazi rule—at that point nearly two thirds of my life—it seemed inconceivable to me that the Third Reich, which Hitler had boasted would last at least one thousand years, had come to such a sudden and ignominious end.

Despite my great excitement, I must have fallen asleep, because the next thing I remembered was the voice of one of my dormmates.

"Hey, wake up! Your friends are here!"

Suddenly, I was wide awake as the meaning of those words penetrated my sleepy brain. It was broad daylight. I rushed to the window to take a look but was cautioned, "Don't let them see you. They might think you are a sniper and shoot up here."

Carefully, I peeped out from the corner of the window. What I saw was too good to be true. In a reversal of scenes depicted in hundreds of Nazi propaganda newsreels, a long row of olive-colored tanks, armored cars, and trucks lined up along our street, which was flanked on both sides by Tommies. They were armed to their teeth and wearing their characteristic flat steel helmets draped in camouflage nets. The long column of vehicles had come to a stop at a twelve-foot barricade in front of the school. Part of a citywide antitank fortification system that had been hastily constructed during the last few months, the barricades were among several last-ditch Nazi efforts aimed at slowing down the approach of the inevitable. They consisted of large cobblestones dug up from the streets and reinforced by heavy steel girders that had been salvaged from bombed-out buildings. Under the Nazis' scheme, *Volkssturm* units and civilians would ambush tanks with Molotov cocktails and small antitank weapons, including the vaunted *Panzerfaust*. Thanks to Kaufmann's decision, that frightening scenario never materialized.

The Tommies were looking suspiciously at the school—the only intact building in a sea of destruction. Next, a small detachment of perhaps ten men climbed over the barricade and approached the school entrance, their automatic firearms at a ready position. Minutes later we heard loud English commandos from the hall. It sounded to me as though someone was shouting, "Everybody outside!"

"Why don't you find out what they want," one of my dormmates suggested nervously. "They won't do anything to you. Besides, you speak English. Just tell them that we're your friends, we're ready to surrender, and that none of us have been Nazis."

I deeply regretted ever having made the highly exaggerated claim of speaking English. At best, my meager vocabulary amounted to just a smattering. It certainly wasn't enough for negotiating terms of surrender with the occupation force. But having been appointed spokesman of the group, I saw no way to refuse the dubious honor. So I quickly dressed and went out into the hall. At the sight of the heavily armed combat soldiers and their grim, dust-covered faces, my courage waned and I wished that I had refused my ombudsman's role. But for that it was now too late.

"Do you speak English?" the leader of the group demanded.

"A little," I replied meekly.

"Smashing," the leader, a tall man with a bushy red walrus mustache and matching red beetle eyebrows snapped without making sense to me. He was the only one in the group who was not pointing a weapon at me. Instead, he was holding a riding whip, while his heavy pistol remained securely inside a canvas holster. I didn't know British military rank insignia at the time, but I gathered that the three big brown stars on the walrus's epaulets were the insignia of an officer.

Introducing himself as Captain So-and-So, the walrus confirmed my guess. "What's your nationality?"

I explained as best as I could that I was part Liberian, part German, in that order.

"How many people are living in this building and what sort of people are they?" the walrus continued while offering me a cigarette. Up to that point I had steadfastly resisted all peer pressure to take up the smoking habit, but now I didn't feel that I should reject this first expression of cordiality from my liberators. So I gratefully accepted and lighted up as a symbolic gesture of solidarity with my allies. I then explained to the officer with what little English I had at my command that the school served as emergency quarters for bombed-out German civilians, of whom approximately 80 percent were women and the other 20 percent mostly elderly men.

"Tell them that I want all of them assembled in the schoolyard immediately so that I can talk to them. And since my German is much worse than your English, I want you to translate for me."

I assured the officer that I would do the best I could. Proud of my new, semiofficial status as interpreter in His Majesty's service, I returned to my dorm and passed on the captain's order. I immediately noticed that a new note of respect crept into my dormmates' voices and demeanor while dealing with me.

As I went from dorm to dorm to relay the captain's order, I was bombarded with anxious questions and requests to act as intermediary. To my amusement, even those neighbors who had always acted distant toward me were eagerly reminding me of what close pals we had always been. Their sudden change in attitude came as no surprise to me, since I knew that many expected harsh treatment from the British, including summary, SS-style executions. Some women, in a state of full-blown hysteria, had locked themselves in the women's washrooms to keep from being raped, as Goebbels had predicted in the event of a German defeat. My attempts to convince them that they had nothing to fear met with only partial success.

It was a miserable-looking bunch that assembled in the schoolyard, with some of the women still sobbing while the men were trying to look as fearless as they could under the circumstances.

"Tell them," the captain told me, "that they are to remove a portion of the barrier in front of the building wide enough for our vehicles to pass through. I want every able-bodied man to meet us in front of the building in half an hour. The women can go back inside."

I was surprised at how much of my school English I had retained. While I didn't understand every word the captain had spoken, I had no difficulty getting the gist of what he meant. When I finished translating, there was noticeable relief among the school's occupants.

Some of the captain's men had confiscated several jeeps full of picks and shovels at a nearby bombed-out construction firm and distributed them among the German men who had assembled at the barricade. The captain instructed them, again through me, to work as fast as they possibly could. He gave them until 4 P.M. to complete the job. That meant they had exactly five hours to dismantle what had taken months to construct—a rather unlikely task.

In spite of the captain's deadline and the steady pace of the workers, it was dark before the breach in the barricade was wide enough for the widest vehicle in the convoy to drive through. After the last truck had reached the other side, the captain asked me to tell the men that they were dismissed and to distribute several packs of cigarettes among them. Before mounting his jeep and disappearing into the night, he thanked me for my help and handed me two round sealed tins containing a total of one hundred cigarettes. I didn't know it then, but I was soon to learn that I had just been paid in Germany's newest currency.

It was way after midnight when I finally turned in. None of my dormmates said a word, making me acutely aware of another shift in attitude toward me. Only this time, it was a negative shift. I immediately understood. In their view, I no longer was one of them, as just a day ago. Instead, I was now "on the other side." It dawned on me that in one fell swoop I had ceased to be what I had always considered myself—a German. But somehow, the thought didn't bother me. The Germans never let me fully share in their happy past. Now I didn't need any part of their miserable present. Lying awake on my bunk and reflecting on the day's events, I concluded that I had reached a watershed in my life. I could sense that the pendulum of fate was swinging my way for a change and wondered what had taken it so long. For the first time in years I felt totally free of the paralyzing fear that my pride had never permitted me to admit to anyone, least to myself, but that had stalked me relentlessly by day and by night. It was not an ordinary kind of fear, such as the fear of being killed in a bombing raid or in a Nazi extermination camp. Instead it was the fear of being humiliated, of being ridiculed, of being degraded, of having my dignity stripped from me, of being made to feel that I was less a human being, less a man than the people in whose midst I lived. Suddenly, that fear was lifted from me like a heavy burden I had carried without being fully aware of it.

Shortly after the daytime curfew had been rescinded, I headed downtown to see what changes had occurred. Still unsure of what to expect from their conquerors, German civilians kept mostly out of sight while the streets swarmed with British troops who were crisscrossing the city in huge olive-drab trucks and small vehicles they called jeeps. Overnight, street signs with arrows and the words UPTOWN and DOWNTOWN had been posted at major intersections, obviously to help British drivers find their way around the city. I noticed that whenever Germans waved at passing British trucks, their occupants did not return the greeting. Instead, the Tommies stared grim-faced ahead or even looked pointedly the other way. I knew that many Hamburgers had been fed up with Hitler's war and regarded the British as their liberators rather than their conquerors. Thus, I was puzzled by this obvious snub. I had to wait two months for an official explanation of this behavior when posters, instructing the city's population on new occupation regulations, contained a special message from British Field Marshal Viscount Bernard Montgomery. Characterizing his countrymen as basically friendly and good-natured people, he explained that his troops did not wave back at Germans because he had ordered them not to fraternize. In view of the bitter struggle that had just ended, he felt that it was too soon for letting bygones be bygones. He further explained that World War I was not fought on German soil but in France and Belgium, and that after the beaten German army returned intact, Germany's leaders concocted the lie that the German army had not been defeated. To prevent history from repeating itself a third time and to prevent World War III, the field marshal said, Germans had to be taught a lesson and be made to understand that a nation has the leaders it deserves. Until that lesson had been driven home, he said, it was too early to kiss and make up. "It is our goal," he concluded, "to destroy the evil of the national socialistic system. It is too early to be sure that this goal has been reached."

However well reasoned, the nonfraternization policy of the man who had outfoxed Erwin Rommel, Germany's famous Desert Fox, contained a fatal flaw: It was conceived without considering one of the most compelling of human characteristics—the sex drive. Before the week was over, certainly long before Monty got around to changing his mind, I witnessed how Tommies and German fräuleins made a mockery of his edict by making out like love-starved fools. Conceding Monty's military genius, I concluded that the good field marshal didn't know a bloomin' thing about the birds and bees.

I had often wondered what had happened to the Giordanos, but kept postponing looking them up out of fear of what I would find. Finally, about two weeks after Hamburg's surrender, I overcame my reluctance and took a walk to their basement on Diesterwegstrasse. To my great relief, I found the entire family relatively well, considering that they had just survived an ordeal of indescribable horror while hiding for weeks in the ruins with barely enough food and water to survive. Even Frau Giordano had shed her worried look and seemed visibly relieved that her family's ordeal had come to an end. All were euphoric about their liberation. They still found it difficult to believe that the nightmare was over and that they had actually survived the Holocaust. In what seemed like a reenactment of our first clandestine meeting, they were all over me, hugging me, slapping my back, shaking my hand, and pinching my cheeks while congratulating me and themselves for the umpteenth time on the death of "that *Nazischwein* Hitler." Somehow the scene reminded me of the conclusion of that old German fairy tale when the seven little goats dance with their mother around the well in which the big bad wolf has just drowned.

After the euphoria had subsided somewhat, Egon, Ralph, and I took a walk to observe our liberators and to discuss the events of the past few weeks. On our way we saw long lines of parked heavy tanks, trucks, and jeeps, with beret-wearing, white-bread-chewing and tea-guzzling soldiers lounging about. They all looked remarkably fit and in excellent spirits. It had been a long time since we had seen so many well-fed-looking men. They contrasted sharply with the long columns of motley-looking German prisoners of war who, flanked by British guards, were being led to discharge centers outside the city. Many hobbled on crutches or wore dirty bandages on their heads and limbs. Some of them showed signs of severe malnutrition. They were a far cry from the goose-stepping young Siegfrieds who not so long ago, in an orgy of conquest, had forced one European nation after another to its knees.

Remembering Goebbels's propaganda newsreels that poked fun at French African prisoners of war by sarcastically referring to them as the "saviors of Western civilization," I could clearly see who had the last laugh.

As Ralph and Egon told me about their plans for the future, I realized that, although we had much in common, we were miles apart in our agendas. Or, more correctly, they had an agenda and I didn't. I was content with having emerged from the Nazi nightmare alive and relatively unscathed, and was now prepared to put it behind me and explore whatever opportunities lay ahead. They, on the other hand, were not about to let go of the past. In fact, they were just beginning their battle with their sworn political enemies, the Nazis and neo-Nazis. Calling me naive and uninformed, they scoffed at my suggestion that with Hitler's death and the destruction of the *Wehrmacht*, the Nazis were history. The Nazis and Nazi ideology, they insisted, were alive and well among the German people; both brothers vowed not to rest until the last *Nazischwein* was dangling from a rope and Nazism was banished from the face of the earth.

While I, too, wanted to see all Nazi criminals brought to trial and all vestiges of Nazism destroyed, I was quite content with leaving everything to the Allies. Not so Egon and Ralph, who were about to launch their careers as hard-hitting anti-Nazi journalists. Already, they had spent the larger portion of the night pounding on a beat-up typewriter they had scrounged up and produced several articles that they hoped one of the city's newspapers would print. Each article demanded a swift and radical purge of Nazi elements by the British occupation force.

But the British wheels of justice, we found out, turned agonizingly slowly, and in many cases ground to a complete halt. Nevertheless, a war crimes trial in Hamburg's Curio House sentenced fourteen SS men and women to death by hanging after they were found guilty of committing unspeakable atrocities in the Neuengamme concentration camp outside Hamburg, where more than fifty thousand inmates perished. Meanwhile, most of the Nazi bigwigs were let go with a slap on the wrist. Hamburg's Nazi *Bürgermeister* Karl Vincent Krogmann, for instance, who from the start of the Nazi regime had been a member of the elite corps of political leaders and a *Gauamtsleiter* (regional leader) of the NSDAP, received a ten-thousand-mark suspended fine. His boss, Karl Kaufmann, fared even better. Although a faithful Hitler follower and confidant until he defied Hitler's order to defend Hamburg "to the last man," he was found unfit to stand trial because of a debilitating angina pectoris condition.

Equally high on the Giordano brothers' agenda was the subject of *Wiedergutmachung* (compensation) to which they insisted all non-Aryans who had suffered in one form or another under the Nazis were entitled. Toward that end, we decided to go downtown and see about our claim.

As we entered British military government headquarters at the former Hotel Esplanade to make inquiries, we were directed to the office of a British major in charge of relief matters. The friendly officer told Ralph and Egon that, as half Jews, they were on the priority list of various Jewish relief measures set up by the Allies. Such relief, he explained, ranged from housing to extra food rations and preferential hiring by the military government. After asking them to fill out several forms, he assured my friends that massive help for them was on the way.

When it came my turn to state my business, I explained that I, like the Giordanos, had been persecuted by the Nazis as a non-Aryan and disadvantaged educationally, economically, psychologically, and physically. Consequently, I said, I, too, would like to apply for some kind of relief. After listening politely to my story and agreeing that my situation under the Nazis was everything but enviable, the major told me that nothing could be done for me. "I'm sorry," he said, "as far as the British military government is concerned, you are a bona fide German. We are authorized to help only Jews, displaced foreign nationals, non-German POWs, and former concentration camp detainees. You can readily see that you don't belong to any of these categories."

So much for the new swing of the pendulum, I thought. In spite of the fact that "my side" had won, I kept being dogged by my old habit of not quite fitting in.

THE RAZOR'S EDGE

I was disappointed by this unexpected rejection, but far from defeated. Nothing could convince me that things would not get better for me now that the Nazis were gone and the war was over. The latest setback was simply a reminder that nothing would be handed to me on a platter. But I was quite willing to do whatever it took to make things happen, although at the moment, I hadn't the foggiest idea what my options were. All I knew was that, if I could help it, I would never work in anybody's machine shop again. I was grateful to my mother, who had sacrificed to give me the opportunity of learning a trade, but after four years of growing calluses while risking life and limb with backbreaking labor amid lung-blistering stench and ear-shattering noise, I was more than ready for a change. By hook or crook, I was determined to make the transition to the white-collar class; in what capacity, I wasn't quite sure. I was convinced, however, that in postwar Germany, most of which was controlled by the British and Americans, I needed more than just a smattering of English to get by and decided right then and there to make the study of English my number-one priority.

I bought a German-English pocket dictionary, which henceforth became my steady companion wherever I went. At first I tried reading the dictionary like a book and memorizing words as I went through the alphabet. That method proved not only boring but largely unproductive. Thus, I made only minimal progress until, quite by chance, I hit on a system that produced dramatic results. A British soldier, with whom I had started a conversation, gave me a much-read-looking paperback copy of W. Somerset Maugham's novel *The Razor's Edge,* with the prediction that once I started reading it, I wouldn't be able to put it down. It was not until a few days later when I tried, quite unsuccessfully, to read the first page that I realized how woefully inadequate my English vocabulary was. My first inclination was to do what the Tommy had told me I couldn't do and put the book down until my understanding of the English language had improved. But instead, I embarked on the tedious task of looking up every single word I didn't understand, line for line, until the entire page made sense to me. After that, I turned to the next page and repeated the process. At first, progress was maddeningly slow and frustrating. Time and again, when a word I had just looked up reappeared, I had forgotten its definition and had to look it up again. But little by little, I got hooked by the action and, as I went deeper into the novel, which deals with a young American's quest for enlightenment in the snow-capped mountains of India, words and their meanings began to stay with me. By the time I was halfway through the novel, after about a month of reading, I was able to read many pages without the aid of my dictionary.

To supplement my reading lessons, I took advantage of every opportunity to strike up conversations with British soldiers. In doing so, I was surprised to notice how quickly some of the English Herr Harden, our much-hated English teacher, had tried to pound into our brains came back to me after I had assumed that it had been irretrievably lost. It wasn't long before I spoke English with a reasonable degree of fluency and felt ready to face the challenges that lay ahead.

Most of my observations regarding the escalating British-German rapprochement I made in violation of the dusk-to-dawn curfew imposed on German nationals by the British military government. Under its provisions, any German caught outdoors after sundown was subject to severe penalties ranging from seven to sixty days imprisonment. Relying entirely on what little English I knew and on my not-so-German looks, I moved about Hamburg at night as if the curfew did not apply to me. Whenever I was stopped by British military police, I told them that they were dealing with a citizen of Liberia, an Allied member state, that I was expecting my Liberian passport any day now, and that I was awaiting repatriation to my homeland as soon as it could be arranged. That always got the MPs off my back. Only once did they take me in, but after I repeated my tale to a superior officer, he apologized for the inconvenience his men had caused and sent me on my way.

Within a few months, the stringent dusk-to-dawn curfew was relaxed and Germans were permitted to stay outdoors until 10:15 P.M. As for me, my liberation wasn't formalized until twenty-one days after General Alfred Jodl signed Germany's unconditional surrender on May 7, which officially ended the hostilities. On May 28, the Allied military government struck down all Nazi laws, including the so-called Nuremberg Laws that were aimed at "the protection of German blood." In a sweeping move, the Allies ordered that "henceforth, nobody may benefit from his connections to the NSDAP or suffer disadvantages because of his race, nationality, or beliefs."

HOME, SWEET HOME

Envious of the occasional gifts of cigarettes and food I was able to scrounge through my rapidly expanding contacts with British soldiers, some of the people at our shelter vented their disapproval of my "consorting with the enemy" through hostile remarks. Since they were too cowardly to confront me, they made their remarks only in the presence of my mother whenever I wasn't around. When I learned about this, I told Mutti that apparently we had overstayed our welcome and that it was time for us to move on. She agreed, then surprised me by formally turning the reins of our small "family" over to me. "You are in charge now," she told me. "With this new British occupation, I don't know my way around anymore. So from now on, you make the decisions for us both."

I was deeply touched and honored, and resolved to skipper our little boat as best I could. The question was, where could we go?

Ralph and Egon told me not to despair and that, in due time, help from somewhere would materialize. I was not convinced. What I badly needed, I felt, was contact with representatives of the Liberian government, but the establishment of a Liberian consulate in Germany, I was told, could still be years away.

Just when I was about to give up hope of finding a suitable place to stay, the Giordanos introduced me to an elderly widow, reputedly a relative of a former Nazi bigwig, who had befriended them and offered her help. The woman immediately agreed to let my mother and me rent a room in her house, not far from the Giordanos' basement. "You and your mother are welcome to stay until you find something more suitable," she told me. I gladly accepted. After that, we grabbed what few belongings we had and, without regrets, left the school that for two years had been our home.

Our furnished room, on the second floor of the woman's home, was barely large enough for a bed, a small couch, a dresser, and a wardrobe, but to my mother and me it seemed like paradise found. For the first time since we were bombed out three years earlier we enjoyed the luxury of privacy within space—however small—we didn't have to share with strangers. But our bliss was short-lived.

It soon became apparent to us that what at first appeared to be an altruistic gesture on the part of our new landlady was nothing but a calculated ploy. I suspected that like most Germans with Nazi connections, she had lived in mortal fear of what the British might do to her once her background came to their attention. By going on record as having helped victims of Nazi persecution like the Giordanos and me, she hoped to earn brownie points with whatever British military tribunal would investigate her case. When, within a few days, it became obvious to her that the Brits were not about to come down hard on Nazis, she totally lost her fear of them and with it, her enthusiasm for helping us. Quite abruptly, her attitude toward my mother and me changed. Instead of friendly greetings, we received the silent treatment coupled with hostile glances. Before the month for which we had paid rent was up, she told me that she really needed her room and would appreciate it if we would move as soon as possible. So anxious was she to get rid of us, she even offered to refund our rent money in full if only we left.

Out of desperation, since we were determined not to return to the school, my mother and I scouted the neighborhood for an unoccupied basement under a bombed-out and abandoned building. Luckily, we found one just a few blocks away from the apartment from which we had been more or less evicted. Invoking an unwritten but widely honored squatter's-right law, we immediately took possession by simply moving in.

Our new "apartment" had several conveniences that would have made it a bargain even if it hadn't been rent-free. It boasted a fully operational flush toilet, running cold water, electric light in the form of a naked bulb hanging from the ceiling, and an entrance door we could secure with a padlock. In addition, it had congenial neighbors, a middle-aged couple who said they had lived next door since they lost their home in the big 1943 air raids.

After storing our meager belongings, my mother and I went furniture "shopping." This was simply a matter of scavenging through several abandoned basements and picking from the things that had been left behind whatever seemed usable to us. After several trips and within less than two hours, we had furnished our new apartment in the most eclectic of tastes with two wooden cots, four nonmatching chairs, a small, three-and-a-half-legged kitchen table, a dresser, an enamel face bowl minus most of the enamel, and a large, badly chipped, but highly functional water pitcher. My mother and I were ecstatic when, surrounded by our newly acquired treasures, we ate our first meal in our very own home. The fact that the meal, which my mother had prepared on a hot plate, was meatless as usual and consisted only of some cabbage boiled in water did nothing to diminish our joy. But something else did.

In addition to the various extras that came with our new residence, there was one my mother and I hadn't counted on: fleas. Even though my contact with these bloodsucking parasites was mercifully brief, they are indelibly etched in my memory as the most worrisome of critters ever unleashed on man.

Despite the fact that we had given the basement a thorough cleaning before we moved in, we had been totally unaware of the fleas' presence at the time. It was not until we turned off the light and went to bed that we realized we had a problem—a big problem. Like an army attacking from ambush, literally hundreds of fleas swarmed all over our bodies, biting and sucking, until we were covered from head to toe with welts and little splotches of our own blood. Totally impervious to pressure because of their armorlike shells, the insects continued their biting and sucking right through our scratching and slapping at them. The only thing, we discovered, that would make them call off their relentless attack was light. As long as we kept the light on and our blankets off, they would leave us more or less alone. Rather than unleash another attack by these Draculas of the insect world, we kept the lights on and braved the night chill while scratching our itching and burning skin until daylight put an end to our misery.

Since we had no other place to go, my mother and I decided right then and there that if anyone had to leave, it was the critters and not us. So as soon as the stores opened, we loaded up with several large bottles of Lysol and started an all-out war on our six-legged invaders. After spending most of the day scrubbing and dousing every nook and cranny of the basement—and most of our possessions—with Lysol, we managed to have the place and us smell like a chemical factory. Whether the smell was as distasteful to the fleas as it was to us remained to be seen. The acid test came at nightfall when we turned off the light. For a while we waited with bated breath while bracing for another attack. But nothing happened. Not one flea made its presence known. When we awoke the next morning, each without a single new flea bite, we congratulated each other for having won another battle with adversity.

HUNGER—THE NEW ENEMY

Throughout the war, the Nazis had managed to keep the German civilian population supplied with food. They did so largely by limiting the occupied nations to cruel starvation diets and shipping the lion's share of their food production to Germany. Thus, we always had food to eat—if not our favorite dishes or as much as we would have liked, at least enough to keep us from starving. All that changed with the defeat and occupation of Germany. Immediately, the Allies stopped the flow of food. Instead of food coming into Germany to supplement the supply produced in Germany, Germany was forced to depend on its own food production. This caused catastrophic food shortages in Hamburg and other German cities and resulted in widespread starvation. For the first time in my life I learned the true meaning of the word *hunger*. The realization that we were now reaping what the Nazis had been sowing was hardly any consolation to my mother and me. With allotted food rations pared down to inhumane minimums that were too little to keep us alive, yet still too much to let us die, we were growing thinner and weaker and more apathetic as the days went by. Making matters even worse was the fact that food-rationing coupons were no guarantee that what little food we were entitled to was actually available. Often, after hearing that a new shipment of meat, bread, or potatoes had arrived at the shops, my mother and I would spend grueling hours taking turns standing in long lines at the butcher's, baker's, or grocer's, only to be told before we reached the counter that the last item of food had just been sold. The disappointment, rage, panic, hopelessness, and depression we felt every time we had wasted our time and what little energy we had left are impossible to put into words. Sometimes my mother and I were so sapped of strength and will by hunger and disappointment that we didn't even try to stand in line after hearing of another food shipment. Our long-held conviction that once the war was over, most of our troubles would be over too evaporated in the face of sobering reality. Suddenly, the irony of having survived Hitler's pogrom and the Allied bombs only to die from hunger during peacetime loomed as a distinct possibility. I remember that during the height of the starvation period in Hamburg, overweight Germans were as hard to find as Nazis. My mother, for instance, who during normal times had always been on the plump side, shrank to a bone-rattling ninety-nine pounds.

During the immediate postwar period, nothing had a more devastating, more debilitating effect on us than the constant hunger that plagued us. It robbed us of our sleep at night and made it impossible for us to function during the day. If we did manage to fall asleep, we often were dreaming of—what else?—food. These dreams usually had me seated at a table, ready to enjoy a scrumptious meal of some kind or another, only to have me awaken abruptly just as I was about to take my first bite. Several mornings Mutti and I woke up to discover that both our faces were swollen and distorted to near-unrecognizable shapes, a temporary condition that my mother diagnosed as hunger edema—an accumulation of fluid brought on by a regular diet of cabbage boiled in water and an extreme lack of protein. Once, I stood weak from hunger on a crowded subway train when all of a sudden, just before reaching my destination, I had the distinct sensation of blacking out, something I had never done in my entire life. Desperately trying not to collapse and make a spectacle of myself, I braced my back against the side of the train and locked my legs before losing consciousness. When I came to, I was surprised to discover that I was still standing, although I had passed my destination by one stop.

I was walking once in my neighborhood when a trucker stopped me and asked me whether I would help him unload his truck, which, he explained, was loaded to the top with boxes filled with bottles of cooking oil. For my efforts, he said, I could keep one of the bottles. Feeling weak from hunger and afraid of ruining my best—and only—suit, I turned him down at first. But after thinking about it a moment, I changed my mind. Cooking oil was, like butter and other types of fat, among the most scarce and therefore most coveted food products, which my mother could surely put to good use.

As I labored like a galley slave in the noon summer heat, carrying one heavy box after another into a warehouse, I could already taste the delicious fried potatoes with which I intended to surprise my mother. After several hours of backbreaking labor, I finally finished the job and collected my bottle of oil. When I surprised my mother with the gift, she told me to rest while she whipped up a pan full of fried potatoes. It wasn't until the first drops of oil hit the heated pan that our happy anticipation turned to huge disappointment. Instead of the appetizing aroma of fried potatoes, thick yellow smoke that had us gasping for air wafted through the apartment. Painfully, I realized that I had been duped, that the "cooking oil" for which I had labored so hard and long was nothing but an industrial oil that was totally unfit for ingesting. Killing mad and eager to even the score, I ran back to the warehouse in hopes of still finding the trucker. But by the time I arrived, the warehouse door was locked and the trucker and his truck were gone.

One day, at the height of the postwar starvation era, Mutti announced cheerfully that she and four of her lady friends, including the irrepressible Lisbeth, had decided to pool their meager resources and prepare a rare culinary treat—a genuine pound cake. We were all looking forward to the following Saturday afternoon, when the feast was going to take place in the apartment of one of the ladies whose home had been spared by the bombs. On Saturday noon, shortly after leaving work, the women congregated in their friend's kitchen and started measuring and mixing whatever ingredients they had been able to scrape together, fudging here and there on the recipe when ingredients were missing, and using their creativity in coming up with substitutes. Each of us had contributed, among other things, one egg, which was our allotment for three months. Just as the delicious-smelling, pale yellow batter was ready to be put into the oven, someone decided that a pinch of vanilla extract was needed to make the cake perfect. So while Mutti and I and the rest of the cooks fanned out over the neighborhood to look for the missing ingredient, Lisbeth volunteered to stay behind and clean up the kitchen. When we returned half an hour or so later, we were totally unprepared for what we found.

Lisbeth was sitting at the kitchen table in tears amid dirty pots and pans. At first we couldn't make out heads or tails of her wailing monologue, except the repeated "I'm terribly sorry." But gradually, we figured out the bad news as we discovered that the cake pan that had held the precious batter was not just empty; it was clean as a whistle. In halting words, interrupted by much boo-hooing and nose-blowing, Lisbeth told us how, after we had left, she had started to clean up. Her mistake, she said, was to allow herself the taste of one teaspoonful of batter. One teaspoon, she said, led to another teaspoon, and another and another, until she had totally lost control. "No matter how hard I tried," she said, "I just couldn't stop eating. That's how hungry I was."

Everyone was stunned and getting angrier by the minute. "I think you'd better leave, Lisbeth," said my mother, "because we are all hungry and if you stay, there's no telling what we might do to you. Right now we are mad enough to kill you."

Lisbeth grabbed her things and ducked out of the door. As soon as she was gone, all the women sat down and released their disappointment and anger in a flood of tears and invectives of which *gemeines Luder* (low-down hussy) was among the more flattering. I didn't cry, but I, too, was angry enough at Lisbeth to reserve a few choice words of my own for her, words I didn't dare to speak in Mutti's presence.

While at the time none of us could find even the faintest bit of humor in what had occurred that Saturday afternoon, years later, after food became plentiful once again, Lisbeth's exploits became one of the funniest stories in Mutti's sizable repertoire.

It was during this period that I was standing at a downtown street corner one day waiting for the traffic light to change. Shivering in my thin, threadbare coat, I was wondering how to silence the indignant growling of my empty stomach.

"What's happening, m' man?" a deep voice interrupted my preoccupation with my misery.

Startled, I looked up and saw a soldier in combat fatigues climb from a heavy-duty U.S. Army truck that had stopped beside me at the curb. He was a black man, the first American "brother" I had seen in all of my twenty years. Dr. Livingston couldn't have been more elated at the sight of Stanley than I was at the sight of this stranger from another continent.

"What in the world are you doing here among these Krauts?" the GI asked me. Eager to practice my budding English, I explained as best as I could that "these Krauts" were my bona fide countrymen and that Hamburg was my native home.

"Where were you during the war?" the GI wanted to know.

"Right here," I replied.

Amazed, the soldier looked at the ruins around us and then at my well-worn German-style clothes. "How are things now?" he inquired. "Still pretty rough, I bet."

I agreed.

After telling me to wait a second, he climbed back on his truck. When he returned, he carried a helmet filled to overflowing with chocolate bars, C-rations, and cigarettes. "I guess you can use these," he said, without my having told him that I was dizzy with hunger. "That'll tide you over for a while."

Unable to express what I was feeling, I stuffed my pockets with my treasures while the eyes of curious pedestrians followed my every move. I felt like dropping to my knees and thanking my black Samaritan, but before I could say anything, he had gotten back on his truck and, with a wave of his hand and a "Take care, m' man," had pulled away.

It was during those few minutes that I first was struck by the sentimental notion to leave Germany and to get to know "my people" in the United States. Undoubtedly, my empty stomach had much to do with my decision to get the hell out of Germany.

Just as crucial as the shortage of food was the severe shortage of coal and other fuel. To supplement their meager allotment, desperate hordes of men, women, and children swarmed like locusts over stalled coal trains, freight yards, and other places where coal was stored or transported in order to fill their sacks, buckets, or baskets. This frequently brought them into confrontation with the police, who fought an uphill battle to curb the pilfering of heating fuel. While the coal rations we received were far from sufficient to keep our home fires burning, my mother and I decided against joining the illegal pursuit of coal after we almost became involved in a battle between pilferers and police in which both sides sustained serious casualties. If need be, we reasoned, we could stay warm by wrapping ourselves in blankets rather than paying for a little extra heat quite literally with an arm or a leg.

The inevitable result of crucial food and other shortages was the rapid spread of a brazenly open black market where everything from food to cigarettes to clothes could be bartered in exchange for jewelry, cameras, binoculars, accordions, and other valuables that some people had managed to hang on to during the war. Within days of the arrival of the British troops, I saw branches of this new, highly volatile economic force spring up at various street corners and in parks and squares throughout the city. Since German cigarette production had stopped, American and English cigarettes quickly filled the vacuum and became the black market's new, not-so-legal tender, with an astronomical exchange rate of one cigarette to five German marks.

In spite of the black market's highly illegal nature, relatively few of its participants were the underworld characters one reads about or sees in crime movies. Most of those I observed furtively trading on the black market were basically law-abiding men and women who had decided to give up their cherished wedding bands or cameras in order to brighten their drab existences with an occasional puff on a cigarette, a feast of canned corned beef, or a few cups of coffee, or to sweeten their hard lives with a couple of chocolate bars. Then there were the small-time amateur suppliers—British soldiers who were looking for bargain souvenirs from Germany, and who were sacrificing a pack or two of their own tightly rationed cigarettes. The real black-market pros, the big-time players, were the suppliers, a bunch of sleazy Germans whose secret warehouses received truckloads of cigarettes from equally sleazy British supply officers for retail black-market distribution. Easily recognized by their long leather coats and enormous gold chronometer wristwatches, they were ruthless wheelers and dealers who, like drug kingpins of generations yet to come, commanded armies of street "salesmen" who retailed the merchandise for maximum profits.

Since I neither was a smoker nor possessed any valuables that I could barter for food, the black market, at first, held no particular interest for me. But that was to change eventually because of several unforeseen events that totally changed the direction of my life.

While I had never formally terminated my employment with Max Roepke, I had no intention of ever returning, since the Allies had declared the compulsory Nazi work laws null and void. Determined to hang up my greasy machinist coveralls for good, I was more than ready to make my move to something better. What that "better" was, I didn't yet know. But I was confident that in the new era of Allied occupation, my color would be less of an obstacle than it had been so far and that, one way or another, I would find a way to put bread on the table for my mother and myself.

A NEW CAREER—MY FIRST GIG

I was still looking for opportunities when I ran into Herr Giordano. When he told me that he was working as a pianist for the British Army Welfare Service, I mentioned in passing that I, too, was a musician of sorts, and that I had taught myself to play the clarinet. "Then you may be interested in knowing that the British are still looking for more musicians to entertain their garrisoned troops," he told me, and urged me to go for an audition. I admitted that I wasn't good enough to play professionally, but he insisted that I couldn't possibly be as bad as some of the "hacks" the British were hiring. I wasn't so sure about that, but figured that with my pockets and stomach empty, what did I have to lose? So the next day, after dusting off my trusty old "licorice stick," which I hadn't touched for many months, I followed Herr Giordano's advice and headed for the Hamburger Staats Theater across from Hamburg's *Hauptbahnhof* and mingled with the musicians who were milling under the theater's marquee in hopes of landing an afternoon gig. They were a varied lot, dressed for the most part in clothing that had seen better days and at best could be described as shabbily elegant. Looking at my own well-worn suit and shoes, I was struck by the irony that at least this time nobody could say I didn't fit in.

When I spotted Herr Giordano, he briefed me on the hiring procedure. Every noon, he explained, the British put together a number of twelve-piece bands from the assembled musicians. "Whenever they call for a clarinet, you raise your hand," he told me. "If you are lucky, you'll get picked. After the gig, you'll be paid a few cigarettes and sometimes they'll serve you tea and sandwiches. So far, I've been lucky only twice, since piano players are a dime a dozen."

After we had waited about an hour, a canvas-covered British army lorry drove up and an officer called off the instruments he needed to form a band. Once he had chosen a dozen musicians from those who had raised their hands, they were loaded on the lorry and, without audition or rehearsal, driven to one of the many British army garrisons in and around Hamburg to provide the troops with an afternoon of musical diversion.

To my surprise, I was among the second truckload that was hired. I felt bad when the truck pulled off and I saw Herr Giordano still standing patiently among the musicians who were left behind. I hoped that he, too, would be lucky, but for the moment I had more pressing concerns. How could I possibly fool the other musicians and pass myself off as a pro? The closer our truck came to its destination, an army installation near Hamburg *Flughafen* manned by several hundred Tommies, the more I regretted having let Herr Giordano talk me into this. But there was no turning back.

When we reached the camp, we were led into a giant Quonset hut–like auditorium, seated on a wooden platform next to an upright piano, and told by our escorting officer that the concert was to start at precisely 3 P.M. That gave us just a little more than half an hour to set up and get our instruments tuned and organized, not to mention rehearse. The officer then distributed several sheets of popular British and American hit tunes and instructed us to choose a bandleader from our ranks. Our unanimous choice was the oldest member of the group, a short, paunchy, bespectacled saxophonist-clarinetist in his middle sixties with thinning white hair and an authoritative demeanor whom everybody addressed respectfully as *Kapellmeister* Fuller. Herr Fuller, I was told, had once had his own orchestra.

Soon the soldiers poured into the auditorium and, after a brief address by the officer, our band blasted off with Glenn Miller's hit arrangement of "In the Mood," a tune that was soon to take occupied Germany by storm. No thanks to me, the band sounded better than one could reasonably have expected under the circumstances. However, it was quite apparent to me that, Herr Giordano's vote of confidence notwithstanding, I was clearly the weakest link in this musical chain.

The fact that I was seated in the first row between *Kapellmeister* Fuller and a brash young tenor saxman who had just pulled off a brilliant solo did little to bolster my confidence in my musicianship. Thus, when a too-dry reed caused my clarinet to let out a piglike squeak in the middle of "At Last," I had to control the urge to walk off the stand before being asked to quit. But instead of the rebuke or ridicule I had expected, Herr Fuller gave me an encouraging wink. "Don't worry about it," he told me between numbers. "You'll be all right." Even Addi Wulf, the cocky tenor saxman, gave me encouragement. Thanks to my new colleagues' moral support, I made it through my first gig.

Following our performance, we musicians were led to a long table that was laden with fluffy white-bread sandwiches and pitchers of sweet, creamy tea and told to eat to our hearts' content. Starved as we were, we hardly needed any encouragement. The fact that nobody mentioned money didn't bother me in the least, since I felt amply compensated for my efforts, especially since I was able to take a doggy bag of sandwiches home to Mutti.

The following day I went back to the theater, hoping to get "hired" again. This time we were told to remain with the same group we had played with the previous day and that henceforth we would stay with that group. In effect, this meant that now I had a steady job instead of each day being at the mercy of Lady Luck. Although the pay was ridiculously small and the working conditions far from ideal, I was happy as a lark. I had access to food and I had achieved a significant breakthrough—the seemingly impossible transition from blue collar to white collar. This time, I felt, the pendulum had truly swung my way.

One evening, upon our return to the theater following a gig, Herr Fuller made me a surprising offer. "You've got what it takes to become a fine musician," he told me, "but as you know yourself, you still have much to learn. If you want me to, I'll give you clarinet and saxophone lessons." He even offered to furnish an E-flat alto saxophone, since all I had was my B-flat clarinet. When I asked him how much the lessons would cost me, he told me, "Nothing. Just promise me you'll work as hard as you can."

I couldn't quite understand what he was getting out of the deal, but I was so elated about what I considered my big break that I immediately accepted, without bothering to ask why he was being so nice to someone he hardly knew.

During several months that followed, under the stern guidance of my new mentor, I threw myself into the study of clarinet and saxophone with an intensity that bordered on obsession. Except for the daily afternoon sessions at British Army camps, I spent tedious hours in our basement "apartment," practicing a wide range of musical fare from the famous clarinet cadenza in Franz von Suppe's "Light Cavalry" to the E-flat saxophone solo in Glenn Miller's arrangement of "In the Mood"—anything Herr Fuller had assigned to me—until I got it right. Twice a week, I went to Maestro Fuller's modest apartment for two-hour practice sessions during which he critiqued my progress, coached me, and assigned new lessons.

One day, after I had finished my lesson and prepared to leave, Herr Fuller looked unusually nervous. "There is something I would like to discuss with you, if you don't mind," he announced, his discomfort mounting visibly.

Pausing repeatedly while groping for the right words, he told me that in order to be certified as a *Kapellmeister* under the Nazis, he had joined the Nazi Party shortly before the war. When the war broke out, he was inducted into the *Luftwaffe* as an officer with the rank of *Oberleutnant* (first lieutenant) and conductor of a concert band. He explained that both as Nazi Party member and as *Luftwaffe* officer, his duties had always been strictly musical, nonpolitical ones.

Since the Allies had announced an extensive denazification program, he continued, he needed an enormous favor from me. Would I sign a letter stating that he had been an old friend of my family who had used his influence to "modify my plight as a person persecuted by the Nuremberg racial laws"?

At first I balked. Lying to help a Nazi get off the hook was the last thing I thought I would ever do. But looking at the pitiful-looking old man who, in the short time I had known him, had been like a father to me, I started thinking. The military government's so-called denazification program in Hamburg had already turned into a big joke, with former big-time Nazis being exonerated without as much as a slap on the wrist. And, I rationalized, Herr Fuller had merely been a tiny party wheel, not a wanted war criminal who had committed heinous crimes. When I considered how much he had already done to modify my present plight by giving me a toehold on a new life when none of my Allied "liberators" had given a damn about me, I reluctantly agreed to stretch the truth a bit and sign the letter, for whatever it was worth. Even though I realized, somewhat sadly, that it wasn't all altruism that had prompted Herr Fuller's generosity toward me, I felt that he had really become fond of me, as I had become fond of him, and that his interest in me was genuine.

Things started looking up not only for me, but for my mother also. Through some of her old friends at the hospital she learned that persons fired by the Nazis for political reasons could apply for reinstatement. Within a few days of filing her application with the hospital, she was notified that she could have her old job back. After thirteen years of absence, she returned to her beloved ear, nose, and throat clinic, where she was welcomed by her colleagues with open arms. One of her former fellow employees and close

friends did not return. Walter Schmedemann, little Erika's Social Democrat
father, who had served time in the Fuhlsbüttel concentration camp for his
anti-Nazi activities, had been elected to the Hamburg Senate in one of the
first political elections held in newly democratic West Germany.

ROBBED

Just when my mother and I thought that, since both of us were more or
less gainfully employed, the bad times were behind us, we were dealt a
catastrophic blow that sent our morale plummeting to another record low.
It was early in the evening and I had just returned from an army camp gig
when, several blocks from our basement, my mother came running toward
me, tears streaming from her eyes and sobbing convulsively. At first, I
couldn't understand a word she was saying. But gradually, as she calmed
down a bit, she kept repeating over and over, "Everything is gone!" It took
me a while to comprehend what she was trying to tell me, namely that once
again we had lost everything we owned. All our clothes, shoes, bedsheets,
blankets, and dishes, everything we had painstakingly acquired since our
home had been destroyed three years earlier, was lost again. Only this time
we weren't ripped off by enemy bombs but by our own countrymen.

Between sobs, my mother told me how she had returned from work at
the hospital less than fifteen minutes earlier only to find the padlock to our
basement broken and the room ransacked clean. Apparently somebody, per-
haps a neighbor who knew that no one was in the apartment during the
day, had taken advantage of that fact. When we questioned the couple who
lived next door, they said they had seen and heard nothing. Unlike three
years ago, when we were able to salvage four suitcases packed with our
belongings, we now had only the clothes on our backs. Fortunately, I still
had my sax and clarinet.

At first we were thinking of going to the police, but we soon dismissed
that idea as pointless, recalling the many accounts we had heard about the
increasing incidents of robbery in makeshift shelters and the police's indif-
ference toward going after the criminals. Since we had every reason to believe

that sooner or later the person who had robbed us would be back for an encore, we decided that we had no other choice but to move as soon as possible. Before we had time to give in to our despair, we got a morale boost in the form of a visit by Egon Giordano. Egon informed us that the British military government had requisitioned a large apartment in a villa in Blankenese for his family and that, as a result, they no longer needed the basement apartment on Diesterwegstrasse. If we wanted it, he said, we were more than welcome to it.

Thanks to the burglar, the move to our new home—about a fifteen-minute walk—was a piece of cake since we were traveling extremely light. The "new" apartment was as devoid of amenities as the one we were leaving behind, but at least it had a front door that could also be locked, and again it came with friendly next-door neighbors, a young family of four, who, the Giordanos told us, were extremely helpful and trustworthy.

Shortly after moving into our home, I made a startling discovery. About a hundred yards from the entrance to our basement, I saw a small group of men who were gathering bricks from the surrounding ruins and, after cleaning them of mortar, arranging them into neat man-high piles. What piqued my curiosity was the fact that, considering the type of work they were doing, all were inappropriately dressed in suits and dress overcoats. Some were even wearing neckties. On taking a closer look, I recognized one of them as my white-maned erstwhile boss, the plant manager at the Harburg rubber factory. The last time our paths had crossed, he had told me that if I didn't shape up and give up my rebellious conduct, he'd have to let the Gestapo deal with me. Now, the tables had definitely turned.

Apparently, he and his coworkers had been caught in the first wave of British "denazification" and ordered, like many compromised ex-Nazis with minor rap sheets, to do penance in the form of menial community work. Although the work he was doing was relatively easy compared with mine when I spent grueling hours inside his factory's suffocating boilers, I could well sense his humiliation. As soon as he recognized me, he averted his eyes. Since I had no particular interest in adding to his misery, I turned around and walked away, leaving him and his cronies to their own consciences. When I passed by that same spot in the evening, the men and their pile of bricks were gone without a trace.

FRED GASS

While taking a leisurely morning reconnaissance walk through my new neighborhood—a mixture of ruins and four-story apartment buildings that had survived the war—I ran into an unusual-looking, slightly built fellow with a pencil-thin mustache and long, slicked-back black hair who looked familiar to me. On taking a closer look, I remembered him as one of the regulars at Café König. Only in those days, I recalled, he had worn a German army corporal's uniform and his arm had been supported by a black sling. Now he was impeccably dressed in prewar-quality clothes, consisting of an elegant glen-check sports jacket, tan gabardine slacks, and a stylish pair of light-brown casual shoes with thick white crepe rubber soles.

"Long time no see, amigo," he opened the conversation. "I see you, too, survived the war." After we compared notes about the good old Café König days, Fred Gass explained that at the time I spotted him at our favorite swingboy hangout, he was convalescing from injuries sustained when Russian shrapnel ripped off his left middle finger. "I still have my souvenir," he said, holding up a four-fingered left hand.

During our subsequent walk down memory lane, I learned that Fred lived nearby with his aged foster parents in a block of apartment buildings that the war had left untouched. Before the war, he said, he had been a uniformed page at Hamburg's prestigious Waterloo cinema, where movie premieres used to be held and featured stars made personal appearances. While a page, he explained, he often had opportunities to ingratiate himself with some of the most prominent people of Hamburg by selling them admission tickets after the box office had sold out. As a result, he said, he was still extremely well connected, and if there was anything he could do for me, I shouldn't hesitate to let him know. With a disdainful look at my outdated, borderline-shabby clothes, Fred suggested that if I were interested in upgrading my wardrobe, he'd be the man to see. "I think I can put you into a brand-new, high-quality suit for relatively little money," he suggested.

That really got my attention, since I had lost the two suits I had when our apartment was burglarized. Looking at Fred's fine threads, I figured that if anyone could put his hands on quality clothes, he was certainly the man, and I agreed to meet him the next day to pursue the matter further.

The next day came and went without Fred being able to contact "the man with the suits." And so did the next day and all the next days afterward. As much as I hated to give up on my dream of having nice clothes to wear, I finally had to admit to myself that Fred, while charming, was about as dependable as the weather in April.

Under normal circumstances, I would have taken the first opportunity to tell him to get and stay lost. But after we had hung around together for a few weeks, he had grown on me, and I had to concede that I enjoyed being around him despite his foibles. Once I had learned never to depend on Fred, no matter what his good intentions, we got along famously, as I found him witty, resourceful, original, and utterly entertaining. As far as he was concerned, I hadn't come empty-handed to the table either. I soon realized that he enjoyed my company because it provided him with an opportunity to share the spotlight with me whenever my exotic looks drew attention. The result was a symbiotic relationship in which each of us got his money's worth, so to speak.

This was particularly true when it came to Fred's uncanny ability to attract good-looking women. Like a general mapping war strategy, Fred never proceeded without a plan when the objective was to ensnare a beauty. On a rainy day, for instance, he would position himself with an umbrella at the entrance of an office building at just about the time the offices would close, keeping a sharp lookout for an umbrellaless damsel in distress. Once he had spotted a likely subject, he would offer to accompany her with his umbrella to the next streetcar stop or wherever she had to go. Most of the girls who accepted his offer and listened to his charming BS were also willing to see him again on a date.

Since Fred usually arranged more dates than he could possibly keep, he generously let me have my pick from the surplus. After describing the young woman and giving me the address where he was supposed to meet her, I would go there, take a look, and, if I liked what I saw, tell her that Fred had been unable to make it, and had sent me as a substitute. Rather than being stood up, they always accepted me as their ersatz date.

Even if Fred exaggerated a lot, he had been uncharacteristically modest when he told me that he had connections. Wherever we went, he was greeted by members of Hamburg's Prominenz, including stage and screen stars, radio personalities, and other high-profile types, who remembered him from his Waterloo days. During each encounter, he generously shared his five-mark-apiece cigarettes although, as far as I could determine, he had no visible means of support.

Hanging out with Fred at the Faun Bar and Haus Vaterland, two prestigious nightclubs that had survived the war, became an enjoyable pastime when I wasn't musically engaged. We'd always gather at one of the more conspicuous tables near the orchestra. Invariably, we were joined by other exotic types, such as Pallah Tuba, a swarthy, devastatingly handsome playboy from Iran, whose working older brothers imported Oriental rugs, and Cookoo, a young Cuban, who, I was told, also owed his leisurely lifestyle to his prosperous working family. Both had only limited German-language skills, so our conversations, if one could call them that, were totally lacking in intellectual content. For the most part, they centered on the latest trends in American music and dress, and—last but not least—which of the girls could be considered prospective love objects. Occasionally, we were joined by Hugo Zeisse, the only true capitalist in our group. Hugo, a tall, impeccably dressed young man whom I had met during the war, was working in his father's ship brokerage firm. Since his father, Tom Zeisse, was English-born, we deferred to Hugo in matters relating to British manners and style. Hugo drove a Mercedes-Benz and lived with his parents in a fancy house in Fuhlsbüttel. In short, he lived the lifestyle to which Fred and I aspired.

In view of the exceedingly modest circumstances in which we lived— Fred in a tiny working-class apartment and I in a basement whose ceiling leaked whenever it rained—I was amused by our café society image and by all the attention our presence attracted. To keep up appearances, Fred would go to extraordinary lengths. Once we were headed for a red-hot double date when, about three blocks from Haus Vaterland, Fred flagged down an elegant car with a distinguished-looking man behind the wheel. Holding up three cigarettes, the equivalent of fifteen marks, Fred asked the gentleman whether he would be kind enough to give us a lift to Haus Vaterland, since we were "running late for an important appointment."

I thought Fred had lost his mind. But before I had a chance to ask for an explanation, the driver told us to get in. When, after accepting Fred's cigarettes, he dropped us off in front of the club, our two dates were duly impressed. Although we had traveled most of the way by streetcar, Fred told the girls that "one of our friends gave us a lift." The entire operation was designed to keep the girls from knowing that we were using public transportation like everybody else.

THE RUBBER BARON

Dropping in on Fred Gass one day, I found my usually impeccable buddy seated in his mother's tiny kitchen, dressed in a pair of work pants and an apron, about to pull a crooked heel from a woman's shoe with a pair of pliers. "What in the world are you doing?" I inquired after surveying the scene.

"I'm repairing a shoe," he replied, as if he had done nothing else in his life.

Suspecting that there was a story somewhere, I asked for an explanation.

"Remember my shoes with the white crepe rubber soles?"

"Yes. What about them?" I replied.

"Remember that I had worn the soles so crooked that I was about to throw them away, since repair shops don't have any crepe rubber since the war?" he kept digging.

"Yes, but what does that have to do with anything?" I shot back impatiently.

"Plenty," he responded, then picked up the shoes in question, but with brand-new snow-white crepe rubber soles.

He then explained that by chance he had passed a junkyard where they sold old, treadworn automobile tires, and he noticed that one of the tires had a cut that revealed a layer of white rubber. For a few marks, he said, the junkman cut him a piece of tire from which he whittled two perfect-looking soles. As proof of his labor, Fred held up a pair of badly blistered hands.

"But that's only half of the story," he added with the excitement of a boy explaining his new toy. "Since I have worn the shoes with the new soles, I can't walk a few blocks without being stopped by all kinds of people who want to know where they can get their shoes fitted with white rubber soles."

Fred said that even after he told them that it would cost them one hundred marks a pair, the requests kept coming. He had already accepted more than a thousand marks' worth of work. When he noticed my skeptical look, Fred opened a closet and several dozen men's and women's shoes tumbled out.

"At this rate," Fred said, with unbridled enthusiasm and characteristic generosity, "I'll be a rich man within a few months. If you want to, you can join me. There's enough work for both of us."

As much as I appreciated Fred's offer, I told him thanks but no thanks. Having just barely escaped the blue-collar brigade, I had no interest in exchanging my carefree musician's lifestyle for working my hands to the bone while being tied down for countless hours to some workbench, no matter how great the monetary rewards. I felt strongly that while it was well-paid and honest work, being a cobbler didn't quite fit the image I had of myself.

To my surprise, dapper Fred, who had written the book on projecting a café society image and cultivating a somewhat creative approach not fully anchored in our grim reality, had no such concerns and threw himself with gusto into his new enterprise. After his mother evicted him from her kitchen, he moved his business to the basement, where he pounded, glued, and carved rubber from morning till night. If he still had any energy left, he would transform himself into the old, supergroomed Fred and join the gang at the Faun Bar or Haus Vaterland, his pockets stuffed with a wad of marks thick enough to support a two-pack-a-day Chesterfield habit. One annoying by-product of Fred's new entrepreneurship was the fact that every Klaus, Karl, and Ilse would stop at our table, not to say hello but to find out from Fred when their long-overdue shoes would be ready.

When business picked up to a point where Fred could no longer handle the volume, he recruited his eighty-four-year-old foster father to help out. Henceforth, the two cobbled away, Papa in the kitchen and Fred in the basement, to reduce the backlog of shoes and to meet the mounting demand for crepe soles, which had clearly become an upscale Hamburg fad. It was inevitable that the junkman who supplied Fred with old tires should become suspicious when the volume of Fred's purchases increased steadily. One day, without any explanation, he upped the price from twenty marks a tire to two hundred marks, a steep increase but one Fred could easily absorb.

I, too, was being besieged by people who wanted me to tell them how they could become the proud owners of white crepe soles like the ones I had cobbled on my shoes. At first, I would send them to Fred, but when Fred and his father could no longer keep up with the demand, I simply couldn't stand by while money was being turned away. I decided to get into the shoe-repair business myself—but the Hans Massaquoi way. Instead of spending my days cobbling, I told potential customers that I could get them the rubber, but that they would have to find a shoe repairman or do the installation themselves. Once I had collected enough orders, I would buy an old tire, then cut it up into sole-size chunks that I would sell to my customers for fifty marks a pair. While I made only half the money Fred made, I had virtually no work to do other than buying and cutting up the tires. I tried to convince Fred that my way was the smarter way of doing business and persuade him to change his modus operandi, but for a reason I have never been able to figure out, he stubbornly stuck to his own arduous method of making a living. Having already paid my dues in the sweatshops of Nazi Germany, I had no intention of giving up my tenuous hold on the white-collar class, and besides, I liked my callus-free hands just fine.

MOVING UP

As a victim of the Nuremberg racial laws, I had repeatedly applied for an apartment for my mother and me without success. Just when I was about to throw in the towel, a letter from the British military government informed me that two rooms had been requisitioned for us in a home in Othmarschen, one of Hamburg's upscale suburbs along the River Elbe, and that the letter would serve as my introduction to the owners of the home.

When my mother and I arrived at the Othmarschen address, a plain, three-story duplex of which one half had been razed by a bomb, I was met by our new landlords, Herr and Frau Flemming, and their two grown sons, the oldest a recently discharged ensign of the German navy. They appeared less than thrilled by the idea of having to take in tenants, but tried hard not to make their displeasure too obvious. I had no idea what had gotten them on the British military government's housing list, since not all Germans were required to take in roomers, but I couldn't have cared less. Since they had survived the bombings unscathed and were spared the loss of their belongings, I found it difficult to feel sorry for them for having to rent out two rooms.

The rooms were minuscule and located on different floors, but they were above ground and had a proper, nonleaking roof over them. To my mother and me, who had become used to living like moles in smelly, dank, and cold basements, they meant no less than a return to civilization. Just being able to walk barefoot for a change on clean wooden floors instead of the rough, always damp, and always cold concrete of our previous "home" seemed like sheer luxury to us.

Othmarschen, like most of Hamburg's suburbs, had been left mostly unscathed by Allied bombs. This meant that we had to get used once more to walking through streets with intact sidewalks and buildings instead of negotiating narrow footpaths through mountains of rubble. I also appreciated having escaped the stigma of living in a rodent-infested basement under the ruins of a bombed-out building. No longer did I have to beat around the bush when someone asked me where I lived. The mere word *Othmarschen* got me immediate respect.

Our new home was conveniently located a five-minute walk from the train station, which was only a half dozen stops from downtown Hamburg. It also was within a few train stops of Blankenese, and thus gave me the welcome opportunity of seeing more of my friends, the Giordanos.

When I paid them a visit, I found them well and, as usual, in a state of excitement. This time the focus of their excitement was a recently arrived addition to the family, a baby sister. Between cooing and talking baby talk, Ralph and Egon brought me up to date on their various journalistic activities. To my surprise, I noticed a drastic change in Ralph's political orientation. Whereas only a few months earlier he had been filled with enthusiasm for our British and American liberators, he now lashed out angrily at capitalists who, he maintained, were exploiting the masses and making common cause with the Nazis. "Wait till you get to your wonderful America," he told me. "You'll soon enough find out what I mean."

In years to come, while observing the wretchedness of America's urban and rural poor, I had ample opportunity to view the less pleasant side of capitalism, but at the time I was truly shocked and disappointed at his political metamorphosis. Ralph told me that he had become a full-fledged member of the German Communist Party, and a correspondent for *Die Hamburger Volkszeitung,* the Communist Party's newspaper. There was no doubt in my mind that behind Ralph's drastic conversion was his resentment over the Allies' lenient treatment of former Nazis. As a victim of Nazi racial hate, I, too, favored the approach of the Soviet troops who, it was widely known, purged the Nazis in their zone of occupation with an unforgiving head-for-an-eye policy. But my orientation was too Western and my knowledge of and interest in dialectic materialism too vague for me to throw out the baby with the bathwater and abandon my American dream.

As much as I regretted Ralph's switch to the Communists, whose slogans and coercive methods seemed no different to me from those of the Nazis, I decided not to let our political differences mar our friendship. We had come too far together to let a little controversy like capitalism versus communism come between us.

ALKAZAR

Bumping into my buddy Addie Wulf, the tenor sax man, one day, he invited me to audition with him for a young bandleader who was putting together a big dance band. The bandleader, Addie explained, wanted nobody older than himself, and he had to have the group ready to go to work in only one month, when he intended to audition for the Alkazar, the biggest theater-nightclub in the city. Without hesitation I picked up my saxophone and clarinet and went along to the audition. The bandleader, a fellow by the name of Rolf Wehlau, took one look at me and decided he wanted me in his band. It was obvious that he valued me more for my decorative value than for my musical ability, of which he knew nothing at the time. I explained to him that I didn't think I was ready to handle first E-flat alto sax parts because of the many solos, but that I played a pretty solid third alto.

After putting a few third alto sheets in front of me and asking me to play contemporary American favorites to his piano accompaniment, he told me I was hired. Addie, too, was hired as second B-flat tenor man. The catch was that the hiring was contingent on the band's passing the Alkazar audition a month hence. To make sure we did, we all agreed to rehearse as many hours a day as it took to get it right.

The Alkazar, in the heart of St. Pauli, was a cavernous ballroom with a huge dance floor that could be hydraulically raised to serve as stage for various acts. It was surrounded by two floors of balconies and its high ceiling permitted aerial and high-wire acts. Although the Alkazar had seen better days before the war, and much of its art deco glitter had faded, its popularity as one of Hamburg's hottest nightspots was undiminished.

We arrived—all fifteen of us—almost an hour early for the noon audition, prepared for hours of musical grilling. We had rehearsed almost incessantly for an entire month until we were convinced that there was no hotter dance band this side of the Elbe. Thus, we were caught totally off guard when a short, skinny fellow with a cigar in his mouth and a hat perched on the back of his head announced that he was the boss of the Alkazar and that he wanted us to play John Philip Sousa's "Stars and Stripes Forever." "I know you all know how to read music and that you know how to play all the latest American hits," he growled. "I don't give a shit about that. Every two-bit musician can do that. What I want to know is how good you are at improvising, and I don't mean playing jazz improvisations. If you want to accompany a variety show program, you've got to be able to think on your feet, be prepared for unexpected problems. An artist may not show up and you have to accompany a replacement act you've never seen or heard before. This means you've got to know how to improvise."

We looked at each other dumbfounded. Nobody, it turned out, had the slightest idea who John Philip Sousa was nor what his "Stars and Stripes Forever" was all about. Exasperated, the Alkazar's boss removed the cigar from his mouth and started whistling a few strains of a march that sounded vaguely familiar to me. Slowly, we picked up our instruments and began to play along—first meekly, then louder and louder as more and more of us caught on. When we reached the end in a rousing finale that reverberated throughout the theater, the man clapped enthusiastically and told us we were hired. "You guys are okay," he praised. "You know how to improvise."

Playing saxophone in a large dance band for 610 marks a month at the Alkazar was more than I had ever dared to dream. I was getting paid—by prevailing standards extremely well—for something I would have gladly done for nothing.

The job consisted of playing two two-hour shows, including two dance sessions, from four to six and from eight to ten, with two hours' intermission. This meant that, except for two weekly morning rehearsals, I could indulge myself sleeping late, then watching the rest of the city work while I strolled about town like a man of leisure. Another fringe benefit of my new lifestyle was the ready access it provided me to the leggiest chorus line appearing on a Hamburg stage at that time. Since most of the young ladies were from out of town and lived scattered over St. Pauli in cheap rooming houses, the job of keeping them happy and contented while away from home fell largely to the band, a responsibility which all of us assumed with the utmost dedication.

It was gratifying for me to note that my skin color, which for so long I had regarded as my major liability, had almost overnight turned into an asset. During my previous, mostly clandestine, encounters with German girls, I rarely could escape the feeling of being used as forbidden fruit— quite willingly, I admit, but used nevertheless. Now I had the new, ego- bolstering experience of being pursued openly and unabashedly because, as far as the fräuleins of the immediate postwar period were concerned, black was definitely in.

Thanks to my new high-profile position as saxophonist in one of Ham- burg's most popular nightspots, I was reunited with many of my old cronies from war and prewar days who happened to be in the audience and recog- nized me. Of all the reunions, however, none was as memorable and heart- rending as one that occurred during a Sunday matinee. As I passed the bar during intermission, I heard an oddly familiar female voice call my name. When I turned around, I looked at a tall, beautiful redhead who turned out to be none other than Gretchen Jahn. In the nearly two years since I had last seen her, her face had become even more beautiful than I remembered, but I also detected a certain hardness around her mouth and eyes that I hadn't seen before. "What are you doing here?" I asked, unable to think of anything more intelligent to say.

Gretchen replied that she was with her mother and took me to their table.

Mrs. Jahn seemed genuinely pleased to see me. "My, have you matured!" she exclaimed, while reminding me that she hadn't seen me since those memorable July days in 1943 when most of Hamburg went up in flames.

There were so many questions I wanted to ask Gretchen and so many things I wanted to tell her, but I felt inhibited by Mrs. Jahn's presence. The same seemed to be true for Gretchen. Sensing our discomfort, Mrs. Jahn suggested that she would catch an early train back to her home in the suburbs so Gretchen and I could talk after the show about the good old days in the Stückenstrasse.

After the matinee and a hasty goodbye from Mrs. Jahn, we went to the bar to bring each other up to date. Seeing Gretchen again stirred up all the old, long-pent-up feelings I had once felt for the girl who was my first love and with whom I had shared my first tender feelings for the opposite sex. Without taking our eyes off each other, we compared notes on what had transformed the young boy Mrs. Jahn used to know into the mature young man, and what had put that certain hardness around Gretchen's eyes and mouth.

"Guess what?" Gretchen prepared me for a surprise. She then told me that she, too, was in show business, as the assistant of a magician who, as part of his act, would saw her in half, then put her ostensibly severed torso back together again. I didn't press her for a more detailed explanation of her relationship with him, but it seemed obvious that he was more to her than just her boss.

I recalled the last time we said goodbye and her insistence on hanging on to her virginity until she was at least twenty-one. Gretchen confirmed that she was no longer a virgin. I didn't know whether I should be glad or sad about her revelation. On the one hand, I felt relief because a big obstacle had been removed. At the same time, I was deeply disappointed and hurt. As if she had read my thoughts, she suddenly said, "No matter what has happened or what will happen, you will always be the first man I ever loved."

The bar was about to close and I offered to walk her home, which, she explained, was just a few blocks away. When we had reached the building where Gretchen rented a small room in a second-floor flat, she told me what I longed to hear, namely that I was welcome to come upstairs. Throughout the night, we both tried hard to rekindle the old magic that we felt when, barely fourteen years old, we exchanged our first kiss. But to no avail. We conceded with some sadness that there was nothing we could do to bring back the magic because our innocence, along with our adolescence, was irretrievably gone.

As we said goodbye, Gretchen told me that she was shortly going on the road with her magician boss. We both felt instinctively that we would never see each other again and that the great love story of Hans-Jürgen and Gretchen had come to an end.

YANKEE WERNER

One night, my fellow bandsmen and I were treated to a strange spectacle. We had just settled down on the bandstand when a waiter ushered an immense black fellow who bore an uncanny resemblance to Louis Armstrong toward a reserved ringside table directly below us. He was wearing a pair of khaki trousers and a U.S. Army field jacket. After waving at me and flashing a wide fraternal grin, he reached into one of the pockets and extracted a sandwich of the most generous proportions, the likes of which I had never seen before. Seemingly oblivious to the people around him, he proceeded to dig his large, snow-white teeth into the delicacy, which, followed by hundreds of covetous eyes, disappeared from view in a matter of seconds. After that, he produced another sandwich of similar proportions from another pocket and, to the envy of the hungry Germans around him, repeated the procedure. Next, his seemingly inexhaustible pockets yielded half a carton of Camels, from which he extracted a pack and, in turn, a cigarette.

By this time my colleagues could stand it no longer. "I'll bet he'll let you have a pack if you ask him," one of them suggested, obviously expecting to benefit from such a move on my part. The thought had already crossed my mind. So at intermission, I made my way to the stranger's table.

"I'm Mickey," I introduced myself. "Are you an American GI?"

"Naw," he replied, "I'm merchant marine. Smitty's the name. How come you're playing in a Kraut band?"

I told him that I was sort of a Kraut myself since my mother was German and Germany was my home.

"I'm from Mobile, Alabama," he informed me. Smitty told me he had just come from New York on the *Appleton Victory* and expected to be in port for two or three days.

Lighting another cigarette, he wanted to know whether I smoked. I thought he'd never ask.

"You bet," I replied, trying out an American phrase I had learned only a few days before. He handed me the near-full pack and told me to keep it. "Musta been rough livin' here during the war," he surmised.

"It still is," I told him, "especially when it comes to getting enough food and cigarettes. Cigarettes are so scarce, you can buy anything you want with them, and," I added suggestively, "I mean anything."

Smitty looked at me incredulously. Then, with a sly wink, he repeated, *"Anything?"*

Handing me another pack of cigarettes, he asked me to do him a favor. "Do you know the tall blonde in the chorus line?"

"I know all the girls in the chorus line," I bragged. "Her name is Gerda; she's the lead dancer."

I didn't like the turn the conversation was taking—or I thought was taking—since I knew that Gerda was not that kind of a girl.

"Ask her if she minds joining us here at the table and having a picture taken with me."

"That's no problem," I assured him with great relief, a bit ashamed for having jumped to the wrong conclusion. I then walked over to Gerda at the bar.

"How'd you like to earn a few cigarettes in a hurry?" I asked her. "All you have to do is have your picture taken with a friend of mine," I explained.

Smitty was happy as a lark when Gerda consented not only to pose with him, but to do so cheek-to-cheek and with both arms wrapped around him. Within minutes, the roving camera girl had captured this touching scene for posterity—as well as, no doubt, for Smitty's envious homeboys back in Jim Crow Alabama. For our "trouble," Gerda and I received our own souvenir snapshots and a pack of Camels each, which brought my loot for the evening to the equivalent of one week's pay.

On a sudden impulse of generosity, I tossed one pack up to my colleagues on the bandstand. Most of them had watched me "operate" and had been eagerly awaiting my return. Before I joined them to resume work, Smitty thanked me for taking care of him and told me that, in return, he would "fix me up" if I came to visit him aboard his ship the next morning. "Just catch the WSA launch and get off when you get to the *Appleton Victory*," he told me. "When you come aboard, ask for Smitty, the messman."

He explained that the launch was a small motor boat that at hourly intervals ferried U.S. seamen between their ships and shore free of charge. I hadn't the vaguest idea where I had to catch the boat or what he meant by wanting to "fix me up," but I was eager to take him up on his offer. Setting foot on an American ship, I felt, was the next best thing to setting foot on American soil. "I'll be seeing you tomorrow," I promised, and he responded that he'd be looking for me.

Except for a few field trips with my class during my early school years, I had never been in Hamburg's vast harbor, the largest in Germany. Consequently, it took me a while the next morning until I had found my way to the wharf near St. Pauli's famous *Landungsbrücken* (landing bridges) where a large sign proclaimed:

> **WAR SHIPPING ADMINISTRATION (WSA) LAUNCH.**
> **ADMISSION RESTRICTED TO**
> **UNITED STATES MERCHANT MARINE PERSONNEL!**

Despite my limited English, I had no problem figuring out that German landlubbers like me were not welcome. But rather than abort my mission, which was to get fixed up by Smitty, I decided to take a chance and meet the challenge head on. There were about a dozen men already waiting for the launch. One covetous look at their new-looking American clothes convinced me that they were Amis, as Germans were fond of calling Americans. Careful not to arouse their suspicion, I boldly mingled with the group as if I belonged, while intensely scrutinizing each man from the corners of my eyes. They behaved exactly the way Amis behaved in the American movies I had seen before the war. Some were smoking cigarettes, while others were chewing gum like ruminating cattle; some did both simultaneously. Except for one man in a navy topcoat and gold-braided white naval officer's hat, the men were dressed in various civilian attires that ranged from suits with huge shoulders, wide-brimmed hats, and colorful geometric-patterned neckties to casual sportswear and khakis. To me, a kid who had only one shabby suit to his name, the group on the landing looked like a male fashion show. Self-conscious, I looked down at my crude-looking "sport shoes" with the home-made "crepe" soles and at the drab-looking, nondescript pants and jacket I was wearing. They were so threadbare and shiny from frequent pressing that on closer inspection one could see the skin of my elbows and knees peeping through. But nobody seemed to pay any particular attention to me or my clothing, or so I thought. Just as I started to feel a bit less apprehensive, a cocky young fellow with what I thought was an all-American face headed straight toward me. He was dressed in a khaki shirt and pants, white socks, and a pair of loafers, and his blond hair was carefully combed into a pompadour in the front and a duck's tail in the back. Before I could figure out what he might want from me, the young fellow said "Hi," and after offering me a cigarette from a freshly opened pack, asked me where I was going. "The *Appleton Victory*," I replied, hoping against hope that he was from another ship.

I had tried to keep our conversation to a minimum so as not to give myself away as a German, but to no avail.

"Where're you from?" he pried.

Before I had a chance to answer, the man in the naval officer's uniform turned to him for a light. After the all-American had lighted the officer's cigarette, the two got into a conversation and for the time being I was off the hook.

"Where're you from?" the officer turned the tables on my interrogator.

"New Jork," the all-American replied.

"New Jork? Where's that?"

Suddenly, the all-American lost his cockiness and for a moment looked quite helpless as he repeated that he was from "New Jork City in the state of New Jork."

"You mean New York," the officer corrected him.

"Yeah, New York, New Jork, whatever."

The officer didn't belabor the point, but I had followed the exchange between the two with increasing interest. It occurred to me that anybody who couldn't pronounce the name of his own hometown correctly wasn't necessarily from where he said he was from.

At that point—precisely at noon—the ear-shattering blast of a foghorn sounded and a motorboat, the Stars and Stripes flying from its stern, approached the shore. With additional blasts from its foghorn, the launch pulled alongside and before it had made contact with the wharf, a young fellow with a thick rope jumped off and skillfully tied the vessel to a massive steel bollard. Acting nonchalant, as if I had spent my entire life at sea, I followed the men as they jumped into the launch. I had feared that there would be some kind of ID check and had wondered whether I would get by if I told them that I was the guest of Smitty, the messman, from the *Appleton Victory*. Fortunately, nobody seemed to care, and after a few minutes of waiting for additional passengers, the launch turned around and headed for the middle of the Elbe, past the bombed-out shipyards of Blohm & Voss and Deutsche Werft. The famous shipyards that once had teemed with the hustle and bustle of thousands of workers and had made Hamburg one of the biggest ship-building centers on the European continent were eerily silent, their cranes and steel structures a tangled, rusting mess.

Soon I was again accosted by the all-American, who, as far as I was concerned, was becoming a regular pest. When he offered me another cigarette, I upgraded his status by a notch or two. "You're not a merchant seaman?" he resumed his interrogation.

"That's right," I admitted. "This is my first time in port. I'm visiting a friend on the *Appleton Victory*."

"That's where I am going, too; I have friends on the *Appleton Victory* also," the all-American confided.

Within a few minutes of comparing notes, I learned that his name was Werner, that he lived with his German mother and a younger brother in St. Pauli, and that his father, whom he hadn't seen since the beginning of the war, was chief purser for an American line. Although Werner had been born near Berlin, he said he had lived for a couple of years with his mother and brother in Rutherford, New Jersey, and in New York City before the war. He also confided that on the waterfront, everybody called him Yankee Werner because of his American pedigree. In the past few months, he said, he had visited many American ships, and that each visit had paid off handsomely.

Reciprocating his candor, I told him about my origins. Werner advised me not to mention my Liberian background to anyone aboard ship and instead say that my father was an American. "All you have to tell them is that you and your mother got stuck here in Germany because of the war, and you've got it made," he counseled. Although I had yet to grasp the full meaning of that little Americanism, "got it made," I took Werner's advice and, in doing so—without realizing it at the time—altered the course of my life in a most decisive way.

Werner explained to me that the *Appleton Victory* was one of three American ships in port and the launch's first stop. "There she is." He pointed toward a distant black freighter with a white-and-yellow superstructure and a massive yellow stack. As the launch approached the ship, the latter's proportions grew rapidly until it towered over us like an enormous mountain cliff hanging over a nutshell. As we circled the giant, I could see its enormous blade partially exposed above the waterline. This, Werner explained, indicated that the ship's unloading was almost completed.

I had been wondering by what means we were supposed to get aboard. When the truth dawned on me, I became horrified and silently cursed Smitty for having gotten me into this mess. The only way to get aboard the *Appleton Victory*, I realized, was to climb what seemed like a mile of rope ladder with wooden rungs that was dangling overboard and swaying back and forth in the wind. To make matters still worse, the launch was bobbing wildly up and down beneath the ladder, requiring any climber to time his ascent to within a second when the ladder and launch came within a few feet of each other. Besides Werner and me, there were three seamen who had indicated they wanted to get off at the *Appleton Victory*. Werner, who had noticed my apprehension, told me not to worry. "Just hold on tight and don't look down," he advised. For a moment I felt like telling the launch skipper that I had changed my mind and that I was staying on, but then I recalled the voice of Herr Wriede, my old Nazi principal, shouting at me, "*Kein Mut! Feigling!* Step aside to make room for the boys with guts!" Suddenly, my fear was gone, and before I knew it, I had leaped into the air, grabbed the ladder, and was climbing and climbing while looking neither up nor down.

After what seemed to me like an eternity, I reached the top and flung myself over the railing and on deck. Werner and the three other seamen followed shortly.

"Hope you'll make out. Be seeing you," said Werner before disappearing through a door.

"What do you want?" a man in soiled khakis and a matching gold-braided hat demanded to know.

"I'm looking for Smitty," I told him as instructed.

"Smitty!" the soiled one hollered. "Somebody to see you!"

Within seconds, Smitty materialized in the door through which I had seen Werner disappear. He was dressed completely in white, including a soiled apron. "See you made it," Smitty greeted me while extending his hamlike hand. "You're just in time for chow."

He told me to follow him, and after a brief walk through a narrow, labyrinthine walkway, during which we had to squeeze by several crew members, we arrived at a narrow room with a long table and chairs that were attached to the steel floor but capable of rotating on their own axis. "This is the crew mess," Smitty explained. "This is where the crew eats."

He then took me to what looked to me like a kitchen but he called a galley. "Chief, I want you to meet Mickey, a friend of mine," he addressed a gargantuan black man who made Smitty, a rather substantial man in his own right, look average size. Like Smitty, he was dressed in white, but in addition he wore a huge white chef's hat. "This is the chief cook, my boss," Smitty explained.

"Hi, Mickey," the profusely sweating giant greeted me while drying his face and hands with a towel.

"How about fixing the kid up with a full house, chief? He hasn't had a decent meal for years," Smitty intervened in my behalf while explaining to me that a "full house" meant a plate filled with everything on the menu.

"Coming up," the chief replied.

Smitty told me to have a seat in the crew mess. Minutes later, he shoved a plate in front of me that was filled beyond the edge with a mountain of food—mashed potatoes, a pork chop, several meatballs, a couple of sunny-side-up eggs, and several different vegetables, all swimming in gravy. When I told Smitty that I had to take some of that food to my mother, he told me not to worry since there was plenty more where that came from. "I'll make you a package you can take home to your mom," Smitty promised. With the last obstacle to my enjoyment of the feast before me thus removed, I started digging in. Soon I was the center of attention as other black seamen who had joined me at the table watched with amazement as I made the mountain of food in front of me disappear.

After I helped Smitty clean up the crew mess, he invited me to his cabin, which he shared with his counterpart in the officer's mess, a tall, skinny fellow with a goatee whom Smitty introduced to me as Slim. A Texan from Galveston, Slim was sitting on one of the two bunks in the tiny cabin, through whose porthole I could see the harbor and Hamburg's shoreline in the afternoon sun. "What's happ'nin', my man?" Slim greeted me.

I had begun to notice that Americans—especially the black Americans I had met—spoke a language that bore little resemblance to the one taught by my English teachers Herr Harden, Herr Neumann, and Frau Dr. Fink. When, at the urging of Smitty, I filled his colleague in on my life under Hitler, Slim was moved to interrupt from time to time with "I dig," "Can you beat that?," "Get a load of that," and "Ain't that a bitch?," none of which made a great deal of sense to me.

Then came my turn to ask questions. From the time I was a child and able to read *Uncle Tom's Cabin,* I had known about the mistreatment of blacks in the United States. Later, I added to that knowledge through newspaper articles about race riots, lynchings, and Jim Crow. But I had never had an opportunity to learn the facts firsthand. When I asked the inevitable question, "How are Negroes treated in America?" both men replied in unison, "Like shit!" They then explained to me that cities in the North, like New York, Chicago, and Detroit, were "halfway okay," but that anyplace in the South—"no matter where"—was "a bitch."

"How are you getting along with the white people on this ship?" I wanted to know.

"We don't," replied Smitty. "We does our work and keeps to ourselves and they does their work and keeps to theirselves. In other words," Smitty summarized, "We don't fuck with them, and they don't fuck with us."

Slim told me that the ship was crawling with "crackers," which, he explained, were racist white people from the South, and he advised me to avoid them like the plague. "That sonofabitch captain of this ship is a cracker from Texas, my home state," said Slim. "He hates our guts but he can't do a fuckin' thing about it 'cause he knows that if he fucks with us, the union will fuck with him. We're all NMU (National Maritime Union)."

When we had exhausted the subject of race relations, Slim started acting peculiar. Although it was stifling in the cabin, he closed the porthole. Then he checked the door to make sure it was locked.

"Do you smoke reefer?" he wanted to know all of a sudden.

"I smoke all brands," I told him, although I was sure I had never heard of Reefer cigarettes before. But instead of offering me a cigarette, he reached for a small can that contained strange-looking, sawdustlike tobacco. Next, he picked up a tiny piece of paper and started rolling himself an even stranger-looking cigarette, which he twirled to a point at one end while leaving it unevenly lumpy in the middle. Then he licked all over his handiwork to keep the whole thing from coming apart.

I couldn't understand why an American, who could buy all the Camels, Lucky Strikes, Chesterfields, and Pall Malls he wanted, bothered with making his own crummy-looking cigarettes. When Smitty noticed my puzzlement, he asked me whether I had ever smoked "weed" or "grass." I told him, quite truthfully, that as far as I knew, I had not. "What about tea?" Slim wanted to know. I naively informed him that some Germans, for want of real tobacco and out of desperation, occasionally smoked tea in their pipes, but "weed" and "grass" I'd never even heard about.

Slim explained that *reefer, weed, grass*, and *tea* were all slang terms for marijuana, a plant whose leaves, if smoked, could get you as high as you would get from drinking alcohol. He then lighted his "cigarette" at the pointed end and started to inhale the strangely sweet-smelling smoke in spastic, hissing increments. Holding his breath, he made weird noises that sounded as if he were swallowing the smoke. After what seemed like minutes, when I felt his lungs must be about to explode, he exhaled in a long breath, then quickly reinhaled the same smoke in brief staccato sniffs. After a while, Slim passed the joint to Smitty, who repeated the bizarre ritual. When most of the joint had gone up in smoke, the two tried to persuade me to give pot a try.

"This here shit is the best shit I've smoked in a long time," Slim assured me.

"Don't come no better," seconded Smitty.

I told them that I'd take their word for it.

Even without knowing at the time that the smoking of marijuana on a U.S. merchant vessel on a federal government mission constituted a serious criminal offense that could have landed all of us in jail, I hadn't the slightest desire to try. The two seamen's bizarre carrying on had been the most effective turnoff for me.

While Slim took his postjoint nap, Smitty and I prepared to return to shore. It was Monday and my day off, and I had promised Smitty I would show him the town. "Town" meant St. Pauli, the portion of the port district where the action was. Before we left the cabin, Smitty "fixed me up" with a huge food package for my mother and me and a bag full of clothing, including a brand-new set of khakis, a set of white underwear, several pairs of white socks, a couple of the loudest neckties I had ever seen, and a whole carton of Chesterfield cigarettes.

I didn't know what to say or how to thank Smitty. The cigarettes alone were worth 1,000 German marks on the black market, more than my monthly musician's pay, and the food was priceless. When I told Smitty that there was no way I could repay his kindness, he told me to forget it. But I never did.

When we hurried on deck in order not to miss the 7 P.M. WSA launch—our last chance to get to shore that night, according to Smitty—several seamen, including the chief cook, were already waiting. I noticed that there were actually two groups waiting, one black and one white. Remembering our talk about race relations back in Smitty's cabin, I realized that the separated grouping was not by accident.

It was a few minutes before seven when we heard several foghorn blasts and saw the WSA launch head full-speed toward us. Luckily, this time the gangway was down, thus sparing me another ordeal on the rope ladder. Just before the motor launch pulled alongside and we started down the gangway, Werner showed up on deck with two white seamen. He, too, was loaded down with packages, which I assumed were "donations" like mine. Mindful of Smitty's pronouncement, "We keeps to ourselves and they keeps to theirselves," I kept my distance. But once in the launch, Werner walked over to me and, pointing at my packages, grinned and whispered, "I see you got some CARE packages, too. I told you you'd have it made."

When I told him that I was about to show Smitty a good time, but that I really didn't know where the action was, Werner advised me to take Smitty

to Harms Bar on Bernhard Nocht Strasse. "There's more action than he
can handle," Werner promised. He then explained that all the girls at Harms
were hookers, no matter what they looked like, and that the going rate was
a pack of cigarettes for a "quickie" and up to five packs for an all-night stay.
"When you get there, ask for Hannelore," he added. "She'll take care of
everything. Pretend that you are an American seaman. If you tell them that
you are German, they won't even give you the time of day." Then Werner
warned me to make sure not to go to the Irish Bar around the corner. "That's
where only white Americans hang out," he explained, "and all you'll wind
up with is a fight."

"Where are you going?" I wanted to know.

"I'm taking two Southern crackers to the Irish Bar," he responded.
"Strictly business," he added, while pointing at his own CARE packages.

When he noticed the carton of Chesterfields sticking out of one of my
packages, he advised me to open the carton and distribute the packs evenly
around my waist under my shirt. "Each seaman is allowed to bring one
intact pack and one open pack ashore," Werner explained. "We'll have to
pass control by British redcaps. Since limeys don't have much to smoke
themselves, they are crazy about American cigarettes. All you have to do is
give them one pack and they'll leave you alone."

I passed that piece of valuable information on to Smitty and the rest of
the crew members, who quickly hid their cigarette cartons in the prescribed
manner.

When we reached shore, we had to file past a stern-faced British military
policeman in white gloves, white belt, and white pistol holster who peered
grimly at us from beneath the visor of his red cap. After each of us handed
him a pack of cigarettes, his grim face melted into a broad grin and a jovial
"Cheerio, Yanks," while letting all of us pass without subjecting us to closer
scrutiny.

I had no problem finding Harms Bar, which was only a short walk from
the boat landing. As soon as we entered, an accordion player launched into
a rendition of an American hit in an obvious attempt to breathe some life
into the place, which was nearly empty with the exception of half a dozen
young women who were sitting around a table, apparently waiting for action.
The way they looked at us and my packages made it obvious that we were
the kind of action they had in mind. After a waiter had seated us at a table

adjacent to the women, several of them gestured their eagerness to join us. Smitty was about to invite the whole gang over, but I told him to take it easy.

The women, some no older than eighteen, looked rather wholesome and unwhorish to my untrained eyes. They seemed to take it for granted that neither of us understood German, for they were loudly speculating about the things that seemed to fascinate them most about us. One woman said that she had never gone to bed with very dark Amis because she was scared of them. "Scared of what?" asked another, who said that for her, blacks couldn't be dark enough.

When I translated the gist of the conversations to Smitty, he exploded with convulsive laughter that drowned out the chatter at the corner table. "You mean all the women in here are hookers?" he asked incredulously.

"Every last one," I replied with the air of someone who knows all the ins and outs of St. Pauli nightlife, when in fact I was just getting an elementary education myself.

Without letting on that I spoke German, I told the waiter in English that we were looking for Hannelore. "Hannelore is right over there, the tall one with the red hair," he replied while pointing to the women's table nearby.

"Would you mind asking her to come to our table?" I asked him as my hand held out an open pack of cigarettes. The waiter was only too happy to oblige.

Hannelore was a statuesque redhead around thirty years old with stunning legs and slightly crossed eyes. When I explained to her that Yankee Werner had told us to get in touch with her, she immediately became friendly and sat down. "Yankee Werner and I are buddies," she said in broken English. "You tell Hannelore what you want and Hannelore will try to help."

Without beating around the bush, I told her in broken German with a phony American accent, "Smitty and I are from the *Appleton Victory*. Smitty is looking for someone real nice and pretty to show him a good time until tomorrow morning when he'll have to catch the six o'clock launch."

"What about you?" Hannelore wanted to know.

"I already met a girl on my last trip," I lied, determined not to get sidetracked since I was anxious to get home and surprise my mother with my culinary treasures from the *Appleton Victory*.

When Hannelore wanted to know what type of girl Smitty preferred, the description he gave—red hair, tall, great legs—came so close to matching Hannelore's looks that she quickly caught the hint. "Okay, what about me?" she asked.

Smitty grinned from ear to ear, "You'll do just fine, baby—just fine."

Without further ado, Hannelore moved her chair next to Smitty's to signal to the other women that, at least for the time being, Smitty was her man.

Gradually, the bar was filling up with more women and other black American seamen, including several from the *Appleton Victory*. Some of the latter joined our table, where Smitty told them, with a proprietary glance at the red bombshell beside him, how well I had taken care of him. Duly impressed, they wanted to know whether I could work the same magic for them, which, with Hannelore's help, was no problem at all. Since neither the men nor the women were particularly picky, it took only a few minutes before each of Smitty's buddies was matched with the fräulein of his choice.

Throughout the evening, I saw white seamen enter the bar, then beat a hasty retreat after taking one look at the raucous interracial scene. Being hopelessly outnumbered, they were smart enough not to voice any objections, but their expressions of undisguised loathing left no doubt in my mind that in their opinion, white women—even prostitutes—had no business mixing with black men.

Satisfied that Smitty and his cronies were well briefed and "squared away," I once more reminded Hannelore to make sure that my pal caught the six o'clock launch the next morning, then told Smitty that I would see him aboard ship the following afternoon. After grabbing the bag of treasures that I had stowed under my chair, I wished everybody a pleasant night and headed for home.

I decided to play hooky from my gig at the Alkazar the following day and instead return to the *Appleton Victory*. Hard times had long taught me not to pass up an opportunity to make hay while the sun shines.

When, dressed in crisp, brand-new khakis, I arrived dockside to catch the noon WSA launch, Yankee Werner, my new buddy, was already waiting. Impressed with my visual transformation, Werner paid me the ultimate compliment. "You really look like an Ami now. If I didn't know you, you could have fooled me."

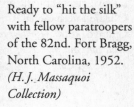

Ready to "hit the silk" with fellow paratroopers of the 82nd. Fort Bragg, North Carolina, 1952. *(H.J. Massaquoi Collection)*

My mother with my two sons, Steve and Hans, Jr. Elgin, Illinois, ca. 1965. *(H.J. Massaquoi Collection)*

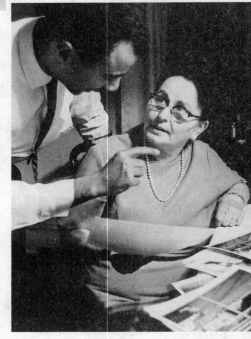

Interview with Dr. Martin
Luther King, Jr., after he carried
his civil-rights crusade up North.
O'Hare International Airport,
Chicago, 1966. *(Photograph by
Isaac Sutton, courtesy of Johnson
Publishing Co.)*

Briefing my mother regarding a
journalistic trip to Germany at
her home. Elgin, Illnois, 1966.
(H.J. Massaquoi Collection)

Living dangerously while horseplaying with Muhammad Ali. Miami, 1969.
(Photograph by Isaac Sutton, courtesy of Johnson Publishing Co.)

At Caesars Palace in Las Vegas with rock 'n' roll star Fats Domino and
ex-heavyweight champion Joe Louis, my childhood hero. Las Vegas, 1970.
(Photograph by Isaac Sutton, courtesy of Johnson Publishing Co.)

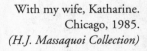

My brother, Morris W. Massaquoi, Liberia's assistant secretary of defense, in his office. Monrovia, Liberia, 1971. *(Photograph by G. Marshall Wilson, courtesy of Johnson Publishing Co.)*

With my wife, Katharine. Chicago, 1985. *(H.J. Massaquoi Collection)*

Aboard the ocean liner *Bremen* flanked by two of my childhood idols, former heavyweight champion Max Schmeling and 1936 Olympic track star Jesse Owens. New York Harbor, 1971. *(H. J. Massaquoi Collection)*

With author James Baldwin at *Ebony* magazine headquarters. Chicago, 1976. *(Photograph by Robert E. Johnson, courtesy of Johnson Publishing Co.)*

Interviewing my friend Alex Haley, aboard a U.S.-bound flight from Dakar, Senegal, 1977. *(Photograph by Moneta Sleet, Jr., courtesy of Johnson Publishing Co.)*

Being greeted by President Jimmy Carter in the White House. Washington, D.C., 1980. *(Courtesy of the White House)*

At the home of Diana Ross. In the foreground *(right)* her then-husband, Robert Silverman. Beverly Hills, 1981. *(Photograph by G. Marshall Wilson, courtesy of Johnson Publishing Co.)*

My mother and I. Elgin, Illinois, 1984. *(H.J. Massaquoi Collection)*

A proud father
with his sons,
"the doctor"
(Steve, left) and
"the lawyer"
(Hans, Jr.), 1988.
*(H.J. Massaquoi
Collection)*

The author, Hans J. Massaquoi. Hamburg,
1996. *(H.J. Massaquoi Collection)*

One-on-one with Namibia president Sam
Njomo during independence
festivities. Windhoek, Namibia, 1990.
*(Photograph by Moneta Sleet, Jr.,
courtesy of Johnson Publishing Co.)*

We again arrived at the *Appleton Victory*. As we had done before, Werner and I split to join our respective friends on different sides of the color bar.

Since Smitty had no shore leave that evening, he invited me to stay aboard overnight. I accepted after Slim told me I was welcome to use his bunk and that he would bunk with a buddy of his in the cabin next door. Before turning in for the night, I listened with envy as the two swapped stories about their adventures in various ports of the world.

I had already undressed and was lying comfortably in Slim's bunk when we heard a loud rap on the door. When Smitty opened the door, a seaman told him that word had reached the captain that there were unauthorized persons aboard and that he wanted them off the ship at once. That, I concluded, could only mean Werner and me.

Smitty apologized for this unexpected turn of events but urged me to dress as quickly as possible and leave. On deck, I bumped into Werner, who had been similarly evicted and who, it turned out, was the reason why the skipper was "pissed."

It seems that Werner had been roaming the deck by himself when he was accosted by a man in soiled khakis who demanded to know what he was doing. Believing the man to be one of several German workers who helped with the unloading and cleaning of the ship, "all-American" Werner responded in his inimitable smart-alecky way, "What's it to you?" That's when the man went ballistic on him. Only after the man kept shouting, "Get your ass off my ship, you sonofabitch!" did it dawn on Werner that he had made a serious mistake, and that the soiled one was none other than the captain of the *Appleton Victory*.

Smitty's assertion that "the old man can be quite an asshole" turned out to be a huge understatement. While Werner and I were resigned to wait on the chilly deck for the day's last launch, which was due in half an hour or so, a young deck officer informed us that the captain wanted us to get off the ship "immediately!" The officer suggested we wait for the launch outside the ship on the rope ladder if we didn't want to run the risk that the captain would have us thrown overboard. Unwilling to test the captain's resolve to commit murder, we reluctantly climbed over the railing and onto the ladder. There, we clung to the rungs for dear life until our arms were numb while swaying precariously in the cold night breeze above the pitch-black, gurgling water of the Elbe. Finally, after what seemed like an eternity, the launch arrived and our ordeal came to an end—or so we thought.

Once aboard the small motor vessel, we were told by the skipper that he would have to drop us off at the *Freihafen* (free port), many miles from our destination. Since we had no cigarettes with which to change his mind, we found ourselves stranded in Hamburg's free port, a vast peninsula reserved for the duty-free transfer and storage of freight. As we stepped ashore, the port was inhospitably dark, deserted, and cold. For want of a better idea, we decided to keep walking in the direction of the city, even if it took us all night to get home. When we saw the headlights of an approaching vehicle, we quickly jumped into a ditch and ducked until the vehicle—a jeep carrying British MPs—had passed. The place, we discovered, was crawling with MP patrols, forcing us to hit the ditch a number of times. As we stumbled on, exhausted and shivering in our thin khakis, we happened upon a small tar-paper shack that at closer inspection turned out to be a chicken house. When we opened the small unlocked door and entered, a vile, acrid stench attacked our nostrils. But the place was warm by comparison with the outside. In the glare of a lighted match, we could make out about a dozen chickens perched on a ledge, clucking at us with displeasure over the nighttime intrusion.

Glad to be out of the cold and out of the MPs' sight, we decided to brave the stench and coexist with the chickens until daybreak before continuing our perilous journey home. After sharing our last cigarette, we huddled together on the ground for warmth, then drifted off into an uneasy sleep.

As soon as we saw the light of dawn shine through the cracks of the shack, we got up. We couldn't keep from bursting out laughing when we looked at each other and discovered that we were covered from head to toe with chicken shit. After cleaning up as much as possible, we left the chickens, whose stench followed us, and resumed our trek. This time there were no more MP patrols to dodge.

We had walked steadily past warehouses, cranes, and boxcars for about twenty minutes when we reached the free port's main gate. Our hearts sank when next to the gate we noticed a small wooden guardhouse marked MILITARY POLICE. Just as we were about to tippy-toe past the post, a bleary-eyed redcap poked his face out of the door and yawnfully wished us a good morning. "You blokes must be Yanks," he guessed, to which we responded in unison with a perfunctory "Yeah." Without bothering to look closely at the papers we had pulled out of our pockets, the MP waved us on our merry way with an unusually cheerful "Cheerio." Had he bothered to take a closer look at our "IDs," he might have raised an eyebrow or two on discovering that one was an expired shore-leave pass Werner had borrowed from an American buddy, and the other was a piece of paper on which Smitty had scribbled his Alabama address.

While Werner was within walking distance from his home, I had to suffer through yet another indignity before my ordeal finally came to an end. Riding the crowded city train to Othmarschen while smelling to high heaven, I had to endure the contemptuous stares of my fellow riders, who were pointedly holding their noses in undisguised disgust. They couldn't even begin to guess the trouble I had just seen.

In the weeks that followed, I underwent an amazing physical as well as psychological transformation. Having been convinced by Werner that there was lots of money—meaning cigarettes—to be made on American ships, and that my exotic appearance made me a natural for negotiating lucrative business (meaning black-market) deals with black seamen, I went all out to make myself look, sound, behave, and think like an American. Soon I had scrounged up an entire wardrobe of U.S-made clothes, complete with penny loafers, boxer shorts, loud ties, and broad-shouldered, peg-legged zoot suits, as well as a couple of broad-brimmed Stetson hats. To complement my American wardrobe, I changed my hairstyle from the long swingboy look, which I had painstakingly cultivated with ample applications of pomade, to a short-at-the-sides-and-back crew cut.

Under Werner's tutelage, I learned to eat the American way, with only a fork in my right hand, instead of the European way, fork in the left hand and knife in the right hand. Werner also helped me Americanize my rapidly expanding English vocabulary by making me discard British terms such as petrol, leftenant, bloke, and lorry in favor of gas, lieutenant, guy, and truck, respectively. What we didn't know about the States, its customs, and speech habits, we learned from watching American movies that were frequently shown in the Urania, a downtown movie theater reserved for Allied personnel, which Werner and I crashed regularly with impunity. Through movies

I learned for the first time about the great American pastime, baseball, and about a roughneck game played largely by carrying a ball, which—inexplicably—Americans insisted on calling football.

To stay in practice and to keep from blowing our cover, Werner and I made it a habit of communicating in English only. Being taken for Americans, we found, had many rewards. One was the ability to ride free of charge to any destination on city trains in uncrowded, comfortable compartments reserved for the Allies. Another was that we got more respect from Germans, especially German officials such as police, who had no jurisdiction over Allied personnel. They never hassled us the way they did their own countrymen.

But there was also a downside to our charade. No matter how hungry we were at times, we were obliged to pass up filling our rebellious bellies at German outdoor food stands in order not to destroy our carefully built identity as Americans. Since it was widely known that Allied personnel were overfed on scrumptious food in their own canteens, nobody would have believed that we were Americans had they seen us wolf down a meal of boiled cabbage.

One time in particular I recall when my impersonation of an American proved a major embarrassment. I had been accompanying a young lady home after we had met for the first time at Haus Vaterland. Unaware that my German was at least as good as hers, she had struggled all evening trying to converse with me in what little English she had picked up since the end of the war. Our slight "language barrier" notwithstanding, things moved right along and I had reason to believe that this was the beginning of a beautiful relationship. We were taking the subway and because of her presence, I deigned for a change to ride in the packed German car. I was chatting engagingly about life in America and she listened with fascination when all of a sudden, at the opposite end of the coach, I spotted an old acquaintance from my pre-Ami days, a wartime factory worker whom I had not seen in a couple of years. For a moment I considered moving to another part of the train to keep him from recognizing me. But it was too late. Before I could move, he was headed toward me and in a loud voice that, I was sure, was audible throughout the coach, hollered in unadulterated Hamburger Platt, *"Hans-Jürgen, bis du dat? Ik hef die bino nich wedder erkannt mit den Bort"*

("Hans-Jürgen, is that you? I almost didn't recognize you with that mustache").

In a futile attempt to preserve my dignity, I looked at my old acquaintance with unrecognizing eyes and said in English, "I don't know what you are talking about." My acquaintance took another look, unsure whether he had made a mistake, shook his head, then walked away while mumbling an apology. I wish I could have explained to him that I was, indeed, Hans-Jürgen from Barmbek but that for the time being I was Mickey from America. But I was caught in my own web.

When we got off the train, my date glared at me with ice-cold, unforgiving eyes. "I don't like being lied to," she said in German, "especially not on a first meeting. *Aufwiedersehen,* Hans-Jürgen or Mickey or whatever your name is."

"Please let me explain," I pleaded.

But she didn't want to hear anything else I had to say, and I really couldn't blame her.

Without giving me a chance to utter another word, she turned around and walked out of my life.

THE THREE AH-YUE HON LOUS

During an intermission at the Alkazar, one of the solo acts, a young Asian-looking tap dancer by the name of Ah-Yue Hon Lou, stopped by the bandstand and asked whether he could have a word with me after the show. We had only exchanged polite hellos in the past. I was curious to learn what was on his mind and agreed to meet him at the bar. When I arrived, he was already seated, elegantly dressed in a tailored double-breasted gray suit and smoking a cigarette through a long silver holder. It was the first time I had a chance to study him up close. He was of delicate, yet athletic build, with large, almond-shaped eyes, high cheekbones, and long, wavy black hair— the kind I would have given my right arm for as a child.

After telling me that his friends called him Yue, he opened the discussion:

"I have a proposal for you that could be beneficial for both of us." Despite his striking, exotic appearance, he sounded like a native Hamburger, a fact that struck me as strange until I remembered that I, too, didn't look exactly like someone who had been baptized with Elbe water.

Yue explained that he had been born twenty-five years earlier in Hamburg. His German grandfather had been a sailor who, during one of his trips to Shanghai, befriended a young Chinese man whom he invited to visit him in Germany. One day, to the sailor's surprise, the young man showed up at his home in Hamburg, where he met and later married the sailor's daughter, who became Yue's mother. Yue's grandfather and father both died when he was still a little boy, but his mother was still living. It was his mother who had enabled him to study tap dance, acrobatics, and acting and become a professional entertainer. He said that he was married, and that despite his racially mixed background, he had been accepted as a volunteer by the German *Luftwaffe* and did wartime service in a parachute outfit.

"I am planning to enlarge my act and to take on two partners," Yue continued. "One of the partners would be a girl dancer and the other would be you."

When I injected that I didn't know the first thing about tap dancing, he told me that I wasn't expected to dance. "The girl and I will do the dancing," he explained. "Your job would be to accompany us on the saxophone." He said that he had already auditioned several girls and that one seemed promising. "Finding a qualified girl is no problem," he assured me, "but finding someone like you—someone who looks like an American and who can play the saxophone—isn't easy in Germany."

Yue explained that he intended to promote his group, the Three Ah-Yue Hon Lous, as "a musical United Nations in microcosm," one Chinese, one German, and one American. He then asked me to imagine myself center stage playing "a wild number" on the saxophone from atop a large, drumlike reflector illuminated from within by a powerful electric bulb, while he and the girl tap-danced on two smaller reflectors that would flank mine. To give the act additional pizzazz, it would be cast against a spectacularly illuminated backdrop of New York's skyline by night.

As an already confirmed Americophile, I liked Yue's concept, except the name he had chosen for the group. A Chinese name, I felt, added neither sex appeal nor box-office appeal. Postwar German youths identified with

Benny Goodman, Louis Armstrong, and Harry James, not with Confucius and Mao Tse-tung. When I tried, as tactfully as I could, to point that out to Yue, he stubbornly disagreed, explaining that it was easier to book an act with an already established name.

What few reservations I had about Yue's proposition were totally dispelled when he told me that he would nearly double my present monthly salary and that instead of working two hours per night I would never have to work longer than fifteen minutes per night. Making twice as much money for one-eighth of the work appealed to my budding business sense. Before Yue and I parted that evening, I agreed to become one of the Three Ah-Yue Hon Lous when my contract expired at the end of the month.

The following month was filled with feverish activities aimed at getting our new show ready and on the road. Through a theatrical agency, Yue had been promised a prominent spot in a British Army Welfare Service–sponsored variety show that was to tour theaters near British army camps in central and western Germany, provided we would be ready to audition a week before departure time. After stepping up his search for a prospective dancing partner, Yue settled for one of his more gifted pupils, a blond seventeen-year-old girl-next-door type named Ilse. Ilse had taken up tap dancing as a hobby but had never danced professionally. Her biggest obstacle was talking her parents into allowing her to go on the road.

Driven by Yue's constant prodding, we three spent hours rehearsing our routines, having our costumes fitted, going over musical scores with an arranger, and taking turns urging a theatrical supply company to meet our deadline for the completion of our stage props. Our tireless efforts paid off. With not a day to spare, the Three Ah-Yue Hon Lous auditioned before a panel of British Army Welfare Service personnel and were signed as opening act for a month-long tour.

Looking back, it amazes me how quickly I adjusted to my new unfettered lifestyle among freewheeling, colorful performers after my drab existence in grimy workshops among staid factory workers. Within a few weeks on the road, it seemed to me as if I had never known another life.

EVENING IN PARIS

One of the more memorable stops I made while traveling with the Three Ah-Yue Hon Lous was at the little town of Helmstedt, which was as prominent a crossing point into the Soviet Zone of Occupation as Berlin's Checkpoint Charlie. Since we had arrived late in the day, when hotel vacancies were limited, Yue and I had been assigned a room in a small inn, while Ilse stayed at another inn nearby.

Upon entering our room, dead tired from hours of travel by truck, we were instantly revived by gramophone music and the voices of two women coming from the adjacent room. Closer investigation revealed that the rooms were separated by only a door and a dresser. Trying to be "neighborly," we introduced ourselves through the door and, to our delight, struck up a lively conversation that ended in the mutual decision to see if the door was locked. When we determined that it could be unlatched from our side, we—again by mutual consent—pushed the dresser aside and opened the door. What we found on the other side was too good to be true—two pretty young women who seemed as bent on having "a good time" as we were. They told us that they came from the countryside of Lüneburg and were on their way to Magdeburg, in the Soviet Zone, where they intended to visit relatives. In turn, we told them that we were entertainers working for the British military and that we could arrange to have them come to our show and see us perform. Although they had planned to leave the next morning, they said they were in no particular hurry and would gladly stay another day.

It wasn't long before we had the lights turned low and were dancing cheek to cheek. What made the encounter especially memorable for me was the heavy fragrance that filled the entire room. It obviously emanated from an electric blue bottle on the dresser with the inscription EVENING IN PARIS. I didn't realize it then, but that name and that fragrance would stay with me for many years to come.

After playing their record for the umpteenth time, the girls reminded us that it was getting late and that, after all, there was still tomorrow. Yue and I decided to be gentlemen and not to press our luck. After the girls agreed to pick up where we left off when we returned from morning rehearsal the next day, we wished them good night, closed the door, and moved the dresser back where we found it. Before going to sleep, we congratulated each other on the extraordinary luck that had guided us to this particular room.

The next morning, on our way to rehearsals, we tiptoed around our room in order not to awaken our new friends. We figured they needed plenty of sleep in order to be up to the program we had planned for them.

At around noon, when we returned to our room from rehearsals, we found the dresser in front of the door pushed aside but the door closed. It was still unlatched, the way we had left it. After receiving no answer to our knock, we opened the door and, to our huge surprise, found the next room completely empty—except for the odor of that confounded, all-pervasive Evening in Paris perfume. Our second, even bigger surprise was that, upon closer inspection of our room, we discovered that most of our belongings were missing, with the exception of our near-empty luggage, which the two thieves were kind enough to let us keep.

When we reported to the innkeeper what had happened, she told us that the two women had checked out shortly after we went to rehearsals, and that in all probability, they were already many miles inside the Soviet Zone, where, because of mounting tension between East and West, pursuit was virtually impossible. Fortunately, I had my saxophone and clarinet with me at rehearsal and we had already dropped off our stage wardrobe at the theater. The loss of those items would have literally killed our act.

After several sporadic outbreaks of impotent rage, Yue and I had to grudgingly admit that we suave and sophisticated men of the world had been duped by a pair of slick country bumpkins. We could never quite decide which was more painful, our bruised egos or the loss of our things, but as with so many adversities, in time we got over our ill-fated brush with the Evening in Paris "ladies" and the adventure that never was.

BETWEEN GIGS

After fulfilling our contract by completing a remarkably successful month on the road, the Three Ah-Yue Hon Lous returned to Hamburg with the understanding that after a month we would hit the road again. Our partner, Ilse, whose parents had only reluctantly consented to her joining us on the road, returned to her original role of girl next door. Yue, the inveterate entrepreneur, picked up where he left off as black-market trader and faithful husband, and I returned to my new hobby of looking for Amis on Hamburg's waterfront.

After contacting my buddy Werner, he told me that I had come back just in time to participate in a juicy deal that involved helping an American seaman bring ashore—meaning smuggle—twenty cartons of American cigarettes. The seaman needed the cigarettes as payment for a brand-new four-hundred-dollar Leica camera that a German man had agreed to sell. For our trouble, Werner explained, the seaman had offered an additional six cartons.

Without hesitation, I agreed to take on the job. I never felt for a moment that I was about to engage in something immoral or dishonorable. After all, everybody, and I mean everybody, had a piece of the black-market action— old ladies who were bartering their good silver for cigarettes; young women who were spending a night with an Ami for a pack of Lucky Strikes; respectable businessmen who accepted cigarettes instead of coupons for scarce merchandise; German cops who shook down black marketeers and kept the cigarettes for themselves; and finally, British and American seamen and soldiers who pestered Germans for their cameras, gold watches, binoculars, wedding rings, and other valuables in exchange for a few miserable cigarettes.

Thus, having long since resolved my moral concerns, I focused all of my psychic energy on pulling off the job smoothly without getting caught. The plan of action outlined by Werner entailed not only smuggling but a bit of bribery as well. Werner felt that the success of our mission depended on not leaving anything to chance, and he wanted to ensure that we didn't run into problems with our contraband once ashore. To implement the plan, we immediately took a walk to the dockside British MP post, where we started a friendly chat with the lance corporal on duty. The redheaded Scotsman, who sheepishly confided that his buddies called him Ginger, turned out to be a dyed-in-the-wool Yankeephile. When we put to him the hypothetical question of what would be the best way to bring "a few extra cartons" of cigarettes ashore from "our ship," he told us, quite hypothetically, that on the following day during certain specified hours, the chances for such a transaction would be optimal since he would be on duty during that time. We thanked him with a pack of cigarettes for the valuable information and promised to see him the next day.

Some twenty-four hours later, around noon, I, Werner, and a black American sailor from Brooklyn named Jeff stepped off the launch and onto the same landing dock, our waists bulging with cigarette cartons and our hearts pounding. In addition to the cigarettes he was carrying around his waist, Jeff was carrying two obviously full canvas bags.

Ginger, it turned out, was on duty all right, but with him was another MP he hadn't told us about. Our first thought was that we had been double-crossed. But just when we were trying to make up our minds whether to jump back into the launch or to face the two MPs, Ginger waved us to come into his tiny sentry station. There, he told us with a smile that the other MP was, like himself, an "okay sort of chap," and that we were free to proceed. Much relieved, Werner handed the Scotsman two cartons of cigarettes and we were on our merry way. The worst part of our mission was over—or so we thought.

We had walked about five minutes beneath the el-train viaduct in the direction of Rödingsmarkt when we noticed three men in dark coats following us at quite a distance. One of them shouted, *"Halt! Polizei!"* "Run for it!" shouted Werner, who intentionally had lagged behind Jeff and me in order to make our group less conspicuous. As the German plainclothes cops began to gain on him, he reached in his jacket and hurled the half dozen cigarette cartons he was carrying at us. Like well-rehearsed circus jugglers, Jeff and I scooped up the cartons and kept running. The last glimpse we had of Werner was when, flanked by the cops, he was led away in the opposite direction. Apparently our pursuers, realizing that German police had no jurisdiction over Allied personnel, had given up on Jeff and me. Other than feeling sorry for Werner, there was nothing we could do for him. After zigzagging through several downtown streets to throw off any cops who might be following us, we went to the address of the German

Leica owner and completed the transaction to the mutual satisfaction of everyone involved. Jeff got the best of the deal, having received a four-hundred-dollar Leica camera in mint condition for twenty-six cartons of cigarettes, for which he had paid seventy-five cents a carton at his ship's "slop chest," or commissary.

That night, after making sure that Jeff and his Leica got back safely to his ship, I went home to Othmarschen with six slightly battered cartons of cigarettes. It was difficult for me to regard the three cartons that were my share of the transaction as ill-gotten "loot" instead of something that con-stituted just compensation for dangerous work, as well as for some of the hardships the Nazis had put me through. It did, however, cross my mind that the street value of the three cartons of American cigarettes that I had earned in one single afternoon was three thousand German marks, almost three months' pay as a member of the Three Ah-Yue Hon Lous. While that kind of quick money seemed to suggest that I was well on my way to getting filthy rich, nothing could be further from the truth. The fact was that big hauls of American cigarettes, like their source—American ships in port—were few and far between, and as a result, my existence was a constant up and down, from famine to feast and back to famine. There was no doubt, however, that the added income from my somewhat unconventional lifestyle went a long way in making up for the hardships Mutti and I had endured immediately after the end of the war.

The day after Werner's arrest by the German cops, I returned to his neigh-borhood to find out what had happened to him. I was prepared to learn that he was languishing in some police lockup, but instead, I found him in front of his tenement, grinning from ear to ear and looking none the worse for wear. Savoring every word, he told me how his frustrated captors had been obliged to set him free after a couple of hours when their superior at the sta-tion explained to them that without the cigarettes as evidence, they didn't have a case. They nevertheless gave him a stern warning to watch his step be-cause the next time he might not be so lucky. When I told him that his three cartons of cigarettes were safe and sound in Othmarschen, Werner decided that he could well afford to lie low for a while and suggested that we keep away from American ships until the heat was off.

GI DAZE

Our decision to avoid American ships for a while was academic, since there was not a single one in port. That fact was easily gleaned from the conspicuous absence of hookers at dockside. Had only one American ship been in port, St. Pauli's ladies of the night (or day, depending on which shift they were working) would have been out in droves, alerted by their unfailing grapevine that stretched from Hamburg to New York and back.

Carefully avoiding the docks, which were crawling with intrusive military and civilian cops, Werner and I decided instead to try our luck in some of our regular waterfront dives. In the absence of American seamen, we were prepared to lower our sights and make do with a frugal limey sailor or, God forbid, with an even less well-heeled Greek. In our highly specialized business, we had quickly learned that beggars can't be choosers. But after a few attempts at establishing rapport with British seamen, we gave up, recognizing that our hearts weren't in it and that the chemistry just wasn't right.

Dropping in at the basement Irish Bar, we spotted a black GI seated at the nearly empty bar. As befitted the only two gentlemen of color in the joint, the GI and I shook hands and introduced ourselves, whereupon I introduced him to Werner. His name was Donald Patterson. He told us that he was from Chicago and was passing through on his way back to his unit in Grafenwöhr, near the city of Nuremberg in Bavaria.

Donald was well built but short, about five foot six, with broad shoulders and a tiny waist. Of medium-brown complexion, he had deep-set black eyes, an aquiline nose, and a wide, generous mouth on whose upper lip he was trying to cultivate a reddish mustache, with only partial success.

On a scale of ten, joining the U.S. Army ranked about eleven among Werner's and my career choices. No wonder that we eyed with a mixture of envy and admiration his olive-drab uniform—the smart, double-peaked overseas cap that he wore low over his right eyebrow, the spit-shined combat boots, the brightly polished brass insignia on his collar, and the Pfc. chevrons on the sleeves of his tight-fitting Eisenhower jacket. We couldn't think of anything we would not have given to be in his place. Of course we hadn't the slightest idea what being a GI was all about. According to our highly idealized fantasy, it meant wearing a sharp uniform; having plenty of good food to eat, plenty of cigarettes to smoke, an inexhaustible supply of girls to bed down, and driving a jeep instead of walking.

When Donald asked the inevitable question, namely what I, a black guy, was doing in Hamburg, I gave him the usual thumbnail sketch of my background, with the usual deviation from the truth—that my father was an American instead of a Liberian. This "little white lie," I had discovered, could make the difference between cordial acceptance as a brother and cold rejection as an unwelcome stranger. It hadn't taken me long to find out that most black Americans I met in the years immediately following World War II considered Africans and Africa backward and thus a personal embarrassment. With slavery just a few generations behind them, they preferred not to be reminded of that aspect of their past. I certainly wasn't going to spoil my chances of building mutually beneficial bridges of international commerce, I rationalized, by trying to impress this black brother from the Windy City with my royal African ancestry.

Donald seemed pleased with my story, especially the true part about "my folks back home in Barrington, Illinois."

"Man, that's only forty or fifty miles northwest of Chicago," he remarked. It was news to me but I agreed as if I had known it all along. Donald told us that he still had three days of furlough left and that he wouldn't mind spending some more time in Hamburg, but he was rapidly running out of cigarettes with which to finance a "swell time."

"How many cigarettes do you have left?" I asked.

When Donald confided that he had two cartons stashed away in his duffel bag, Werner and I assured him that with our savvy of the lay of the land, two cartons of cigarettes would be more than adequate to finance any kind of swell time for all three of us.

When Donald agreed to join us, I was ecstatic. Hanging out with Donald offered me a perfect opportunity to learn more about the country of my dreams—its customs, language, and racial attitudes, as well as what was hot and what was not. I also figured that being seen in public with an American soldier in uniform could only enhance the credibility of my Ami impersonation ploy.

After finishing our drinks, Werner and I took Donald to all of the city's hot spots, from the popular Faun Bar to Haus Vaterland. Since in British-occupied Hamburg an American uniform was a rarity, our interracial trio invariably became the center of attention. Whenever I ran into acquaintances, I made sure they met Donald, who, to my infinite delight, introduced himself as my cousin from Chicago. I couldn't have asked for more. It seemed that Donald was as proud of having a cousin in Germany as I was of having a cousin in the United States.

The day Donald had to return to his unit in Grafenwöhr, he invited Werner and me to come along. When we asked him how he figured he could get us to ride with him without tickets and without any papers of authorization or a passport, he told us, "Just let me worry about that and let me do all the talking." Before we knew it, we were riding on a Nuremberg-bound train in a wagon reserved for Allied personnel. We were understandably nervous when an officer, whom Donald identified as a U.S. Army first lieutenant, approached us and demanded to see our papers. After a brief exchange during which Donald told the lieutenant a heartrending story of how his poor cousin and his American friend had gotten·stuck in Germany during the war, the visibly touched officer welcomed us aboard the sparsely occupied wagon and asked us to make ourselves comfortable. That we did. We rode toward Nuremberg in a style to which we hoped to become accustomed—smoking American cigarettes, reading American magazines, listening to American big band sounds over the train's intercom, and, in the diner, eating delicious American food. Careful not to blow our cover and get thrown off the train the way we were evicted from the *Appleton Victory,* I meticulously followed Werner's sage advice to eat with my fork only instead of the European way.

Comfortably, we arrived at Nuremberg *Hauptbahnhof,* which was crawling with black and white GIs, including a disturbing number of MPs. When we reached the street, Donald had us stand at a curb while he held out his right arm and poked his thumb in the direction of the traffic. "Do you mind telling me what you are trying to do," I inquired.

"I'm trying to hitch a ride." Before he had a chance to go into details about the time-honored American custom of hitchhiking, a jeep stopped in front of us.

"You men goin' back to camp?" a white army captain inquired.

"Yes, sir," was Donald's reply.

"Hop on!" the captain responded.

Cautioning us to hang on, he floored the gas pedal and, to our great delight, the vehicle took off like a bat out of hell. Soon, we had left Nuremberg behind us and, following a dizzying drive on a two-lane cobblestone country road, we reached the main gate of the U.S. Army installation at Grafenwöhr. A white-helmeted military policeman in a glass-enclosed booth saluted the captain, and without bothering to ask for our IDs, signaled him to proceed. The captain returned the sentry's salute, and after a short drive past row upon row of wooden barracks, dropped us off in front of a shedlike building that a sign on the door identified as ORDERLY ROOM, COMPANY A. After Donald checked in with the sergeant on duty to report his return from furlough, he took us to his barrack to let us take a look at his home away from home and to meet some of his buddies. The barrack was empty, with the exception of one orderly.

Neither Werner nor I was prepared for what happened next. All of a sudden, the barrack was teeming with GIs, but instead of the smart Eisenhower jackets and overseas caps that had made American soldiers look so glamorous to us, they were wearing drab fatigues. They were soaking wet with perspiration and covered from hat to combat boots with grease and dirt. It was quite obvious that they had been working hard at some less than glamorous task. Donald explained that they were Signal Corpsmen who had just been digging trenches and laying cables. As we looked at the primitive barracks and the motley soldiers, it became increasingly clear to us that serving in the U.S. Army—our most cherished fantasy—was a far cry from what we had imagined.

While the discovery of GIs' lowly lifestyle came as somewhat of a culture shock to me, it was not nearly as disturbing as another discovery. It dawned on me that all the soldiers in Donald's unit were black, and—even more disturbing—that all of the officers we had seen were white. Donald had never mentioned to us that black soldiers were serving in racially segregated units. I recalled the pithy words of Smitty, the messman on the *Appleton Victory,* who had said of race relations aboard ship, "We keeps to ourselves and they keeps to theirselves; we don't fuck with them and they don't fuck with us." I had no idea, and it didn't make the slightest bit of sense to me, that the same social order prevailed in the U.S. Army, which had just fought a brutal war for the stated purpose of making the world free for democracy.

It took me a while to psychologically digest my introduction to the American dilemma—America's inability, or unwillingness, to live up to its creed of "liberty and justice for all." I had known for quite a while that white people in America, especially in the South, did not always live up to that creed and, indeed, had committed some of the most brutal atrocities against their black fellow citizens, but I had no idea that racial discrimination was not only condoned but openly practiced by the United States government. As much as I hated the Nazis for it, somehow, their overt racism and refusal to accept me in their military ranks seemed more honest to me than the United States' lip service to democracy and eagerness to recruit blacks while keeping them at arm's length in segregated, low-status service units commanded primarily by whites. I found it difficult to admit to myself, but my newly created ideal of an America that had mounted and won a crusade to free the oppressed had received a severe, perhaps fatal blow.

But at age twenty, I was not about to let philosophical differences come between me and my determination to survive as best I could. Regardless of how poorly black GIs were treated compared with their white counterparts, I realized that physically, they were incomparably better off than the vanquished Germans. Having discovered that my resemblance to a black American had decided advantages in war-torn Germany, I resolved to continue my efforts to learn how to sound and act like one. Being able to study black GIs close-up, in their own habitat, struck me as serendipitous.

The next morning Werner and I heard the voices of two men entering the barracks, then footsteps coming up the wooden stairs. We were confronted by a white captain and a black sergeant with a clipboard. The two were apparently conducting an inspection. "Who are you and what the hell are you doing here?" the captain demanded to know.

When I explained that my "cousin," Pfc. Donald Patterson, had gotten permission from a sergeant to let me and my friend spend the night in the barracks, the officer turned on his heel without saying a word and, trailed by the sergeant, stormed out in a huff.

With an acute sense of foreboding, I hastily substituted an overdue shower with liberal splashes from a bottle of Old Spice. Both Werner and I agreed that the captain's sudden exit was a bad omen. We were right. Within less than ten minutes, Donald showed up. He was wearing unflattering fatigues and an uncharacteristic troubled expression on his face. "I'm sorry, but you guys have got to leave the post right away," he blurted out, half worried, half embarrassed. "The company commander has been pitching a bitch; he says he won't have unauthorized people staying here."

I had never heard the term "pitching a bitch," but I got the idea. "So what are we supposed to do?" I inquired. "It takes almost twenty minutes to walk to the main gate. And how do we get to Nuremberg?"

"It so happens that there's an officer leaving for Nuremberg in a few minutes," Donald explained. "He agreed to give you two a ride, but you've got to hurry."

While Werner and I hadn't contemplated a long visit in Grafenwöhr, neither had we expected that we would overstay our welcome quite that soon. Mindful of our untimely expulsion from the *Appleton Victory*, we quickly grabbed our overnight bags, said so long to Donald, then jumped on the waiting weapons carrier whose driver, a black first lieutenant, was impatiently checking his watch. Exceedingly handsome and meticulously dressed in officer's twill, he was the first black U.S. Army officer I had seen. His friendly smile gave no indication how much, if anything, he knew about our plight. It filled me with an extraordinary sense of pride when I watched the white MP at the gate come to attention and salute the black officer as we were leaving the post.

Easily succeeding in breaking whatever speed record the captain had set the previous day, the lieutenant kept flooring the accelerator of the weapons carrier. "Sorry I was a bit in a rush," the lieutenant apologized as he stopped in front of the Nuremberg *Hauptbahnhof*. "I hope I didn't scare you guys with my driving."

We assured the lieutenant that we liked nothing better than a fast ride, and then entered the crowded station. Our unexpected eviction from the army post had made us gun shy and seriously diminished our enthusiasm for passing ourselves off as Americans. So instead of honoring the waiting hall reserved for Allied personnel with our presence, as had been our habit, we went to the German waiting hall instead. Dilapidated and bereft of any amenities, this hall was packed with weary German travelers with battered suitcases and knapsacks. Many were munching on homemade sandwiches that they must have brought along since there were no food vendors anywhere within sight. We were almost hungry enough to swallow our pride and ask a German to let us have a couple of sandwiches in exchange for some cigarettes. But instead, we lighted up ourselves to appease our growling stomachs. We immediately became the target of envious, if not hateful, stares from people who obviously felt that affluent Americans had no business in "their" waiting hall.

They weren't the only ones who felt that way. Two black MPs in white helmets and white belts had entered the waiting hall and headed straight for us. "Can you read English?" one of the MPs accosted me with an air of sarcasm. When I didn't quite get what he was driving at, he repeated his question, "Can you read English?"

"Of course I can read English," I finally replied, more annoyed than frightened by his interrogation. After all, I hadn't done anything wrong— for a change.

"Then read that," he ordered while pointing a mean-looking nightstick toward a large sign on the wall. The sign read, OFF LIMITS TO ALL ALLIED PERSONNEL.

Before I could follow my inclination and respond with a flippant "So what?" the MP good-naturedly told us to stop giving him and his buddy a hard time and to take our you-know-whats to the Allied waiting room on the other side of the station where we belonged. He said he couldn't understand why we wanted to stay in this "dump" and hang out with the Krauts.

Werner and I couldn't either, for that matter, and within minutes we were enjoying—quite illegally—the generous hospitality of Uncle Sam in the waiting hall's comfortable USO canteen. There we ate delicious, freshly made hotcakes and sipped aromatic coffee served by friendly USO ladies who went out of their way to make "our boys" feel at home in what seemed to be the only waiting room where we weren't bothered by pesky MPs. Only this time, the sign on the wall read USO—NUR FÜR ALLIIERTES PERSONAL (USO—FOR ALLIED PERSONNEL ONLY).

After we had dined sufficiently and caught up on our hygiene in the men's room, we decided to go for a walk and take a look at Nuremberg before returning to Hamburg.

As we walked through the bomb-ravaged streets of Nuremberg, I was reminded of the significant, though largely negative, role the city had played in my life. It was at the 1935 Nazi convention in Nuremberg, billed ironically as the "Party Day of Freedom," that the legal groundwork for the pogroms against Jews and other so-called non-Aryans like me was laid.

Known as the Nuremberg Laws, the enacted measures stripped Jews and other persons of "non-German blood" of their German citizenship, while forbidding them to marry Aryans or have sexual relations with them.

Thanks to film director Leni Riefenstahl, whose documentaries captured much of the drama, Nuremberg, the official city of the Nazi Party, stood out in my memory more than any other German city, including Berlin, as the quintessential Nazi showpiece where each year, for an entire week, the Party staged an orgy of self-congratulation with spectacular mass rallies, pro-Hitler demonstrations, and endless marches that lasted into the wee hours of the night. Through the creativeness of Albert Speer, Hitler's architect and wartime munitions chief, the nightly scenes were further enhanced by the dramatic placement of searchlights that formed what some described as a "cathedral of lights."

I wondered how many hundreds of downtrodden people who were passing us in the streets had been among the fanatically screaming throngs who had cheered their beloved Führer on to ever-greater excesses until they had convinced him that he could take on the entire world. I looked hard into the faces of the men and women to see if I could detect some remnants of the old Nazi arrogance, that air of assumed racial superiority. But neither their faces nor their demeanor gave clues to their infamous recent past. All I saw in their bland expressions was resignation, an unquestioning acceptance of the status quo.

It was only fitting, I felt, that the Allies had selected Nuremberg as the site of the Nazi war-crimes trials that had just concluded a few months earlier. Twelve Nazi reprobates were sentenced to death by hanging, including (in absentia) Martin Bormann, Hitler's chancellery chief. He was rumored to have fled to Argentina, but his remains were found in Berlin decades later, supporting the theory that he killed himself in May 1945. Göring also cheated the hangman by swallowing a cyanide pill, which, it was rumored, his wife had passed to him with her goodbye kiss. As in the case of Hitler's death, there were no public expressions of sorrow—and probably no private ones either. Ex-Nazis and Nazi sympathizers kept their mouths shut out of fear of calling attention to themselves, while "ordinary" Germans said "*Gott sei Dank* (Thank God)," for want of a German equivalent for "good riddance."

It was late afternoon by the time Werner and I felt we had seen enough of Nuremberg and decided to return to the *Hauptbahnhof*. On our way, we ran into three black GIs, who wanted to know what we were doing in civilian clothes. "We're merchant marines sightseeing in Bavaria," explained Werner, without seeming to arouse suspicion.

"You guys are welcome to come to a dance at our barracks tonight," one of the GIs offered.

We were in no particular hurry to get back to Hamburg, and sensing new adventure, we accepted the invitation.

The GIs were stationed in Nuremberg's former SS *Kaserne*, a complex of massive three-story brick barracks that not too long ago had housed a division of Hitler's military elite. Except for the missing swastika, which had been chiseled from the wreath in the claws of the giant stone eagle emblem above the entrance gate, the barracks seemed untouched by the war.

Expecting to be asked to leave at any moment, Werner and I were on a constant alert for inquisitive MPs or other military officials who might object to our presence. But everyone treated us like long-lost brothers. The only hitch came when we were about to enter the auditorium for the dance and an officious soldier seated behind a table at the door stopped Werner to ask, "You sure you're colored?"

Without hesitating for even a split second, blond and blue-eyed Werner indignantly replied, "What do you think?"

The soldier shrugged apologetically and let Werner pass.

The huge hall was jam-packed with hundreds of black GIs and their German dates. Never in my life had I seen so many blacks. And what a wide range of complexions, from white to deep ebony and all the shades in between.

When the dance band, consisting of a dozen or so black GIs, blasted off and the tenor saxman stepped to the mike and effortlessly improvised incredibly intricate variations of the tune's main theme, my pride in my own musicianship was literally blown away. Grudgingly, I had to admit to myself that I would never be that good and that eventually I needed to look for some other kind of work.

It was quite apparent from the choreographed-looking jitterbug acrobatics put on display by the fräuleins and their black GI partners that they had had plenty of practice. Watching the rapturous expressions on the young

women's perspiring faces as they "jived" to what the Nazis had always de-
rided as *Negermusik,* I was sure that if the Führer hadn't blown out his
brains, the mere sight of his cherished *Deutsche Mädchen* with the "apelike
creatures" would have killed him.

The band struck up a stirring, upbeat tune that I had heard for the first
time some ten years before during the 1936 Olympic Games in Berlin. At
the first strains of the tune, all the GIs came to attention, and Werner and
I followed their example. One of the soldiers had stepped up to the micro-
phone and in a rich baritone sang the words, which, although I didn't fully
understand at the time, I listened to with deep-felt reverence, especially the
final ". . . o'er the land of the free, and the home of the brave." Never did
the idea of becoming an American citizen one day appeal to me more than
at that moment.

The dance came to an end and the GIs and their fräuleins filed out of
the auditorium. Since we were dead tired, we gladly accepted when one of
our new GI friends suggested that we spend the night in the barracks, and
we followed him to another floor. Stopping at a door, he told us that two
of his buddies were asleep inside but would be going on duty in an hour or
so. Motioning us to be quiet, he opened the door and, without turning on
the light, steered us toward two empty bunks. "I'll be back for you in the
morning," he promised. Werner and I were too tired to let the loud snoring
of the two GIs bother us and were soon fast asleep. By the time I awakened,
it was daylight and the two GIs were gone. Werner was still sleeping peace-
fully in the next bunk.

Lazily, my squinting eyes swept across the room to take inventory. There
were several neatly made bunks, a small table flanked by four chairs and
several wall lockers. When my eyes beheld the lockers, they did a double
take. Perched on top of each was a white helmet liner, and each helmet liner
displayed in large black type the familiar and much-feared letters *MP.* Along
one wall, neatly aligned on hooks, was a row of white belts with empty white
pistol holsters. This could mean only one thing—the GIs we had befriended
the previous day were off-duty military cops.

As soon as the full impact of my discovery had hit me, I woke up Werner
with the news that we had been sleeping in the lion's den. Within seconds
we were fully dressed and, after a brief facial bath in the washroom next
door, we briskly walked along the endless corridors, down several flights of

stairs, and out of the swastikaless gate. Only after the *Kaserne* was completely out of sight did we dare to run. When we reached Nuremberg's *Hauptbahnhof,* we were tempted to pay another visit to the Allied personnel waiting room, but thought better of it when we learned that a train to Hamburg was leaving momentarily.

Without the benefit of Donald's company, we were obliged to ride in the train's no-frills German car, instead of the Allied car to whose sumptuous amenities we had so easily become accustomed. "Where are the MPs when we need them?" I wondered, hoping that an MP patrol would make the rounds and send us to the Allied train where we felt we belonged. But no such luck. The only official who made the rounds was an old, grumpy-looking German conductor who checked all passengers but us, obviously assuming that we were Allied personnel and entitled to a free ride.

After a long and eventless train journey, during most of which Werner and I caught up on some sorely needed sleep, we returned to Hamburg.

WERNER LEAVES FOR AMERICA

Shortly after our Nuremberg adventure, in the spring of 1947, Werner surprised me with an extraordinary bit of news. After literally years of futilely petitioning the U.S. government for repatriation, he had finally received a favorable response from Washington.

"The Germans won't have to put up with Yankee Werner much longer." He grinned, showing me a letter from the U.S. State Department stating that an examination of his submitted documents had fully established his claim to U.S. citizenship and that travel arrangements from Bremerhaven to New York City at U.S. government expense were being processed. If all went well, the letter said, he could be on his way to the United States within the next three months. He was also advised that he would shortly receive notification from the U.S. Consulate General in Hamburg to pick up his U.S. passport.

Werner's good news triggered a welter of emotions in me. While I was happy for him to be so close to the fulfillment of his—no, our—dream, I dreaded seeing him leave, since we had become almost inseparable. We had known each other barely a year and a half, but to me it seemed as if we had been friends for a lifetime. I had always fantasized that one day we would somehow embark on our journey to the United States together. I had played the role of the black American stuck in Germany for so long and with so much conviction that I had somehow convinced myself that I had a right to be repatriated to the U.S. like Werner. Werner's good news had been a reality check. It drove home to me the fact that I had only been playing charades, that I had not only been fooling other people but myself as well, and that I was no nearer to being admitted to the United States than the day I first met Werner and he planted in me the idea of seeking my fortune in the United States.

I had difficulty concealing my disappointment over the discouraging fact that my own dream of one day going to the United States was just that, a dream, with nothing to justify my expectation that it would ever come true. It occurred to me that for Werner, the charade of impersonating an American that had been the total content of our postwar life had suddenly come to an end. With a U.S. passport in his pocket, he no longer had to pretend to be an American citizen; he *was* an American citizen. He now could go into any Allied service club or movie theater, and board any Allied train without having to look over his shoulder for U.S. or British MPs. By simply claiming his birthright, he could now—delight of delights—plant his feet in true Yankee fashion on any seat in front of him without having to apologize to anyone.

Under no circumstances did I want Werner to think that I was jealous of his good fortune, although I had to admit to myself that I would have preferred if the State Department had delayed his return just a little longer. Luckily, Werner was too preoccupied with his newfound happiness to notice my halfhearted response to the news.

Fortunately for all involved, my mind was soon taken off Werner when Yue called me to get ready for another two-month-long British Army Welfare Service tour of central Germany. It spared me lengthy goodbyes and the impossible task of pretending that I was truly happy that Werner was sailing for the U.S. By the time I returned to Hamburg, Werner had left and, according to his first letter to me, had safely arrived in New York City, which, he explained in glowing terms, exceeded all of his expectations.

Werner's departure was, if nothing else, a wake-up call for me. I suddenly realized that if I were ever going to get out of Germany, I had to stop dreaming and playing games and instead start doing. Since, unlike Werner, I had no legitimate claim to U.S. citizenship, I decided that I had to play the cards that fate had dealt me. Under no circumstances was I ready to resign myself to being stuck in dead-end Germany for the rest of my life.

Ever since the war ended, I had tried to establish contact with my father in Liberia. Since at that time regular postal traffic between Germany and Liberia had not yet been resumed, I had given my letters—addressed for want of an address to "Mr. Al-Haj Massaquoi, Monrovia, Liberia, West Africa"—to British soldier friends with the request to mail them for me through the British postal system. In the letters I explained that my mother and I had survived the war, that I was making a living as a musician, but that we were still facing many serious problems and were eager to leave Germany. When I hadn't received a reply after more than half a year of anxious waiting, I almost gave up hope of ever again hearing from my father.

Since with Werner's departure my dream of a future in America had evaporated, I decided to give writing to my father another try. With the help of my friends Ralph and Egon Giordano, who were beginning to make names for themselves as budding young journalists and who let me use their battered manual typewriter, I pecked out a dozen or so letters to my father. This time I requested to have my letters forwarded by the International Red Cross, the United Nations Relief Agency (UNRA), and several consulates in Hamburg, including that of the United States.

I also resumed writing to my cousin Martha, the daughter of my aunt Clara in Barrington, Illinois, and to my cousin Ilse, the daughter of Uncle Paul in Chicago. I wrote both that my mother and I wanted to come to America and asked for their help.

Unsurprisingly, I didn't hear from my father, but after a few weeks I received letters from Martha and Ilse. Martha's letter was positive. She told me that as soon as she and her mother received my letter, they had gone to a lawyer to see what could be done to get us to come to the States. Unfortunately, the lawyer explained to them that the main obstacle to our coming was the fact that no formal peace treaty had as yet been signed with Germany, and that as a result, it was still subject to Allied military law. Consequently, Germany did not have a U.S. immigration quota. Without such a quota, he had told them, immigration by German nationals was impossible. Martha ended her letter on an optimistic note, writing that her mother would not give up trying to get us to come and had already scheduled a meeting with her congressman on our behalf.

The letter from Ilse was quite different. Unlike the usual chatty tone that characterized her previous letters to me, she merely offered a few polite platitudes about being glad to have heard from me again. At the bottom of her letter, Uncle Paul had written a few remarks whose gist was "Dear nephew, whatever you do, under no circumstances come to Chicago." The reason was to spare me disappointment, he explained, since I, like most Germans, seemed to labor under the misconception that the United States was the land of milk and honey when, in fact, Americans had to work extremely hard for what they owned and also that many things, including certain foods, were still scarce. Therefore, he concluded, my mother and I would be much better off staying where we were and sticking it out until things got better.

When my mother read her brother's note, she was seething with rage and disappointment at her sibling, whom she had always loved from the bottom of her heart. "Here we are starving and often don't know where our next meal is supposed to come from," she fumed, "and this dear brother of mine has the nerve to tell us not to come to his precious America because people in America have to work hard for what they own and because certain foods are still scarce. I don't recall ever having written him that we expect not to work." She became even angrier upon receiving her sister Clara's letter, which explained that the real reason Uncle Paul didn't want us to show up in Chicago was that "he was afraid his sister and her black son would be an embarrassment to him in his all-white community." Paul, according to Aunt Clara, had married a woman from the South following the death of his first, German-born wife, the mother of his children, and was seemingly acting under her racist influence.

That's all my mother needed to hear. "Paul," she raged, "has forgotten that twenty-five years earlier he was a starving, dirt-poor immigrant from Germany, who would never have made it to the United States were it not for the help of our sister Martha and our brother Hermann. Now he has the nerve to look down on other people because of their race. But he doesn't ever have to worry about being embarrassed by us. As of today, I no longer have a brother named Paul. As far as I am concerned, he's already dead!"

It was a vow my mother kept for the remainder of her life. Paul, for his part, lived up to Clara's allegations of racial prejudice and never extended himself to my mother or me. Although Mutti eventually did move to the United States, where for twenty-five years she lived a mere forty-minute car ride from Paul, she never visited or called him, and when he died, she refused to attend his funeral.

BUSTED

Taking care of business on the waterfront without Werner at my side for logistical and moral support was difficult at first, but I managed. One day, however, when I least expected it, I ran into my first case of potentially serious trouble.

Having just returned from an American ship, I had taken a small group of black seamen to a bar for the usual combination of business, booze, and babes. It was broad daylight and already the bar was packed. We could not have been there more than fifteen minutes when we heard shrill whistles and loud commands outside. Looking out of the window, I saw several jeeps lined up at the curb. Seconds later, blue-uniformed, white-hatted, pistol-toting men from the British Port Controller's office poured through the door. Indiscriminately, they picked several Americans, both black and white, and hustled them out of the door and onto the waiting jeeps. Unfortunately, I was one of the captives. After a short ride to the Port Controller's office, we were told to wait in a large room from where we were called individually into an adjoining room for interrogation.

When it was my turn to be questioned, I was confronted by several officers who were seated at a long table. One of them ordered me to empty the contents of my pockets on the table. When I produced a fresh carton of Chesterfields from under my jacket, the officers grinned gleefully, obviously pleased with themselves for having caught at least one culprit redhanded.

"Let me see your shore-leave pass!" the officer demanded.

"I don't have a shore-leave pass," I replied.

"So you left your ship without permission?" the officer insisted.

"No, I did not," was my stubborn reply.

"If you are not in possession of a valid shore-leave pass from your purser, you are on shore illegally and thus subject to arrest," the officer lectured me.

Realizing that I really hadn't broken any law, I was beginning to enjoy playing cat-and-mouse with the haughty British officer.

"Do you have any identification on you?" the officer demanded irritably.

I pointed to my blue, photoless German *Kennkarte,* which I had put on the table with several other objects, including a lighter and a pack of chewing gum. The officer picked up my ID card and carefully studied the writing.

"According to this you are a German national and not an American seaman?" the officer continued.

"That is correct," I conceded.

"Then how did you come into possession of this carton of cigarettes? How did you pay for it? And what had you planned to do with it? You realize that black marketeering is a serious offense?" the officer inquired, convinced he had driven me into a corner from which there was no escape.

"I didn't pay anything for the cigarettes," I responded. "They were a gift from an American seaman who gave them to me when I visited his ship."

Turning sarcastic, the officer asked, "Are you saying then that all I have to do is board an American ship and the people will give me free cartons of cigarettes?"

"I doubt that seriously," I told the officer.

"Then why you and not me?" the officer pressed on.

This time I responded with a bomb. "Because you are white and I am black! The seaman who gave me the cigarettes was a black man who felt sorry for me when he heard that I had lived in Nazi Germany during the war."

My explanation was followed by embarrassed silence on the part of my interrogator until another officer apologized for the inconvenience they had caused me and told me that I was free to leave with my belongings, including the cigarettes. But before I had made it out of the building, I was followed by another of my interrogators, a young lieutenant. For a moment I thought that the officers had changed their minds about letting me go, but the young officer reassured me that I had nothing to worry about. "I wonder whether I could talk to you for a moment."

Realizing that I really didn't have much of a choice, I followed him into a small, empty office. There he told me that his office had received reports that four "colored" American soldiers had deserted their post in Bremen and apparently were hiding out on Hamburg's waterfront with the help of some German women. He said that according to reports, these men were responsible for several burglaries and holdups in the area and must therefore be considered dangerous. I recalled that several days earlier I had run into three black GIs accompanied by three German women as they were strolling through St. Pauli. We had said "hi" to each other as we passed, but since they had shown no interest in getting to know me better, I had walked on. American soldiers, especially black American soldiers, were exceedingly rare in British-occupied Hamburg, and I had no doubt that the three GIs I had seen were part of the quartet the British authorities were looking for.

The lieutenant told me that his office suspected that the deserters were hanging around the waterfront in hopes of befriending black seamen from a U.S.-bound American ship in order to stow away. "I know you do not approve of robbers and burglars," the officer continued in a transparent effort to butter me up. "That's why I thought that you might want to help us apprehend these men. In return, we would issue you a dock pass that would authorize you to enter the dock area and ships without interference from the port authorities. All you have to do is be on the lookout for any colored American soldiers." With that, he filled out a dock pass made out to me and valid for one month. He also handed me a piece of paper on which he had written his rank, name, and telephone number. "If you see or hear anything, you can reach me at this number. I don't care what time of day or night," he said, "just call. Will you do that for us?"

"I'd be glad to," I lied. I hadn't the slightest intention of becoming a Judas to black American soldiers who, perhaps because they were treated like second-class citizens, had become fed up with army life and were trying to make it back home. Not for one second did I believe those "reports" about robberies and holdups by black soldiers. But even if they were true, I was not interested in becoming a stoolie for the British.

In the weeks to come, the dock pass came in mighty handy, since it enabled me to enter and leave the dock area without having to worry about inquisitive MPs. With every MP in port on the lookout for black deserters, my complexion had quickly reverted from an asset to a serious liability. But thanks to my pass, I was able to slip into and out of the dragnet at will and without a hitch.

I soon learned through the waterfront grapevine that one of the four deserters had been captured and sent back to his unit in Bremen for court-martial proceedings, while three were alive and well but lying low at the homes of some of Hannelore's friends. The men reportedly were biding their time to make their move. The lieutenant was right about one thing. Hannelore confirmed that they were trying to stow away on an American ship. She told me that her friends had fallen madly in love with the fugitives and would do anything to help them get away, but she denied the claims that they were thieves.

A few weeks later, while on my nightly round of some of my favorite waterfront hangouts, I watched a dozen or so jeeps loaded with British MPs pull up in front of an apartment building that Hannelore had pointed out to me as the hiding place of the black GIs. After dismounting, the MPs unholstered their sidearms and, on a hand signal from an officer, rushed into the building. Within a few minutes a small crowd of passersby had gathered across the street from the building's entrance. Wondering what the commotion was about, some ventured that it was a black-market raid. Although I had a pretty good idea otherwise, I kept my mouth shut. I hoped that the raiders would find the nest empty, but no such luck. When they emerged a few minutes later, they were surrounding three handcuffed, sullen-looking black GIs. As quickly as they had come, the jeeps sped away, the crowd dispersed, and the street turned back to normal as if nothing had happened.

I had no idea what was in store for them, but whatever their fate, I was glad that I had nothing to do with their capture.

AFRICA-BOUND

I had almost given up ever hearing from my father again when one day an airmail letter arrived that was impossible to overlook because of its large size and the brilliant colors of its exotic-looking postage stamps. It was the long-awaited letter from my father.

A flood of conflicting emotions took hold of me as I prepared to open the letter, the first tangible link in almost eighteen years with the man my mother had taught me to call *father* despite the fact that from the time he left us, while I was still a little boy, he had been largely a stranger to me. Time and absence had not made my heart grow fonder of him. If I felt anything about him, it was detached curiosity. Who was this Al-Haj Massaquoi, the man I had heard so much about throughout my life and whom, my mother kept insisting, I resembled in so many ways? Why had he left us in Germany without bothering to help when we badly needed help?

The letter, typed in English, started simply, "Dear Hans-Jürgen." Thanking me for my letter dated January 8, 1948, my father explained that he was much relieved learning that my mother and I had survived the war, since he had feared for some time that we had both been killed. Immediately upon receipt of my letter, he wrote, he had applied for a Liberian passport for me in preparation for having me come to Liberia. To expedite matters, he asked me to send him a set of passport photos of myself as soon as possible. He suggested that I should come to Liberia first, and that if I found the country to my liking, he would arrange for my mother to follow.

Then came the bad news, which I had suspected and dreaded for some time. "I am sorry having to tell you that your grandfather, Momolu, has been dead since 1938." I recalled how, when I was a little boy, my grandfather promised me that one day when I came to Liberia he would show me the crown he had worn when he was king of the Vais. For a moment I could hear his roaring laughter in response to my stories; next, I could see us once again strolling along the Alster and feeding cantaloupe leftovers to the swans. Realizing that he was gone for good filled me with a sense of irreparable loss. Then I read on. "Due to the political situation that prevailed in this country," my father wrote, "I was not able to do much between the years 1930 and 1943. But things are somewhat better now with a president (William V. S. Tubman) who is friendly disposed towards me."

Underplaying his wealth, my father wrote that he was doing all right as an entrepreneur involved in import-export trade with Denmark, a steamship agency, and several transportation ventures that included a few diesel-powered trucks and buses and a large diesel-powered motor vessel used for passenger service along the coast.

Confiding that he and Auntie Fatima were no longer on speaking terms since her return from her studies in the United States, he explained that "all at once she had it in her head that your grandfather left millions that should come to her. Instead of approaching me in a decent manner, she joined a certain wretched brother of mine [Nat] in legal actions against me. They are still spending the few dollars they have on lawyers and have gotten nowhere with the matter as yet. Now she is ashamed and does not come around me anymore. She will, perhaps, tell you all about it when you come out."

After this bit of family dirt, my father explained that he had contacted his Danish friend and business colleague, Harold Nissen, as the Liberian consul general in Copenhagen, who would be in touch with me shortly to arrange my passage to Liberia via Denmark on the Danish freighter *Bornholm*.

Promising to write again very soon, my father concluded sheepishly, "Why does your mother not write me herself? Perhaps she does not care for me any more?!!!"

While my big dream had always been to one day go to the United States, I quickly made the necessary mental adjustment and settled—for the time being at least—for Africa. My father's plan of having me join him in Liberia received the full approval of my mother, who had long resigned herself to the certainty that there would come a time when I would leave her. Firmly convinced that it was necessary for me to get out of Germany in order to reach my full potential, she had always encouraged me to pursue my dream of a future abroad, even if it meant that we would have to separate for a while.

As much as I had wanted to leave Germany, I had mixed emotions about going to Africa. But after discussing the matter with various people, I became convinced that moving to Liberia was better than being stuck in devastated

Germany, and, besides, if I didn't like Liberia, I could always go to the United States.

Within a few weeks of hearing from my father, the U.S. Consulate General in Hamburg informed me that it represented Liberian consular interests and that a Liberian passport in my name had arrived, which I should pick up at my convenience. It had to be signed in the presence of a consul and, as a result, could not be sent through the mail. A Liberian passport would once and for all end my existence in the nationality twilight zone in which I had lived for so long under the Nazis. Most important, my passport would enable me to leave Germany legally any time I felt like it, a privilege that, during the immediate postwar years under Allied occupation, was denied German citizens.

Next, as announced by my father, I received a letter from Consul General Nissen, informing me that the necessary arrangements for my trip to Liberia had been completed. He explained that the *Bornholm* had just left Liberia and was scheduled to make a brief stop at Hamburg prior to returning to its home port in Aalborg, Denmark. He advised me to take that opportunity to meet with Captain Hartmann, the ship's master, to discuss details of my trip.

Having visited dozens of American freighters during my beachcomber days on Hamburg's waterfront, I felt quite at home when I stepped on the deck of the *Bornholm* for my visit with Captain Hartmann. It occurred to me that this was the first time I had entered Hamburg Harbor on legitimate business.

The captain, a burly man with thinning gray hair and a ruddy complexion, seemed annoyed at first at the interruption, then mellowed after I told him who I was. "So you are young Massaquoi—well, well," he remarked. I had no idea what "well, well" meant in this context, and he didn't bother to explain. Hartmann told me to be ready within two months to travel by train to Aalborg in order to board the *Bornholm* for my trip to Liberia. Now that my departure was imminent, I suddenly had mixed feelings about leaving Germany so soon, but I assured the captain that I would be in Aalborg on time.

When I asked him whether he knew my father and what life was like in Africa, the captain told me that he had been doing business with my father for many years and that, as far as my future lifestyle was concerned, I would have it made. "Your father is very well fixed," he insisted. As if to back up his words, he fetched an envelope from a desk drawer and handed it to me. "He asked me to give you this to tide you over until you get to Monrovia and in case you need to buy a few things for the trip."

As soon as I had left the *Bornholm,* I tore open the envelope and counted the money. There was five hundred dollars in crisp ten-dollar bills—a veritable fortune by prevailing black-market rates. At first I was moved by my father's generosity, until I reminded myself that this was the first money he had spent on me in nearly twenty years.

From the moment I learned my departure date, I started counting the days with eager anticipation. Then something happened that I hadn't foreseen, something that almost changed my plans.

Fred and I had been making our usual rounds of Hamburg when we stepped on the el-train platform at Kellinghusen station in order to change trains. As we looked to the next platform across the tracks, we spotted two women, one young and remarkably pretty with shoulder-length blond hair, the other middle-aged and, as far as we were concerned, nondescript. We smiled at the young woman to let her know that we approved. To our surprise, she not only smiled back, but waved at us invitingly. As my testosterone production kicked into high gear, I deliberated feverishly what could be done to keep this angel from simply slipping away. In a matter of seconds her train would arrive and take her to an unknown destination where I would never see her again.

Suddenly, I had an idea. Pointing toward the large station clock, which indicated around 4 P.M., I held up eight fingers, then pointed toward me and the platform on which we stood. To my great relief, the blonde signaled back that she had understood and that she, too, would be back at 8 P.M. A few seconds later, her train arrived and she was gone.

Four hours later, after endless speculation whether or not the blonde would keep our date, Fred and I were back on the platform. To our surprise, the blonde was already there. This time, she was accompanied by a tall young redhead with a nice figure but a rather ordinary face. Close up, the blonde was even more stunning than I had imagined her to be from across the tracks.

Although Fred did most of the talking, her smiling blue eyes that examined me with undisguised curiosity relieved me of the nagging fear that she might be interested in Fred instead of me. Fortunately, Fred was quite content to pursue the redhead, whose name was Hannah. After inviting Hannah to accompany him to a movie, he left the field wide open for me to get better acquainted with Ingeborg, the blonde. Ingeborg told me that she was eighteen years old—four years younger than I—and that she lived with her mother (the woman we had seen her with earlier), her handicapped father, and a younger sister and brother.

I had only once experienced love, with Gretchen, and never at first sight, but this time Cupid's arrow struck me like lightning and with tornado force. The fact that Ingeborg told me before the evening was up that she felt the same way about me made my feelings for her even more intense. There was no rational explanation why I would feel that strongly about a person I had known only for a few hours, but reason didn't figure much in the emotional quagmire into which I had slipped head over heels.

Just as I was about to build dream castles about a life with this angel by my side, I realized that I was scheduled to leave Germany in less than a month. Suddenly, my desire to roam had evaporated. How could I take off for some unknown part of the world and leave this beautiful creature behind for someone else to appreciate? For a moment I weighed the possibility of postponing or canceling my journey to Liberia, but I immediately dismissed the thought, realizing that my opportunity to leave Germany might never come again.

When I told Ingeborg that my days in Hamburg were numbered and why, she started crying. "I knew from the first moment I saw you that this was too good to be true, that somewhere there would be a catch. So this is it," she sobbed.

I told her that this didn't have to be "it," and that I would either send for her after I had gotten settled in Liberia, the way I planned to send for my mother, or return to Germany. For the time being she was satisfied with my solution and we decided to make the most of the days we had left together. Since I had no more show business obligations and had long turned my back on the beachcomber life, I had nothing but time on my hands.

Like two star-crossed lovers, we crammed what seemed like a lifetime of living and loving into three short weeks. Ingeborg introduced me to her family, who welcomed me with open arms, and I introduced her to my mother, who immediately bonded with her. During the day, we went for romantic walks in some of the many forests surrounding Hamburg, and in the evening, we wound up in intimate bars or the cavernous Haus Vaterland. Wherever we showed up, we were the immediate focus of attention, obviously because of the hard-to-ignore contrast we presented. People who liked what they saw smiled at us with approval, and people who didn't were smart enough not to let their disapproval show.

Before we knew it, the day had come for me to leave Germany for Africa. To spare my mother and me painfully long goodbyes, we had agreed that I would take my leave from her in our apartment and that Fred and Inge would accompany me to Hamburg *Hauptbahnhof,* where I would catch the train for Aalborg, Denmark. Suddenly, the thought of leaving my mother behind all by herself seemed unbearable to me, but when she noticed that I was fighting with myself to overcome my scruples, she told me firmly that she would be all right and that my leaving for Africa would eventually benefit both of us. Thus assured of her blessing, I hugged her one more time, then followed Inge and Fred into the street. When I looked up, I caught one last glimpse of my mother waving from the window.

By the time we arrived at the station, the train that was to take me to Denmark was already waiting on the tracks. I immediately boarded, stowed my luggage in my compartment, then rejoined Inge and Fred on the platform for final farewells. Minutes later, I was waving at the two as my train pulled out of the station, wondering whether I would ever see them again.

DAKAR

I was much too preoccupied with my thoughts about what I had left behind and what would be in store for me to pay much attention to Aalborg, a large seaport and one of the oldest cities in Denmark, during my brief cab ride from the train station to where the *Bornholm* was docked. After I boarded the seven-thousand-ton ship, I was greeted by the ship's chief steward, who instructed a boy of about fifteen to take me to my cabin and to show me to the captain's private stateroom, where, he explained, all my

meals would be served, since the freighter had no dining facilities for pas-
sengers.

When I arrived at the captain's salon for the first scheduled evening meal,
Captain Hartmann introduced me to a young Danish fellow by the name
of Aage Kelstedt, who, he said, was a friend and guest of the *Bornholm*'s
owner and the only other passenger besides me. Aage and I hit it off. He
told me that he had just finished his first semester of college, and that he
had never been in Africa before either and looked forward to the experience.

Until our arrival in Dakar, where the *Bornholm* was to go into dry dock
for several days of repairs, our journey was pleasant and uneventful.
Throughout the days, Aage and I would roam the ship, chat with off-duty
crew members, read books, or lounge in easy chairs on deck. At night, we
would sleep in our cabins, which seemed tiny compared with the ones I had
seen on the American freighters I had visited in Hamburg.

The only interruptions in our monotonous routine were our mealtimes
as guests of the captain. Captain Hartmann stood on punctuality, we were
told by the cabin boy. So to keep him happy, we made it our business to
be seated at our designated places at the table at least ten minutes before the
skipper's scheduled arrival.

Despite his resemblance to old St. Nick, the captain turned out to be a
humorless, dour man who seemed to dislike the idea of having to give up
some of his privacy for two young men who didn't interest him in the least.
As a result, the table conversation dragged like molasses, mainly about the
increasingly oppressive heat. When the captain noticed that I was perspiring
profusely, he advised me cheerfully, "You better get used to it, because where
you are going, it's even hotter."

Somehow, I got the impression that Captain Hartmann didn't like me
very much. All I can say to that is that the feeling was definitely mutual.

The first land we sighted after several days at sea was the Canary Islands.
One of the ship's officers explained to Aage and me that the islands served
Christopher Columbus as bases during his exploration of America and that
Generalissimo Francisco Franco launched his Nationalist revolution from
them. "It won't be long now," the officer said encouragingly, "and we'll be
arriving at Dakar."

As the *Bornholm* tied up dockside in Dakar Harbor, I got my very first, long-awaited glimpse of Africa. Looking down from the *Bornholm*'s deck to a freighter being unloaded adjacent to us, I saw a strange, seemingly endless procession of spindly figures carrying huge bags of a grayish powdery substance on their heads to nearby trucks. The spindly figures, it turned out, were near-naked workers, and the substance, which covered them from head to toe, was cement.

Despite the dizzying heat, they were loudly chanting in harmony and moving to the rhythm of their chant while their feet churned up clouds of lung-searing cement dust. As if totally oblivious to their wretched condition, they gave no indication that they were anything but comfortable. From time to time, a khaki-clad black overseer would hose down the workers with a stream of water, instantly transforming the gray figures into glistening ebony-hued young men, some barely in their teens.

I was appalled that these youths, who should have been playing and going to school, worked under such inhumane conditions, most likely for exceedingly meager wages.

"Well, how do you like Africa so far?" the voice of Captain Hartmann interrupted my thoughts. When I told him how I felt about the spectacle before us, he cautioned me not to be too rash in my judgment. "Your father controls an army of laborers, some no older than these. As you will soon see, it made him a very rich man."

The captain's remarks did nothing to endear my father to me, but I decided to reserve judgment until I had a chance to see things with my own eyes. Somehow, I was suspicious of the captain's motive for telling me what he did, although I couldn't think of any good reason for doubting his words.

Three young Danish ship's officers I had befriended invited me to go with them ashore that afternoon. I gladly accepted, as I could hardly wait to set foot on Mother Africa. Because of my African family ties, I subscribed to neither the Eurocentric image of the "Dark Continent" nor Hollywood's romanticized Tarzan jungle idyll. Yet I could still respond to Africa's exotic lure and promise of high adventure. On the latter score, I was not to be disappointed.

The Dakar of 1948 was a bustling, cosmopolitan city still rife with symbols of France's deeply entrenched colonial authority. French tricolors were flying from every government building of Senegal's capital and black soldiers and their white French officers, as well as detachments of the French Foreign

Legion, were a common sight. The markets teemed with gesticulating people in flowing robes and an occasional camel or donkey carried oversize loads. In addition to the many exotic sights that helped convince me that I had finally succeeded in getting out of Germany, a pervasive sweet smell of tropical vegetation heightened my sense of being a long way from what used to be home.

As we approached a fruit stand, my attention was drawn to a display of beautiful plump bananas. Due to the severe curtailment of tropical food imports in Germany during and after the war, I hadn't seen, much less eaten, a banana for at least eight years. When I asked the vendor how much he wanted for a half dozen bananas, he communicated with his fingers a certain number of colonial francs. While I counted out the required number of large-size bills, another fruit merchant pulled me to the side and gestured that he would give me the same number of bananas for half the price. The Danes advised me to go with the better deal, but before I could finalize the transaction, the first vendor started such a ruckus that it attracted people from all over the marketplace. Eventually, a black policeman showed up. After listening to the vendor's complaint, he ordered us with an unmistakable gesture of his baton to follow him to the police station. With the screaming vendor in tow, we wound our way through the thick crowds of people who were eyeing us with hostility. Since the vendor did all his ranting in French, we hadn't the slightest idea what he was complaining about. While I could sympathize with his disappointment over having lost out to a competitor, I couldn't imagine what made him think he had a right to demand that I buy from him.

At the police station, we were herded into a large room with several desks occupied by African policemen. While we were waiting our turn to be brought before the police prefect, a white detainee in one of the cells behind us whispered to us in English to keep our cool and "for God's sake not make any waves" unless we felt like joining him. Identifying himself as a Dutch seaman, he told us that when he refused to pay a bribe to two policemen whom he had asked for directions at night, they arrested him for disorderly conduct. "I've been in here for over a week already," he said despondently, "and my consulate still hasn't been able to get me out."

When finally we stood before the police officer in charge, a Frenchman in khaki uniform, he invited the vendor to state his case. For several minutes the vendor ranted and raved, the way he had done outside, while frequently pointing toward my companions and me. When the Frenchman gestured that he had heard enough, I assumed he was now ready to listen to our side, but I assumed wrong. Before I could finish my first sentence, the official shouted rudely, *"Ferme ta gueule,"* which even I knew meant "Shut up." Remembering the advice from the Dutch seaman, I did just that.

The Frenchman then ordered us in fluent, yet heavily French-accented English to empty our pockets of all money and put it on his desk in front of him. After counting the thick wad of bills, the prefect handed the vendor the amount he had asked for his bananas, put the rest into his desk drawer, then pointed at the door and shouted at us, *"Allez!"* which, we figured out instantly, meant "Get out!"

The ship's officers and I were livid, but we wisely kept our anger and commentary regarding the Gallic system of justice in check until we were well out of hearing distance of the police station. The only way we could explain what had just happened to us was that we had been the victims of a scam played by the vendor and the police official at our expense.

Bananas, it seemed, were a cursed commodity that forever eluded my grasp. At that moment, I really didn't care, since during our short adventure I had totally lost my banana appetite. It took several months before I was able to look at bananas without feeling a sense of rage and even longer before I could stomach the idea of eating them.

The following evening, when the officers invited me to come along for a night on the town, I was ready to give Dakar another chance. At night, the city seemed even more exotic and mysterious than during the day. Except for an occasional furtive figure and several homeless persons sleeping on the sidewalks, the dimly lighted streets were empty. Fortunately, we were able to hail a taxi. After we asked the native driver in Danish, German, and English whether he could take us to where the action was, his eyes lit up in sudden comprehension. *"Oui, Monsigneurs."* He smacked his lips and kissed the joined fingertips of his right hand. *"Beaucoup* beautiful *la femme."* After what seemed like a never-ending ride through Dakar—no doubt along the "scenic route"—we stopped in front of a nightclub called Le Moulin Rouge, a place that had little in common with its famous nineteenth-century Paris namesake except its ill repute.

Our waitress, a pretty Eurafrican girl with olive skin and a close-cropped

Afro, let us know in perfect English that she and her colleagues were "at our service," ready to heighten our comfort level. All around us were white men and African women openly engaged in behavior that made St. Pauli's waterfront bars seem tame by comparison. We opted for champagne and listening to the seductive French tunes of a velvet-voiced African piano player.

It was quite late when we went back to the *Bornholm*. As I felt in no mood to face old sourpuss over breakfast, I quickly scribbled the words, PLEASE DO NOT DISTURB! on a piece of cardboard and attached it to the outside of my cabin door before falling into a comalike sleep.

When I awakened and looked through the porthole, it was broad daylight. A glance at my watch informed me that it was almost time to get ready for lunch. Apparently, the cabin boy had heeded my message and left me alone. Still feeling a bit hungover, I congratulated myself on my quick thinking, which had allowed me several precious extra hours of sleep. As I left my cabin to have lunch in the captain's quarters, I noticed that my cardboard sign was gone.

Aage was already seated at the captain's table when I arrived. "The captain had a fit this morning when you didn't show up," Aage told me. "He said you insulted him by putting a do-not-disturb sign on your door."

While it was true that it was with Hartmann's unpleasant attitude in mind that I had decided to forgo breakfast, it had never occurred to me that he would take my absence so personally. I resolved to apologize and unruffle his feathers, if that's what it took to clear the air between us. But my opportunity to negotiate a reconciliation with him never came. "The captain will not be coming," the captain's steward informed us. "You may go ahead and eat."

When he didn't show up for supper or for breakfast the following morning, it dawned on me that he intended to deprive me of the dubious pleasure of his company for the rest of my stay on board. That was fine with me. I could never stand the old geezer anyway, and the less I saw of him, the better.

One sizzling hot morning, the repaired *Bornholm* slipped out of Dakar Harbor and headed for the open Atlantic. After a couple of days, the African coast came back into view, and before long, we could see the hilly city of Monrovia, baking in the West African sun.

Throughout our journey from Dakar, I had seen Captain Hartmann only from a distance standing on the bridge, and the few times our paths crossed on deck, he pointedly ignored me. My Danish friends aboard told me not to let the captain's hostility get to me. They explained that he hated the idea that I didn't kowtow to him and that he couldn't bully me the way he bullied his crew.

The deck officer told me that Monrovia Harbor, which was under construction by the U.S. Navy, would be completed in a few months. Until then, he explained, the *Bornholm* had to anchor a few miles off the coast. He said that my father would come aboard by rowboat. "That's him now," he exclaimed, pointing to what looked like a tiny boat in the distance. As the boat came closer, I could make out eight oarsmen who were chanting rhythmically in response to their helmsman's shouts. Their tattered, soiled clothes were in sharp contrast to the immaculate white suit worn by the black man who was seated just below the helmsman. I couldn't make out the man's face because it was covered by a white pith helmet, but there was no doubt that the man under that helmet was a person of considerable authority.

As my father walked up the gangway that had been lowered for the occasion, he was greeted by Captain Hartmann, who welcomed him aboard like a visiting potentate while the *Bornholm*'s crew members on deck looked on with undisguised curiosity. The only thing missing from the scene, I thought, was a multiple-gun salute. I found that the officers had not exaggerated when they described my father as an extremely formal, no-nonsense type of man. Although I noticed that he was slightly shorter than I, I already felt intimidated by the air of authority that emanated from him. Hundreds of times I had rehearsed in my mind my pending reunion with him—I would simply give him a big hug and tell him how happy I was to see him. But when I actually came face-to-face with him and looked into his eyes, which were noncommittal after nearly two decades of separation, he seemed like a total stranger to me and I froze.

"It's good to see you made it all right," he said while formally shaking my hand.

After an awkward pause during which I groped in vain for the right words, I finally managed to come up with a self-conscious "How do you do, sir?"

which was not at all what I had intended to say. Somehow, I couldn't escape the feeling that we were both disappointed by our first encounter.

But my discomfort was far from over. I had yet to decide how to address the man to whom I owed my existence, and who, until a few minutes ago, had been an absolute stranger to me. The German *Vati* (Daddy), which is what I had called him when I was a little boy, sounded too foreign in an English-speaking country and inappropriately affectionate. *Father* seemed too formal, while *Dad* didn't seem formal enough. For the time being, I decided to wing it and avoid addressing my father until I came up with a better idea.

While I said goodbye to my Danish friends, my father and Captain Hartmann went to the captain's stateroom to take care of business. The transaction, I had been told, involved the *Bornholm*'s temporary hiring of more than twenty African dockworkers through my father's steamship agency.

When my father returned from the captain's quarters, his face registered annoyance. In his hand I saw the cardboard sign I had left on my cabin door. "What have you done?" my father demanded in an agitated voice. "The captain told me that you were extremely rude to him and warned me that I would have my hands full with you."

So that was it. Captain Hartmann, in his childish need for revenge, had bad-mouthed me to my father and thereby made an already difficult reunion even more difficult. Rather than letting my father discover for himself what kind of person I was, he compromised our relationship before it had even begun.

While I groped for some kind of explanation, my father cut me off. "We'll talk about it some other time," he said ominously.

FAMILY REUNION IN MONROVIA

As the rowboat took us back to shore, my father's anger seemed to have evaporated. With obvious pride, he pointed out various gleaming white government buildings in the distance that dotted the hilly landscape of Monrovia, including the U.S. Embassy at Mamba Point. On shore we were met by a young, barefoot man in khaki shorts and shirt whom my father introduced to me as his "houseboy" Jason. "This is my son, Mr. Hans," my father told Jason.

"Pleased to meet you, Meesta Haans," said Jason with a deferential nod, then grabbed my suitcase and led the way. The house, my father explained, was located on the same street just a short distance away.

The street was teeming with people, some dressed in African garb while others wore Western-style clothes. Most of the buildings were ramshackle structures of cinder-block walls with corrugated iron sheet roofs. What struck me most about the people was that they seemed to be an unusually jovial lot, happily laughing, slapping each other's backs and pumping hands. All along the street, rows of squatting women in colorful dresses were offering a vast variety of wares that ranged from hand-woven "country cloth" to freshly baked bread. They were engaged in loud chatter in their native languages that at first sounded to me like arguments, but that I later learned was just normal talk. Some of the women, wrapped tightly in colorful *lapas* that revealed their curvaceous bodies, sauntered along at a leisurely pace while balancing all types of objects on their heads, from boxes to buckets to sewing machines, all the while chatting up a storm. Some women, I noticed, carried sleeping babies strapped to their backs.

"This is it," my father announced, pointing at a large, rather plain, two-story stucco house on the side of the road. "The first floor holds my office and garage and upstairs are the living quarters."

Then he instructed Jason to show me to my room before getting my bath ready. "When you have cleaned up and rested a bit, we can have some chop," my father suggested, explaining that *chop* was Liberian slang for food. "Let Jason know when you are ready. I'll be in my office."

My room was large and cheerfully bright. It was dominated by a huge bed that was covered by a mosquito net whose apex was attached to the ceiling. A large ceiling fan kept the air in motion, but not enough to provide an escape from the stifling heat.

"Your bath is ready, Meesta Haans," Jason announced.

"Thank you, Jason. How long have you been working for my father?"

"Four years, sah," Jason replied.

I was soon to discover that the term *houseboy* did not begin to describe

the myriad of functions Jason performed with the greatest aplomb and ef-
ficiency. A true factotum, he was also my father's chauffeur, his auto me-
chanic, his messenger, his launderer, his valet, his appointment secretary,
his finder of lost or misplaced objects, and his memorizer of important facts.
After getting to know Jason, I became convinced that had he had just a few
years more than his three years of missionary schooling, he would easily have
been able to run my father's steamship agency.

Refreshed by a lukewarm bath, I put on the freshly laundered white shirt
and slacks Jason had laid out for me and, on his direction, went to the large
living room where a long table was set for two. Soon I was joined by my
father, who told me that he was closing his office early in honor of my
arrival.

Jason had placed a huge, cloth-covered tray in front of me that contained
several delicious-looking dishes, including chicken in gravy, collard greens,
plantains, and mountains of rice. A few seconds later, I experienced my first
visceral culture shock. I had a monstrous appetite, having forgone breakfast
on the *Bornholm,* and so I swallowed with great relish a mouthful of chicken
and gravy. All of a sudden, my mouth and throat turned into a fiery inferno
that had me coughing and gasping for breath. "I guess you're not used to
pepper," my father chuckled after I had recovered my breath and composure.
"For a moment I had forgotten that my son is a European and not an
African. But don't worry. I'll have some more chicken prepared for you in
no time, this time without pepper." He then instructed Jason to tell Maima,
the cook, to hurry up and fix some pepperless chicken. "Tell her that I want
to see her cousin, the one who used to cook for the Americans."

My father explained that he intended to solve my problem by hiring a
male cook who had been working for American missionaries and, as a result,
knew how to cook nonspicy dishes.

While I waited for my food, I watched my father turn his attention to a
second tray that Jason had put before him. It was filled with unfamiliar
African dishes, some of which smelled fishy and exceedingly unappetizing
to me. Pointing toward a puddinglike dish that gave off a pungent, unpleas-
ant odor, my father told me that this was an African delicacy called *fufu.* It
was made from fermenting starch extracted from cassava roots, he explained.
He ladled a liberal helping of a dark-green, okra-based sauce over it that
followed the spoon from plate to mouth in slimy strings. "This we call

palaver sauce," he explained. "It's called that because once you get it on your clothes, you're in for a lot of 'palaver'—arguments and trouble—with your woman since the stains are difficult to come out." He followed his explanation with a hearty laugh.

It suddenly occurred to me that this was the first time I had heard my father laugh. It made me quite happy to discover that there was another, less formal side to him.

Taking advantage of what I thought was a propitious moment, I expressed my concern over the run-in with the captain. Once I assured him that I had not meant any disrespect, my father told me to forget it and promised me that he would too.

He told me that, first thing the following morning, I was to see his personal physician, Dr. Jean Baptist Titus, head of Liberia's Department of Health, for a complete checkup and instructions on how to avoid catching any of the many tropical diseases, especially malaria. He then cautioned me to never sleep without a mosquito net. "I wish I had heeded that same advice when I came back from Europe almost twenty years ago," he said, "because the malaria I caught at that time still flares up occasionally and puts me out of commission for several days."

While I was finally enjoying my pepper-free chicken, a young, slender man with striking, chiseled dark features entered. "How are you doing, Brother Lahai?" he greeted my father, using another version of my father's first name, "and how is my little nephew?" He turned to me with a big grin, mockingly adding, "My, have you grown!"

I realized that this must be Fritz, my father's baby brother and, although six months my junior, my uncle, whom I hadn't seen since he and I were barely past the toddler stage in Hamburg's Johnsallee. Fritz welcomed me to Monrovia, telling me that his sisters, Fasia and Fatima, and brother, Arthur, couldn't wait to meet me. "I'll be back tomorrow after you've had some rest to take you to meet them and to show you around Monrovia," Fritz promised.

After Fritz had left, my father elaborated on the "family palaver" with some of his siblings, especially sister Fatima and brother Nat, to which he had alluded in his letter. When "the old man" (Consul-General Momolu Massaquoi) was running unsuccessfully for president, my father explained, he mortgaged his sizable properties to finance his campaign. When he died in 1938, he had left only debts behind, which, after years of hard work, my father said he had been able to pay off. "Now Fatima and Nat feel that a share of the redeemed properties belongs to them," my father complained. "They don't want to understand that our father didn't leave us anything but debts. They've been wasting a lot of their money on lawyers in order to force me to share with them what is mine. But each time we go to court and I plead my case, the judge sides with me."

My father told me that, although he and Fatima hadn't been on speaking terms, he had no objections to my visiting her. "I put no restriction on with whom you can associate," he assured me, "with one exception. There's a fellow by the name of Morris. He has told everybody that he is my son. Well, he is lying. He is no good. He'll probably approach you and tell you he's your brother. I don't want you to have anything whatsoever to do with him. If you ever decide to make common cause with that rascal, you are on your own, because I won't have anything more to do with you."

In spite of his rather harsh terms, I anticipated no problem living up to my father's condition and assured him that, as far as I was concerned, Morris didn't exist. But my father's strange demand had aroused my curiosity. "Besides claiming to be your son and being no good, what kind of a guy is this Morris fellow?"

Although obviously uncomfortable with the subject, my father told me a story that made me regard Morris in quite a different light. "If Morris weren't such a screwball, he could have been one of the most powerful men in Liberia today," my father said. "One thing I have to give to him, though, he has more guts than he has sense." He then explained that a couple of years ago, Morris had landed a job as a heavy-equipment operator on the construction site of Monrovia's harbor. When the native workers grew dissatisfied with their meager wages and grueling working conditions, they went on strike and marched en masse to the Executive Mansion to demonstrate. Worried about the prospect of social unrest and the impact of the strike on the scheduled completion date of his pet harbor project, President Tubman asked the workers to send him a representative to state their grievances. None of the workers had the courage to face the president, my father said, except Morris. "Here comes this little runt of a fellow and tells the president that he and his fellow workers won't go back to their jobs unless they get a substantial pay raise along with shorter work hours," my father recalled.

After the president promised to meet their demands, Morris persuaded the workers to return to their jobs. From then on, my father recalled, Morris was "riding high" in his chauffeured government-supplied jeep and with a government-supplied office at the port as the official representative of the workers. Had Morris taken care of business, my father said, he could have become powerful as the first organizer of a Liberian labor union. Instead, Morris "acted the fool," with nothing on his mind but chasing after women. Rather than tending to the concerns of his fellow workers, my father said, he showed up at his job only when he felt like it. One day, when on a rare occasion he did go to his office, according to my father, a delegation of workers informed Morris that he had been replaced as their spokesman. "To my knowledge," my father concluded, "he hasn't had a job since."

I realized that my father's account of Morris's fifteen minutes of fame was intended to turn me against him, but it did just the opposite. I was immensely impressed with the courage it must have taken Morris, at age twenty-six, to stand up to the most powerful man in the country.

The following morning, after another lengthy breakfast chat with my father, I went to see Dr. Titus, a handsome, middle-aged Haitian. He told me that we were soon to be related, for he was all set to marry a cousin of mine, Emma Shannon, daughter of Supreme Court Justice Eugene Shannon, who everyone in Monrovia knew was Momolu's illegitimate son. After giving me a complete physical, he advised how best to survive in the tropics and prescribed a daily dosage of atabrine antimalaria pills, which were more effective than the old quinine pills.

That evening, my father took me for a ride through Monrovia. After we made the rounds of several nightspots where he introduced me to some of his male and female friends, I told him that I was beginning to see a big problem.

"What kind of problem?" he asked solicitously.

Reluctantly I told him that I hadn't seen a single woman in Liberia who appealed to me. "How can I live in a country that doesn't have any women I like?"

My father laughed when he heard that. "If that's all that's bothering you, forget it," he counseled. "I felt exactly the same way when I first arrived in Germany." None of the women he saw looked beautiful to him, he said, but if I needed proof that he got over his "visual prejudice," he suggested I take a look in the mirror. "After a few weeks, your perception, and with it your beauty standards, changes," he assured me. "Just be patient." It didn't take me long to discover that, at least in this instance, Father knew best.

Following our little man-to-man chat, we decided to call it a night. When my father got behind the wheel of his brand-new twelve-cylinder Lincoln sedan, he was approached on the driver's side by a man. Without uttering a word, the man reached through the open window and slapped my father's face. That was all I needed to see. Enraged by the unprovoked act, I jumped out of the car and confronted my father's assailant. With a combination of well-aimed head punches that would have done me proud during my amateur boxing days, I knocked the attacker to the ground. "You've been messing with the wrong guy," I heard myself growl. "The next time you feel like messing with my father, come mess with me." Instead of trying to even the score after getting back on his feet, the assailant took flight as fast as his wobbly legs would carry him, then shouted obscenities from a safe distance.

Although the incident lasted but a few minutes, it attracted a small crowd of curious onlookers. "Get in the car and let's get out of here!" my father shouted.

As we sped away, I felt proud of myself and glad I had an opportunity to demonstrate to my father my loyalty and readiness to face danger in his behalf. But instead of thanking—not to mention praising—me for coming to his defense, he berated me, telling me that I overreacted and that my action could cost him a lot of money if the fellow decided to sue. I was crushed.

The following day, as he had promised, Fritz stopped by to pick me up for a reunion with Aunt Fatima and Aunt Fasia, both of whom were still living with Ma Rachel, Momolu's widow and the Massaquoi matriarch. Aunt Fatima, who had recently returned from years of studies and teaching at Fisk University in Tennessee, was now a full professor at Monrovia's College of Liberia, where she taught most of the sciences known to man. She had hardly changed since I last saw her in Germany shortly before the outbreak of World War II. Neither had Ma Rachel, who still looked the same except for a few extra pounds on her never-skinny frame and considerably more gray in her hair.

Also on hand to welcome me was Arthur, my uncle and playmate from our childhood days on Johnsallee. Now Liberia's influential and affluent director of mines and natural resources, Arthur, a graduate of the Colorado School of Mines, presented the biggest visual surprise to me. He had ballooned to over three hundred pounds. Also beyond recognition was my youngest aunt, Fasia. The tiny tot in diapers had grown into an attractive young lady of twenty. I met Uncle Abraham, a high official at the agriculture department and future head of Liberia's Maritime Commission, which licenses a large portion of the world's oil-tanker fleet.

When all of my relatives had their turn hugging and welcoming me, Aunt Fatima announced that she had a surprise for me. Leaving the room momentarily, she returned leading a short, skinny young man by the hand. For a moment I thought my eyes were playing tricks on me as I looked into the rejuvenated face of my father. "This is your brother Morris," Aunt Fatima announced, "and this, Morris, is your brother Hans." As we shook hands, I took a closer look at Morris. In spite of what my father had told me, there wasn't the slightest doubt in my mind that this fellow who walked and talked like my father and who had my father's face was indeed his son and my brother. Consequently, I knew what my attitude toward Morris should be.

"Do you know that on account of you I almost landed in jail?" Morris wanted to know. He explained that the previous night he had been aroused from sleep by police. They ordered him to get dressed and took him to the police station, where they confronted him with a man with a bloody mouth, who had complained that the son of Al-Haj Massaquoi had knocked out one of his teeth. "That's not him," the man told the officers after taking one look at Morris. "The one who did it was taller and lighter; he looked and talked like an American."

Morris said that all of a sudden it dawned on him that the man the police were looking for must be his brother from Germany. "I had heard that you had arrived in Monrovia," Morris said, "but I didn't let on that I knew who you were and where to find you."

"Sorry about that," I told Morris, after explaining to him what had happened and why I had become physical. "I guess I owe you one." Although my father had told me only negative things about Morris, I immediately liked him. During the afternoon, as he told me the story of his life, I was glad that my boyhood wish of having a big brother had finally been fulfilled.

Morris told me that he was born in a hut on the outskirts of Monrovia. His mother was a native woman from the Kru tribe who never learned to read or write and who died when he was still a boy. Before she died, she told him that his father was a rich Vai man by the name of Al-Haj Massaquoi who lived in a big house on Water Street. Since an older aunt who "inherited" him had no use for a ten-year-old boy, she "gave" him as a houseboy to an Americo-Liberian couple named Williams. They named him Morris Williams, sent him to a missionary school, and all but formally adopted him. When he was in his teens, Morris said, he went to the big house on Water Street that his mother had told him about and presented himself to Mr. Al-Haj Massaquoi as his loving son. "The old man wanted no part of me and told me to get lost." Instead, Morris continued, he went to all the other members of the Massaquoi clan and told them who his daddy was. He said they took only one look at him and told him, "Say no more; we know who your daddy is." After welcoming him into the fold, he said, they told him not to let his "crazy daddy" upset him and that sooner or later, he'd come around. Morris said he made it a habit to drop by our father's house at least once a week and wish him a cheerful "Good morning, Pa" or "Is there anything you want me to do for you, Pa?" Eventually, his persistence paid off. One day, to Morris's surprise, our father gave him an errand to run. From that time on, he said, "the old man" gave him more and more things to do until, for all practical purposes, he was working for him. They got along so well, Morris recalled, that when he dropped the name Williams and substituted it with Massaquoi, our father not only didn't mind, he himself began to refer to Morris as "son."

When I asked him why the relationship went sour, Morris mumbled something about "some woman palaver." When I pressed him for details, he at first refused, but then told me, "What the hell, you might as well know."

According to Morris, our father had sent him on an extremely delicate mission, which involved fetching a young Kru woman he intended to "court" from her village in Liberia's interior. To facilitate the mission, which was to take less than a day, and to impress the young lady, our father let Morris drive his brand-new American luxury car.

Morris claimed that he had every intention of carrying out the mission faithfully and expeditiously, but when he saw the comely Kru maiden, he was so smitten that he decided to win her for himself. Since he spoke Kru fluently and our father didn't, he said, that was easy.

A week later, our father found his car, minus Morris and the Kru maiden, dirty and with an empty gas tank parked in front of his house. He let it be known throughout the Republic of Liberia and beyond that "that damn Kru rascal" who called himself Morris Massaquoi was not his son. Morris said that it took months before he dared to face our father, but that when he finally did, "the old man called me every kind of sonofabitch he could think of and told me to keep away from him for good. That was about four years ago," Morris explained, "and I've stayed away from him ever since."

Morris concluded his story with a mischievous grin that showed everything but remorse. "I guess the old man told you not to have anything to do with 'that damn rascal Morris,'" my brother said, aping our father's British accent.

"Can you blame him?" I shot back. "That was a rotten thing to do."

Morris agreed, still without showing any remorse. "I figured one week of fun with his car and girlfriend wasn't too high a price to pay for all the years he neglected my mother and me," Morris reasoned. Thinking of the hardships my mother and I endured in Germany, I decided that Morris definitely had a point.

We agreed to keep in touch, but secretly, so as not to jeopardize my position. I had no doubt that our father would pull the rug from under me if I made "common cause" with Morris. To facilitate our future secret meetings, we enlisted Fritz as our go-between. I felt terribly guilty for having to deceive my father in this way, but the alternative of shutting my own brother out of my life seemed even less acceptable.

When I returned home from my visit with my family, my father informed me that the police had been looking for me. "Don't worry," he added, when he saw my anxiety. "I took care of it." He then explained that two policemen and the man whom I had beaten up the night before had come by to talk to me. "The man claimed you knocked his tooth out. I knew what they wanted, so I paid them some money and told them to forget the whole thing." He then added, "In the future, don't be so hasty with your fists, or I'll wind up in the poorhouse."

"Right," I thought, having just learned from my relatives that my poor-mouthing father was not only the owner of a most lucrative steamship agency, he was also the sole importer of Danish Tuborg beer, one of the country's most popular brands. I didn't let on that I had already heard about the knocked-out-tooth story from Morris. Instead, I apologized to my father for having caused him such inconvenience, but my heart wasn't fully in my apology. I still felt that he should have been more appreciative of my coming to his defense and resolved that the next time he got into similar trouble, he would be on his own. When I asked my father what the attack had been all about, he explained that the attacker had once worked for him and claimed that he was owed some back pay. "He was mistaken," said my father, "but I paid him what he asked for, just to get him off my back."

MEETING THE PRESIDENT

Looking unusually pleased, my father informed me that his friend President Tubman had invited us to come to the Executive Mansion because he wanted to meet me. At first I was elated about being the subject of such a high honor, but as the Sunday of the meeting drew near, I came down with a serious case of the jitters. "What am I supposed to say when I meet the president?" I asked my father. "I've never met a president in my life."

"Don't worry," he counseled. "The president is not going to bite you. All you need to remember is to speak only when spoken to, and always to say 'Yes, sir' and 'No, sir,' instead of just 'yes' and 'no.' Otherwise, just be yourself."

On the day of the appointment, armed with that piece of paternal wisdom, my hair freshly cut, and dressed in pristine tropical white, I accompanied my father to the Executive Mansion, my growing anxiety giving way to full-blown panic. I still hoped that the president would send a message calling the whole damn thing off. But no such luck. Precisely at 4 P.M., my father informed a uniformed presidential guard of our arrival. Within minutes, we were greeted by the president's bespectacled aide-de-camp, Colonel Alexander Brewer, who led us to a spacious veranda on the second floor where the president was in the midst of an animated conversation with two white gentlemen. When he saw my father, he got up from his chair, grasped my father's outstretched right hand, and snapped interlocking fingers and thumbs in Liberia's traditional salute. "I'm so glad you could make it, Mass," said the president, then, turning to me, he shook my hand with the same enthusiasm while gazing at me with eyes that seemed to penetrate my soul. "This must be the young man we've heard so much about. I can see, Mass, that you didn't waste your time while in Germany," the president cracked, with a sly wink at my father.

"I can't say I did, Mr. President," my father agreed.

After introducing us to his other two guests, a captain of the U.S. Navy in charge of the construction of Monrovia Harbor and a young Ivy League–type American businessman by the name of Stettinius, the president invited us to be seated. Lighting a huge Havana cigar, he resumed the conversation, mostly about subjects that were miles above my head. When a butler offered me a cigar and a glass of Vat 69 Gold, the president's favorite scotch, I had sense enough to turn down both offers. As much as I wanted to appear sophisticated and debonair, my instincts told me that since I had never tried my hand at drinking whiskey or smoking cigars, this was not the place to start practicing. It bothered me, however, to see that the Stettinius fellow, who seemed hardly much older than I, was conversant in topics such as the U.S.'s financing of the multimillion-dollar Monrovia port project, the gold standard, and Soviet Russia's intentions since the end of the war. I, on the other hand, had never given as much as a single thought to these matters. In addition, I noticed with envy that the young businessman was a poised whiskey drinker and cigar smoker to boot.

I felt like a mule among thoroughbreds. Painfully aware that my education was woefully lacking, I resolved that afternoon to do whatever was necessary to correct this deficiency. Just as I resigned myself to sitting out the afternoon on the sidelines in embarrassed silence, President Tubman came to my rescue. "Now let's hear from young Massaquoi, who has just arrived from Germany after spending the war years over there," he broke the ice. "I understand you lived in Hamburg. How in the world did you survive the bombing raids?"

Suddenly, I was given an opportunity to talk about a topic I knew more about than anyone present. Within minutes, I had the president and his guests at rapt attention as I related some of my experiences during the British and American air attacks. Occasionally, my listeners interrupted me with questions about certain details. When President Tubman asked at what point the German people realized that the war was lost, I answered him that it depended entirely on which Germans we were talking about. Die-hard followers of Hitler didn't believe in an Allied victory until Allied troops actually marched through Germany's streets, I explained, while Germans opposed to Hitler predicted a German defeat from the very outset of the war.

"Very interesting," the president commented. "You are a lucky fellow to have come out of all this alive and without a scratch." At the conclusion of the afternoon visit, the president thanked my father for bringing me. "Mass, you have to promise me to bring your son back soon so he can tell us more about his interesting experiences during the war."

"I certainly will, Mr. President. I certainly will," promised my father, his chest swelling with unmistakable fatherly pride.

As we were driving home, my father congratulated me on the way I had conducted myself and told me that he was proud of me. "By the way, that young man we met at the Executive Mansion is the son of former U.S. Secretary of State Edward Stettinius, a multimillionaire industrialist." When I confessed that I had felt woefully ill-prepared, mainly because of young Stettinius's polish, my father promised to help me make up for my educational deficiencies by having me attend college, perhaps in the United States. His words were music to my ears, and I intended to do everything I could to earn his continued support and trust.

Shortly after our meeting with the president, my father had another event planned for me. "It's about time that you meet our people," he announced, "so next Sunday, I will take you to Vai Town." Vai Town, he explained, was the small settlement of thatch-roofed clay huts we had passed many times. It was scenically located on a stretch of Atlantic Ocean beach a ten-minute drive outside Monrovia. The real homeland of the Vai people, my father added, of which his father had once been king, straddled Liberia and the British colony Sierra Leone.

I had never been too crazy about meeting "our people," if by "our people" my father meant people who lived in clay huts instead of homes with indoor plumbing. "Our people," in my book, were people like Aunt Fatima, Fritz and Arthur, and my grandfather Momolu, not people who could not read or write. Because of my European upbringing, most of it during the racist Nazi era, my regard for "primitive natives" was woefully lacking.

When my father and I drove up to the town, we were greeted by deafening drums, men and women in colorful robes, and potbellied children with broad smiles and shaven heads. Obviously, we had not arrived unannounced. As we slowly made our way through the crowd, the people were reaching out to shake our hands.

At the center of town, we were greeted by the settlement's chieftain, a grizzled man in an immaculate white robe and a gold-embroidered black cap. He invited us into his large thatch-roofed meeting hall and motioned us to be seated on two richly carved wooden stools beside him and in front of a semicircle of seated elders. The chieftain gave a lengthy address in Vai, during which, I was told later, he paid homage to my grandfather and father and welcomed me "home." My father responded briefly, also in Vai. We then were served a milky beverage called palm wine and large chunks of corn bread. This was followed by a seemingly endless procession of men and women who filed past us, shaking our hands while wishing us a long life and happiness. It was almost dark when the last person shook our hands and the chieftain and several elders accompanied us to our car. As we drove away, the sound of the drums followed us even after Vai Town was out of sight. Although I hadn't understood a single word that had been spoken, I had felt the sincerity of the speakers. Listening to the drums, and recalling the massive outpouring of love and devotion from Vai Town's humble people—our people—I suddenly felt a deep sense of appreciation and pride about my Vai heritage.

Despite my father's low opinion of "American Negroes," who, he felt, looked down on Africans, he accepted an invitation for us to attend a social gathering at the home of a high-ranking official at the U.S. Embassy, which was almost exclusively staffed by black Americans. From the moment we arrived, it became clear to me that my previous social experiences with Americans, which were limited to merchant marine seamen and GIs, were of absolutely no use in this new environment. If anything, they were counterproductive. The black embassy staffers were a far cry from the uninhibited, jive-talking, zoot-suit-wearing hipsters I had hung out with on Hamburg's waterfront and whom I had tried my level best to emulate. Without exception, the embassy folks were refined, articulate, conservatively dressed, and college-educated.

To get by in this sophisticated milieu without making an absolute fool of myself called for quick adjustment. Remembering my visit with President Tubman, I resolved to be a good listener and to open my mouth only when I thought I knew what I was talking about. Before long, I was mixing with the guests with appreciable ease, exchanging how-do-you-dos and I'm-so-very-pleased-to-meet-yous as if I had graduated *summa cum laude* from a charm school.

Since virtually all the black Americans I had met before had been male, I was pleased to discover what to me was an entirely new species—black American women. Most were embassy employees and embassy wives. Besides being refined, sophisticated, and impeccably groomed, I found many of them extremely pleasing to the eye. Thus, with only a little encouragement from my father, I took to the dance floor, where, to the strains of a piano and the delight of my partners, I managed to reenact some of the fanciest steps I had learned at Herr Lucas's dance classes in wartime Barmbek.

Attracted by the beautiful piano playing, I joined some guests who had gathered around the player and were singing along to some of the most popular American hit tunes of the time. The musician, to my surprise, was a blind man, who, someone explained to me, was a Liberian music professor known far and wide as Prof Hayes. While I got caught up in the sing-along, my father tapped me on my shoulder and told me that he had to leave in order to take care of "some urgent business" and promised to return shortly. "Just go on having fun," he urged. I had no problem with that.

When he returned a short while later, he handed me my saxophone case. "Show them what you can do," he urged. "I know Prof Hayes won't mind."

Since a few glasses of wine had wiped out any inhibitions I might have had, I gladly complied. Within minutes my alto sound blended seamlessly with Prof Hayes's rendition of "Till the End of Time." After his initial surprise, a broad smile on the face of the blind musician let me know that he thoroughly approved of my collaboration. At the end of the tune, while the guests were applauding and calling for an encore, Prof Hayes got up from his seat and gave me an enthusiastic hug.

That evening I made another new friend, Vice Consul Charles Hanson from New York, a horn-rimmed six-footer with degrees from Harvard and

Yale and a genuine appreciation for all people. "Come and see me at the embassy after work hours any time you feel like it," the thirty-something bachelor told me. "Perhaps you can help me polish up my German, which is getting mighty rusty."

I told him that we had a deal if he would help me spruce up my English.

My father, who had been strutting about all evening like a peacock with a that's-my-boy kind of attitude, assured me that I had done well and again told me that he was proud of me. There was nothing I enjoyed hearing more.

Most of my "normal" days in my new environment started around 8 A.M., when my father and I would meet for a light breakfast consisting of toast, some fruit, and tea. Freshly out of the shower, still dressed in his bathrobe and slippers, my father would pace the floor between sips of tea and puffs on his cigarette while expounding on just about every subject under the sun. It was during these daily breakfast talks that we came as close to father-and-son bonding as we ever would. Grinning mischievously, he would tell me all about his ongoing legal skirmishes with his brother Nat, whom he called the brain trust of the family's rebellion against him. "They have gotten nowhere so far," he explained, "and now that you are here, they are beginning to realize that they'll never get their hands on my money."

He often regaled me with stories of his days as a student in England and Ireland. He never tired of showing me an old and brittle newspaper clipping with a photo that showed him, "Prince Al-Haj," seated beside Edward, Prince of Wales and future king, at a dinner in Buckingham Palace. He also delighted in informing me that it was he who brought the first automobile, a Mercedes-Benz, to Liberia, sometime during the early twenties, long before there were paved roads.

"Too bad that your grandfather is no longer with us to see what has become of you," he would say, then give me a detailed account of his father's distinguished life. Unlike other Vai children, Momolu was required to begin the study of Vai early, my father explained. By the time he was eight years old, he had mastered the Vai's sophisticated, self-developed system of writing, whose alphabet of more than one hundred characters sets the Vais apart from the vast majority of analphabetic African tribes. His royal Muslim parents placed him under the tutelage of a Mohammedan priest to receive instruction in the Koran. Two years later, at age ten, he was sent to St. John's Episcopal School at Cape Mount, to learn English. While under the influence of his Christian tutors for several years, Momolu adopted the Christian faith and was baptized and confirmed. At age sixteen, in 1888, the precocious boy was sent to the United States, where he enrolled as a freshman at Central Tennessee College in Nashville. The sudden deaths of his mother in 1892 and his father four years later put him in line for the leadership of the Vais, but he declined and instead became principal of his alma mater, St. John's Episcopal School. After six years in that post, he finally accepted the kingship, and in a spectacular ceremony attended by indigenous dignitaries and British colonial officials, he was crowned King Momolu IV, then set up court in the Vai territory, an area about three hundred miles long and two hundred miles wide, extending along the Atlantic seaboard from Gallinas in Sierra Leone to Cape Mount in his native Liberia. Eventually, my father concluded, intratribal quarrels instigated by the intrigues of British colonials who feared the rise of a strong, charismatic, and educated indigenous leader undermined Momolu's reign and caused him to abdicate in favor of a less-effective cousin.

To reciprocate, I described my mother's and my survival of the Nazi persecution and the war. He never tired of hearing these stories.

During our daily discussions, which were more like liberal-arts lectures that ranged from the judicial concept of habeas corpus to Mendel's laws of heredity, I learned to respect his formidable intellect and breadth of knowledge. I also began to detect a likable side in him that had escaped me earlier. At the same time I became increasingly aware of his many foibles. When it came to his religious beliefs, it appeared that he hadn't quite made up his mind whether to call himself a Christian, a Muslim, or what, and nimbly quoted from either the Bible or the Koran, depending on which came closer to supporting his argument. He was consistent, however, in three areas: his contempt for "American Negroes" (from which his close friend the former U.S. Minister Plenipotentiary William P. Lanier was exempted); his disdain for a career in government (triggered, no doubt, by the misfortunes his father encountered as a longtime member of the Liberian government); and his worship of President Tubman, whom he quoted at every opportunity. "White or black," he would say, "Tubman is the greatest statesman alive, barring none." He would back up his statement by explaining the two major measures on which President Tubman had staked his administration and which, my father claimed, had yanked Liberia out of its antebellum existence into the twentieth century: Tubman's Open Door Policy opened the country to foreign investment and his Unification Policy brought tribal people, who had been intentionally isolated and kept ignorant by the ruling Americo-Liberians, into the political life of the country.

My father had another good reason to feel favorably toward the president. Under the previous administration of President Edwin Barclay, he and the rest of the Massaquois had been down and out. Tubman, who became president in 1944, turned things around for the Massaquois. Reversing Barclay's policy of neutrality toward Germany and declaring war on the Nazi state, he sent German diplomats and residents in Liberia packing, then made my father the sole executor of the sizable holdings the Germans were forced to leave behind. As executor of the confiscated property, my father's task included inventorying all German assets, office buildings—including an entire legation—homes, yachts, and warehouses stacked with goods, then selling them for the government, primarily to wealthy foreign and Liberian businessmen, for a handsome commission of ten percent. The resulting windfall was sufficient to put my father back on his feet and enable him to redeem the various properties Momolu had mortgaged before his death. They included numerous rented-out houses in and around Monrovia and considerable tracts of land. "Very soon," my father promised, "I shall take you around and show you what will one day be yours."

Despite my father's affluence, he was a workaholic who toiled single-mindedly from the moment he went down to his office at 9 A.M sharp until late at night. The only diversion in which he indulged himself was attending weekly meetings at the exclusive seaside SAC (Saturday Afternoon Club) Pavilion, where President Tubman and his all-male inner circle would socialize with the help of fine brandy, fine whiskey, and fine cigars.

ADJUSTING

My father repeatedly expressed hope that my arrival in Monrovia would make it possible for him one day to take things a bit easier and even enable him to take a vacation for a change. He wanted to pay a long-overdue visit to his aged mother in Lagos, Nigeria, whom he hadn't seen for many years. After divorcing Momolu long before I was born, my grandmother had moved to the British colony, where she married a Mr. Sonii, a Liberian-born foreman at a Lagos shipyard. "I have promised your grandmother that I will send you as soon as you get settled a bit. She can hardly wait to see you."

All that sounded interesting and exciting to me, but it didn't help my present situation much. Each morning, I dreaded the moment when my father would go downstairs to his office, leaving me to figure out how to stay occupied the rest of the day.

To keep from getting bored, I usually took long walks along Monrovia's bustling waterfront or hung out with Fritz and his pals, all of them sons and daughters of Monrovia's Americo-Liberian elite. They included Sewell Brewer, son of President Tubman's top military aide; his cousin Herbert Brewer, whose father was the Liberian ambassador to Paris; Calista Dennis, niece of Liberian Secretary of State Gabriel Dennis; and other similarly privileged characters. All of them were graduates of or students at the College of West Africa, a high school–level institution, and slated to study at various colleges or universities in the United States on Liberian government scholarships. After they had earned their degrees and returned home, each was assured a high position in the Liberian government. Fritz was scheduled to leave shortly for the United States to study dairy farming at the University of Iowa. Somehow, I couldn't imagine fastidious Fritz coming within miles of a cow, to say nothing of milking one.

The group's constant chatter about proms and debutante balls didn't interest me, but I envied their carefree life. They made me realize how much of my own youth I had lost struggling to merely survive. I also envied the way their careers, and often their future marriages, had been carefully arranged by their families while I had to keep flying by the seat of my pants.

It was clear to me that without formal training I would never amount to anything in status-conscious Liberia, but whenever I broached the subject with my father, he became evasive and told me to be patient.

I also spent considerable time pounding a manual typewriter, for the dual purpose of improving my typing speed in preparation for joining my father's business and to keep my mother, Inge, and others abreast of how I was making out. My mother wrote that shortly after I left Hamburg, the highly inflated Deutsche Reichsmark was declared worthless. In its place a new currency, called the Deutschmark, was introduced and everyone received forty D marks with which to sink or swim. Overnight, shops that had been chronically empty were suddenly stocked to the ceilings with all types of "scarce" merchandise that she had not seen since the outbreak of the war. Her letter ended on an optimistic note, expressing her confidence that the worst seemed finally over in Germany and her hope that I would like Liberia so that we could be reunited soon.

Inge wrote that she and my mother had hit it off unusually well and were spending much of their free time together, attending movies and talking about (who else?) me. Inge promised that there was no way in the world she would ever even as much as look at another man and wanted to know what Liberia was like, especially Liberian women. My immediate response to her question was a sincere, "Stop worrying about Liberian girls. They're simply not my type."

It took a while, but as my father had predicted, slowly but surely something in my perception changed. Before I had become fully aware of it, some Liberian girls started to look rather enticing.

Morris for some time had been teasing me to get serious and test the waters. He said that as far as my social life was concerned, I should leave everything to him. He already knew several young ladies who were interested in making my acquaintance. The more I said that I wasn't quite ready, the more he praised the virtues of his female friends. One of them, he explained, was especially eager to meet me. He said she was the girlfriend of a very influential married Liberian who visited her maybe once a month. "But as you can imagine," Morris added, "once a month doesn't cut it."

When I kept pressing him to tell me who her boyfriend was, he finally told me that it was the president.

"Are you crazy or something, trying to get me hooked up with one of the president's old ladies?" I replied. "If he finds out, he'll have me assassinated."

Morris tried to assure me that the president wouldn't find out, and even if he did, he wouldn't care. "He keeps women all over the country and has a hard time getting around to them on a regular basis," Morris argued. "Why don't you just come along and meet her? She lives only a couple of blocks from here."

Morris was delighted when I ignored my better judgment and let him talk me into meeting his friend. "Strictly to say hello," I admonished.

When we arrived at the lady's house, I saw an ample-bosomed, bathrobe-clad woman leaning over the banister of her second-floor veranda.

"That's her," whispered Morris.

"Is that your little brother, Morris?" asked the woman, with a childlike, coquettish voice.

"Yeah, that's my baby brother from Germany," Morris replied.

"Why don't you come up and let me meet him?" she suggested.

After joining the woman on her veranda, I noticed her truly beautiful face but also that, to me, she was at least forty pounds overweight. "Too bad," I thought, because without the extra weight she had real possibilities.

Another turnoff for me was a life-size photograph of a stern-faced President Tubman that dominated the living room. It served me as a grim reminder that I was over my head and living dangerously.

Morris introduced Eva and me.

"You didn't tell me that your brother is almost a head taller than you," the woman chided Morris. She then disappeared into her kitchen to fetch us something cold to drink. Morris muttered something about having left his wallet somewhere and, before I could stop him, spun around and rushed down the stairs and out of the house. "Don't go anywhere. I'll be right back," he hollered from the street, then disappeared around the corner. I was certain that I had seen the last of Morris that day.

I vowed to get even with Morris for getting me into a jam like this. While the woman and I made small talk, I wracked my brain to come up with an excuse for following Morris out the door, but nothing plausible came to my mind. Meanwhile, my accommodating hostess was plying me with glass after glass of spiked punch. When I complained that I was feeling excessively hot, she suggested that I take a refreshing bath. After another glass of punch, that suggestion made a lot of sense to me, and without giving the matter any further thought, I was soon luxuriating in a tub of refreshing lukewarm water. As Eva was leaning on the floor beside the tub to wipe perspiration from my face with a towel, her bathrobe came open at the front, revealing an expanse of smooth brown skin that, at least for the moment, totally changed my mind about overweight women.

When, a few hours later, I walked into the bright street, literally punch drunk and physically drained, my anger at Morris had completely disappeared.

But even Morris's tireless efforts toward enlivening my social life could not keep me from craving a more purposeful lifestyle. When I complained one day to my father that boredom was killing me and asked him to give me something constructive to do, he became agitated. "This is Africa, not Europe," he lectured me. "People here take their time. You barely got here and want to become rich overnight. That's not the way we do things here."

I hadn't said anything about wanting to get rich overnight, but endured his lecture without argument. A few days later, he took me to a nearby warehouse crammed with what looked to me like junk. In one corner were a dozen or so large, dusty commercial scales, the kind used to weigh sacks of produce. "This used to be a German warehouse," my father explained, "and these metric scales were left here by German businessmen during the war. They seem in pretty bad shape, but if you think you can fix them, you've got yourself a job."

After a brief inspection of some of the rusty scales, I told him that I thought I could put them back in working condition.

In good repair, my father explained, each of the scales would be worth about $50. "I'll make you a deal," he said. "I'll hire a couple of helpers for you. If you repair the scales, I'll sell them for you and we'll share the proceeds fifty-fifty." Quickly figuring that I stood to make about three hundred bucks, I eagerly agreed.

One early morning, after I had selected some tools from my father's garage, I went to work on my new project with my newly hired two-man crew. I hadn't felt as good in weeks. All of a sudden I felt useful again. It amazed me how a few rusty scales could restore my sense of purpose, which

I had lost completely during my idle existence since my arrival. So with considerable enthusiasm, I threw myself into the task at hand.

My two helpers, both barefoot and about my age, told me they belonged to the Bassa tribe. What they lacked in mechanical expertise they made up with their quick grasp and eagerness to please me. After I carefully explained to each his task, they went about their jobs chanting cheerfully and with total disregard of the stifling heat and the dust churned up by the work.

Each noon, in keeping with a custom I had observed since I joined the workforce as a machinist apprentice at age fourteen, I told my helpers to take an hourlong break while I joined my father for lunch. A week or so into the project, my father inquired about the work. "Take a look," I invited him, proud to be able to show some progress. As we walked into the warehouse, my helpers were sitting on crates while eating their meager lunch, consisting of raw cassava roots.

"What's going on here?" my father demanded, pointing at my helpers. At first, neither the men nor I understood what he was getting at until he told them harshly, "Get back to work!" Without betraying the slightest displeasure, the men immediately resumed their work. When I tried to explain to my father that, on my instruction, the men were still on their well-deserved lunch break, he took me outside the warehouse and treated me to a long lecture about the way things were done in Africa as opposed to the European way. "These people don't know anything about lunch hour," he insisted with a perfectly straight face. "You are confusing them by introducing them to highfalutin' foreign ideas. I am paying them good money to work—not to take lunch breaks."

I thought it inconceivable that "these people" didn't know anything about lunch hours when every day they saw their rich bosses take noon breaks. When I confronted my father with my logic during one of our subsequent breakfast chats and suggested that perhaps he feared that after being "confused" by me, others might insist on taking a lunch break, he got angry. "You just don't understand Africa and how things are done here," he told me, "so stop meddling." I thought I understood very well, but kept my mouth shut for peace's sake. Later, I asked my helpers how much they were getting paid. They told me that their daily wage was twenty-five cents, at the time the price of a pack of cigarettes. Recalling this episode some three decades later, I was hardly surprised to learn of Sergeant Samuel Doe's bloody 1980 revolution against the ruling Americo-Liberians.

After three weeks of steady work, my helpers and I finished the job. Before we parted, I told them to look me up discreetly in about a month so that I could pay them a bonus once I had gotten my share of the proceeds from the sale of the scales. Perhaps they didn't believe me, because they never took me up on my word and I never saw either of them again.

My father was duly impressed when I showed him a dozen gleaming and freshly painted scales. After testing the scales' accuracy with some standardized weights, he pronounced me a mechanical genius and told me that he already had buyers lined up. A few days later he handed me thirty ten-dollar bills, the first money I had earned since I left Germany.

A WEDDING

News of an upcoming event hit my father like a hurricane. Fatima had announced her betrothal and impending marriage to an electrician from British-ruled Freetown, Sierra Leone. While the rest of the Massaquois weren't exactly overjoyed by what all considered a monumental mismatch, they gradually adjusted to the idea and went on with their lives. My father, on the other hand, regarded the impending marriage as one of the big disappointments of his life. Although not on speaking terms with Fatima because of the "inheritance palaver," he was quite proud of her scholarly achievements and often bragged about his "brilliant baby sister." As the oldest son of Momolu and titular head of the Massaquoi family, he felt entitled to have a say-so in his younger sister's choice of a spouse. He might have forgiven her not consulting him, which he viewed as an act of defiance, had she chosen to marry someone he considered worthy. To him, the man she chose, "a bloody bushman with a slave name, Freeman," was at best a joke and at worst an insult to him. In his elitist view, Fatima had disgraced the family and the memory of their father, Momolu.

Fully aware of her brother's sentiments, Fatima went ahead with her wedding plans anyway. The wedding coincided with Liberia's Independence

Day, July 26, 1948, which also happened to be the republic's 101st birthday. Conspicuously absent from the ceremony, my father had let it be known that he couldn't dignify such a "ridiculous spectacle" with his presence, but nevertheless had wished me a "jolly good time." Even the fact that, as a concession to her own Vai nobility's sensitivities, Fatima translated her married name into Vai and henceforth called herself Mrs. Fatima Massaquoi Fahnbulleh did not cause my father to look more favorably upon his sister's nuptials.

The church ceremony ended just in time for Fritz, Morris, and me to catch the Independence Day parade along palm-fringed Broad Street. The street was lined with spectators, some of whom, Morris explained, had come from distant villages to witness the annual event. It reminded me of my childhood and my affinity for Nazi-style parades.

The parade was led by an off-key military band, followed by a ragtag contingent of khaki-clad men with outmoded bolt-action rifles, each seemingly marching to the beat of another drummer than the one in their band. Only the saber-brandishing officers at the head of each platoon wore shoes and long pants with their ill-fitting, U.S. Army–style tunics. With undisguised pride, Morris told me that I was looking at the vaunted Liberian Frontier Force, the nation's entire military might. I was tempted to voice an unflattering comparison with Nazi and Allied military parades, but thought better of it.

The high point of the parade was a walk-by by President Tubman and his cabinet. In spite of the oppressive heat, the men were formally attired in black tailcoats, striped gray pants, and black top hats. In addition, they wore colorful silk sashes and were bedecked with decorations of glittering stones and metal, with the president being the most bedecked. Even on a formal occasion like the one at hand, the president refused to part with his beloved Havana cigar, which he held in his left hand as he waved to the cheering crowd with his right, while sending off large puffs of smoke.

Immediately trailing the president were Vice President Clarence Simpson and Secretary of State Dennis, who, Fritz explained, were "the two most powerful men in Liberia after the president." I recalled my father telling me that both men, like the president, were old chums of his and that Secretary Dennis had personally arranged for a Liberian passport to be issued to me and sent to Hamburg. I now understood what he meant when he told me about the advantages of being a big frog in a little pond, like Liberia, versus the other way around. With chums like these, my father had to be a pretty big frog.

Before I returned home, I asked Morris whether he could help me find a job, since I was tired of loafing all day. Morris said he was "between jobs" and was looking for a job himself. "I've heard the Liberian Mining Company, a subsidiary of Republic Steel, is hiring people at their new installation in Brewerville," he told me. "If you are interested, we can apply tomorrow." I surely was interested and agreed to meet him the next day.

That evening, after I left Fatima's reception, I had to give my father a detailed account of the wedding—who was and who wasn't there and what people had been talking about.

"How did you like the parade?" he then wanted to know. Having been weaned on high-precision SS goose-stepping, I had to suppress a snide remark. But my father caught my look of condescension. "What are you looking all smug about?" he asked.

"Well, if you really want to know," I replied, bracing myself against an angry rebuttal, "I think your Frontier Force is a big joke."

Instead of getting angry, however, my father agreed with me. "I know those Frontier Force people are no soldiers," he conceded. "They were recruited straight from the bush and never received any military training worth mentioning. The president knows that. Not only that, he wants to keep it that way."

Having been raised in a country where military might was the main yardstick of national worth and prestige, I failed to understand the president's lack of military ambition until my father explained. Tubman, he said, who had seen many Latin-American leaders toppled by their generals and colonels, decided from the start of his administration that he would have the weakest military establishment of any regime—"people so incompetent and disorganized, they couldn't overthrow their own grandmas."

That explanation made sense to me and I began to look at the shrewd president with renewed respect until another question occurred to me. "What would the president do if Liberia were to be attacked from the outside?" I wanted to know.

"That's a risk," my father explained, "the president is more than willing to take, since the likelihood of such an attack by any of Liberia's three neighbors, British Sierra Leone and French Ivory Coast and Guinea, is virtually nil. Tubman knows that the borders were guaranteed by both European powers as well as the United States and that he can depend on that."

BREWERVILLE

The next morning, as soon as my father had gone down to his office, I met Morris outside the employment office of the Liberian Mining Company. After I had turned in my completed application, a blond Dutchman called me into his office. He was studying my application with great interest before telling me that on the basis of my German journeyman rating, he could offer me an excellent machinist's job for ten dollars a day. I felt as if I had hit the jackpot. With that kind of money, I could easily support myself and even send money to my mother in Germany.

After agreeing to start the following Monday, I was about to leave his office when he handed me my application and reminded me that I had neglected to indicate my nationality. "I'm Liberian," I said.

Suddenly, the Dutchman squirmed with embarrassment. Apologizing that he had acted too hastily, he said he thought I was an American citizen. "This is actually an American outfit. We have an agreement with the Liberian government that allows us to pay only so much to Liberian citizens. Because of your German background, I can make an exception and offer you five dollars a day at the very most."

I was devastated. Because of a crooked agreement the Liberian government made with foreign companies, I had to work for a fraction of the money I could have earned. But realizing that I wasn't in a bargaining position, I accepted the job in spite of my misgivings.

When I rejoined Morris, he told me gleefully that he had landed a three-dollar-a-day job as an auto mechanic, a trade he had picked up during the war while working in a GI motor pool. When he heard my story, with 20/20 hindsight, he told me that I should have lied about my nationality. He said that if foreign companies were allowed to pay higher wages, no Liberians would want to work for the slave wages paid by Liberian-owned rubber plantations and by the Liberian government. As a result, he explained, foreign companies like Firestone get away with paying only twenty-five cents a day to thousands of rubber tappers who broke their backs harvesting rubber for the American rubber millionaires.

When I told my father that I had accepted a job in Brewerville and who would be going with me, he hit the ceiling. Ranting and raving about my "act of treason," he reminded me of the *Bornholm* skipper's prophecy. "Now I know what he was talking about," he lamented. "After I send for you, and take you into my house and let you eat as if I had a meat factory, you make common cause with my enemies. That's how you repay me."

I hadn't realized that staying with my father for three months after he hadn't spent a dime on me for nearly my entire life put me that much into his debt. Nevertheless, I tried to be conciliatory and apologized for disappointing him. I tried to state what I considered a reasonable case for getting a job—so that I wouldn't have to ask him for every penny I needed in order to buy a tube of toothpaste or go to the movies, and to keep from being bored loafing all day.

I might as well have spoken to the wall, for my father didn't hear a thing I said and repeatedly accused me of betraying him.

Since Morris and I didn't have any transportation, we gladly accepted when Charles Hanson, our friend from the U.S. Embassy, offered to give us a ride to Brewerville. On the morning Charles and Morris came to pick me up, I tried to tell my father goodbye, but he was nowhere to be found. Jason confided that "Meester" had left early that morning in his car without telling anyone where he was going or when he would be back. So I left a brief note, telling him in effect that I was sorry that my taking a job was so upsetting to him, but that I couldn't stop being my own man just because I had come to Africa. I ended the letter on a conciliatory note, "I shall miss our morning chats. Take care of yourself. Love, your son Hans."

Since Charles had decided to travel the primitive bush route instead of the newly completed highway, he was driving one of the embassy jeeps rather than a sedan. As soon as Charles pulled away from my father's house, I felt as if I had been released from prison. I realized that what I had been missing was my freedom and that I had been afraid of my father, who had dominated me as if I were his property. I decided then and there never again to put myself in that predicament.

For the time being, I decided to give my adventurous nature full rein and make the best of a bad situation. My friends in Hamburg, especially Fred Gass, should see me now, I thought, as, khaki-clad and sun-helmeted, we three adventurers careened along the bumpy path, far from any discernible signs of civilization.

When I wanted to know what our chances were to encounter some lions or other local fauna, Morris told me that our chances were better than good of meeting up with a "bush cow"—Liberia's most ferocious buffalo. Just as I expressed skepticism regarding his monster cows, my brother told Charles to stop the jeep. "Take a look," Morris invited, pointing to the ground. What I saw made a believer out of me in a hurry. "Let's get out of here," I shouted after looking at the gigantic footprints and similarly gigantic droppings of what unmistakably was some kind of bovine animal.

Eventually, the winding road came to an end at the bank of a broad river. "This is it," announced Morris. "This is as far as we can go by jeep. Brewerville is just a short ways upstream on the other side."

"How do we get across?" I wondered.

"Not to worry," assured Morris. With that, he let out a piercing yell that sent flocks of colorful birds shrieking into the sky and monkeys and other creatures scrambling for safer perches in the trees. Before long a canoe with two villagers approached and pulled alongside the shore. After handing our few belongings to the two men, we thanked Charles for the ride and boarded the canoe.

"Watch out for bush cows!" I hollered at Charles, who was waving at us from the shore until we turned at a crook in the river and he disappeared from sight.

Except for the splashing of the oars, the canoe cut silently through the water. Occasionally, we passed a small village of huts in which occupants went about their simple daily chores of cleaning, pounding corn kernels into flour, baking, cooking, washing, and child-rearing, exactly the way they had done for centuries. At each village, little children waved at us and we waved back at them.

As we neared our point of disembarkation, I noticed a large, dark object floating in the river directly ahead. When I suggested to Morris that we might be headed for a capsized canoe, he grinned. "Some canoe," he quipped.

On closer inspection, the horrible truth dawned on me. What I had taken for a canoe some fifty feet in front of us turned out to be a large crocodile. My instincts told me to get the hell away from the beast that watched us lazily through two narrow slits under the lids of its bulging eyes. But instead, our canoe came to a dead stop. Morris whispered to me to be quiet and not to move. "Don't worry," Morris tried to reassure me on noticing my terror. "He won't bother us as long as we don't bother him."

Morris seemed to know what he was talking about, because "he" kept his distance and, after several more minutes of scrutinizing us closely, disappeared with an audible swoosh into the deep, murky water of the river, leaving behind a boat-size wake that made our flimsy canoe rock precariously.

I was much relieved when our canoe ride ended and we continued the final leg of our journey on foot. Within a few minutes we reached the Liberian Mining Company office, where we were assigned our living quarters and told to report for work assignment the next day. Our new home away from home consisted of a room in a wooden barracks whose only amenities were two wooden bunks, two metal lockers, and a sink with running water we were warned not to drink. Too tired to give our miserable surroundings much thought, we sacked out immediately, despite the torrid heat and the swarms of mosquitoes that kept up a constant hum about us.

The next morning, I was given an arc-welding job and Morris was assigned to the motor pool. At first I was a bit nervous, since I hadn't welded for more than three years. But after a few sputtering attempts, my hand became steady, and before long I was putting down respectable-looking seams.

Before I knew it, the first workday was over and Morris and I were back in our barren, inhospitable barracks. Just when I was about to get depressed over our shabby surroundings, Morris suggested that we forget about the squalor and check out the action in Brewerville's only tavern. He didn't have to twist my arm. The tavern was packed with people, mostly Liberian Mining Company workers like us and local women who, I surmised, were Brewerville's equivalent of Hamburg's waterfront queens. Some of the couples were dancing to the hillbilly tune, "Be Honest with Me, Girl," that was blaring from a loudspeaker. Decidedly not a fan of that particular genre of music nor of the type of available females, I politely declined when one of the young women invited me to dance. "My baby brother's just bashful," explained Morris, who shared none of my misgivings and totally misinterpreted my lack of interest. While I stood on the sidelines nursing a can of beer, Morris grabbed the hand of the girl I had rejected and in no time was on the dance floor, proving that lack of dancing talent was no obstacle to having a ball.

For the next week, the tavern became our regular and only diversion after work. We could either face the squalor of our barracks and go mad from boredom and the constant hum of mosquitoes or drown our misery with hillbilly music, beer, and the company of easy women. One night, after Morris and I turned in, I had a strange feeling of dizziness that I attributed to the long hours of welding in the heat and the possibility that I might have inhaled some of the toxic welding fumes. But when I awoke the next morning shaking uncontrollably with chills, I knew something was seriously wrong. When I told Morris how I felt, he touched my forehead and felt my pulse. "You have malaria, bro," he announced with authority, "and I've got to get you out of here right away." With that, he was out of the door and I heard him running toward the plant.

He returned a few minutes later and said that he had made arrangements for us to catch a ride on a company truck that was leaving for Monrovia within the hour. After piling several blankets on me, he told me to lie still and leave everything to him. He also assured me that this time we would travel the highway route, which did not involve crossing a river by canoe and facing crocodiles.

I slept through most of our journey and didn't fully awaken until the truck stopped in front of my father's house. After walking into the office, Morris returned with my father and Jason. I was wondering how my father would act now that I was back under his roof and depending on his hospitality, but I was much too sick to be bothered by the prospect of being at his mercy again. All I wanted was to be left alone and sleep. I remember Morris and Jason lifting me off the truck, carrying me upstairs, and, after changing me into my pajamas, putting me on my bed. "Take care, bro," I heard Morris saying. "I'll be seeing you soon."

The next thing I knew, Dr. Titus was examining me. "You've got a nasty case of malaria, son," confirmed Dr. Titus. "But don't worry. You'll be back on your feet in no time." Then, turning to my father, he said, "Make sure he drinks a lot of soda pop and regularly takes the medicine I'm leaving here."

As soon as the doctor left, my father let go with a barrage of recrimina-tions. "Do you realize that if I wanted to, I could see to it that you'll never receive a single letter from your mother again?" he snarled. It was a threat to punish me in the most cruel way his mind could conceive. Mercifully, my mind and ability to comprehend became numb and my father's voice drifted away as I fell into a deep, delicious sleep.

Jason was obliged to add nursing to his already full calendar. Whenever I awoke from my fitful sleep between bouts of chills—whether during the night or during the day—he was sitting by my bedside, dabbing my forehead with an ice-water-soaked towel or spoon-feeding me soup and making me drink soda pop and gall-bitter medicine.

One time, in the middle of the night, I was awakened by a scratching noise on the door. I asked Jason to go see what it was. Slowly the door opened a crack and I could make out a hand, then an arm. The long fingers of the hand were outstretched toward me as if about to grab me. But no person materialized. Instead, the arm grew longer and longer as the hand came closer. I had pressed myself against the headboard in order to escape the grasping fingers that seemed to reach for my throat. Just as they were about to touch me, I screamed, "Jason!"

"You okay, Meester Haans?" I heard Jason's quietly reassuring voice, and it dawned on me that my fever was playing tricks on me. A few seconds later, my father poked his head through the door, but withdrew abruptly when Jason told him that Meester Haans had a bad dream. As far as I could determine, it was the first time in several days that my father had checked on me, although I had been acutely aware of his oppressive presence through his many discourses with Jason and others beyond my bedroom door. Sud-denly, I was hit by an absurd thought. The hand that had followed me in my delirium and had threatened to strangle me, I decided, was the hand of my father.

Gradually, my fever subsided and the interludes during which I drifted away became fewer and shorter. I was still too weak to get out of bed, except for a few steps to the bathroom, but I was definitely past the critical stage of my illness. As a result, Jason stopped his round-the-clock bedside vigil and instead visited me only at intervals.

ESCAPE

I was still bedridden when I heard my father return from one of his occasional evenings on the town. But this time was different. He was accompanied by a female who was not a native Vai woman, the only kind he normally associated with. I could tell because, as the two walked up the steps and into the living room, he sounded uncharacteristically solicitous. "Can I offer you anything—perhaps some whiskey?" he asked. A female voice replied, "Whiskey and water would be lovely."

The woman spoke a cultured English that was neither Liberian nor American. Yet I could not place her rather appealing lilting accent. Finally, the woman gave me a clue when she told my father that she still felt a little homesick for Kingston. I surmised that she was one of a group of Jamaican immigrants who had recently arrived in Monrovia.

At first I felt embarrassed to be eavesdropping on my father and tried hard not to listen to their conversation. But since my father didn't make the slightest attempt to lower his voice, that became impossible. Eventually, I listened intently as the subject of my father's conversation shifted to "that damn rascal son of mine who since he arrived from Germany hasn't given me anything but trouble." He then unleashed a tirade during which he described me in very unflattering terms, starting with my "near criminal behavior" aboard the *Bornholm*. "To top it all," he concluded, "my son had the nerve to come back full of malaria and take advantage of my generosity when he was in need of food, shelter, and medical care."

By that time I had heard quite enough. This privileged life had become a private hell. My first impulse was to walk into the living room and tell my father that he could stop worrying about my being a burden to him, that I would leave in the morning, never to return. Trembling with rage and feelings of powerlessness, I decided on another course of action.

After an hour or so the two finally wound up their "date" and my father prepared to drive the woman home. As soon as I heard his car pulling away from the house, I hastily got dressed, threw my few belongings into my suitcase, and rushed downstairs past Jason, who looked dumbfounded by my hasty departure but dared not question me. I told him not to worry about me and thanked him for all his help. My plan was to go to Aunt Fatima, who lived a few blocks away, and ask her to put me up for a while until I could make other arrangements. To avoid running into my returning father, and although it was pitch black outside, I climbed the rather steep, muddy hill behind my father's house instead of taking the road. My knees were trembling, my heart was pounding, and I could literally feel sweat gushing out of my pores. I felt like fainting, but the fear that my father would catch me and somehow force me back drove me on. I knew that in my weakened condition I would have been unable to resist him. At one point I lost my grip on my suitcase and it slipped down the muddy hill, causing me to repeat part of my strenuous climb all over. It reminded me of the legendary King Sisyphus of Greek mythology, whom the gods condemned to push a huge rock to the top of a steep hill in Hades, only to have the rock slip from his grasp and roll back down the hill, forcing him to start his backbreaking labor over again. I recalled that Sisyphus, a former Mount Olympus insider, had offended the gods by cheating death, and wondered what I had done to suffer a similar fate.

After what seemed to me one of the longest foot journeys I had ever undertaken, although I had walked no more than a few blocks, I arrived at Aunt Fatima's house. Despite the late hour, she was still up taking care of her new baby daughter, named Püppchen (Little Doll) in memory of her years spent in Germany. Unable to utter a single coherent sentence, I was grateful when Aunt Fatima, after taking one look at my sweat-drenched clothes, my feverish appearance, and my suitcase, told me to go to bed and give her the details in the morning.

Despite my exhaustion, it took me a long time before I was able to fall asleep. Each time I heard a car passing, I imagined it was my father looking for me. I knew I had hit him where it hurt him the most—his pride. Monrovia was a small community, and news of my having left him was bound to travel fast and raise a lot of questions.

When I finally awoke the next day, it was past noon. I hadn't felt so good in weeks. Remembering the last twenty-four hours, I felt buoyed and invigorated, both physically and mentally, as if I had tapped into a new source of energy. All at once I felt free again—free from the oppressive dominance of a father who, although he had never supported me as a child, couldn't get it into his head that I was an adult with a mind of my own and long used to responsibility and independence.

A few days later, when I was well on my way to recovery, Aunt Fatima convened an informal Massaquoi family council in her parlor to decide on a course of action. Fatima's husband, a permanent outsider, was barred from the meeting, as he was from all Massaquoi family affairs. Uncle Nat, the architect of the family's legal war against my father, made a special trip from Bundeway, on the Firestone plantation, where he was the reigning district judge. Also present were Uncle Abraham, a high-ranking agriculture department official, and my brother, Morris. All agreed with my decision to leave my father and confided, belatedly, that they were surprised that I had been able to live with him as long as I did.

When I told them of my concern that my mother would be terribly worried once she learned that my father and I were on the outs, Uncle Abraham wrote her a detailed letter explaining that my decision to leave my father was inevitable since "Al-Haj is a man with whom nobody who has a mind of his own can get along" and that she shouldn't worry about me since the rest of the Massaquoi family would look out for me. Then Aunt Fatima suggested that I write a letter to my father explaining why I found myself unable to continue living with him. Glad to get things off my chest, I composed a letter that spelled out my hopes and dreams when I arrived in Liberia and my disappointment when I realized that he was not the wonderful father my mother had kept alive in my memory during all those years. "If you wanted me to be reared as your unquestioningly obedient son," I concluded, "you should have been there for me from the time I was a small child. Now, you are exactly twenty-two years too late." Everybody thought the letter was right on the money.

From the moment I moved in with Aunt Fatima, it was understood that the arrangement would be for only a few days, since the arrival of Püppchen had left her with little extra space. Anxious not to overstay my welcome, I accepted Morris's offer to stay at his place.

Little did I know that I was in for a gargantuan surprise. Morris's casual admission that his place wasn't much to look at was the understatement of the year. Located near the oceanfront on Camp Johnson Road, in a shantytown of clay buildings topped by corrugated metal roofs, the "place" was a one-room shack that had the audacity to boast a tiny porch with several wooden crates that, I surmised, served as patio furniture. The only window had a wooden shutter that could be placed in an open mode with the help of a wooden stick. There was no evidence of water, running or otherwise, or, for that matter, any indoor plumbing. To my mild amusement, I noticed that there was no dearth of reading material, since indoors the straw-mat walls were covered with several layers of newspapers that, on close inspection, proved several years old. The entire inventory of the room consisted of a mattress, which was covered by sheets and a GI blanket, and a battered kerosene lamp standing next to it on the concrete floor. When I asked about the dark little pellets that covered the bedsheets, the blanket, and the floor, Morris replied, rather succinctly, "Rat shit."

Morris's shack made our basement refuge in bombed-out Hamburg look inviting. I had trouble concealing my shock at the squalid conditions in which my brother had been living and shuddered at the thought of having to call this hovel my home. But I decided not to sound too negative. Besides, I had long ago learned from my mother that "in a pinch, the devil eats flies."

He explained that he had inherited the shack from his Kru mother's sister after she died a few years before, and that he only slept here "now and then." Most of the people in the area were Kru, he said, while assuring me that I would be as safe at night as if I were sleeping in Abraham's lap. "I never lock this place and nobody has ever tried to rob or bother me. It's just like with the rats—we all know and respect each other here."

I was not impressed by Morris's liberal philosophy of peaceful coexistence, especially when it came to rats.

After acquainting me with some of the shack's conveniences, such as a nearby outhouse and a hand-operated water pump, Morris told me that I was welcome to use the place any time and as long as I had a need for it. "You may even bring visitors," he added with a crooked grin.

I couldn't imagine how much pride I would have to lose to bring company to this dump, but thanked Morris for being there for me when I needed him.

My first night in my new "home" was an adventure I would never forget. Since Morris had told me he hadn't planned on coming home that night, I had intentionally arrived late in order to make my overnight stay as brief as possible. As soon as I got between the not-so-pristine sheets and blew out the kerosene lamp, all hell broke loose between the hollow straw walls. What seemed to be an army of hundreds of rats rushed above and around me in an endless chase that was punctuated by frantic squeals.

Since sleep was out of the question, I lit the lamp. As if I had uttered a magic word, the racket stopped. The only reminder of the rodents' presence was a cloud of droppings that drizzled from the ceiling. To keep the rats quiet, I decided to sleep with the lamp burning. Since I had no other alternative, I spent many a night in the company of my rodent neighbors, and eventually learned to ignore them entirely by adopting Morris's philosophy, "If you don't bother them, they won't bother you."

UNCLE NAT

Fortunately, I didn't have to depend on Morris's hospitality for long. Just as I was getting used to the rats, Uncle Nat showed up at Aunt Fatima's house and invited both Morris and me to live with him for a while on the Firestone rubber plantation. Nat promised to use his influence to help us find jobs with Liberian International Airways, an American company that flew a small fleet of DC-3s out of Robertsfield adjacent to the plantation.

It turned out that, unlike my uptight father, Uncle Nat was a lot of fun to live with. From the moment Morris and I moved into Nat's spacious bungalow on the government compound in the middle of the rubber-tree-studded plantation, he treated us more like an older brother than an uncle. Since his wife, Julia, was staying in Monrovia with their little daughter, Maria, while awaiting the arrival of another baby, Nat, an otherwise devout Catholic, celebrated his temporary bachelorhood by bedding down a young lady from a nearby village. Extramarital shenanigans, I had discovered, were a time-honored custom among Liberian men. When Nat told Morris and me that he had no objections if we, too, entertained female company, we rose to the occasion and found two attractive women who helped keep our plantation life from becoming dull.

Despite his deceptively jolly private demeanor, there was another, no-nonsense side to Uncle Nat. I discovered that side unexpectedly one morning. As we were chatting over breakfast, our conversation was interrupted by a loud scream. Looking out of the large picture window, I saw across the yard in front of the tiny jail a huge uniformed policeman bent over a cowering, shackled man on the ground, unmercifully flogging him with a long wooden cane. Uncle Nat resumed his breakfast as if nothing was happening, while both the beating and screams increased in intensity. When I asked him whether he wasn't going to put a stop to this barbaric spectacle, Uncle Nat informed me that he hadn't the slightest intention of doing so and that the prisoner whom he had sentenced to be flogged had deserved every lick he was getting and more. "Some of these natives," Uncle Nat explained, after noticing that I was visibly shaken by the morning's events, "don't respect anything but brute force because they were reared that way. Reasoning with them and telling them not to do it again would be a total waste of time."

"What about putting them in jail and letting them serve time?" I tried to argue.

"We simply don't have the resources to incarcerate thousands of lawbreakers for any length of time," Uncle Nat responded. "The best way to deal with most of the criminal elements on this plantation is to give them a good whipping that, hopefully, they won't forget very soon."

Maybe Uncle Nat had a point when he said that Liberian tribal people are reared in a brutal fashion. I recalled seeing one of Morris's aunts tie up a little boy about six years old, wash his eyes, mouth, and nose with a rag dipped in a solution of pepper, then whip him unmercifully with a stick. His crime: denying that he had embezzled a nickel, which he spit out during his ordeal.

Gradually, the screams subsided and changed to moans as the policeman finished his gruesome task. Next, he grabbed his victim and dumped him down a hole, which he covered with a wooden plank and weighed down with a heavy steel drum.

I was about to resume my argument for more lenient treatment of prisoners, but Morris gestured me to keep my mouth shut.

"Tomorrow, if you like, you and Morris can come with me to court and see what it's like," Uncle Nat suggested. "But I want you to keep in mind that this is Liberia, not Germany. We have different standards here."

We gladly accepted his invitation. As far as different standards of jurisprudence between Germany and Liberia were concerned, I recalled some of the known atrocities of Nazi justice and was convinced that Liberian jails must seem like luxury spas compared with the horror chambers of the Gestapo.

I had already learned that my uncle, as highest representative of the Liberian government on the Firestone plantation, was regarded by the thousands of plantation workers as the ultimate authority and that the awe in which he was held was not confined to blacks. White American Firestone staffers, too, had learned to respect the short, rotund man whom they called "the German judge," because he delighted in letting them know that he had received much of his legal training in pre-Nazi Germany. Unlike his predecessors, who had treated white lawbreakers on the plantation with kid gloves, Nat had built his reputation as a tough and impartial judge by being the first judge to have white troublemakers arrested and thrown in jail. Most of these cases involved the blatant mistreatment of African workers. In each such case Nat would stay incommunicado for several days, ostensibly while "visiting his farm in the country," to prevent Firestone officials from springing their wayward employees from jail by hastily making bail. Such antics had the full backing of President Tubman, who enjoyed regaling his Saturday Afternoon Club pals with the German judge's original way of dispensing justice.

The tiny courtroom next to the compound's jail was packed with villagers in native dress when Uncle Nat, followed by Morris and me, entered. A policeman serving as bailiff told the crowd to "stand up and be quiet" as Uncle Nat, dressed in a white suit, took his elevated seat on the bench and Morris and I sat down in two ringside chairs that had been reserved for us.

For the next three hours, a long procession of plaintiffs stepped forward with complaints that ranged from theft of a goat to adultery. In each case, Uncle Nat listened patiently to both sides, asked a few questions—often in country people's jargon, which he mastered to a T—then, after a brief moment of reflection, announced a verdict based mostly on common sense rather than on the written law. In the majority of cases, the verdict was a compromise aimed at satisfying both parties. An adultery case was thrown out and the husband was denied the traditional compensatory reward he had been seeking because testimony revealed that he had actually encouraged his wife to have an affair with the defendant, a plantation foreman, in order to collect damages. "This is the second time you are pulling this stunt," Uncle Nat admonished the plaintiff. "The next time you come into this court with the same story, I'll throw you in jail for pimping."

In keeping with the notoriously low plantation wages of twenty-five cents a day, the fines leveled by Nat rarely exceeded three dollars. In some cases he ordered the defendants to pay their fines in chickens or goats, or make restitution by helping a plaintiff build a new hut. I could clearly see now what Uncle Nat meant when he told me, "We have different standards here."

ROBERTSFIELD

The day following our introduction to country-style justice, Nat took Morris and me to Robertsfield for job interviews with Mat Adams, the president of Liberian International Airways. It was obvious from the start that Adams, a stocky Yankee from New York City, was less interested in obtaining Morris's and my services than in winning political brownie points. Before Morris and I had a chance to fully explain our respective qualifications as machinist and auto mechanic, he told us that we could start the following day for ten dollars a day and thanked Uncle Nat profusely for giving him a chance to be of service.

While hanging out with black sailors on Hamburg's waterfront, I had been told of the concept of "Uncle Tomming," obsequious behavior exhibited by blacks toward whites. What I had just witnessed clearly demonstrated to me that blacks had no monopoly on this sort of behavior. It occurred to me that power, not skin color, was the determining factor, and that since in Liberia blacks held the power, Tomming often became the province of whites.

Life at Robertsfield turned out much more to our liking than our wretched existence in the mosquito-infested jungle of Brewerville. Robertsfield had served U.S bombers as a base from which they launched raids on Field Marshal Rommel's Panzer units in North Africa. It was by no means the hub of world air travel, but it boasted a few amenities that were missing in Brewerville, including a small restaurant and a post office.

Morris and I were assigned to the repair shop of the airport's motor pool, headed by Mike Omsted, a forty-something California-born Swede, who had drifted on the base from who knows where. He had been hired on the spot after a day's demonstration that he knew his stuff. Mike, a lanky six-footer with long sideburns and a pockmarked face, was responsible for keeping the company's small fleet of pickups, jeeps, and sedans running. When it came to autos, he had the reputation of being a genius, capable of taking any old broken-down vehicle that had been declared dead and breathing new life into it. Even Morris, himself no mean auto mechanic, was impressed with Mike's mechanical genius.

Since new spare parts were often impossible to come by, Mike solved that problem by cannibalizing parts from some of the hundreds of vehicles the U.S. Army had left behind to rot at the edge of the airstrip when it pulled out at the end of World War II. But often Mike was stymied when he was unable to get his hands on a certain metal part. That's where I came in. Following Mike's rough sketch of the missing part, I'd put my German machinist's skill to work and usually had no problem making the part he needed. Morris, too, quickly impressed upon Mike that he knew his way around engines. It gave both of us a great deal of satisfaction to be able to demonstrate to the company's head that having hired us not only made good political sense but also good business sense.

For the most part, Morris and I were pretty satisfied with our lifestyle at Robertsfield. On weekends, we usually caught a ride to Monrovia to catch up on our social life, which, thanks to our new status as gainfully employed bachelors, was beginning to prosper. But just when we felt that things were going fine, we were rudely reminded of the precariousness of life.

The reminder came in the form of an explosion that could have crippled us for the rest of our lives. Like many times before, Morris had been trying to coax a car engine to overcome its reluctance to start by pouring a cup of gasoline down its carburetor. When, after a brief start, the engine stalled again, Morris asked me to stand by with another cup of gasoline to help him feed the carburetor and thus keep the engine running. But instead of the car starting, a huge flame burst from the carburetor that instantaneously

jumped to Morris's cup of gasoline. In an involuntary reflex action, Morris
threw the burning cup into the air, unfortunately in my direction, where it
ignited the gasoline cup I was holding. Instantly, both of our hands were in
flames like torches. Flailing our arms about in an effort to extinguish the
flames only made matters worse, and the flames grew bigger with the added
oxygen our movement supplied. After burning up all the gasoline that had
spilled on our hands, the flames died as suddenly as they had erupted. But
our ordeal had just begun. Initially numb, our hands suddenly started to
hurt with a ferocity that made us want to scream at the top of our lungs,
but we merely allowed an occasional moan as a driver from the motor pool
rushed us to the Firestone hospital. How I managed to remain conscious
during the twenty-minute ride as the pain grew more and more intense, I
shall never know.

While a Liberian nurse cleaned and bandaged our hands, a young white
American doctor administered painkillers and told us that we had been quite
lucky: we sustained only second-degree burns, which, he predicted, should
heal within two weeks, provided we didn't have any complications from
infection. After emergency treatment we were wheeled to the overcrowded,
segregated "native ward" of the hospital, where I had difficulty deciding
which was worse, the loud chatter of the patients or the smell of food and
disinfectant.

When it was time to eat and two nurses tried to feed us some ill-smelling
slop that went for food in the "native ward," both Morris and I balked.
"Tell them we can't eat this stuff," Morris told the nurses, who dutifully
took our bowls back to the kitchen. When there was no response to our
protest, we started to have second thoughts. Maybe we acted too hastily, we
speculated; perhaps bad food was preferable to no food. Eventually, a white
hospital administrator informed us that he had just received instructions to
move us to a private room. Profusely apologizing for the "mistake," he said
he would personally see to it that everything possible would be done to make
our stay at the hospital comfortable. Later, when Uncle Nat showed up to
pay us a visit, we began to understand what "mistake" the administrator
had been talking about. When we were admitted, the hospital staffers had
no idea that we were nephews of the all-powerful German judge until Uncle
Nat, having learned of our accident, telephoned the hospital to find out how
we were doing. The hospital then realized that the two emergency cases they

had put into their native ward were actually relatives of a Liberian VIP. Since at that time, even in black-ruled Liberia, it was unthinkable to put black patients in a white ward, the customary alternative was to put black VIPs into private rooms within the white ward. That was fine with us, especially since the food that was served immediately after our transfer smelled, looked, and tasted much better.

Recovering, Morris and I had ample time to reflect on our sad predicament. One minute we had felt on top of the world; the next minute we found ourselves in a substandard section of a hospital, shot full of morphine, with our arms bandaged to the elbows. Grateful for the doctor's assurance that the accident would cause no permanent damage, I decided to let bygones be bygones and not blame Morris.

For want of something better to do with our time, we cultivated the friendship of several nurses on the ward. Before long, several of them would drop in on us more frequently than their job required in order to chat and keep us company. One beautiful nurse in particular had caught Morris's and my eye. On several occasions she had let me know that she was interested in getting better acquainted. Since I knew what was on Morris's mind, I decided to beat him to the punch—a small payback, I figured, for two burned hands.

It was her duty to look in on us each night and to hand each of us two sleeping pills before turning off the lights. Each time, I'd whisper to her that as soon as my bandages were off, we'd have our date. In response, she would stroke my cheek and, with a look that seemed to promise paradise, wish me good night.

One morning, as I awoke, Morris was sitting upright in his bed across the room grinning at me from ear to ear. Suddenly it dawned on me—he had scored with the nurse while I was asleep. He gleefully confessed that it had been relatively easy. When the nurse passed out the sleeping pills, he waited until I swallowed mine while merely pretending to swallow his. After that, he said, it was literally like taking candy from a baby. All he had to do was wait till I had fallen asleep before making his move.

That interlude, which as far as Morris was concerned was supposed to have ended after our discharge from the hospital, had a more lasting effect than either of us had anticipated. Several months after we left the hospital, Morris was informed by the nurse that he was about to become a proud papa. As a sort of consolation prize to me, Morris named his firstborn son Hans, after his uncle, who had been present, albeit fast asleep, during his conception.

A few days after we had resumed working at Robertsfield, Morris informed me that he was quitting his job. He planned to appeal to President Tubman to give him a government job and urged me to come along and do the same. "I know the old man will help us if we ask him," he said. "Anyway, I'm sick and tired of this grease monkey business. This time I'll get me a real job. And I know exactly how," he told me before packing his few belongings and catching a ride to Monrovia.

Having gotten used to having a brother around, I futilely tried to change his mind, since I had no intention of giving up my job before I had found a better one.

Morris had often told me that you couldn't get ahead in Liberia unless you joined the Masons. Thus, I was not surprised to learn when he visited me several months later that he had become a Mason and that, thanks to his connections, he was rapidly rising in the Masonic hierarchy. When I asked him for details, my usually talkative brother turned uncharacteristically tight-lipped. He did tell me that he had just accidentally run into President Tubman, who, he explained, was to Liberia's Masons what the pope is to Roman Catholics. Morris said that when he shook the president's hand and gave him that secret signal that revealed his Masonic degree, the president's eyes popped. Seizing the moment, Morris then asked the president for an appointment for the following week, intending to ask the president to give him a government job.

"You can put in a word for me, too," I said, more in jest than earnest, since the last thing I could imagine was sitting behind a desk all day. Little did I realize then that there would come a time when, as a journalist, I would spend a considerable amount of time doing just that.

SAMMY

Although I wasn't making a lot of money, I was satisfied with my job, at least for the moment, because it gave me a sense of security and independence. It had even made it possible for me to hire a houseboy, a bright young fellow from the Bassa tribe by the name of Sammy. Sammy, who said he thought he was about fifteen, had knocked on my door one day and asked whether I needed someone to keep house. I told him that there really wasn't a great deal of work to be done and, more important, that I didn't earn enough money to afford hired help. Sammy said that it didn't matter how little I paid him as long as I would also "teach (him) book," meaning to read and write. I agreed to pay him five dollars a week, by prevailing Liberian standards an astronomical sum, and to teach him all the book he could absorb. In return, he would sweep my room, wash and iron what little laundry I had, and for the rest of the day sit around with his houseboy colleagues and shoot the breeze. After I'd return from work, I'd switch to my teacher's hat and, for an hour or so, help Sammy demystify the alphabet. Fortunately, he was a quick study, and although he had started from scratch, he rewarded my efforts by reading simple sentences in less than a month.

Overall, I was quite pleased with Sammy's job performance. For a guy who didn't own a watch, he was punctual like Benito Mussolini's trains, always arriving shortly before I had to leave for the shop, and in his own way he was scrupulously honest, although his definition of the word *stealing* differed somewhat from mine. Never mind that my clothes were several sizes too large for him, Sammy couldn't resist his annoying habit of "borrowing" my shirts, pants, and socks to wear on special occasions at his village and return them—ring around the collar, funk and all—the next day. No matter how often I told him that taking things that didn't belong to him was stealing, even if he intended to return them, Sammy was irresistibly drawn to my clothes. One day, when I lectured him for the umpteenth time about borrowing my things, and even threatened to fire him, he confided to me that among his peers, "white man clothes" like mine, especially long pants, were status symbols without which a man would always be treated like a "small boy."

The next time I went to Monrovia, I bought a pair of khaki slacks and a couple of shirts. "These are yours," I told Sammy, "under the condition that from now on you leave my stuff alone."

Sammy beamed like a lighthouse beacon as he changed into his new clothes and promised to mend his ways. It was the first time I had seen him in long pants; I had to agree that even without shoes, which he detested, they made him look more respectable. "I guess I'll have to call you 'Mr. Sammy' from now on," I joked. Ignoring the joke, Sammy nodded consent. So from then on, I was careful never to call him *Sammy* without the prefix.

RECONCILIATION IN THE NICK OF TIME

Since my father had not replied to my long letter of complaint, I surmised that our breakup, as far as he was concerned, was irreconcilable. Having proved to myself that I could survive in Liberia without him, I no longer feared him and his wrath. Rather, I pitied him for being such a small-minded person who lived an isolated existence, virtually without close friends or family, in his own mental prison. Eventually, I realized that perhaps I should be the one to extend the olive branch. Morris seconded the motion, and we decided to use the pending New Year's Eve as the occasion to visit our father.

When we arrived at his house, Jason let us in. "Your pa is alone. Go right upstairs." I hadn't set foot in my father's house since that fateful night seven months before, when I made my hasty getaway. "What do we have here?" Our father chuckled as he got a glimpse of us. "If it isn't my two rascal sons."

I could tell he was pleased to see us. Holding out my olive branch in the form of a bottle of good whiskey we had bought with our hard-earned money, I told him that we happened to be in the neighborhood and thought we'd drop by to wish him a happy New Year. "Let's see what kind of cheap whiskey you chaps have brought me here," he joked, in a transparent attempt to hide his emotions. Neither Morris nor I took offense, and after a brief exchange during which none of our problems were mentioned, we said goodbye. Before we had a chance to walk away, our father reached into his pocket, extracted two $100 bills from his wallet, and handed them to us. "Happy New Year, sons. Have yourselves a drink on me. By the way," he added, laughing, "did I ever tell you that you two remind me of Pat and Patachon?" Our difference in height reminded him of the popular European comedy team from the twenties and thirties. Morris and I took our father's jovial attitude as a sign that he was mellowing and that, perhaps, there was still hope for working out our differences.

We never had a chance to find out. Two months later, I was awakened in the middle of the night by a knock on my door. It was my foreman, Mike Omsted. He had learned from the airport's radio operator that my father had been in a serious automobile accident in the interior of the country and that the tiny dispensary in Ganta where he had been taken for emergency treatment had radioed an urgent request for oxygen. "Just get dressed and let's go!" Mike hollered. "I already have two oxygen bottles in the pickup."

Taking turns behind the wheel, we raced silently through the night over unpaved clay roads through small native settlements and across rickety bridges, some of which consisted of only two parallel flattened tree trunks. "He mustn't die" was my only, incessant, thought. By dawn, we reached Ganta, a small village of clay huts. Someone showed us to the village dispensary, where, in one of the rooms, my father was lying on a large bed. His neck and chest were covered with blood-soaked bandages. When we entered the room, he opened his eyes and a sign of recognition came over his face as he spotted me. He moved his lips, but no sound came from his mouth. All I could do was grab his hand and hold it. I was amazed at the strength with which he returned my grasp. It seemed as if he were afraid to let go of me. I looked down at his right hand, the one that had pursued me in my absurd, fever-induced hallucination, and found it difficult to imagine that I had ever been afraid of him.

After we left the room, a medic from the dispensary briefed us on my father's condition. He had a cut windpipe and had sustained major injuries to his chest. If he could be transported to Monrovia to undergo surgery, the medic explained, he had a good chance of recovery. Unfortunately, because of the rough and extremely dusty roads, it had been determined that my father would not survive the long trip to the capital. To compound the problem, the small airplane frequently used to shuttle people to and from

Monrovia needed major repairs and was out of service. Our only option was to have one of the dispensary's visiting physicians attempt emergency surgery to stabilize my father, then move him to Monrovia when he had improved somewhat.

We learned that my father, in his endless pursuit of business deals, had been driving a van that was loaded to the top with bags of rice when an oncoming truck drove by. Since the truck left a long trail of red dust behind, my father did not see that a second oncoming truck had moved into his lane in order to pass the first truck. The second truck struck his van head-on. My father was critically injured and his van totaled, while the oncoming truck and its driver were barely fazed. Miraculously, one of my father's houseboys who was riding in the back of the van also escaped injury.

Mike reminded me that there was nothing for us to do but return to Robertsfield. But before we did, we went to the scene of the accident a few miles outside Ganta. What we saw made me shudder. There was still a great deal of dried blood at the scene, which had to be my father's. His van, what was left of it, was a tangle of twisted sheet metal, steel beams, engine parts, and broken glass. The wheels, it appeared, had already been picked clean of tires by "salvagers," as was the interior of the van, which showed no trace that it had loaded with rice. It reminded me of the old saying, "One man's meat is another man's poison." For the hungry bellies of the poor villagers of Ganta, my father's accident and several thousand pounds of rice must have been a welcome windfall.

After ten days of anxiously waiting, Morris and I learned that our father had died. All that remained for us to do was bring his body back to Monrovia and mourn. As much as I tried to find solace by telling myself that he had never been much of a father, especially during all those years when I needed a father the most, I felt an overpowering sense of sadness and the excruciating pain of having sustained an irreparable loss. He may not have been the father I had craved as a young boy and especially when I reached my teens, but he was the only father I had.

The funeral, which had been arranged by Uncle Nat, was attended by hundreds of mourners from the Vai community as well as by members of the Liberian government, including Vice President Simpson, who represented the out-of-town President Tubman. After the funeral, Morris and I learned that our dear Uncle Nat—while publicly posing as the bereaved and inconsolable brother—had been busy behind our backs with another agenda. Using his influence and his knowledge of the law, he had himself appointed sole administrator of our father's estate. He was aided by the fact that, as far as we could determine, my father had died without leaving a will.

Since we had always been on friendly terms with our uncle, Morris and I didn't contest his grab for power, although we considered his action highly inappropriate, since we were both of legal age and didn't require a guardian. It didn't take us long to discover that Nat intended to cheat Morris and me out of our rightful inheritance. Recalling my father's disclosure to me that Nat was the leader of a family conspiracy to steal his money, I confronted Nat and demanded that he keep us informed of anything regarding the estate, especially its size and what he was doing with the proceeds from renting our father's house to Lebanese traders. Nat readily agreed, but kept stalling. Figuring we had waited long enough, we kept pressing him for some information. Finally Nat told us that to his great shock and dismay he had discovered that our father, instead of being a millionaire, had actually died a pauper, with hardly any assets to his name. The best thing to do under the circumstances, he advised, was to keep our mouths shut and not let the public know about this "embarrassing situation."

Convinced that he was lying and that he had somehow tampered with the books and juggled our father's properties into his own accounts, we told him that we had no intention of keeping our mouths shut or giving up without a fight. We were up against a most cunning and politically powerful adversary, but we had nothing to lose. With that in mind, we sent a short note to President Tubman, explaining our plight and asking him in the name of our late father, his friend, to intervene in our behalf. Within a week, President Tubman responded and arranged for a meeting with us and Nat.

Our uncle was visibly uncomfortable when the president asked us to take seats in his opulent office in the Executive Mansion. After lighting his inevitable Havana, he asked me to state my case. With a trembling voice I thanked him for having agreed to see us in this extremely personal matter, then, encouraged by the president's fatherly smile, told him that Morris and I had lost confidence in our uncle's handling of our father's estate, especially his claim of its meager size.

When I had finished, the president explained that he had no legal powers to intervene and that he was acting merely as a private citizen and a personal friend of the Massaquoi family. "But," he added, turning to Nat, "I'm appealing to your sense of fairness to see that the right thing is done, especially with regard to this young man who has just arrived from Germany and was totally dependent on his father."

I could see Nat squirm as the president spoke, but he quickly recovered. "Before you feel too sorry for this boy, Mr. President," he responded, "I want you to look at this to give you a better idea of what kind of person my nephew really is." With the triumphant expression of a prosecutor producing the smoking gun in court, Nat reached into his pocket and came up with a letter, which he handed to the president. "Please read this very insulting and disrespectful letter, Mr. President, which he wrote to my brother just before his death."

I immediately recognized the letter, which I had written at my family's encouragement shortly after leaving my father. To my deepest embarrassment, the president read the letter aloud. When he had finished, he complimented me on my English. Then, turning to Nat, he said, "Judge, I don't think this letter is insulting or disrespectful, but even if it were, it doesn't alter the fact that you are obligated to see to it that this young man is taken care of. His father sent for him and he can't be left here to his own devices. I'm sure you'll be able to work something out. As far as Morris here is concerned, I'm not worried. He'll get by with or without money from his father's estate."

"I'll take care of everything, Mr. President," was all Nat could mumble before the president dismissed us.

When we reached the street, Nat turned to us with an expression of undisguised hatred. "Both of you will pay for this," he snarled. "Don't think you dragged me before the president and embarrassed me for nothing. I can promise you one thing—just as I had to wait for your father to die before I could get my hands on my father's estate, you will have to wait until I'm dead before you'll see any of your father's property."

I was not impressed. At age twenty-three, I couldn't even imagine what it meant to be rich. So my uncle's threat failed to get me upset. Morris, on the other hand, became livid, and would have started an altercation had I not pulled him away and reminded him that by assaulting a judge in front of the Executive Mansion we would have literally handed our father's estate to Nat and landed ourselves in jail.

LAGOS

Several weeks after our meeting with Nat and the president, I received a brief notice on Executive Mansion stationery informing me that the president wanted to see me on an important personal matter at my earliest convenience. I called on President Tubman within the hour.

Without referring to our last meeting, the president came right to the point. "I have received a letter from your grandmother, Mrs. Mary Sonii, in Lagos, Nigeria. She has heard of your arrival in Liberia and of your father's death and now wants me to arrange for you to visit her." My grandmother had asked him to advance me the necessary funds for sea passage from Monrovia to Lagos, which she promised to refund upon my return to Monrovia. With that, he extracted a wad of twenty-dollar bills from an envelope and handed it to me. "This should be quite sufficient," he said. "Please give Mrs. Sonii my best regards." After I thanked the president, he shook my hand and wished me a pleasant trip.

Foreseeing a lengthy absence from Liberia, I returned to Robertsfield and quit my job. After saying goodbye to Sammy and my friends at the motor pool, I caught the next available ride back to Monrovia. When I told Morris, who had visited our grandmother on several occasions, he enthusiastically approved of my going to Lagos. But as far as my passage was concerned, he told me that he had a better idea. Instead of my buying an expensive ticket, he said he could arrange with some of the Kru people on a freighter to have me stay in the crew quarters for a few dollars and thus save most of the money the president had given me. At first I objected. His plan didn't sound quite right to me. But after Morris explained that this was the way everybody with connections travels in Africa, I relented.

On the day of my departure, Morris accompanied me to Monrovia's newly completed seaport, where we boarded a Lagos-bound British freighter.

There, after briefly negotiating in Kru with the foreman of the "deck boys," Morris assured me that everything was arranged, that I would have a cabin to myself and that I would take my meals with the crew. Before long I was off to a new country and a new adventure.

The British tub that was to become my home for the next three days was a far cry from the spic-and-span American ships I had gotten to know and love in Hamburg. Everything was dirty and in ill repair. The bunk in my cabin was filthy and crawled with roaches, and a nauseating smell permeated everything. Already I regretted having listened to Morris and cursed his idea of saving a few dollars. But my regrets turned to outright anger mixed with revulsion when mealtime came around and my "hosts" invited me to help myself to a dirty-looking bowl of rice and some putrid-smelling, unidentifiable gravy, an offer that I politely refused. The next morning, the same gravy and rice were served for breakfast. This time, however, hunger had made me more receptive to the menu and I managed to eat a bit. That afternoon, we reached the port of Takoradi, in the Gold Coast (now Ghana), where I went ashore for a quick, uninspiring sightseeing tour. It was the first time I had ever stepped on British colonial territory. The next day we reached Lagos, the capital of Britain's largest and most populated African colony. I was glad to get off the ship and vowed to make better arrangements for my return to Monrovia.

After a short taxi ride at breakneck speed through left-hand traffic, past teeming Tinubu Square, to my grandmother's address at 157 Igbosere Road, I stepped into the courtyard of a one-story row house where I was greeted by a slender old lady with a pretty, light brown face and a head full of short white curls. As she hugged me, she was crying uncontrollably while repeating over and over, "My son, my son, my poor, poor son," in a pronounced British accent. She seemed to refer to my late father as well as to me. When she had regained her composure, she introduced me to a kind-looking elderly gentleman with fine chiseled features. "This is Pa Sonii, your step-grandfather," she explained. As we shook hands and he welcomed me, I immediately took a liking to the old gent.

When Pa Sonii wanted to know whether I had had a pleasant trip, since I had traveled on one of his company's freighters, I confessed Morris's money-saving scheme and how it all had backfired with a trip straight from hell. I immediately offered to fork over the amount of money I had saved, but Pa Sonii wouldn't hear of it. "You keep it," he said. "You've earned it— every penny of it. But Morris should have known that you shouldn't be traveling like that. I always said that boy doesn't have good sense."

Then, pointing to two slender teenage girls, Ma Sonii said, "These young ladies help me run the house. This one here is Howa and that frisky one over there is Kpakanya." Both girls had smooth, velvety brown skin, doll-like, dimpled round faces, and flawless white teeth.

"After you have taken my grandson's luggage to his room, I want you to prepare his bath," my grandmother continued.

"Yes, ma'am," the girls replied in unison before going giggling about their chores.

It was only then that I noticed that my grandmother seemed paralyzed on one side. Her left arm dangled limply at her side and she dragged her left leg while walking, with great difficulty and the help of a cane.

"Yes, I'm an old wreck," she said, noticing my unintentional staring at her infirmity. "Since I had a stroke about a year ago, I haven't been much use for anything."

After taking a bath and changing into fresh clothes, I spent the rest of the evening feasting on a wide variety of African delicacies, shaking hands with a seemingly endless line of my grandmother's friends and neighbors who had heard of my arrival, and answering questions about my life in Germany, "that rascal Morris," and my father's accident. Inevitably, the matter of Nat's having taken control of my father's estate came up. "Leave that to me," my grandmother assured me. "Nat will not get away with that. I shall see to it."

I had no idea of what my frail old grandmother had in mind, but I was soon to find out. A few days after my arrival, shortly after Pa Sonii had left for work at the shipyard, a strange group of about a dozen tall men arrived at the house, dressed in tribal robes. At my grandmother's request, they took seats in her spacious parlor, where Howa and Kpakanya served them freshly brewed tea.

"I know you will laugh at what I tell you now," my grandmother whispered to me after she had asked me to sit beside her and face the men, "but these men have the power to keep your uncle from stealing your father's money. You don't have to believe it and you don't have to do anything but sit here and watch." Despite my skepticism and out of deference to my grandmother, I did as she told me. The next hour or so, I became privy to a strange ritual consisting of a great deal of chanting and the passing around of various small objects that looked to me like ordinary stones, beads, and sticks, and that, as far as I could determine, didn't have a thing to do with anything, certainly not with my late father's money. When the ceremony was over, the men filed by me and touched me, then pocketed the "dash" (tip) that my grandmother handed them, before leaving as quietly as they had come.

That evening, when Pa Sonii returned from work, he greeted me with a big grin. "How did you like all that mumbo jumbo this morning?"

"I thought it was interesting," I replied diplomatically, in an effort not to hurt my grandmother's feelings.

"Your grandmother is a strong believer in all this juju rubbish," he continued, not caring that she was standing directly beside him. "All that education in England was a total waste. She's more superstitious than a bushwoman."

"You can laugh all you want, Sonii," my grandmother replied, unfazed. "I know what I know."

After taking a leisurely bath, Pa Sonii changed from slacks and shirt to a comfortable African robe, then joined us for supper. "Sometimes I wonder which problem is worse, colonialism or superstition," he said, returning to what seemed to be two of his pet peeves. He then explained that a few years ago, the city administration had installed electric streetlights along Igbosere Road, but that "superstitious bush people," who feared that the spirits might become offended when "the night is turned to day," kept destroying the lamps with stones and sticks until the city gave up on repairs and left the street dark.

He then withdrew to his favorite chair and settled down to his day's favorite pastime, reading his *West African Pilot,* a militant, anticolonialist newspaper published by his hero, Nnamdi Azikiwe, a member of the Ibo tribe, known throughout Nigeria as Zik. "Zik is the only Nigerian the British are afraid of," explained Pa Sonii. Through his hard-hitting editorials against the colonial government, Pa Sonii said, Zik had become so popular among the people that the British didn't dare to mess with him lest they set off a huge explosion. "If he plays his cards right, he can be the first president of independent Nigeria," Pa Sonii added wistfully.

Unfortunately, Pa Sonii didn't live to see his prediction come true. He couldn't know that only fourteen years hence, as an *Ebony* magazine journalist, I would be conducting a personal interview with President Nnamdi Azikiwe on his yacht anchored in Lagos Harbor, within walking distance of Pa Sonii's home.

Much of my time I spent chatting with my grandmother, who by her own admission was "quite a card" in her young years in England, and who kept me in stitches telling me about her various antics as a young woman. At one point, she confided, she was being pursued in the most obnoxious way by three different gents, none of whom knew of the others' existence. After they kept refusing to take "no" for an answer, she agreed to a rendezvous with each of them at exactly the same time on the same bench in London's Hyde Park. Still chuckling when imagining the faces of her suitors when they realized that they had been duped, she said none of them ever bothered her again.

My grandmother confided in me that my grandfather, Momolu, was really the love of her life, but that he was an intolerable ladies' man. "Nobody would believe that man's woman palaver," she recalled, incredulity and admiration mingling in her voice. She said that the more than twenty children Momolu admitted having fathered in and out of wedlock were only the tip of the iceberg. Years after she broke up with Momolu and my father was in college, she met Pa Sonii in Monrovia. He had just been offered a foreman's position in Lagos, and when he proposed marriage, she jumped at the chance and never regretted her decision. "Pa Sonii is a good man," she said, "but Momolu was a king."

Occasionally, I would walk through the streets of Lagos and watch with fascination the pulsating rhythm of a big African seaport city. Unlike Monrovia, which in the late forties was a town that had yet to be awakened from its hundred-year sleep, Lagos teemed with traffic and people that crowded to overflowing its sidewalks and streets.

The streets were lined with government office buildings and commercial enterprises that ranged from one-woman peanut vendors to huge department stores. My walks would take me along Lagos's popular Marina, a scenic, palm-lined thoroughfare along the lagoon from which the city derived its name, and through the hustle and bustle of Tinubu Square, the hub of the city's commercial life. Noting the consistent pattern of Africans holding low-prestige, often menial, positions under the supervision of whites made me feel fortunate that I was not a colonial subject but a free Liberian.

Except for my run-in with the French colonial authorities in Dakar, I had had no personal contact with colonialism. I was soon to get firsthand experience of the British variety. It happened when I tried to buy some postage stamps. A discouragingly long line of customers, all Africans, awaited me when I arrived at the post office in downtown Lagos. Exposed to the city's brutal noon sun, the queue stretched more than half a block to a small service window manned by an African clerk. I decided to get in line and await my turn. Not so a white Britisher who, dressed in colonial khaki jacket and shorts, knee socks, and sun helmet, marched straight to the window and demanded to be served. I could hear some muffled murmurs of protest from the crowd, but no open challenges. Enter Hans Massaquoi. "Who the hell do you think you are?" I heard myself address the Britisher. "Why don't you wait your turn like anybody else?"

Suddenly, the crowd became unruly and other voices chimed in, demanding that the Britisher get in line. The white man seemed incredulous that someone had dared to challenge what he considered his birthright. He must have concluded that he was dealing with a mentally deranged person, for as soon as he spotted me, he turned around and, to the humiliating cheers of the crowd, marched away.

That evening, when I told Pa Sonii and my grandmother of my encounter at the post office, Pa Sonii gave me a long and stern lecture. "You are lucky that white man didn't come back and have you arrested and thrown in jail on some trumped-up charge like inciting people to riot," he said. "This is not Liberia, where black people are in charge. This is a British colony where whites are very jittery because they sense that their rule is coming to an end. Right now they are looking at every little incident as the spark that might set off an explosion. They will do anything—and I mean anything—to prolong their rule as long as they can. So the next time you see some Britisher do something you don't like, keep your mouth shut, at least for your grandmother's and my sake."

Pa Sonii's advice was well meant, but it hastened my decision to leave Nigeria and return to Liberia as soon as possible, since I had no intention of living in a racist colony. During twelve years in Nazi Germany, I felt I had more than paid my dues.

My decision to return to Monrovia, after more than four months in Lagos, came as a great disappointment to my grandmother. Secretly she had hoped that I would get to like Lagos enough to stay with her. Pa Sonii had already found a machinist opening for me at his company, the Elder Dempster Line, with "excellent pay"—at the nonwhite rate, of course. I told him thanks but no thanks. Although I felt sorry for my grandmother, who had hoped that I would replace the son she had lost, I still cherished my dream of one day going to America.

So one day, with a heavy heart, I said goodbye to my grandmother and Pa Sonii, of whom I had grown quite fond. As my taxi pulled up, I gave my crying grandmother one final hug. She whispered, "I'll miss you a lot, son." Something told me that I would never see her again.

RETURN TO MONROVIA

This time, I booked a cabin passage on an American steamer that was stopping at Monrovia before crossing the Atlantic to New Orleans. After stowing my luggage in my cabin, which had a bunk with inviting snow-white sheets, I went on deck to take one last look at Lagos.

At once I felt at home on the ship, which, like all American ships I had visited in Hamburg, was meticulously clean and smelled of fresh paint. As usual, the steward department, with the exception of the chief steward, was black. As most freighters, the ship had only limited passenger space. I had two fellow passengers, whom I met at suppertime in the small dining room for passengers. One was a young Nigerian student, Felix Osi. The son of a Yoruba chieftain, he was bound for his freshman year at a black college in the southern United States. The other passenger was Virginia Langston, a pleasant thirtyish blonde with a twangy Southern drawl, who insisted we call her Ginny, and who said that she was returning to her hometown of Mobile, Alabama, after spending two years in Nigeria as a Methodist missionary.

Just as we were about to eat, the chief steward told Ginny that the captain had given instructions that, beginning at once, she was to take all her meals

with the officers. Visibly annoyed, the missionary left with the chief steward
after telling us that she had been looking forward to dining with us and
would miss our company. Recalling that the ship's home port was the seg-
regated Southern city of New Orleans, Felix and I were convinced that the
captain's special invitation to the missionary was intended to spare a South-
ern white woman the ordeal of dining with two black men. We were still
discussing the insult to us, especially in view of the fact that we were traveling
in African waters, when Ginny returned and told us with a big smile that
she was going to dine with us after all. She said that when she had been
seated beside the captain in the officers' mess, the black messman, in an
ironic twist, refused to serve her, saying that it was against union rules for
him to serve passengers, something the captain had apparently overlooked
in his zeal to uphold Southern tradition.

We spent the next three days lounging lazily on deck while the ship's
white crew worked steadily to keep the ship in tiptop shape. They bom-
barded us with hostile looks suggesting that they did not like the idea of
two black men in the company of a white woman relaxing while they
worked. Since they were merely scrubbing and painting, I failed to see what
Felix found so fascinating as he watched the seamen for hours with undi-
minished interest. When I finally asked what he found so intriguing, he told
me that in all of his twenty-two years he had never seen a single white person
do menial work. "In Nigeria," he explained, "white people only supervise
or do office-type work. Dirty or menial work is done only by Africans."

"Well, in the United States, things are different," Ginny assured him.
"You'll find that white people do all kinds of dirty, menial work. Strangely
enough," she added, "the same thing is true in England. Only in the colonies
do white people regard menial work as beneath them."

Ginny explained that at the various missions where she had been sta-
tioned, many white missionaries, men and women, had been doing menial
work. But Felix, a Muslim, wasn't satisfied. Turning on her with sudden
anger, he asserted that Christian missionaries were mostly to blame that
Africa was colonized by European states. Had it not been for Christian
missionaries who taught "us heathens" to turn the other cheek and made
black warriors docile, he charged, whites would never have succeeded in
conquering an entire continent.

"If you want to blame us Christian missionaries for helping to prepare Africa for colonialism, you Muslims must accept the blame for getting slavery started," Ginny shot back. She then gave Felix a long lecture on how Arab Muslims led raiding parties throughout Africa and either captured or bought from greedy African chiefs large numbers of slaves, whom they then sold to eager European and American slave traders.

When we arrived in Takoradi in the Gold Coast, where I had briefly visited on my way to Nigeria, a deck crew of several dozen Africans was chanting dockside in the heat while preparing to load the ship with a large cargo of cocoa.

"Just look at them," a tall blond ship's officer in a khaki uniform invited me in a thick German accent. "They're nothing but a bunch of lazy bums!"

"Why do you say these people are lazy?"

"Because they don't want to work. All they want to do is dance and sing. To load this ship takes them three times as long as it would take an American crew in the States."

The officer's comments were typical of the prevailing attitude of whites toward blacks in the colonies. Africans were expected not only to submit to being exploited, but to do so cheerfully and under conditions no white person would tolerate.

I didn't feel like arguing with this smug *Landsmann.* If he couldn't figure it out by himself, how could I make him understand why people who were forced to survive in a system that paid them only a starving wage didn't feel motivated to work as hard as workers who received literally fifty times the pay, plus union-guaranteed benefits of all kinds? It was impossible for these Africans to buy homes and automobiles. How hard would he work in the grueling sun if all he'd have to show for it at the end of the day was the price of a pack of cigarettes or a bottle of beer?

When the ship docked in Monrovia, I said goodbye to Felix and Ginny, whom I envied for soon being in the land of my dreams. I told them that I hoped to see them again one day in the States, but that it would have to be "up North," since I had no intention of ever setting foot in the Jim Crow South.

In Monrovia, my first mission was to keep my promise to my grandmother. I returned the money President Tubman had advanced for the trip.

This time I did not get to see the president, but left the amount with Colonel Brewer, his aide-de-camp.

Then I intensified my efforts to get out of Liberia and emigrate to the United States. I no longer felt that my staying in Africa served any useful purpose. I resumed my correspondence with my Aunt Clara in Barrington, Illinois, explaining to her that I was more than ever interested in coming and imploring her to complete the necessary paperwork to support my application for a U.S. visa. In her reply, she assured me that she had already set things in motion, but that the best she could do at the time was get me a temporary non-quota student visa rather than a permanent immigrant visa. The German immigrant quota was still suspended, it was explained to her, since U.S.-German relations had yet not been normalized.

In order to obtain the student visa, Aunt Clara explained, she had enrolled me at the Aeronautical University of Chicago, a trade school, which she hoped would meet with my approval. I frantically responded that I approved of anything that would get me into the United States.

POLICE INSPECTOR MORRIS

The next time I saw Morris, I was in for a big surprise. He was wearing a crisply starched khaki uniform with the insignia of a ranking Liberian police officer. When I demanded to know what he was doing in that uniform, he explained that President Tubman, his Masonic brother, had granted his request and commissioned him an inspector in Liberia's National Police Force. "One word of disrespect out of you, bro," he joked, "and your sorry ass goes to jail."

Turning serious, Morris said that his new duties consisted of patrolling the roads of the interior in a police pickup truck and making sure that the loads of commercial trucks were within the weight limit. The idea was to prevent Liberia's road and bridge system from being overstressed and prematurely damaged. "If you want to," he added, "you can hit the road with me tomorrow. I'll be leaving early in the morning for the interior."

I took Morris up on his offer and became his unofficial traveling companion as he drove hundreds of miles over the dusty clay roads in search of overweight rice trucks. Once he had caught up with a suspected vehicle, he would order the driver to follow him to the next weigh station, where he'd assess the correct fine and direct the driver to jettison the excess rice bags. Usually, the owners of the rice trucks were Lebanese or Syrian businessmen from Monrovia. Invariably, they would argue that the government scales were inaccurate. When that failed to make an impression on Morris, they would try to settle the "small misunderstanding" with a bribe. Morris was familiar with President Tubman's permissive policy on graft, which expected government employees to steal a little as long as they remembered to reach into the government till no farther than their elbows instead of all the way to their armpits. Consequently, Morris kept only a tiny percentage of the fines he collected; his ethics, on the other hand, made him steadfastly refuse any bribes. This, he assured me, was well within the parameters of President Tubman's "wrist-to-elbow policy."

One evening, we stopped at a village. I was fast running out of steam after a long day of taking turns at the wheel, and the next government compound was still more than two hours away. Morris could go for extraordinary lengths of time without food or sleep by chewing on a bitter raw kola nut, but not I. As we drove into the open square of the small settlement, our pickup was surrounded by a swarm of children who were reaching out their hands for some kind of "dash." After divesting ourselves of all our pennies, Morris asked the kids in their native language for the chief. They pointed toward a group of men sitting around a fire eating their evening meal. Seated apart from them was a group of women who were also in the midst of supper.

There was no mistaking who was the chief. An old man, he was seated on an elaborately carved chair, while everyone else sat on the ground. After Morris introduced himself as a police officer and me as his brother, he told the chief that we were looking for some food and a place to spend the night. The chief immediately invited us to join him as his honored guests and urged us to help ourselves. I noticed two gigantic bowls in the center of the human circle; one containing rice and the other meat with gravy. Morris, in effect, urged me to do like the Romans when in Rome. So I followed his example and scooped up some rice with my hand, made it into a ball, then dunked it—hand and all—into the other bowl of meat and gravy. It smelled and tasted delicious, and I was soon munching as fast as my teeth could chew. But then I noticed one of the men wipe his sweaty brow and use the same hand to reach into the bowl. Suddenly, the food got immovably stuck in my throat. Morris snarled, "You can't insult these people by puking up their food."

"Don't bet on it," I snarled back, but bravely kept chewing and swallowing until the last bit cleared my throat. Just in case someone had noticed my struggle with the food, Morris explained that I had just come from a "far-off white man's land" and hadn't yet become accustomed to delicious African food.

Later, a young boy took us to a hut that, he explained, the chief wanted us to use for the night. As we stepped inside, I noticed the clay floor and walls were immaculately clean. Glancing at the skinned carcasses of several small animals with long tails hanging from the ceiling rafters, I inquired what they were. "Monkeys, sah," the boy replied. "Monkeys make very good chop."

A sense of revulsion grabbed me for the second time that evening. "Who in the world would eat monkeys?" I wondered.

"You would," replied Morris with unconcealed glee. "What do you think you were eating tonight? It tasted pretty good, didn't it?"

Grudgingly I had to admit he was right. "Your father warned me you were no good," I joked. "Now I know what he meant." After we put the monkey palaver to rest, we made up our cots and went to sleep.

Soon we were awakened by loud shouts. Looking out, we saw a huge column of fire rising from one of the nearby huts. Several people tried frantically to douse it with buckets of water from a well, but to no avail. Within minutes, the hut was consumed by fire and only the clay walls remained.

The next morning, when we tried to thank the chief for his hospitality and to take our leave, we found the entire village assembled in front of the chief's hut. Our little friend from the previous evening explained that there would be "a big palaver" regarding the fire. Arson was suspected and three suspects had already been apprehended. Each denied the deed, the boy said, so the chief asked the village shaman to do his magic and identify the culprit.

Since we were in no particular hurry, Morris suggested that we stick around and watch. "You'll find this interesting," he promised, "especially since you Europeans believe that only Jesus can do magic."

We maneuvered ourselves to a front-row position. After the chief and some of the elders had taken their seats, the crowd went silent. At a hand signal from the chief, the circle opened and three "constables" in tattered khaki uniforms entered. Each was leading a distraught-looking suspect by a rope. The suspects, hands tied behind their backs, were made to sit on the ground in the center of the circle.

On a second signal from the chief, amid murmurs of veneration, the circle opened again and a frail man with a scraggly white beard whom everyone referred to as "the wise one" entered. Dressed only in loose white pants and leather sandals, he revealed a chest and back covered with white painted markings. Strapped to his right side was a huge antique cavalry saber whose rusty curved steel blade still managed to look menacing. While the wise one was slowly walking around the arson suspects, several men built a waist-high pile of kindling wood and started a fire. When the fire reached its peak, the wise one held the blade of his saber over the flames. After several minutes, he withdrew the blade and viewed it critically. I could see the blade turn a dark red and the air around it vibrate from the heat. The wise one took the red-hot blade and held it to his cheeks, chest, and back, without any adverse effects. He then walked around the circle and asked for volunteers. Immediately, several villagers stepped forward and offered their cheeks, hands, and legs to the blade, with the same result—no visible burns. When the wise one stopped in front of me and gestured to me to join the volunteers, I hesitated, but Morris stepped forward and took the plunge. "If you didn't set the fire, the saber won't hurt you," he promised.

"Why not?" I wanted to know.

"Because of magic, African magic," was his response.

Having gotten severely burned once because of Morris, I wasn't about to give him another chance. But curiosity got the better of me. Emboldened by what I had just seen with my own eyes, I let the shaman touch my cheek with his blade. The blade felt cool on my cheek, although it still looked red hot.

While the wise one reheated the blade, the chief conducted a brief interrogation of the suspects during which each maintained his innocence. After the chief gestured him to continue, the shaman advanced with his saber toward the suspects, who eyed the weapon with horror. With a swift motion, the wise one laid the blade on the first suspect's cheek, then repeated the procedure with suspect number two, each time without producing burns or pain. But before he could turn to the last man, the suspect suddenly jumped to his feet, pulled away from the constable who had held him on a tether, and made a mad dash through the crowd, his hands still tied behind him.

In only a few minutes, the constables had caught up with the fugitive and returned him to the center of the circle. There, the wise one resumed his task of administering the test of fire to the captive. This time, however, the result was quite different. As soon as the blade touched the man's cheek, he let out a loud scream, and when the wise one withdrew the blade, it left behind a blistering red wound from ear to chin. The wise one repeated the procedure on the other cheek, again with the same results. As the crowd roared its applause, the prisoner admitted his crime before being hauled away by the constables.

"What you just saw was juju," Morris explained. "It's the same thing they call voodoo in Haiti."

"I don't know how he did it," I allowed, "but I'm sure there was some trick involved. Don't tell me about magic; there simply is no such thing."

Openly, I held on to that view, but secretly, I was no longer convinced. Could it be that Africans had come up with something that defied Western logic and could only be explained as magic? In time I was to learn that in Liberia nearly everybody, from the president on down, believed in and feared the power of juju, although most educated people refused to admit it.

Morris decided one day to patrol Saniquellie, on the French Guinea border to the north, and pay our respects to Uncle Jaiah. One of Momolu's numerous sons, Uncle Jaiah held the exalted position of provincial commissioner. He represented the Liberian government throughout Nimba County along Liberia's frontier. I had met Uncle Jaiah only briefly during my father's funeral and looked forward to getting to know him better. According to Morris, he was a decent man who had achieved his position through diligence and dedication to duty instead of political maneuvering. Yet he was not held in high esteem by the rest of the family. One reason was that while Jaiah had the Massaquoi name, unlike many of his siblings, he lacked the polish of a European education. The other was that he was officially married to several native women, a custom frowned upon by "civilized" Liberians.

When we arrived at the gate of the commissioner's compound, which consisted of several office buildings, a private residence, and military barracks, a rifle-toting soldier from the Liberian Frontier Force saluted Morris and let us pass. Once inside, another soldier led us to an office. Uncle Jaiah, a stocky dark man with a massive bald head and dimpled cheeks, got up as soon as he recognized us. "Hello, big shot," he greeted Morris, with obvious reference to Morris's new status. "And how are you, Hans?" he asked as he shook my hand. "Unfortunately," he said, "I have to leave in less than an hour for a meeting with some colonial officials at the Guinea border and won't be back for about a week. But you two are welcome to stay here as long as you want. Just make yourselves at home."

He then introduced me to one of his wives, a slender beauty less than half his age, and instructed her to look after our comfort and to make sure that we had plenty to eat. Following a brief chat during which Uncle Jaiah assured us that he didn't approve of his brother Nat's handling of our father's estate, a soldier announced that the commissioner's "motorcar" was ready. Through a window we could see a jeep with three soldiers, including the driver, waiting outside. He invited us to come back soon, then rushed out of the door and mounted the jeep, which soon disappeared in a cloud of dust.

WATCH OUT, COLONEL SANDERS!

The next time we arrived in Monrovia for Morris's periodic report at Police Headquarters, I learned that Mr. and Mrs. Johnson, a native Liberian and his German wife who had recently arrived from Europe and whom I had met at Robertsfield, had opened a small restaurant. The two welcomed Morris and me with open arms and proudly showed us their cozy establishment. It was packed to capacity, mostly, Mr. Johnson confided, because of the popularity of his wife's chicken soup. After each of us had wolfed down a bowl of the delicacy, we agreed that they had a winner.

"I wish you were right," Mr. Johnson replied, "but my problem at the moment is that the demand for our chicken soup is much greater than our supply of chickens. If I could only get my hands on enough chickens, this place would be a gold mine."

"How much do you pay for one chicken?" Morris asked.

"Depending on the size, I'd say on average about one dollar," Mr. Johnson replied.

"Then how about you letting us worry about the chickens?" Morris asked, pointing toward me and himself.

For a moment I thought Morris had flipped. Where in the world was he going to get chickens? But he motioned for me to keep my mouth shut. Later he reminded me that each of the villages we had visited so far had a small flock of chickens. According to Morris, we could stop at a number of villages on our way to the interior and let the people know that on our return trip we would buy as many chickens as they could scrounge up for fifty cents apiece. Then we would drive to Monrovia and sell the chickens to Mr. Johnson for a profit of fifty cents each. In order not to arouse unnecessary attention that would let people know that the Liberian National Police Force was a partner in a chicken-transport venture, he would schedule our arrivals in Monrovia late at night when traffic was at a minimum.

Morris's plan worked like a charm. The next time we returned to Monrovia, the police pickup was loaded to the sky with coops of cackling live chickens. We were ecstatic as Mr. Johnson paid us nearly a hundred dollars. "Just keep the chickens coming," he urged.

We decided to reinvest our entire profits in chickens, and in a few days had amassed five hundred dollars, a veritable fortune by our standards. We talked about nothing else but chickens while dreaming of ever greater chicken fortunes. Morris was seriously considering turning in his police badge, buying a pickup truck, and going into the chicken business full time. But as quickly as it had started, our chicken dream bubble burst when our suppliers told us that they were fast running out of merchandise. We simply had bought up their chickens faster than new ones could be hatched and grown. In each village we visited, the number of available chickens dropped steadily until we were told the dreaded news, "Sorry, no more chickens for sale." That ended our high expectation of becoming chicken tycoons. Yet before I had a chance to mourn our great loss, my spirits received an unexpected lift that no chicken fortune could have given me. I was informed by my friend, Consul Hanson of the U.S. Embassy, that he had been authorized to issue me a one-year student visa to the United States.

When I wrote Aunt Clara that my student visa had arrived, she promptly mailed me a six-hundred-dollar airline ticket and urged me to make my travel arrangements as soon as possible and to telephone her as soon as I had arrived in New York. I didn't need any urging, although I wondered why she wanted me to fly, since ship's passage was considerably cheaper. I finally reasoned that since she had also enrolled me at a university although she knew that I had no money and would be prohibited from working, she probably was wealthy. Whatever her reason for giving me the royal treatment, it was all right with me.

IN THE "HOME OF THE BRAVE"

On May 22, 1950, carrying the obligatory battered suitcase containing my best (and only) suit and a half dozen shirts and neckties, and with about a hundred dollars in cash—the remainder of my share of the chicken proceeds—in my pocket, I prepared to board a New York–bound Pan Am clipper at Robertsfield, eager to join my pal Werner and the rest of the tired, poor, and huddled masses yearning to breathe free and make a buck.

The only thing that dimmed my joy over having finally attained my goal was the thought of leaving Morris. During my two-year stay in Liberia, we had become all but inseparable. Although reared in different cultures on different continents and not aware of each other's existence until we were adults, we had bonded more closely than some brothers who had grown up together.

Eager not to betray any emotions, we made small talk in the small passengers' lounge while I awaited the signal to board for my first airplane ride.

"Take good care of yourself, little brother," Morris admonished, as always ignoring the four inches in height that actually made *him* the little brother. "And write me all about how you're making out." He promised to visit me in the States as soon as he was financially flush again. Remembering my brother's chronic shortage of cash, I sadly said goodbye, suspecting that it would be a long time before I'd see him again.

From the moment the plane took off, I became so fascinated with the new experience of flying that my somber, reflective mood was soon replaced by excited anticipation. After a brief stop in Lisbon, Portugal, we continued our flight to the United States. The closer we came to our destination, the more impatient I became and the more I wondered whether the idealistic image I had of the United States had any basis in reality. Although Werner's letters had painted a rosy picture of life in New York City, some of my black American friends in Liberia, including Charles Hanson, had told me that race relations were far from perfect and warned me that I might never get used to that side of the "American Way."

My negative thoughts were dispelled temporarily as, in the wee hours of morning and about an hour behind schedule, we approached LaGuardia International Airport and a gigantic carpet of millions of lights came in sight. I had written Werner when I would arrive and wondered whether he had received my letter in time to meet me at the airport. But as soon as I had reached the bottom of the gangway a uniformed airline employee asked me whether my name was Hans Massaquoi. When I told him yes, he said, "Thank God! A young fellow by the name of Werner has been bugging us for hours trying to find out whether you have arrived."

I saw Werner waving at me among a crowd of relatives and friends waiting for passengers. After I cleared immigration and customs, we finally had a chance to hug and to take a good look at each other after nearly three years of separation. Werner looked great. Unlike in Hamburg, where his taste ran from electric blue pin-striped suits to hand-painted ties depicting bathing beauties, he was conservatively dressed in a neat gray double-breasted suit and a carefully color-coordinated tie.

I was duly impressed when we arrived at 210 Riverside Drive, where a uniformed doorman greeted us like royalty. I wondered how, on his meager office clerk's salary, he could afford to live in such a lavish style, until an elevator operator took us to the eleventh floor and I saw the size of his super-neat apartment. Although minuscule, it boasted a spectacular view of the Hudson River and the never-ending traffic on Riverside Drive. "I'd rather live in a small apartment in a great neighborhood than in a huge apartment in a slum, especially when the price is about the same," Werner reasoned.

In the following days, Werner showed me *his* New York—Broadway, Central Park, the Empire State Building, Rockefeller Center, the Statue of Liberty, the Village, Germantown, Chinatown, the Bowery, and Grand Central Station. As we strolled through Manhattan, I immediately felt at home. It seemed as if I were experiencing déjà vu, as if I had been there before. Everything seemed so familiar to me, undoubtedly because of the many Hollywood movies I had seen. New York was exactly as I had expected.

Venturing out on my own in Harlem, where I had promised Charles Hanson I would say hello to his father, I had my only surprise. Instead of the menacing slums with lurking shadowy figures I had seen so often in U.S. films, I saw neighborhoods peopled by active, working-class folks not much different from those in my old Hamburg neighborhood. The only difference was that everyone—from the mailman to the barber to the policeman to the garbage collector to the occasional big shot in a Cadillac convertible—was black. As I walked along busy 125th Street totally ignored by the people around me, I had the brand-new experience of really blending in. At the same time I realized that I was still light-years away from feeling that I belonged.

Before I left for Chicago, Werner made me promise that if things didn't work out for me in Illinois, I would head back to New York and stay with him. When my bus arrived in downtown Chicago, I was met by Aunt Clara, my cousin Martha, and her husband, Rudolph. I recognized them immediately from the pictures Martha had sent me while I still lived in Germany. Although three years younger than my mother, Clara looked much older and bore little resemblance to her. Martha, a statuesque brunette with a pretty doll face, and her husband, a tall, studious-looking fellow with horn-rimmed glasses, made a striking couple. Undeterred by the curious stares of black and white bystanders, they all hugged me and seemed delighted that I finally had arrived.

To help me get situated, Rudolph and Martha, who lived in Chicago, said they would ride with us to Barrington, the Chicago suburb where Clara lived with her youngest son, Willie. During the one-hour train ride to Barrington, I sat beside Rudolph. When I told him how much I had looked forward to coming to Barrington, he told me, with a side glance at his mother-in-law, "You have my deepest sympathy."

That remark jolted me.

"What do you mean?" I asked.

"I can't tell you, but you'll soon find out."

He was right. Arriving in Barrington, we walked about half a mile along the railroad tracks and passed several respectable-looking homes before we came to what at first looked like an empty lot but what on closer inspection turned out to contain a low-slung, jerry-built wood-and-tar-paper shack.

"This is it," whispered Rudolph, "your new home. Welcome to Barrington."

I was stunned. Unable to say anything, I followed my aunt into the shack, whose interior turned out to be no more than its outside appearance suggested. Suddenly I felt sorry for my aunt and at the same time sorry for myself. How, I asked myself, did my aunt, who obviously lived in abject poverty and could barely take care of herself, intend to put me through college? Why hadn't she leveled with me? Where did she get the six hundred dollars to buy my ticket?

Totally oblivious to the thoughts racing through my mind, Aunt Clara invited me to make myself at home. "You can take Hermann's room," she said, referring to her oldest son, who had married and, like his sister, had moved to Chicago. Later that evening, after Martha and Rudolph had left, my cousin Willie arrived. Unlike his mother and sister, he greeted me with unconcealed disdain, which, I learned later, had nothing to do with race but everything to do with economics. A strapping blond six-footer who made his living as a tree surgeon, Willie made no secret of the fact that he considered me a worrisome burden on his mother's already overtaxed budget and that she needed another mouth to feed like she needed a hole in her head. I couldn't blame him for feeling that way, although the problem I obviously presented wasn't of my making. My only mistake had been to assume my aunt knew what she was doing when apparently she did not. Had she given the slightest indication of her true financial status, that the six hundred dollars for my airline ticket had been advanced by my uncle Hermann, my mother's oldest brother, or that she eked out a meager living cleaning homes for Barrington's rich folks, I would never have accepted her unrealistic generosity.

In due time I would learn that at the root of Aunt Clara's personality was a common-sense-defying belief that—in the face of staggering evidence to the contrary—things would turn out the way she wanted. It was that naive belief that caused her to enroll me in college, although she hadn't a clue what to do about tuition. By the same token, she had encouraged me to apply for a student visa although she had been told that foreign students were not ordinarily permitted to work. "We'll worry about that *after* you get here," she had blithely written. Unfortunately, when things didn't turn out the way she visualized, she looked for a scapegoat, which in this case turned out to be me.

After a couple of weeks of putting up with her and her son's growing hostility while trying to adjust to my new life in a little shack on the outskirts of an affluent, all-white suburban community, I looked back with longing to the carefree days when Morris and I were roaming the Liberian country-side. But just as I was contemplating the new mess in which I found myself and wracking my brain figuring how to get out of it, we were visited by my Aunt Hedwig and her husband, Gust Galske. The two had driven from their small farm in nearby Bartlett, Illinois, in their Model A Ford—a gift from Uncle Hermann, who had given up driving—to get a glimpse of me. I took one look at Aunt Hedwig, an older version of my mother, and she at me, and it was mutual love at first sight. I also took an immediate liking to Uncle Gust, a ruddy-faced, coverall-clad giant with a gray mop of hair and a boom-ing voice, which, to the constant chagrin of Aunt Hedwig, he used invariably to cuss and to laugh infectiously at the end of each of his ribald jokes.

While Gust kept Aunt Clara in stitches, Aunt Hedwig took me aside and told me that even before I had arrived in the United States, she and Uncle Gust had been quite aware that I was coming into an impossible situation. "Uncle Gust and I want you to come and spend some time with us on our farm," she told me. "We have plenty of space and plenty of food. You don't have to, but if you like, you can help Gust with the chores. Then we can figure out what to do next."

I felt like hugging her on the spot. "But how do I tell Aunt Clara?" I asked. "After all, she started the ball rolling in getting me to the States."

"You just leave that to me," Aunt Hedwig assured me. "I'll tell her the truth, which is that I'm your aunt, too, and entitled to have you spend some time with me, simple as that. If I know my sister, she's probably glad by now to get rid of you."

Aunt Hedwig was right. Aunt Clara didn't show the slightest misgiving when Hedwig told her that she wanted me to spend some time on her farm.

Aunt Clara even helped pack my things. When I told her goodbye, I had the distinct feeling that our relationship had gone as far as it could.

Helping Aunt Hedwig feed her flock of chickens and Uncle Gust his cows and mules soon made me forget the trouble I had seen in Barrington and reminded me somewhat of my childhood visits in Salza with Tante Grete and Onkel Karl. Aunt Hedwig turned out to be the living doll she appeared to be when we first met, as did Uncle Gust. I also got along well with my cousin Johnny, a quiet World War II navy veteran with a permanent five o'clock shadow, and his wife Shirley, a dark-haired woman who also lived on the farm with their infant boy, John, Jr.

Talking about her own marriage, Aunt Hedwig confided in me that after a failed marriage to an alcoholic Swiss farmer who gambled their farm away and left her stranded with two boys, Lothar and Johnny, she took a job as housekeeper for bachelor Gust and his blind mother. Shortly before her death, the mother asked Hedwig to stay on the farm and marry her son.

"Gust is a good man," she concluded, "just a little rough at the edges."

"What do you mean, Toots," bellowed Gust, "rough at the edges? The trouble with you women is that you have no sense of humor, no sense of humor at all. Isn't that right, Junior?" Without waiting for me to agree, he slapped himself on his thigh and let out a burst of laughs between shouts of "Jesus Christ!"

After that, he plunked his massive frame on a chair in the kitchen, rolled a lumpy cigarette with his *Bratwurst*-size fingers, then lighted it with a huge farm match that he ignited on a metal button of his coveralls. "No sense of humor," he kept repeating while filling the kitchen with big puffs of smoke.

"See what I mean?" Aunt Hedwig addressed me, convinced that Gust had helped her make her point.

One weekend we were visited by my uncle Hermann, Mutti's oldest brother, whose generosity to his relatives I had heard so much about and had unknowingly experienced myself. A stocky, suspendered man with short-cropped gray hair, he told me not to lose any sleep over it when I told him that as soon as I was able, I would pay him back the six hundred dollars he had advanced me for my airfare. "Don't you vorry about it. You pay me when you have ze money," he said with a thick German accent. "I know I can trust you because you are Bertha's son." It made me feel good to hear that. Although they had not seen one another for more than thirty years, he still trusted her to have passed on her honesty to me. Immediately I resolved to prove to him that his trust in his sister and me was not misplaced and to pay off my debt as soon as I could.

While the wholesome lifestyle on the farm was therapeutic, I couldn't forget that in four months I was scheduled to enroll at the Aeronautical University or forfeit my student status. I figured that if I could find a job during that time, although legally I was not supposed to work, I could make enough money to pay at least a part of my tuition. When I asked Johnny to help me find a job in the Elgin Watch Company in nearby Elgin, Illinois, where he worked, he told me that they weren't hiring but that he would take me to Woodruff and Edwards, a foundry in Elgin, where he had heard they were looking for lathe operators.

The next morning, Johnny took me to the foundry in his shiny, near-new Hudson. When Johnny introduced me as his cousin, the personnel manager registered only a flicker of surprise but made no comment. After a ten-minute interview, he took me to the foundry's machine shop, where row upon row of medium-size lathes were humming away. Interestingly, all the lathe operators were white; the few blacks I saw were pulling hand trucks and operating forklifts.

"You can start next Monday," the personnel manager told me, and shook my hand.

Monday, bright and early, I reported for work. The personnel manager introduced me to my new foreman, who explained what he wanted me to do, a rather simple operation of cutting lengths of raw pipe down to shiny bushings of specified dimensions. Although I hadn't touched a lathe since I worked for Lindner A. G. in Nazi Germany, it took me only a short while to feel at home behind the cranks and levers of the machine in front of me. My mother was right, *gelernt is gelernt* (learned is learned).

Before I had a chance to rejoice over the way things had turned out, the foreman informed me of a disturbing development. "I am really ashamed to tell you this," he started, "but we have learned that most of the operators have walked off their jobs because we hired you. We never had a colored lathe operator before."

It was only then that I noticed that, with the exception of a few operators, the machine shop was empty.

"I don't want you to be upset," the foreman continued. "You seem to be doing fine. Just keep working as if nothing has happened. In the mean-time, management has taken a very firm stand and informed the operators who walked out that if they don't return right after lunch break, they can look for other jobs."

It was not the first time since the destruction of Nazi Germany that I encountered racism again, only this time it was racism American style, in the reputedly racially liberal North. Recalling Charles Hanson's and other American blacks' admonitions in Liberia, I couldn't say that I hadn't been warned.

At lunchtime I was sitting dejectedly beside my lathe, listlessly munching on one of Aunt Hedwig's sandwiches, when several workers, including some women, stopped by to chat. They wanted me to know that they strongly disapproved of their colleagues' action and told me to hang in there because not all of the people at the plant were bigots.

That was encouraging news to me, but even more encouraging was the fact that gradually the machine shop started to fill up as workers who had walked out returned to their machines. The firm stand taken by the Wood-ruff and Edwards management, and with it common decency, had won out. Within a few days the incident seemed forgotten. At least nobody openly challenged my right to work in the shop. While I was convinced that the company's action did not change any hearts, it certainly went a long way to change behavior.

Aware of race bias in America, I had made it a practice to keep a low profile whenever Uncle Gust and Aunt Hedwig, or Johnny and Shirley, had visitors. Usually I stayed in my room upstairs while they were entertaining in the living room below. This went on for some time, until Uncle Gust noticed my absences at social gatherings and put two and two together. "Let me tell you one thing, Junior, and I'm not telling you again," he roared. "This is your home. I don't give a shit who doesn't like it. The next time we have company, you come down and sit with us like everybody else. Anyone who has a problem with that is an *Arschloch* (asshole) from Pitts-burgh and can go straight to hell." Having thus laid down the law while at the same time demonstrating his German linguistic ability, such as it was, he slapped himself on the thigh, as usual, and shouted "Jesus Christ!"

Uncle Gust's plainspoken declaration went a long way to make me feel wanted and at home. It also convinced me that true human decency is not a function of education or religion, but simply a matter of the heart.

Fall eventually arrived and it was time for me to enroll at the Aeronautical University. The school's curriculum, which was intended to lead to certification as an aircraft mechanic, was divided into two parts, the theoretical part taught at the school's main building, an old villa at Eighteenth Street and Prairie Avenue, in Chicago, and the practical portion taught in a hangar at Chicago's Midway Airport, at the time the world's busiest.

Since I didn't want to quit my job at the foundry, I had myself transferred to the second shift. This meant that I had to get up in the wee hours of the morning, catch the first commuter train from Bartlett to Chicago's Union Station, transfer to a bus that would take me to Eighteenth Street, and attend classes until noon, catch a bus back to Union Station and board the next train to Elgin, work from 2 P.M. until 10 P.M., then catch the next train to Bartlett and walk about a mile to the farm, only to repeat the entire cycle all over again the next day. It didn't take me long to decide that if I kept this up, I would simply die of exhaustion. But I didn't know how to escape this vicious cycle and the dilemma I was in. If I quit my job, I'd wind up without tuition money and would be barred from school. If I quit school, I would lose my student status and be deported.

Just when I didn't know whether I was coming or going, Aunt Hedwig handed me a letter that had just arrived. It was sent by a relative of sorts known far and wide as Uncle Sam. After what sounded like tongue-in-cheek "greetings," the letter invited me to report for a physical examination at my draft board in downtown Chicago. It reminded me that when I received my U.S. visa in Monrovia, I had signed a statement directing me to register with the draft board upon arrival in the United States. This I had done. At the time I was informed that registration with the draft board was "merely a formality" since, as an alien student, I was not subject to the draft. Thus, I attributed the notice to a clerical error.

But instead of being sent home as I had expected, I was examined, found fit as a fiddle, and ordered to report for active duty on February 19, 1951, well into the Korean War. On that day, despite the fact that I was neither an American citizen nor a permanent resident of the United States, my erstwhile wish of becoming an American GI finally caught up with me. I could have gotten off by calling attention to my student status, but decided to go along with the program, because facing bullets in Korea seemed preferable to dying of exhaustion during my around-the-clock commute. I also thought that serving in the United States Army would one day look good on my résumé when I applied for U.S. citizenship.

Only nine months after my arrival in New York, I was riding a southbound train from Chicago to Camp (now Fort) Breckenridge, Kentucky, as a newly inducted recruit of the United States Army. If I still harbored any notions about the glamorous life of an American soldier, I was thoroughly disabused of them during the fourteen weeks of basic infantry training. I certainly found nothing glamorous about running until my tongue hung out, hiking until I had excoriated the skin off my butt and thighs, cowering in a foxhole while being run over by a monstrous tank, and crawling on my belly in a muddy field while .50-caliber machine-gun bullets whistled over my back.

Efforts at transforming me into a soldier were momentarily interrupted when my first sergeant summoned me to the orderly room and ordered me to report to the provost marshal's office immediately. Although I could not think of a single thing I had done that warranted my concern, I worried anyway, especially after a receptionist in the provost marshal's office pointed toward two plainclothesmen who were waiting for me. Identifying themselves as INS officers, they had come to check on me because I had failed to make my annual alien registration report as required by federal law. They told me that my one-year student visa had expired and that for a while, I had been considered at large until they learned from my relatives that I had joined the armed forces. They then proceeded to scold me for my "negligence" and mentioned the possibility of immediate deportation proceedings.

That did it. Releasing my pent-up anger, I told them to go ahead and deport me, since I was sick and tired of the army anyway. When I mentioned that joining the army wasn't my idea, but that I was merely complying with orders sent by somebody who didn't know what he or she was doing, they apologized. They told me that a letter from my commanding officer verifying that I was a soldier in good standing and a valuable member of his unit would satisfy the INS, at least as long as I remained on active duty. When I asked my commanding officer to write such a letter, he was happy to comply.

Race relations in our integrated basic training companies were exceptionally good. We black recruits got along well with our white comrades-in-arms, and many interracial friendships were formed. But midway through basic training, I received a jolt that shattered one of my fervently held beliefs about the United States. One night, while pulling guard duty with one of my white buddies, he started complaining about the fact that the Jews in our company—about half a dozen—enjoyed duty-free time during Christian holidays as well as during Jewish holidays, while non-Jewish soldiers had time off only on Christian holidays. "I'm sick and tired of these fucking Jews," he lamented. "I wish we'd do the same thing Hitler did in Germany and get rid of them."

I couldn't believe what I had just heard. I had always assumed, quite naively, that the reasons America went to war against Hitler were to stop aggression, wipe out totalitarianism and racism, reestablish democracy, and free the Jews. Now an American used the same language of hate and intolerance that I knew so well from Nazi Germany. Anti-Semitism, I reluctantly concluded, was alive and well in the good old U. S. A.

When I tried to persuade my buddy that getting rid of millions of people just because he begrudged them a few extra holidays was rather extreme, he told me that I was naive for taking the side of Jews. "You just don't know them the way I do," he insisted. "If you did, you'd know that they'll steal you blind if you give them half a chance. I know. My father and I worked for Jews, and we rented from Jews."

I told the soldier that I didn't care to hear any more of his bigoted ramblings. It took a while to readjust my thinking to the point where I no longer felt the need to idealize the United States. For the moment, I felt terribly disappointed and betrayed regarding my view of "the land of the free and the home of the brave."

Toward the end of basic training I was given further reason to be skeptical about the American way. When time came for us recruits to be assigned to permanent units, a pattern emerged. By the strangest of strange coincidences, all the white soldiers were sent to peaceful Europe, while all the blacks were shipped to places like Chonju and Kanggyong in war-torn Korea, where the odds of being returned in a body bag were exceedingly good. When some of us blacks queried our white company commander about this rather strange roll of the dice, he told us that racial bias had absolutely nothing to do with it and that the orders "came down from Washington" by people who had no idea whether the soldiers were black or white. Right! Sure!

As a foreigner, I was not quite ready to shed blood for the United States, at least not before having lived in the country for a while and enjoyed some of the benefits of U.S. citizenship. Therefore, I frantically looked for a way to stay in the States a little longer. I was told that there were two alternatives that had priority over being shipped overseas: Officer Candidate School (OCS) and airborne training at Fort Benning Infantry School. As a noncitizen I was ineligible to apply for OCS, so I opted to volunteer for airborne training. This, I understood, was only a temporary solution, since airborne training lasted only three weeks and I had no way of knowing what other assignments would follow.

A tall Mississippian by the name of Bill Toler had ridden the train with me from Chicago to Kentucky and during basic training had become my close buddy. Sharing my reluctance to become a statistic in Korea, Bill followed my lead by volunteering for the paratroopers. Neither of us had a clue what we had gotten ourselves into.

At the first formation following our arrival at Fort Benning, a muscle-bound airborne instructor in a tight, snow-white T-shirt, starched fatigue pants, and spit-shined jump boots went nose tip to nose tip with me. "What's that under your nose?" he bellowed.

I had no idea what he was talking about.

"All of you who are growing whatever it is you are growing under your noses have exactly ten minutes to get rid of it," the muscleman hollered. After checking his wristwatch, he announced that the time was 820 hours and he wanted us back in formation clean-shaven at exactly 830 hours— "or else!"

Like a stampeding herd of buffalos, I and all the other mustache wearers—which meant all of the black soldiers or, in effect, half of the platoon— made a mad dash for the barracks washroom, where we armed ourselves with razors, then hacked away at the mustaches that had been our pride and joy. Bill and I just barely made it back to the formation in time. Those who didn't found out what the muscleman had meant by "or else!" They were ordered to do ten pushups for every minute they overstayed.

After Bill and I returned from our first day of airborne training, which consisted largely of running until we were blue in the face, we carefully viewed our handiwork in the mirror and immediately went into shock. Strangely unfamiliar and bland, the images that looked back at us looked not at all like the dashing machos we had gotten used to seeing. When I tried to console Bill by reminding him that the clean-shaven look was merely temporary and that as soon as we were done with airborne training, we were free to grow new mustaches, he merely shrugged. Then he explained to me that for a black man to lose his mustache was a catastrophe, since black women like their men to have mustaches. "For a black woman, to kiss a man without a mustache," he further explained, "is like eating an egg without salt." I immediately got his point, and have worn a mustache ever since the army permitted me to grow mine back.

Unable or unwilling to take the accelerating pressure of airborne training, Bill told me a few days later that he had decided to quit. I hated to see him go, as I had hoped we would go through military life together, but his mind was made up. His volunteering for airborne duty paid off nevertheless, since he was reassigned and shipped to a unit in, of all places, Germany.

During three weeks of catching hell under Georgia's blazing July sky while contemplating the inevitability of exiting an airplane from an altitude of twelve hundred feet, I, too, considered calling it quits. Our cadres assured us that if a parachute failed, we could always exchange it for a good one once we were back on the ground. This joke did little to boost my morale. But after a few pep talks from our airborne officers, I kept slogging along, more afraid of being called a quitter than I was of "getting wasted" in a parachute mishap. Under the relentless prodding of mean-spirited cadres who kept us trainees at the edge of physical and mental exhaustion, I mastered punitive pushups, the staple of airborne life; the PLF (Parachute Landing Fall); suspended harness exercises known for some strange reason as the "Nutcracker Suite"; simulated parachute jumps from 34-foot and 250-foot towers; and finally the real McCoy—five qualifying parachute jumps from an Air Force C-46.

I have never tried bungee jumping and have no plans to do so, but I'd bet its thrills are modest compared with the exhilarating, adrenaline-boosting feeling one gets from jumping into the prop blast of an airplane during flight. Although we had practiced it hundreds of times on the ground, it was an altogether different feeling when, after reaching our jump altitude, our jump master shouted, "Stand up! . . . Hook up! . . . Sound off for equipment check!" then ordered the first man in the "stick," "Stand in the door!" and finally "Go!" The first time I hurled myself out of the gaping opening and into thin air, my exhilaration level—some call it plain fear—had reached such a pitch that I totally forgot to count the mandatory "one-thousand, two-thousand, three-thousand" before my main parachute opened. Within seconds I was relieved to discover that there are few sights, if any, more beautiful than a recently opened expanse of canopy above. After that, it was all fun, as the chute carried me rather gently toward earth and, having carefully maneuvered away from trees and other obstacles, I made a perfect PLF. Before long, parachuting ceased to be something to be feared, as we quickly became conditioned to fearing each other's suspicion that we were afraid more than fear itself. At the conclusion of airborne training, we graduates stood tall in our class-A uniforms and our first pair of spit-shined Corcoran jump boots, while an officer pinned our silver airborne wings on our stuck-out chests; mine, I'm sure, stuck out the farthest.

Following the completion of airborne training, I and six fellow jump school graduates were sent for permanent assignment to Fort Bragg, North Carolina, home of the 82nd Airborne Division, which had distinguished itself in World War II in actions against the Germans from the Battle of the Bulge to the Battle of Berlin. Our new unit was B Battery of the 80th Airborne Anti-Aircraft Artillery Battalion, an all-black Jim Crow outfit headed by Captain Jefferson S. ("The Man") Boone, the meanest-looking and -acting officer I had encountered since I put on a uniform. Short and paunchy, with a permanent scowl, he strongly reminded me of a black version of my erstwhile English teacher Herr Harden, that unforgettable character from my childhood. Instead of welcoming us, Captain Boone gave us newcomers a withering glance that sent shivers down my spine in spite of the July heat, then let us in on a little idiosyncrasy of his. "There are two things I hate from the bottom of my heart," he announced menacingly, as if he had already caught us red-handed at both transgressions, "an AWOL and a VD!"

My first night as a bona fide paratrooper was hardly more auspicious than my first meeting with "The Man." Sometime after midnight, I was awakened by a tremendous racket. When someone turned on the lights, I saw two of my new buddies in a serious fight over who knows what. Everyone watched, but no one interfered as the two bloodied one another with heavy punches and kicks. Eventually, the fight ended after one of the combatants, Oscar Ford, picked up the other, Robert Stone, and threw him down a flight of steep barracks stairs. There he remained, moaning occasionally, but motionless. My immediate impulse was to summon help, but when I prepared to go downstairs I was told by my barracks mates to "stay out of it." After that, someone turned off the lights and everyone, including the apparent victor of the brawl, turned in as if nothing had happened.

I found it difficult to fall asleep, worried that the badly beaten soldier at the bottom of the stairs might not survive. But I need not have worried. The next morning before reveille Stone walked in, his eyes bloody and nearly closed from the fight. He carried a steel rod that he had ripped from one of the bunks. Before anyone realized what he was up to, he walked up to his enemy, who was sitting on a footlocker engrossed in shining his boots, and struck him from behind at the base of his neck. Without uttering a sound, Ford keeled over and fell facedown to the floor, where he remained as motionless as he had rendered Stone the night before. This time, a platoon sergeant appeared, and within a few minutes, an ambulance rushed the comatose Ford to a hospital while the MPs hauled Stone to the stockade, where he was held pending murder charges in case Ford did not survive. But in a few days Ford recovered, and Stone was released. To my surprise, both resumed their duties as if the whole thing had never occurred. The incident taught me one valuable lesson—in my new environment, people played for keeps.

That lesson was driven home even more forcefully when, a few months later, our division was in convoy on its way to Texas for extended maneuvers dubbed Exercise Longhorn, up to that time the largest military training exercise ever held in the United States. Following a "pit stop," one of my buddies, an exceptionally nice guy from New York by the name of Homer Travis, got into an argument over a coveted seat at the tailgate of the truck we were riding. When Homer, claiming squatter's rights, refused to relinquish the seat the other had occupied prior to the stop, the enraged trooper jumped off the truck, picked up a rock the size of a coconut, and hurled it at Homer, hitting him squarely in the forehead. By the time the medics arrived, Homer was dead. For this senseless killing, which was officially listed as "involuntary manslaughter," the trooper received a miserly sentence of four months.

In the 80th triple A Battalion, a man's worth and standing in the pecking order was determined simply by how many parachute jumps he had made, or, as they said in the 80th, how many times he had "hit the silk." By that measure, I and other fresh-out-of-jump-school troopers were relegated to the bottom of the totem pole and contemptuously dismissed as "five-jump Charlies." This made us ready targets for bullies who tried to impress themselves and others with their "badness." It was only a question of time before it became my turn to have my mettle tested. It happened when a trooper with an impressive number of jumps under his belt decided to get personal with me after noticing a framed picture of my mother on a shelf above my bunk. "What's this nigger doing with a white woman's picture?" he hollered loud enough for everyone to hear.

"That woman is my mother," I informed him in a stern tone that was meant to tell him to back off.

On hearing the word "mother," everyone in the barracks went silent.

"How come yo's a nigger and yo' mama's white?" the soldier persisted.

By this time one could hear a pin drop. Everyone seemed curious to find out how I would handle this ultimate intrusion into my private life. Realizing that anything less than an immediate and forceful response would brand me a coward and subject me to insults for the rest of my stay in the 80th, I decided to teach this brother a lesson he wouldn't soon forget. With the confidence of someone who knew that he was in top physical condition, I hurled myself at the sneering soldier and attacked him with several hard blows to his head that took him totally by surprise. Instantly, his knees buckled and he hit the floor. His bewildered look as I hovered over him told me that, at least for the time being, my attack had broken his fighting spirit.

"Be cool, bro! I didn't mean no offense," he mumbled in a conciliatory tone that was quite a departure from his earlier cockiness. "No need to get yo'self all worked up."

Strangely enough I believed him, but remembering Stone and his steel rod, I didn't turn my back on him for months. The effect of my quick reaction was as intended; word got around not to mess with "that nigger from Germany," and for the rest of my time in Uncle Sam's Army, nobody did.

I got along well with all of my fellow black troopers from the 80th, whom I came to appreciate in spite of their ever-readiness to go "upside somebody's head." They were a varied bunch, some good old country boys from Alabama and Mississippi, others streetwise city slickers from the Harlems of America, and a few well-read and college-trained at both black and white institutions. All of them, without exception, were outstanding soldiers, dependable buddies, and fearless paratroopers with whom I would have gladly "hit the silk" if ever I had to face an enemy overseas.

Serving in a segregated unit was as much a learning experience for me as was army life itself. I soon learned that the axiom so eloquently expressed by Smitty, that sage messman from the *Appleton Victory,* held true not only for our Jim Crow battalion, but for the entire 82nd Airborne Division. "We don't fuck with them, and they don't fuck with us," was Smitty's brilliant assessment of race relations aboard his ship. The same, I discovered, held true for life at Fort Bragg, where it seemed one hand didn't know what the other was doing.

Between reveille and retreat, we went about our various duties and hardly saw our white comrades-in-arms who were doing identical duties in other parts of the sprawling post. Except for our white battalion commander, Lieutenant Colonel Lawrence Linderer, and a sprinkling of white officers, we had no contact with white people whatsoever. President Truman's executive order to integrate the armed forces had not yet caught up with the sleepy old Southern ways of Fort Bragg. Jim Crow still ruled supreme in virtually all post installations, including the PX barbershops. That is, until one day when the commanding general of the 82nd Airborne Division needed a haircut. He noticed that the only black barber in the shop cut both black and white soldiers' hair if his white colleagues were busy but that the four white barbers stayed idle if there were no white customers, even though black soldiers were waiting in line. When the general demanded to know why the white barbers didn't cut black soldiers' hair, they told him that they didn't know how. "In that case," the general told them, "you have until tomorrow morning to learn. If you haven't learned by then, don't bother to come back." Only one of the four white barbers returned to his job.

Segregation was even more strictly adhered to during our hours off the post. As soon as we reached nearby Fayetteville, North Carolina, often on the same bus, white soldiers headed for the nearest honky-tonks that lined the town's main drag, where white women waited for them. We black soldiers had to hike "way to the outskirts of town" where the pavement ended and where, in a few rundown barns that passed for nightclubs, black women waited for us. If we got into trouble with the law while off the post, our officers had warned us that we would be strictly on our own, since there was nothing they could do for us. Having barely squeaked by the Gestapo, I was determined not to act foolhardy and wind up in some redneck sheriff's slammer. I had heard too many accounts—many, I'm sure, true— of how hapless black soldiers who had rubbed a white lawman the wrong way were "made examples of " or simply disappeared.

Most of my black fellow soldiers seemed resigned to our Jim Crow status, and some preferred it that way. For me, however, it was utterly ludicrous that a nation that prided itself on its democratic traditions and looked down on the Nazis for their racial attitudes would segregate soldiers who served in the same army and who were expected to fight the same enemy. Despite my misgivings, I learned to take the bitter with the sweet.

One day, the mail clerk from the orderly room handed me a telegram that made me the happiest man among the twenty thousand troopers of the 82nd Airborne Division. In it, my mother informed me that she had safely landed in New York Harbor and was on her way to her sister Hedwig's farm in Bartlett, Illinois. Words are inadequate to describe what I felt. The moment I had waited for from the time I left Hamburg four years earlier—the moment I feared would never come—had finally arrived. We were both in the United States, and although we would not be able to live near each other right away, we could take comfort from knowing that we were no longer divided by foreign borders and an ocean.

With the intervention of the Red Cross, I was able to obtain a short emergency furlough, and on a beautiful summer afternoon, I got off a train in Bartlett and ran half a mile up a country road while carrying a heavy duffel bag on my shoulder. Meanwhile, knowing my arrival time, my mother had set out running toward me on that same road. Somewhere at midpoint, in what seemed like a reenactment of the climactic scene of the movie classic *Wuthering Heights,* we ran into each other's outstretched arms. We hadn't seen each other for four years, four years that seemed like four eternities.

Not long after returning to the post, I heard the familiar sounds of musical instruments coming from inside a barrack. I learned that the occupants were members of the Division Artillery (Divarty) Band, the black counterpart of the all-white 82nd Airborne Division Band. It didn't take much for the bandsmen to convince me that blowing a saxophone at parades beat digging huge craters for 40-mm antiaircraft guns, and with their encouragement I requested a transfer to the band and a change of my Military Occupational Specialty (MOS). A couple of weeks after passing an audition, my wish was granted and I moved in with members of the Divarty Band. My new duties were much more pleasant than my grungy antiaircraft-artillery chores. They consisted mainly of keeping my jump boots and brass shined, attending rehearsals, standing and marching tall at parades, playing classical concerts, participating in airport ceremonies for arriving dignitaries from Washington, and making an occasional parachute training jump.

Not long after I joined the Divarty Band, we were ordered to pack our gear and move to other barracks near the main post. Integration of the United States Armed Forces had finally arrived, and with it the integration of the Divarty Band with the 82nd Airborne Division Band. In spite of the apprehension of some of my buddies, many of whom had never had any close contacts with whites, the move went smoothly. Before we knew it, we and our new white buddies were like peas in a pod. I found it amusing to watch how eagerly our white comrades tried to sound "colored," something they hoped to achieve by prefixing the *f* word with the word *mother*. It never sounded quite right to us blacks, but we accepted our comrades' good intention of absorbing black "culture." More important, after several joint rehearsals, our newly integrated band not only looked like one harmonious ensemble, but it also sounded better and richer than either of the two groups had sounded alone.

The only thing that could have put an end to my relatively blissful existence in the newly integrated 82nd Airborne Division Band was an order to ship out for combat duty in Korea. But that order never came. After serving the mandatory two years of a draftee in U.S. Army garrisons of the South, with its shantytowns reserved for blacks, I received my honorable discharge and returned to Chicago and civilian life. In the years ahead, there were many times when my infatuation with the United States would be severely tested, when I began to wonder whether my long-harbored vision of succeeding in the New World had been nothing but an adolescent's pipe dream, and if my coming to America had been a monumental mistake.

Unfortunately, I couldn't escape my blue-collar status by becoming a musician. A country that had produced hundreds of saxophone giants of the caliber of Ben Webster, Chick Webb, Ornette Coleman, Dexter Gordon, Coleman Hawkins, Charlie Parker, and Johnny Hodges was hardly looking for a kid from Germany whose main musical credentials were that he had played saxophone with the Three Ah-Yue Hon Lous. As much as I despised blue-collar jobs, I was lucky that there were plenty of them to keep me afloat, including driving a delivery truck for a liquor store and—what a comedown—working as a machinist *helper* in factories.

After several years of paying dues, including journalism studies at two universities, things started to look up and fall into place. Ever so slowly, I began to see the light at the end of the long, long tunnel. I knew I had not only survived but succeeded when I went on my first major assignment for *Ebony,* to interview President Sekou Touré of newly independent Guinea at the Libertyville, Illinois, home of UN Ambassador Adlai Stevenson. When the two world figures sat down for an animated chat with me, the "racially inferior" dead-end black kid from Nazi Germany, it seemed to me that my coming to America had not been such a bad idea after all.

GERMANY REVISITED

The year was 1966. Eighteen years had elapsed since I had left war-ravished Germany to seek my fortune, first in Africa, then in the United States. We were cruising at about thirty thousand feet somewhere between Chicago and Frankfurt on a Germany-bound Lufthansa Boeing 707. As always during long plane rides, I had dozed off.

"Are you feeling all right?" The concerned voice of the flight attendant interrupted my dream about the spine-chilling event nearly two decades ago when I narrowly escaped being lynched by a German mob that had mistaken me for a U.S. pilot.

"I'm fine," I assured the young woman, while wiping the beads of perspiration from my face.

"Do you care for a pillow?" the flight attendant inquired.

"*Ja, bitte, wenn's Ihnen nichts ausmacht* (Yes, please, if you don't mind)." I showed off my unadulterated German, amused at her surprise. African-Americans, I had long since discovered, weren't expected to speak accent-free German.

I would soon be back in Germany, the country of my birth, which I had left without regrets. I could still hear the taunts of children and their inevitable chorus, *"Neger, Neger, Schornsteinfeger!"*

During the nearly two decades I spent away from my homeland, much had happened to me and the rest of the universe. After scuffling and "paying dues," I was snugly ensconced in the so-called middle class, married to an African-American professional woman and the proud father of two adorable boys, aged ten and six. In addition to a journalism degree from the University of Illinois and a well-paying job as managing editor of *Ebony* magazine, I had acquired a home in one of Chicago's "desirable" neighborhoods and with it a mortgage that negated any thoughts of early retirement. In short, I had found my American dream.

With a dull screech, the wheels of the Boeing 707 touched down. The long-anticipated moment was here. Throughout my years in self-imposed exile, I often wondered whether racial attitudes in onetime Nazi Germany had changed and whether so-called non-Aryans were finally getting a fair shake.

Hundreds of questions crowded my mind. Now that they were once again the masters in their land, what was the attitude of Germans toward blacks? Were they saddled with guilt over the extermination of six million Jews and other racial and ethnic minorities, or had their newly acquired material success and NATO membership made them callous and revived their old racial arrogance? I had exactly three weeks to find out.

My first impression of Germany, gleaned from Frankfurt's modern airport, was dramatic. Mingling with the airport crowd, I was engulfed in a whirling mass of colors and a cacophony of languages. The terminal buzzed with people from all corners of the earth. It was the typical cosmopolitan crowd one finds at international crossroads throughout the world. But to the traveler who remembered only the drab, dead-end Germany of the late forties, a Germany that had neither airports, airplanes, nor air passengers, it was an unexpected and refreshing sight.

After a comfortable seven-hour train ride, I arrived in the city of my birth. "Hamburg *Hauptbahnhof*!" a blue-uniformed conductor shouted outside the compartment in the aisle. With a loud squeal, followed by a jolt, the train came to a stop.

With the picture of a burned-out Hamburg still vivid in my mind, I was hardly prepared for what I found. The Hamburg I left had been a vast pile of rubble and empty building shells among which people, demoralized by hunger and defeat, eked out a questionable existence plying a furtive black-market trade. It was a city in which women sold their bodies for a pair of nylons, where mothers bartered the favors of their teenage daughters for food and husbands the affections of their wives for a pack of cigarettes. Had the British foreseen the far-reaching effects of their air attacks, they could hardly have thought of a more fitting name for their handiwork than their code name "Gomorrah."

It was inconceivable to me that anyone would be able to put Hamburg back together again. A slightly rebuilt Gomorrah I had expected to find, but instead I found a breathtakingly beautiful metropolis with brightly lit boulevards on which a bumper-to-bumper stream of shiny automobiles passed endlessly. There were miles of streets bustling with well-dressed shoppers and lined with row upon row of stores that bulged with quality merchandise.

On fashionable Jungerfernstieg, Hamburg's answer to New York's Fifth Avenue, pleasure-bent throngs queued up under a movie marquee that in large letters proclaimed WAS GIEBTS NEUES, PUSSY? (WHAT'S NEW, PUSSYCAT?), another reminder of that all-pervasive American influence. Germany's widely touted "economic miracle," primed by Uncle Sam's dollar-studded magic wand and sustained by German industriousness, had not been exaggerated.

But there were other, quite different sights, also. Visiting my former neighborhood on the north side of town, I stood stunned before a crate-littered vacant lot where on that memorable summer night twenty-three years earlier my home had been razed in an air attack. It seemed that the "miracle" hadn't quite reached this point. Briefly, I paused at the site of the air-raid shelter where I had survived the crucial attack that had turned my neighborhood into an inferno. I remembered the charred corpses of the unfortunate people who had been unable to reach the shelter in time. On that site there now stood a spanking-new housing development with green play lots and children playing the same old games I had played as a little boy. As I watched them, I wished, somehow, that at least one of them would give me once again the old *Neger, Neger, Schornsteinfeger* routine, just for old time's sake. But either German children had changed, or I no longer rated. Like a latter-day Rip van Winkle, I walked the vaguely familiar-looking streets where once I had known just about every lamppost, every tree, and every face, unrecognized by the people I met and recognizing none of them. For me, who had once been a celebrity of sorts in Barmbek, whom everybody had known, if not by name, certainly as *der Negerjunge,* it was an unfamiliar feeling. At that moment the full truth of Thomas Wolfe's famous assertion hit me: you can't go home again.

I went to Ohlsdorf Cemetery to pay my respects to the forty-one thousand fellow Hamburgers who had not been as fortunate as I during the air raids of July 1943, and had lost their lives in the raging infernos. I was stunned when I saw the seemingly endless rectangular mass graves, marked only by the name of the city district in which the remains of the deceased—frequently burned beyond recognition—had been found. As I walked in awe along the peaceful, beautifully landscaped paths, I wondered why I had been spared and why the occupants of the mass tomb below had met with such a wretched death.

As a black person born in Germany, the most interesting group of Germans to me was the country's burgeoning population of thousands of so-called "brown babies," mostly illegitimate offspring of black GIs and German women. With U.S. occupation troops firmly entrenched in the country, "that old black magic" kept fräuleins in a perpetual spin, with the result that brown babies kept a-coming. West German authorities, for the most part, insisted that they kept no records regarding race and that all persons born in Germany were absolutely equal under the law. American authorities washed their hands altogether of illegitimate children fathered by U.S. occupation troops, since they were German citizens.

To learn more about Germany's brown babies, I ventured to the Munich apartment of Al Hooseman, the man who, I was told, knew more about the

subject than any other person alive. The expatriate former heavyweight con-
tender from Waterloo, Iowa, was founder and president of the organization
Help for Colored and Parentless Children. Originally he had come to Ger-
many in 1950 to bolster a sagging boxing career, but when he was given the
part of a brown baby's GI father in a German movie called *Schwarzer Engel
(Black Angel)*, he was so touched by the plight of these children that he
hung up his gloves and took up their cause in real life. In the process,
between additional movie and stage stints, he fell in love with Germany and
its people and decided to stay. By the time I caught up with Hooseman, he
was a Munich personality whom everyone recognized and respected, from
the city's lord mayor on down.

"Come on in," boomed a voice, and I found myself confronted by a
bearded brown giant of a man in his mid-forties. "Don't look around,
though," he cautioned as he led me into a cluttered, one-room bachelor
apartment whose walls were literally covered with a photographic record of
his adult life. There were photos of his fights, snapshots of him with various
brown babies and of his meetings with an impressive string of celebrities,
from Eleanor Roosevelt to Dr. Martin Luther King, Jr.

Throwing wild punches at an imaginary foe while footworking his way
around the room, Hooseman first recalled some of his prouder moments in
the ring before venting his old grudge against Joe Louis: he blamed the
Brown Bomber for having finished his boxing career by knocking him out
cold in an exhibition match and causing permanent eye damage. Then he
sat down to talk about his social work. His battle-scarred, still-handsome
face twitched with emotion as he explained his frustration over having seen
his efforts bog down because of a lack of funds. "If I could only get my
hands on some money—ten thousand dollars would do for a start," he
moaned. "I would show 'em what can be done. But what little money I've
been able to raise is not enough for hiring professional help or keeping the
organization alive.

"The biggest problem," he continued, "is that most of these children's
mothers or grandparents or foster parents belong to the low-income group
and as a result, the children enter life unprepared to compete with other
children who have had the benefit of an enriched home life. Germany is a
cultured country of art, music, and literature. Any child who is not steeped
in these has already a strike against him. What little money the guardians

of these children get in welfare assistance from the West German government is the bare minimum and not enough to give them opportunities to develop whatever special talents they might have.

"Another unfortunate circumstance is the class-consciousness of Germans. Too often in Germany you stay in the class in which you were born. Brown babies, therefore, even apart from their color, are automatically a part of the lower class.

"This, in a nutshell, is the problem of many of the brown babies. But it isn't a matter of race, because any child in Germany who is born poor and illegitimate faces the same problems. In general, the children are accepted as individuals. I would say without hesitation that black children of comparable backgrounds in the United States don't come near the degree of social acceptance which the children enjoy here. As for myself, I don't make a lot of money, and movie parts are getting scarcer by the day, but here I am at peace with myself. Somehow, I just don't get the same vibration anymore from that 'Hi, baby,' and slap-on-the back routine at home that I get out of that firm, old-fashioned German handshake."

After visiting the major population centers of West Germany, I recognized one incontrovertible fact: the former Third Reich, once a shrine to a spurious racial-purity cult, had ceased to be a "white" nation. In addition to black GI-fathered children, it was well-nigh impossible to walk the streets of the Federal Republic without seeing people of color—Americans, Africans, West Indians—all of whom had become as ubiquitous and as integral a part of the German scene as *Knackwurst*, beer, and Mercedes-Benz automobiles. This contrasted sharply with the racial situation that had prevailed up to the end of World War II, when the mere sight of a black person was a noteworthy event.

The new generation of Germans seemed to enjoy a carbon copy of "the American way of life." This was most evident in young people's fanatic display of American-style clothes, dance, and music, especially soul and jazz. Unlike the Nazi days, when playing or listening to jazz were sure ways to land in jail, jazz appreciation was totally unfettered. From the windows of record shops throughout the nation, I was greeted by the faces of black jazz and pop artists, most of them at least as popular and renowned in West Germany as back home in the United States.

"Get a load of how these cats are digging the sounds. You'd think you're in one of them Harlem joints," remarked a black soldier as he and I peeped through the door of a jam-packed Munich discotheque. For several minutes I watched the enraptured young faces of this new breed of Germans as they "frugged," "swam," and "monkeyed" to a Count Basie beat. Vividly remembering the rigid, goose-stepping brownshirts of my childhood, and the taunts I endured because of my brown skin, I was filled with renewed hope for the country of my birth.

REFLECTIONS

Unfortunately, since I made those observations back in 1966, times have changed again. Subsequent developments on Germany's racial front, characterized by the alarming rise in hate crimes and the proliferation of a variety of neo-Nazi groups with racist agendas, have rendered my optimistic sentiments woefully obsolete.

While it would be an exaggeration to say that, racially speaking, Germany is back at square one, the sad fact remains that racism in Germany is far from a thing of the past. My encounter in 1997 with about one hundred young German-born black people from a wide spectrum of educational, social, and economic backgrounds, all members of the ISD (Initiative Black Germans), has convinced me that much work still needs to be done—by the German federal government and the private sector, as well as individual citizens—to assure the absolute equality and complete economic and social integration into German mainstream society of Germans of African descent and other racial minorities. It is only through constant and concerted vigilance that Germans can hope to prevent repeating the horrors of the Holocaust.

I hope that my story will convey the inescapable lesson I have drawn from the slice of history I was destined to witness from uncomfortably close range: if it happened once, it could happen again; and if it could happen in Germany—a country raised on the wisdom of intellectual giants like Goethe and Schiller and enriched by the timeless contributions of musical geniuses like Beethoven, Bach, and Brahms—it could happen anywhere.

Terrorism and brutal pogroms in the name of racial, religious or ethnic cleansing, and tribal dominance as practiced by the Nazis in Germany have been reenacted by the Afrikaners in South Africa, the Serbs in Kosovo, the Tutsis in Rwanda, and the Protestants and Catholics in Northern Ireland, to name just a few. Initially, the purveyors of racism need no more than the silent acquiescence of the public. In the case of Nazi Germany, first Germans and then the entire world turned a deaf ear to the flagrant human rights abuses until it was too late to prevent the architects of racial madness from carrying out their evil schemes. That sad chapter in history suggests that it is never too soon to confront bigotry and racism whenever, wherever, and in whatever form it raises its ugly head. It is incumbent upon all people to confront even the slightest hint of racist thought or action with zero tolerance.

Those of us who have experienced the depravity to which a country can sink under a government controlled by unscrupulous manipulators owe it to our fellow human beings to keep this unholy specter vivid in the public's mind.

WHERE ARE THEY NOW?

I am frequently asked by people who are familiar with my life story what ever happened to that disparate group of relatives, friends, and adversaries in Germany, Liberia, and the United States who at one time or another played major or peripheral roles in my life. Because of the massive population shifts following the destruction of major parts of Hamburg and other German cities and because of the heavy casualties among German military personnel and civilians during World War II, the fate of a great many of them will never be known to me. In many cases I lost track of people simply because of distance, both in terms of time and space. I call myself fortunate, however, for having been able to maintain close ties with some of my relatives and friends and, in some cases, to reestablish contact after an interruption of many years.

My mother's two sisters, Clara and Hedwig, and her oldest brother, Hermann, all of whom helped me to gain a foothold in the United States following my arrival from Liberia in 1950, have died. Except for Onkel Hermann, who remained a bachelor until the day he died, they left me with an army of second and third cousins too numerous to count.

During frequent trips to Germany while on assignment for *Ebony,* I used to cross into Communist East Germany to visit my widowed Tante Grete, who lived with her granddaughter, Karla, Karla's husband, Bernd, and their two teenage daughters in Nordhausen. After predicting her pending death each year from the time she reached middle age, Tante Grete didn't make good on her prediction until she was well into her late eighties. Her daughter, my cousin Trudchen, who was like a sister to me during my childhood summer vacations in the Harz Mountains, died while still a young woman, long before her mother.

In the mid-sixties, I had a huge surprise when then–U.S. Secretary of Defense Robert McNamara's office invited me to attend a reception at Chicago's Sheraton Hotel for Liberia's deputy secretary of defense, the Honorable Morris W. Massaquoi, and several Liberian generals in his retinue. When, after passing several security checks by U.S. military officers, I was finally admitted to my brother's VIP suite, I had another surprise coming. Instead of the wiry police inspector I had left behind in Liberia's hinterland, I was met by a rather portly, meticulously attired gentleman, who seemed quite at home amid the opulence that surrounded him. Neither of us could get over the quantum leap that had brought us from abject poverty and a rat-infested shack to the measure of comfort and respectability each of us had achieved.

When President Tubman died, in 1971, I went to Monrovia to cover the funeral for *Ebony.* I flew on the government plane that carried a delegation of U.S. officials who were to represent President Nixon at the state funeral. On our arrival at Robertsfield International Airport, I had a second reunion with Morris. Like Morris, Monrovia had prospered. The sleepy town of my memory had awakened and had turned into a bustling city, replete with a skyline and traffic jams.

During the viewing of Tubman's body, Morris and I recalled how the president had listened to our plight when it became obvious to us that Uncle Nat was ripping us off. Morris told me that since Uncle Nat had died in 1962 from a host of severe health problems, his battle had shifted to Aunt

Fatima, who, he claimed, was fighting him tooth and nail for our late father's property. I was glad I had made up my mind long ago to forget about the inheritance, especially after seeing that years of worrying about it hadn't gotten Morris anywhere.

During my brief stay in Monrovia, Coast Guard boss Morris gave me the VIP treatment by personally accompanying me on a short "inspection cruise" in one of his speedy Coast Guard cutters. As he showed me around his domain, he told me that he had been conducting a private war with Stephen Tolbert, the new president's younger brother and head of the Tolbert family's fishing enterprise. Morris insisted that Stephen Tolbert was using Coast Guard docks for his own private fishing fleet. "Each time I catch one of his boats at our docks," Morris bragged, "I have it impounded at his expense."

When I pointed out to Morris that it didn't seem to make good political sense to annoy the brother of the president now that his benefactor and protector, President Tubman, was gone, Morris scoffed, "Don't you worry. Tolbert will serve only what little is left of Tubman's term. After that we'll vote him out. It's already been taken care of."

Having just conducted an exclusive interview with President William Tolbert during which he assured me that he planned to continue President Tubman's policies, I was not so sure. "Maybe so," I said, "but I still think you should take it easy with Stephen Tolbert."

Unfortunately, my good advice came much too late. As soon as I had returned to Chicago, I learned that President Tolbert had fired a number of Tubman appointees and that Morris had been among the first.

In retrospect, Morris's firing turned out to be a blessing in disguise, since it removed him from the line of fire nine years later, when Samuel Doe purged President Tolbert and other top members of Liberia's ruling class in a bloody massacre that shocked the world. Instead, Morris lived quietly as a businessman, occasionally visiting me in the States, until illness claimed him at age sixty-eight in 1985, his fervent wish to recoup our father's legacy still unfulfilled.

In keeping with my resolve to leave well enough alone, I never mentioned the estate when I briefly visited with Aunt Fatima, who by 1971 was dean of the University of Liberia and one of the most respected educators in the country. She proudly told me that her daughter, Püppchen, was a student in Germany. Through Fatima, who died in 1978, I learned that Ma Sonii, my paternal grandmother, had died in 1958 after she moved from Lagos to Monrovia following the death of her husband. I didn't catch up with Fritz and Fasia until 1991. Following Sergeant Doe's coup, they had moved to Knoxville, Tennessee, where Fritz was able to establish himself as an artist and art dealer. Both he and Fasia live near their children and grandchildren and it seems doubtful that they will ever return to Liberia. Their mother, Ma Rachel, and brother Arthur, Liberia's former director of natural resources and mines, died in 1986 and 1984, respectively.

Throughout my odyssey on three continents, I never lost touch with my old coconspirator "Yankee Werner," who launched me on my beach-comber's career on Hamburg's waterfront more than five decades ago, and who is partially responsible for my early obsession with America. From the moment I arrived in the United States in May 1950 until this day, we have kept our friendship alive through phone calls, holiday cards, and occasional visits. Werner, divorced, remarried, and the father of a grown daughter, put in many years as a purser of a major airline and now lives happily in retire-ment with his wife, Birgid, in sunny California.

The most prominent survivor of that old gang of mine is my fellow non-Aryan Ralph Giordano. Disillusioned with the Communist Party, which he served for eleven years as a correspondent and publicist, he established him-self as a popular presenter of TV documentaries before chronicling the story of his family's survival under the Nazis in his novel *Die Bertinis,* in 1982. The novel, which immortalizes a certain character named "Mickey Massa-kon," became a best-seller in Germany and made the name Giordano a household word and Ralph a rich man. Widowed and remarried, Ralph lives with his wife, Rosie, in Cologne, grinding out additional books at the rate of one per year on such disparate subjects as Israel, Ireland, and Germany—past and present. Both of his parents died, as did his older brother, Egon, who succumbed to a heart attack shortly after Ralph's first literary success in 1982, and his younger sister, Gabriela, who was born after the war. His younger brother, Rocco, still lives in Hamburg.

In 1992, after seeing an article about me in the Hamburg press, Erika, my erstwhile childhood playmate, was able to reestablish contact with me. Having put her precocious past as a four-year-old stripper behind her, Erika, daughter of the late Hamburg senator Walter Schmedemann, has long been a housewife, mother, and grandmother who spends her time with her retired security-agent husband, Harald Stobbe, traveling to exotic spots around the world—including my home in the United States—or at their comfortable home in Hamburg-Fuhlsbüttel.

Inge, the last woman to capture my heart before I left Germany as a young man of twenty-two was among the survivors. After promising to love me forever, she had what she thought was a better idea and married a British Royal Air Force officer with whom she led a nomadic but interesting life in some of the most exotic places throughout the British colonial empire. Eventually divorced, she returned to Hamburg. It was at that stage, more than twenty years after I had left Germany, that a mutual friend reintroduced us and we were able to compare notes. Since then, I have been told, she has left Hamburg without a trace.

One of my former buddies, whom I had mourned for several years after I was told that he had died in a traffic accident, surprised me by turning up very much alive. Stopping briefly in Hamburg while on an *Ebony* assignment in Germany in the late sixties, I accidentally came across the name *Fred Gass* in the local telephone directory. Although believing Fred, my erstwhile crony in Haus Vaterland and other Hamburg hot spots, to be dead, I dialed the number out of curiosity and found myself talking with a woman who informed me that she was Frau Giesela Gass, the wife of postal worker Fred Gass.

Within the hour, I was hugging my old buddy, who not only had risen from the dead, but who had changed from a skinny wisp of a man to a tubby grandfather type. Since that fateful reunion, Fred and Giesela, at the time an insurance executive, have lived in retirement in their cozy apartment in Hamburg, where I have been a regular dropper-in whenever my addiction for an occasional whiff of foggy Hamburg air has brought me to the city of my birth. In the fall of 1989 I accomplished what until then had been considered an impossible feat—I succeeded in persuading Fred to overcome his fear of flying and to come with Giesela to spend time with my family and me in Chicago and with Yankee Werner and his wife in California. The two had the time of their lives and have promised us to come back for an encore.

Another member of my old inner circle who literally landed on his feet is Ah-Yue Hon Lou, my former partner in the show-biz act the Three

Ah-Yue Hon Lous. Following the disbanding of our group, Yue kept up his tap-dance act as a solo artist, but eventually branched out into acting in major films that call for Asian characters—Chinese, Japanese, Korean, Vietnamese, et cetera. Widowed, remarried, and the father of two grown sons and a daughter, Yue now lives with his wife, Giesel, in Hamburg's suburb of Blankenese, where I visit them whenever I happen to be in the neighborhood.

Of the Morell clan, headed by Nazi *Blockleiter* Wilhelm Morell, only my friend and former classmate Karl is still around. To my big surprise, I found him living by himself in retirement in an apartment only a few blocks from the neighborhood where we grew up. He told me that after he had been reported missing in action, he returned belatedly from a Soviet POW camp one night half-starved and in rags only to find his parents and brothers reveling at a party at their home. "I had always pictured them grieving for me," he recalled, "and instead I found them living it up." At least Karl was spared the indignity suffered by many German POWs who, upon their return home, found that their wives had replaced them with an English or American soldier—true to the saying, "To the winner go the spoils."

Karl's disappointing homecoming, he explained, alienated him forever from his family, especially his father, whose Nazi politics, he said, had always disgusted him. Shortly after Karl's return from the POW camp, his brother Gerd, a talented drummer with his own band, slumped over his drums and died of a heart attack during a gig at a Baltic Sea resort. Following Gerd's death, Herr Morell, then Frau Morell died. Hans, the oldest of the Morell boys, survived combat in the Soviet Union. He died only a few years ago after ailing for several years, according to Karl.

A depressingly long list of members of my former circle of relatives, friends, and acquaintances who did not survive include my former classmate Fiffi Peters, the waiter at the *Ratskeller*, who, I have learned only recently, was killed in action, as was our former teacher Herr Henry Herbst. One of the most tragic fates brought to my attention is that of my first great love, Gretchen Jahn. After appearing as a guest on the popular Hamburg television program *Die Schaubude* in 1976, I was deluged with telephone calls from people who had recognized me, including a woman who identified herself as Gretchen's cousin. Through her I learned that Gretchen, her mother, and her brother had planned to emigrate to the United States, but that Gretchen had to remain in Germany because she had contracted tuberculosis and was refused a U.S. immigrant visa. Left to her own devices, she made a living as a barmaid in a Hamburg nightclub. A few years following our last meeting in St. Pauli in 1946, she died destitute and alone.

I never heard what happened to the two major villains in my life, Kätnerkamp principal Wriede and teacher Dutke. Judging by their ages, I must assume that one way or another, they have moved on to their just rewards, which I hope are in keeping with the sadistic pleasure they derived from tormenting me.

It is of considerable comfort to me to know that my mother, who followed me to the United States in 1952, finally lived a happily married life before she died in 1986 at the ripe old age of eighty-three. In Mileta Nikodijevic, a hardworking Serb who had been freed by the Allies from a German POW camp, she found the love and companionship she so richly deserved. The two lived an idyllic life in their comfortable, friend-filled (and, Mutti used to stress, "all paid for") home in a suburb of Chicago. It was exactly the kind of home with a small vegetable garden she and I used to dream about in Germany, when home ownership was totally beyond our reach. Their happiness lasted until, on the eve of their twenty-fifth wedding anniversary, Mileta succumbed to a heart attack.

There was no better way I could have repaid my mother for all she had done for me than to "make something of myself" and to present her with two grandsons, Steve Gordon and Hans Jürgen, Jr., who likewise have made something of themselves. Following Steve's graduation from Harvard Medical School and the enrollment of Hans at the University of Michigan Law School, nothing gave her more pleasure than to brag about "my grandson, the doctor, and my other grandson, the soon-to-be lawyer." As she always used to say, *"Ende gut, alles gut."*